D1267978

THE NOTABLE MAN

THE
NOTABLE MAN

The Life and Times of
Oliver Goldsmith

JOHN GINGER

HAMISH HAMILTON
LONDON

First published in Great Britain 1977
by Hamish Hamilton
90 Great Russell Street, London WC1B 3PT

Copyright © 1977 by John Ginger

SBN 241 89626 6

The publisher acknowledges the financial assistance
of the Arts Council of Great Britain in the publication
of this volume

Printed in Great Britain by Elliott Bros. & Yeoman Ltd.,
Liverpool L24 9JL

'It was very soon after my first arrival in London, where everything appeared new and wonderful to me, that I expressed to Sir Joshua my impatient curiosity to see Dr Goldsmith, and he promised I should do so on the first opportunity. Soon afterwards Goldsmith came to dine with him, and immediately on my entering the room, Sir Joshua, with a designed abruptness, said to me, "This is Dr Goldsmith; pray why did you wish to see him?" I was much confused by the suddenness of the question, and answered, in my hurry, "Because he is a notable man." This, in one sense of the word, was so very contrary to the character and conduct of Goldsmith, that Sir Joshua burst into a hearty laugh, and said, that Goldsmith should, in future, always be called the notable man.'

JAMES NORTHCOTE, *Life of Sir Joshua Reynolds*

To my parents

CONTENTS

Preface   xiii

1 THE PORTRAIT—AUGUST 21, 1766   1
2 THE DANCING BOY   35
3 FICTION   52
4 THE PHILOSOPHER WHO CARRIES ALL HIS
   GOODS ABOUT HIM   71
5 EMPIRIC   94
6 AN AMPHIBIOUS CREATURE   121
7 GOOSE-PIE AND GOOSEBERRIES   157
8 COMEDY OF HUMOURS   186
9 THE GOOD-NATURED MAN   221
10 EXILES   248
11 NOBODY WITH ME AT SEA BUT MYSELF   276
12 HODGE   296
13 BETWEEN THE COMIC AND THE TRAGIC MUSE   328
14 AFTERMATH   355
   Appendix   363
   Notes   371
   Bibliography   395
   Index   401

A*

ILLUSTRATIONS

Between pages 128 and 129

1a   Oliver Goldsmith by Reynolds, 1766

1b   Sir Joshua Reynolds, Self Portrait, 1768

2a   Green Arbour Court, with the opening onto Breakneck Stairs. Goldsmith lodged with the Butlers in the house on the right.

2b   Fountain Court, the Middle Temple

3a   Mrs Butler by Hogarth

3b   Ralph Griffiths

3c   Thomas Davies

3d   William Kenrick

4   Samuel Johnson by Nollekens

Between pages 224 and 225

5   *The Times I* by Hogarth, September 7, 1762

6 and 7   *Members of The Club*

6a   Robert Chambers by Reynolds

6b   Edmund Burke

6c   Bennet Langton

6d   Topham Beauclerk

7a   Thomas Percy

7b   Samuel Dyer

7c   John Hawkins

7d   Anthony Chamier by Reynolds

8a   Mary and Catherine Horneck by Reynolds, 1766

8b   Robert Nugent (Lord Clare) and family

Between pages 288 and 289

9a   Hugh Kelly

9b   Arthur Murphy by Dance

9c   George Colman by Gainsborough

10a James Boswell by Willison

10b Mrs Thrale by an unknown Italian artist, circa 1784

10c Horace Walpole by T. Lawrence

11   Oliver Goldsmith by Henry Bunbury

12   David Garrick between the Comic and the Tragic Muse,
     by Reynolds (Mrs Abington as the Comic Muse)

Illustrations 1b, 2a, 2b, 3a, 3b, 3c, 3d, 5, 6c, 7a, 7b, 7c, 9a, 11 and 12 are reproduced by kind permission of the trustees of the British Museum; 1a, 4, 6a, 6b, 6d, 7d, 9b, 9c, 10a, 10b, and 10c by kind permission of the National Portrait Gallery; and 8b by kind permission of a private collector, England.

PREFACE

OLIVER GOLDSMITH was an infrequent letter writer and all but a handful of his personal papers were dispersed, apparently beyond recall, at the time of his death in April 1774. The friends who had been thinking in terms of his biography as early as the spring of 1773 mysteriously failed to produce a record until 1801 when Thomas Percy's *Memoir* appeared as a preface to the *Miscellaneous Works* published by Cadell and Davies. The first major biography, by James Prior, was produced in 1837, and in the circumstances Prior must be considered exceptionally lucky to have been able to extract a few first-hand accounts of Goldsmith from elderly men and women who had known the writer slightly in their youth.

Fortunately, he had been too celebrated a figure during the last ten years of his short life for the literary world to allow him to disappear without trace, and several short biographical sketches had been written before Percy at last produced his *Memoir*. They tend to be inaccurate and sometimes as lacking in interpretative qualities as the *Memoir* itself, but they embody useful insights and stories from which a fragmented portrait emerges. The most useful are the sketch published by J. Swan in the year of Goldsmith's death (generally believed to have been written by William Frederick Glover), and a longer study by another tavern companion of Goldsmith's, William Cooke, who had been his neighbour in the Temple. This was published in three parts in the European Magazine for August, September and October 1793.

As a member of the Johnson circle, Goldsmith was in the full view of two avid collectors of impressions, talk and personalities, James Boswell and Hester Thrale. He is to be encountered too in the recollections of Fanny Burney, George Colman the Younger, Thomas Davies, Joseph Cradock, Sir John Hawkins, Fanny Reynolds and James Northcote. Perhaps the most valuable of the first-hand accounts is Sir Joshua Reynolds' perceptive essay about the man who had been his intimate companion for several years.

Whereas the Goldsmith to be found in the pages of Boswell and Mrs Thale is seen through a distorting lens of prejudice and jealousy, in Reynolds' study he is both a likeable and, even more important, a credible figure.

My debt to these predecessors is of course considerable. In the Notes I have tried to keep as accurate a record as possible of my obligations to them and many other commentators on Goldsmith, the Johnson circle and the political, social and artistic background to the age. When the precise nature of the debt is more difficult to define the reader is referred to the book *in toto* rather than to a specific page.

I should like to thank all those who have brought their minds to bear on the specific task of producing this book. Miss Livia Gollancz, Canon D. W. Gundry, Mr Christopher Morris, Miss Mary O'Hara and Mrs Antonia White helped it forward in various ways by suggesting lines of research; and Lady Cairns, Dr Raymond Crawfurd, Mr Humphrey Day, Mrs P. Lowe and Dr Charles Newman were kind enough to answer written enquiries from a stranger.

I am particularly grateful to the specialists who have allowed me to pick their brains in areas where my own were found wanting. They include Mrs Mavis Batey, who introduced me to the site of the demolished village at Nuneham Courtenay, Mr Wallace Breem who put his knowledge of the Inner Temple at my disposal, Mr Patrick Considine, Mr N. W. English, the Honorary Secretary of the Old Athlone Association, who very kindly lent me his manuscript notes and helped to throw light on the Goldsmith country of counties Roscommon and Westmeath; Mr Fairfax Hall; Mr Eric Freeman; Mr Henry Joyce; and Brother David Lawson, O.P. I am indebted to Mr James Kemble, Ch.M., F.R.C.S. for an interpretation of the symptoms of Goldsmith's final illness.

For their kind co-operation in my research I must thank the librarians of All Souls College Oxford, the Representative Church Body of Ireland, the Royal Academy, the Royal College of Surgeons and the Royal College of Physicians, together with the London Borough librarians of Brent and Barnet, the research assistant at Holborn Library and the county archivist at the Essex Records Office for their answers to my enquiries. Miss Ruth Vyse of the Oxford University Archives helped me with the problem of Goldsmith's *ad eundem* degree, and Miss Margaret Griffith, MSS assistant of the University of Dublin, provided details of Henry Goldsmith's career at Trinity College. To both I am deeply indebted. I should also like to express my appreciation for the facilities made available to me at the British Library, the Bodleian, the libraries of Cambridge and Bristol universities, the London Library, the Guildhall Library and the India Office Library. Mr Reginald Williams kindly helped me to locate material in the Prints Room at the British Museum. Mrs Agnes Burrett generously devoted her professional skills to the transforming of my own troubled typescript into something legible and pleasing to the eye. Mrs June Wyton did invaluable work on the index.

Lastly I owe a special debt of gratitude to Professor Ian Jack, not only for encouraging me to write this book and for reading a chapter in typescript but for the stimulating influence of his scholarship and dry wit and his unflagging patience both now and twenty years ago as teacher and friend.

ONE

The Portrait—August 21, 1766

O N AN August afternoon in 1766 two men were shut up together in a studio on the west side of Leicester Square. The man on the dais in the centre seated in a plain mahogany arm-chair without his wig and with shirt open at the neck was thirty-eight years old, and for the third time since June was finding himself in the unusual role of client. The octagonal room with its handsome fireplace, couches and solitary window above eye-level was well known to him, and the portrait painter, Joshua Reynolds, was his greatest friend, a bachelor like himself whose company could be relied on for an evening at the theatre, a stroll through the lamp-lit groves of Vauxhall or under the chandeliers of the assembly rooms in Soho Square. They were both disfigured by the traces of small-pox, though the bland-faced Reynolds with his unvaryingly benign expression was not considered ugly like the sitter.

It was the last of three appointments[1] and, at 2 o'clock when the face of the previous client had been removed from the easel and that of Oliver Goldsmith brought in from the adjacent room, the portrait was already in its outlines the work that can be seen today at Woburn: the nose prominent and coarse with wide nostrils, the upper lip heavy; the forehead, strongly marked with that vertical cleft which created the impression of habitual anxiety, bulging out to overhang eyes, which, naked-looking and dark, seem to need any protection that can be provided. The strangest feature is the mouth, wide, deflected at the corners, undershot, the full lips jutting forward like nose and temples; if it had been the mouth of an unweaned baby rather than a man of thirty-eight it might be imagined searching hungrily for a breast which was unable to provide much nourishment.

Standing with the light behind him and keeping at a distance from his canvas with the aid of a marl-stick and a nineteen-inch brush[2] Reynolds was at the height of his career, celebrated for a technique which lent itself to the accurate recording of every contour. But

I

perhaps the spark of life which glimmers out of this portrait and those of Johnson and Sterne has less to do with technique than with the psychological insights which were revealed when a forgotten manuscript containing his word portraits of Goldsmith, Johnson and Garrick came to light in 1940—insights which made him the ideal person to commemorate on canvas a man who was too often taken at his face value.

Already, that afternoon, Goldsmith's features would have been built up on the white ground with pigments of lake, black, flake-white and Naples yellow selected from the square palette. The outline of the figure, to be worked over later by assistants who painted draperies in an adjoining studio,[3] would also have been sketched in. The choice of a Hamlet-like pose, white fingers keeping a place in the book while the reader pauses in reverie, would strike some contemporaries as inappropriate. They had come to rather different conclusions about the sitter's puzzling character.

*

47 Leicester Square was an unusual house behind its conventional London façade. The heavy door with its cobwebbed fanlight, the three rectangular drawing-room windows on the first floor, the third-floor dormers half-concealed by a shallow parapet, suggested the typical L-shaped terraced house of the time, and so concealed its real size. In 1760, after acquiring long leases on this property and another that backed on to it from Whitcomb Street, Reynolds had spent £1,500 on extensive alterations, including the construction of a suite of rooms on the site of the yard and domestic offices between them.[4] Through a door on the first half-landing of the staircase at the Leicester Square side of the establishment, clients entered a narrow picture-gallery and passed between Reynolds' Titians, Vandycks and Rembrandts[5] on their way to the octagonal painting-room. Beyond were stores and another studio for the drapery-man, Peter Toms, and resident pupils.

Reynolds' house, which survived until 1937, was in the middle of a terrace on the west side of what was then known as Leicester Fields. In keeping with the general 'improving' trend of the period the open ground had recently been enclosed with iron railings, and the vagrants who had until then congregated here and sometimes lighted fires, had been thrust back into one of the evil warrens near at hand, the notorious St Giles' slum to the north-east with its teeming and filthy lodging-houses and the equally unsavoury neighbourhood of the Royal Mews on the site now occupied by the National Gallery and Trafalgar Square. London was a small city by modern standards and the transitions from squalor to Georgian elegance were abrupt.

In spite of the proximity of St. Giles' and the Mews, 47 Leicester Square was the kind of address to signify both wealth and social arrival. Other houses in the late seventeenth-century terrace were owned by aristocrats and high-ranking military and naval men. On the north side of the square in a courtyard behind a row of single storey shops was Leicester House where the present king's parents, Prince Frederick and Princess Augusta of Saxe-Coburg, had held their court in active opposition to George II in the 1740s and 50s, and where the Princess, now in the fifteenth year of her widowhood, still lived, unpopular and suspected like her equally unpopular adviser and friend Lord Bute, of being an *éminence grise* behind the throne of the twenty-eight-year-old George III.

From his drawing-room windows Reynolds could look out across the gravel walks and lawns of the new gardens, beyond the gilded equestrian statue of George I, to the opposite terrace where another widow, Hogarth's, had recently allowed the young painters and engravers who now lived there to set up a billiard table in her late husband's studio. Next door to her, two of the King's younger brothers shared an establishment created out of two houses in the middle of the row. The royal influence was also felt at number 53 where until recently the royal jeweller had resided, and at number 20, the home of the royal dancing master. But apart from the fashionable *bagnio* next door to the young princes, the predominant influence in the square was artistic, and Reynolds had only been conforming to the pattern of the times when he went to live in a square where many other exponents of his craft of portrait-painting were already residing. A few hundred yards to the east, between the Fields and the piazza of Covent Garden, the principal north-south thoroughfare, St. Martin's Lane, was still a focal point for the fine craftsmen of the age, including Chippendale near the corner of Long Acre. It was here, a quarter of a century earlier, that Hogarth had organised a group of forty artists into an academy[7] which met regularly in a basement to draw from the naked figure—an initiative which, however much he himself would have disliked the idea, helped to prepare the way for the foundation of the Royal Academy under the presidency of Reynolds in 1768.

At the back of Leicester House was a tavern in appearance very like Reynolds' house: the Turk's Head in Gerrard Street where Reynolds and Goldsmith had a weekly engagement to dine with Dr Johnson, Edmund Burke and other members of what was known with almost arrogant simplicity as 'The Club'. To the north again stretched without interruption the pleasant dark-brick terraces of Soho, a predominantly middle-class area with its sprinkling of craftsmen, sometimes immigrants. The mansions of Golden Square and Soho Square had been only recently abandoned by their aristocratic owners in favour of the developing western end of town where late seventeenth century speculations like St James's Square, Berkeley Square and Hanover Square were already held fast in their gridiron of wide streets, lined with those deceptively modest house-fronts which Dickens was to find, still staring each other out of countenance' seventy years later. A correspondent to the Public Ledger in 1774 could record the gratifying fact that a brace of woodcocks had been flushed by the gardener who looked after the plantation in Grosvenor Square—an indication that the London of Goldsmith's time began at the eastern edge of Hyde Park and ended with the fields to the east of Whitechapel. To the north, Oxford Street was still the effective boundary, though by the early 1770s the village of Marylebone had been absorbed and the fields to its east were being invaded by the northern extension of Harley Street and by the development in the neighbourhood of the Middlesex hospital. To the south of the river there were still stretches of common land, fields, private and market-gardens within the quadrant between Southwark and Vauxhall. As there were still only two bridges (though a third, Blackfriars, was nearing completion), a trip to the southern bank of the Thames, perhaps in the care of one of the watermen who were famous for their bad manners and satirical tongues,[8] must still to many people have represented a change of scene if not an adventure. Vauxhall was at the height of its popularity and there were other south-bank resorts like the Dog and Duck in St George's Fields which offered dubious society but where even a famous actress like Mrs Bellamy might be found on occasions when she was experiencing difficulty with her creditors.

*

The summer months of 1766 were a period of intense political speculation, and it may have been in July that Reynolds and Goldsmith were interrupted in the studio by Edmund Burke. In the account of this (undated) incident which Northcote passed on to Hazlitt, Goldsmith left the room rather than be forced to listen to their friend's tirade against the King.[9] Six weeks before the final sitting George III had dismissed the Rockingham ministry, with which Burke was closely associated, and invited William Pitt to form a coalition government. To people like Goldsmith, who admired the monarchy and sympathised with the young King's avowed intention to free the country from corruption and wrest back from powerful factions of Whig aristocrats some of the constitutional power which his grandfather had surrendered, it must have seemed that the nation had turned a corner. Reynolds, who shared Burke's Whig philosophy, would have been less sanguine, and within only a few months he was to be proved right, for the appointment of Pitt as first minister and Lord Privy Seal marked only one of many stages in the power struggle which dominated the early years of the new reign.

George III had come to the throne in the middle of a world war which had begun with a series of disasters for Britain and been transformed under the leadership of Pitt into a war of colonial expansion at the expense of the French in Canada and India. The last phase of such a war was not the ideal time for a change of ministry however impatient the new King might be to inaugurate a reign of political virtue. It was important that Pitt, the minister of 'Measures', and the nominal head of the government, the Duke of Newcastle, minister of 'Means', i.e. the controller through the Treasury of a complex system of political patronage and family alliances, should be given every encouragement to complete their task. But a mixture of tactlessness, personal dislike and dilatoriness on the part of the King and the Marquis of Bute, a Scots nobleman whom he treated as a friend and father confessor, had sparked off the resignations of, first Pitt, and then Newcastle himself. The concept of Opposition had not yet entered political life and Pitt, whose influence lay in his ability to mesmerise the House of Commons and in a personal popularity which stretched from the merchant interests of the City of London to the American colonies, was prepared to abide his time and await future developments, but Newcastle, encouraged by the King's uncle, the Duke of Cumberland, managed to suppress his qualms of conscience to the extent of leading his followers in the active harrassment of his successor, Lord Bute.

Bute had been unprepared for the tornado of hostility which was let loose against him. He was represented as a feudal laird intent on imposing an autocracy and on importing hordes of Scots vassals who would seize profitable jobs and places from true Englishmen. The mob gleefully took up the cause and Bute's coach was pelted whenever it rumbled out of South Audley Street, while pamphleteers and cartoonists, representing the new first minister as a leather riding-boot and the forty-three year old Princess Dowager as a petticoat, insinuated that the two were lovers. As the government attempted to negotiate a settlement with the French, the departed ministers used the press and their place-men and supporters in the upper and lower chambers to condemn the very clauses they had shown themselves willing to accept when in office. Bute, who had had no practical experience of politics beyond the intrigues of the rival 'court' during the preceding reign, had endured the onslaught until April 1763 when his resignation was prompted by a redoubled outburst of public fury on the imposition of an excise tax (on cider) which was represented as a threat to privacy and all the most sacred liberties of Englishmen.

It was a few days after the departure of Bute that the notorious 45th number of the *North Briton*, an anti-ministerial journal edited by a member of parliament, John Wilkes, accused the King of having lied to the country in describing the proposed peace treaty as honourable, and acting through his new first minister, Grenville, George III set in motion proceedings which would drag on until the end of the decade, bringing the House of Commons into disrepute and transforming a witty rake into a popular hero.

By March 1764 the first phase of the Wilkes affair was over. He had been arrested on a warrant of dubious legality, imprisoned in the Tower, released amid popular acclaim and, after his escape to Paris while awaiting trial on a new charge of obscene libel, expelled from the House of Commons. Boswell fell under the spell of his raffish charm in Naples in 1765 (but revised his opinion on being shown a letter that Wilkes had written to a discarded mistress).[10] One of the victims of the violent feelings aroused by this first round of the Wilkes affair was Hogarth, the last two years of whose life were soured by the squibs and lampoons which he drew down on himself by his support of the government in its attempts to conclude the Seven Years War.[11]

A year before Goldsmith's sittings in Leicester Square, when the King had no longer been able to tolerate being bullied by Bute's successor George Grenville, the Marquis of Rockingham had been invited to form a ministry. Rockingham was as much a part of the Whig tradition of land and family alliances as the Duke of Newcastle himself but he had a reputation for honesty and a quiet magnetism which was to hold together a group of politicians, including Burke, during years of political eclipse and allow them to convince at least themselves that they represented policies and ideas rather than mercenary interests. The Marquis had rarely spoken in the House of Lords and played such a passive role in cabinet that his ministry had become known as a 'round robin' administration, but as the owner of vast estates in Yorkshire and Northamptonshire (and all that this entailed with regard to suggestible tenants, neighbours and friends) he headed a formidable clique which commanded power in both Lords and Commons. He was also one of the largest Irish absentee landlords of his day. In 1765 he had made the decision from which so much of the prestige of the group was ultimately to derive when he asked Edmund Burke to become his private secretary. Rockingham was not the last politician to discover that a cause embraced in opposition is better dropped in office and, ironically, one of Burke's first tasks had been to buy off Wilkes, whose 'martyrdom' the Rockingham group had energetically exploited. He had reappeared in London on the formation of the new Ministry and it became expedient to purchase his prompt return to Italy.[12]

After his election to the seat of Wendover in time to introduce the legislation for the repeal of the Stamp Act so deeply resented by the American colonists, Burke had become the group's spokesman in the Commons. The reputed £30,000 which Rockingham settled on his secretary would prove an extremely sound investment.[13] Seen through the medium of Burke's oratory and political essays, the Rockingham administration really did appear to be a ministry in which principles mattered more than places.

Rockingham had been defeated, this summer, by the mercantile interests whose support he had deliberately courted. It was a period of slump, and for the first time in British politics foreign policy became subservient to economic interests. In 1765 Burke was warning readers of the *Annual Register* that 'the Nation has lost its good Humour and unless things are set to rights, it is become a matter of great Indifference to the Publick, and will be more so every day "who have the places".'[14] The repeal of the Stamp Act had been inspired by merchants who could gauge the strength of colonial hostility to it in the pages of their own ledgers; and Burke had acted as liaison officer between the cabinet and a committee of twenty-eight merchants under the chairmanship of Barlow Trecothick which had been established, with ministerial encouragement, to organise commercial opinion throughout the nation. But by the early summer of 1766 the merchants, having tasted success, were in a bullying mood and Rockingham found himself squeezed between rival factions representing the divergent interests of American and West Indian trade. It was at this point, when the Ministry had already been weakened by the death of the Duke of Cumberland, that the King had decided to intervene.

William Pitt, who had had his first audience on July 12th, was no favourite of the King but at this moment he seemed a highly acceptable substitute for the man who had earned himself the title 'King Rockingham' through his attempts to undermine the royal prerogative. Pitt, the great Commoner, had as few reasons for welcoming the perpetuation of oligarchical rule as George III himself, and may even have been shocked by Rockingham's attempts to further undermine the constitutional position of the monarchy. The King and the Commoner acted from very different motives however: while Pitt envisaged for himself a role of tremendous political power, by-passing his cabinet colleagues and acting through direct consultation with the King, George III appears to have been aiming at the destruction of 'faction' and a reassertion of royal authority by means of the access of extra-parliamentary popularity which Pitt would bring him. This August the two men were in agreement: the new administration was to be 'of all parties and no parties'.

Unluckily, Pitt was by now a semi-invalid and quite unable to cope with the rôle to which he had committed himself. The excitement of July 12th had hardly had a chance to die down before the public was astounded to learn that he had accepted a peerage and become Lord Chatham. For a House of Commons man it was an act of political self-immolation. The news was received with incredulity in the City where until now he had had a powerful following, and very quickly it began to appear that the main factors of his foreign and colonial policy—support for an alliance with Prussia, and the belief that the appeal of his name alone would lead to an improvement in relations with the Americans—were dead issues. Unperceived in the gossip and speculation of this summer were elements of Greek tragedy. By the following February Chatham would have suffered a mental breakdown on discovering his inability either to split up the Whig alliance that was forming against him or to secure the loyalty of his own political associates in the Commons. Between June 1766, when Goldsmith sat to Reynolds for the first time, and this afternoon of August 21st, were sown the seeds of a troubled political future which would include the American war and the loss of an empire.

The political crisis of July had coincided with a spasm of social unrest. The hard winter of '65/'66 had been followed by a cold and wet summer. The effects of the continuous rain throughout May and June were seen in the shortage of hay and the loss of livestock in summer floods.[15] In spite of a fine July and August the harvest failed and the price of bread and other commodities rose steeply producing riots and the inevitable attacks on flour mills up and down the country. The anger of the poor, on whom the burden fell most heavily and whose prospects of employment had already been worsened by the economic recession which followed the Peace of Paris, exploded in mindless acts. Corn sacks were ripped open and the grain scattered. Butter, cheese and bacon were seized from shops and thrown into the street.

In the world of the arts, painters and sculptors were also experiencing hard times, though, in a society as split as that of eighteenth-century England, the likelihood of their experiencing the harsher realities of subsistence living was small. In April the one annual exhibition of the works of living painters, at the Society for the Encouragement of Arts, Manufactures and Commerce, had been dominated as usual by portraits, the only contemporary art form which was really profitable. There had been no entries this year

from Richard Wilson, the merits of whose classically sober landscapes of Wales and the Roman Campagna had been under-rated
in the exhibitions of the previous three years.[16] Reynolds now
charged 30 guineas for a head, 70 guineas for a half-length and 150
guineas for a full-length portrait. Wilson was delighted if he got as
much as £30 for a landscape and at the end of his life, according to
James Northcote, was 'obliged to borrow ten pounds to go and die
in Wales'.[17] This year, Benjamin West's large historical and
mythological canvases, 'The Continence of Scipio', 'Pylades and
Orestes', and 'Diana and Endymion' had been widely discussed,
and West's servants had profited when carriages had arrived to
collect them for a private view; but no-one bought.[18] Finding that
there was no sale for the paintings of 'modern moral subjects' with
which he had hoped to wean the public from its narcissistic taste
for portraiture, Hogarth had spent the last years of his life as an
engraver, thus tacitly admitting that his real patrons were further
down the social scale. But in 1764 a sympathetic observer was
fearful that Fuseli's poverty would throw him into company 'every
way unsuitable, or, indeed, insupportable to a stranger of any
taste: especially as the common people are of late brutalised.'[19]
Reynolds himself recognised the problem and helped painters in
distress, either through a timely purchase (he owned Gainsborough's 'Girl with Pigs' for example) or through gifts of money.
But while modern painters languished, the dealers in Italian masters
thrived and the rage for antiquity which had been noticed earlier in
the century continued unabated, creating a tribe of educated rogues
who, if the journalists and playwrights of the age are to be credited,
would pillage Italian churches, purloin each other's more moveable
treasures[20] or, like Samuel Foote's *Carmine* and *Puff*,* fake a
Correggio, a Roman medal or a mutilated head 'fresh from Her-
culaneum'.[21]

Theatrical entertainment was now provided by four theatres, two
in Covent Garden and two facing one another across the Haymarket.
The former were licensed for the performance of plays, Drury Lane
under the managership of David Garrick and Covent Garden under
that of the singer John Beard. Covent Garden, built in 1732, was a
comparatively modern building but was just as small as Drury Lane,
where the principal acting area in front of the proscenium arch was

*Characters in his satire on the art market, *Taste* (1753)

only thirty feet wide and twenty feet deep,[22] a factor which assisted Garrick in his development of a more natural style of acting. At capacity, eighteen hundred spectators would be crammed mercilessly into a space originally designed to take less than half this number. The Italian Opera House in the Haymarket, designed by Vanbrugh, was a larger building and, on the other side of the street a few yards to the north of the present Haymarket Theatre, was the Little Theatre in a yard behind private houses, where for several seasons the authorities had turned a blind eye on Samuel Foote's illegal presentations of farce. A good part of the repertoire at both Drury Lane and Covent Garden consisted of classical revivals (Shakespeare made 'polite'; Congreve, Vanbrugh and Farquhar made decent); the rest consisted largely of thin comedies of sentiment and contemporary manners, and flaccid historical dramas based on stories from Greek and Roman antiquity—though the long theatre evenings would end in a livelier vein with a short musical entertainment or farces like Garrick's *Miss in Her Teens* and Foote's satirical commentaries on current affairs. The middle classes who had taken fright at Jeremy Collier's attacks on the 'lewdness' of the theatre at the turn of the century, had long since been wooed back, but the influence of their tastes in drama still impinged heavily on the repertoire. Fortunately their musical appetites were more robust and Covent Garden regularly performed a series of Handel oratorios at Easter, usually attracting a sizeable Jewish audience for *Judas Maccabeus.*[23]

Garrick had been in charge at Drury Lane since 1747 and his career was now entering its last phase. He had left England at the end of the troubled '63/'64 season and was not seen again on the stage until he appeared as Benedict in November '65. From now on he would make only one or two appearances a week, as opposed to the three or four of his busiest years and, denying himself new parts, would concentrate on keeping at their highest pitch such famous roles as Richard III, Hamlet, Macbeth, Lear, Ranger (in Hoadley's *Suspicious Husband*) Don Felix (in Mrs Centlivre's *The Wonder*) and Abel Drugger (in *The Alchemist*). The great success of the season that was ending as Goldsmith sat for the first time to Reynolds was *The Clandestine Marriage* which Garrick had assisted his business partner George Colman to write.

A summer company under the direction of Barry and his wife

Mrs Dancer, the leading players at the Theatre Royal, Dublin, was now in residence at the Italian Opera House with a repertoire which included *Othello*, *King Lear*, *Romeo and Juliet*, Otway's *Venice Preserved* and Richard Steele's answer to Jeremy Collier, *The Conscious Lovers*. Goldsmith would have had mixed feelings about Steele's play, which was still an active influence in the promotion of the sentimental style in comedy but, as an admirer of Jacobean and Restoration drama, he would have approved of their other choices. The night before his final sitting, Barry had played Romeo to Mrs Dancer's Juliet: it was one of his great rôles[24] thanks to Garrick who had revived the play after a silence of eighty years. Barry would almost certainly have performed it in Garrick's own 'improved' version which allowed him protracted death agonies and a brief last act reunion with Juliet—an opportunity which Shakespeare had missed. This had been followed, according to custom, by an after-piece—on this occasion Samuel Foote's satire on Methodism, *The Minor*, in which the author himself played the rôle of a Covent Garden madam with immortal longings.

Foote, the most brilliant impersonator and comedian of his age, was himself a topic of conversation this summer. Earlier in the year he had lost a leg as a result of a fall from a frisky horse on which the King's brother, the Duke of York, had mounted him. He had quickly returned to the stage, showing off his wooden leg to some comic effect, and appearing to enjoy the prospect of endless punning which the accident had opened up to him. In the second week of July he had received some compensation for his loss in the form of a royal patent which legalised his productions at the Little Theatre.

Reynolds and Goldsmith had been at Drury Lane on the evening of January 23rd to see Garrick play Lusignan in a royal command performance of Aaron Hill's *Zara*. The King had been less anxious to see the play than to have a chance to look at Jean Jacques Rousseau who, having run into difficulties with the Geneva authorities, had come to England at the invitation of David Hume. Rousseau had been placed, by design, in Garrick's box, opposite the King's, where he had alarmed Mrs Garrick by bowing to the audience until he seemed on the point of tumbling into the orchestra pit. Rousseau was now staying at Wootton in Staffordshire, but he was no longer on speaking terms with Hume. A rather vapid hoax of Horace Walpole's in the form of a letter apparently addressed to the philosopher by Frederick the Great had done its work on raw nerves and driven the always susceptible Rousseau into another bout of paranoia. But he had been received with enthusiasm by men and women who had read *Emile* and *La Nouvelle Eloise*—both of which were now available in English. Society had embarked upon a flirtation with ideas not quite compatible with the Age of Reason, as can be sensed in the gushing tones of the Scots lady who begged Hume to bring Rousseau with him on a visit: 'Oh bring him with you; the English are not worthy of him. Sweet old man, he shall sit beneath an oak and hear Druids' songs; bring dear old Rousseau.'[28] Not everyone shared Mrs Cochrane's feelings. Burke met Rousseau this year and conceived a strong dislike of him, while Johnson told Boswell that he would 'sooner sign a sentence for his transportation than that of any felon who has gone from the Old Bailey these many years'.[29]

The principal event in the world of publishing over the last twelve months had been the long-overdue appearance of Dr Johnson's edition of Shakespeare. This work had been subscribed for on the issue of a prospectus in 1756 but by Christmas '57, the promised publication date, the list of subscribers had been lost and the money spent. In 1763 Charles Churchill had drawn attention to Johnson's indolence in his satirical account of the Cock Lane Ghost affair, reaching the most uncharitable of conclusions:

> He for subscribers baits his hook,
> And takes your cash; but where's the book?[30]

Johnson was at last goaded into activity; but the eight volumes that Jacob Tonson had brought out the previous October had had a restrained reception. There was disappointment that this was not the definitive edition which Johnson's reputation for scholarship had led people to expect. As a commentator, Johnson was too much within the Augustan classical tradition to feel completely committed to Shakespeare's eclectic exuberance or to an art which swept away every landmark of critical theory like a river in flood, and as the emendator of a corrupt text he was too much of a scholar not to be inhibited by a knowledge of the pits into which his immediate predecessors had fallen. 'I do not propose this with much confidence,' he adds revealingly after his failure to respond to a simple pun has led him to burden a phrase with an over-ingenious explanation.[31] The breakdown which overtook Johnson this summer may have been connected with the recent burst of editorial activity and perhaps with his sense of having failed in a project which had been in his mind for twenty years. But in other terms, which no one in Johnson's circle would have despised, the *Shakespeare* had been a success: it had earned the editor at least £1,300.

In January the public which was eagerly awaiting the ninth and last volume of *Tristram Shandy* had been offered *Mr Yorick's Sermons* as a stop-gap. Goldsmith was deeply offended that Sterne, who had started work on the new volume of his novel in July and would finish it in November, should still be taken seriously as a clergyman. His own publisher John Newbury had concentrated this year on moral edification of a quite unequivocal kind. Apart from a *history of Mecklenberg*, evidently written in honour of the Queen, *The Vicar of Wakefield* and a little book called *Goody Two-Shoes* ('See the original Ms. in the Vatican at Rome and the Cuts by Michael Angelo') which was to show a capacity for survival almost as strong as Goldsmith's novel, his list was predeominantly theological. It included topically enough, *The Truth of the Christian Religion vindicated from the Objections of Unbelievers, particularly of Mr John James Rousseau. By the editors of the Christian's Magazine.*[32]

*

Londoners, this year, were as intent on improving their city as on improving their minds. The war with France had been followed by a period of cheap money[33] which made this an age of speculative building and 'improvements'. The emphasis on gentility that can be felt in the repeated appearance of the word 'polite' throughout the decade in the titles of magazines and anthologies was echoed by the desire for a cleaner, quieter and safer environment. A French visitor,[34] the previous year, had been impressed by the shops of the Strand and Fleet Street, and the even finer ones tucked away in the quiet courts which provided pedestrians with convenient traffic-free routes between Holborn and Fleet Street. He liked their large windows and glass-paned doors and reported that they were finer than any he had seen in Paris. But he had been surprised that the citizens who were busy purveying works of fine craftsmanship to the rest of Europe should tolerate imperfectly paved and dirty streets with a filthy central gutter (the 'kennel') and cobbled footways. The cobbles were unsatisfactory because they were imperfectly bedded (the rammer was little used, but coaches and wagons with wheels broad enough to act in this capacity were encouraged by means of tax exemptions). M. Grosley believed that the average Londoner's black stockings, drab blue surtouts and wigs of brownish curling hair had been chosen with an eye to the dirt and standing water with which they were frequently spattered. Outside St Clement Dane's church he had taken note of a puddle between three and four inches deep. Some attempt seems to have been made to save the pedestrian from the worst effects of the puddles, and, at the expense of the carriages, the Strand had been ribbed with small 'causeways' of larger stones which linked the two footways.

During M. Grosley's visit, the Westminster Council had set up an Improvements Committee with the result that concerns like paving, lighting and sanitation (the new houses of Mayfair and St James's had outside privies which communicated with sewers and thence with the Thames or, less fortunately, with the pond in Green Park) had now been taken out of amateur hands and confided to the care of paid Commissioners. An act of parliament stipulated that householders were to be responsible for cleaning the footway in front of their houses each day, and were to provide two oil-lamps to light the street in front of their houses.[35] A major undertaking of 1765 had been the rationalisation of St James's Street, which until then had descended from Piccadilly to the gates of the Palace in a series of bumps. Its footways had now been terraced, but cries of anguish echoed through the newspapers, for householders found their front doors either above or below the level of the pavement.[36] Whitehall and Pall Mall had been paved with free-stone and, by 1766, the work of re-paving the Strand had begun. Goldsmith might have decided, this August afternoon, to walk from the Temple to Leicester Fields by way of Covent Garden and Long Acre, to avoid the worse than usual congestion in the Strand.

In June, this year, the City of London had followed Westminster's example and committed itself to re-paving the streets in Aberdeen granite and removing 'inconveniences and obstructions'. Whatever was to be gained in convenience, a certain amount of colour was about to be lost, for 'obstructions' included not only the regularly spaced posts which divided the pedestrian area from the carriageway but also the elaborate trade signs of painted or gilded wrought-iron which hung above them from Whitechapel to Temple Bar advertising the activities of barbers, mercers, surgeons, fishmongers or wigmakers, with razors, westphalia hams, lancets, salmon and golden periwigs.[37] Bow windows projecting on to the street were also to disappear, but nervous pedestrians may have accepted fairly cheerfully the loss of colour implied by the ban on 'penthouses loaded with flower-pots'. Traffic restrictions were introduced. Carts were allowed to remain for a limited unloading period after which they risked impounding. Ash and euphemistically designated 'refuse' (the City lacked even the primitive sewers of the West End) were to be deposited in proper 'dust-holes' to await collection.[38] In spite of such improvements, the Thames remained the principal source of London's water supply, each house receiving piped water three times a week. The City of London improvements committee was arranging for the names of every street and alley to be inscribed on their corners and for houses to be numbered. In St James's and Mayfair, brass plates displaying the names of the occupants were already appearing and the obligatory oil-lamps were incorporated elegantly into the design of railings which culminated on either side of house entrances in iron pillars or sometimes met in an ornamental arch. The approach to Reynolds' house was particularly imposing as his lamps were supported (like some of the others in the square) by stone obelisks standing where the edge of the pavement would now be.

Not all Englishmen would have regarded the changes simply as the march of progress. Some saw in them a dangerous new softness and even decadence. A reader of the *London Chronicle* in June 1765 was alarmed by the signs of Trade sweeping all before it: 'Have we now any shops? Are they not all turned into warehouses? Have we not the English warehouse, the Scotch warehouse, the Irish warehouse, the shirt warehouse, and even the buckle and button warehouse?';[39] and a City man picking up an unfounded rumour that Mrs Cornelys planned to open a branch of her Soho Square assembly rooms in Bishopsgate, wrote in alarm to the *Public Advertiser* on March 14, '66: 'What an age of depravity and corruption do we live in; how opposite are we getting to that industry, uprightness, and proper management of business, for which this Metropolis has ever been so famous'.[40]

There was an element of snobbery in the frequently voiced objections that working class people were spending money on commodities like tea, which within living memory had been exclusively a luxury item, or that, as the result of a thriving second-hand trade in clothes and wigs, servants, apprentices and small tradesmen on a Sunday jaunt to a tea-garden were not immediately distinguishable from people with very different incomes and expectations. At the same time commentators were beginning to notice that blurring of differences in manners and living standards between the nobility and the increasingly prosperous middle class, which can still be sensed today in the family resemblance of the Georgian village house to the red-brick mansion, or a Pembroke table to one of the fine pieces that Chippendale's workmen were producing to order. In his *London Eclogues* of 1772, Charles Jenner laments the spread of 'luxury' and ascribes rising prices to the expensive tastes that tradesmen are acquiring. The Mercer

> Must raise his soap and candles, to afford
> To dress himself, on Sundays, like a lord;
> Whilst that pert puppy, with the powder'd queue,
> Must pay his barber out of me or you'

and while his apprentices scull up stream to drink wine in the taverns of Richmond and Windsor, his daughter's tastes are clearly leading her to the very brink of debauchery:

> Whilst Miss despises all domestic rules,
> But lisps the French of Hackney boarding-schools;
> And ev'ry lane around Whitechapel bars
> Resounds with screaming notes, and harsh guitars.'[41]

Amongst prosperous City people there was an eagerness to acquire a weekend retreat or 'box' to which the family could retire armed with cold chickens, bottles of brandy punch and clean linen when business ceased in the early hours of Saturday afternoon. A typical box would be found not more than three miles from the Mansion House and, although detached, might be part of a row bordering one of the main roads. Sometimes a little summer-house actually topped the boundary wall so that refugees who found the country too isolated could sit and observe the passing traffic. In the garden, a fountain might be found together with statues of such popular pantomime characters as Harlequin and Scaramouche, and also a little wooden temple ornamented with spires or battlements, set in a grove of shrubs, which would prove on closer inspection to be the 'necessary house'. These pioneer commuters were easy prey for writers like George Colman and Charles Jenner who drew a contrast between the still idyllic countryside of England and this hinterland which, by their standards, was already beginning to suffer from urban blight. From the attic window of his box, Colman's *cit* enjoys 'a beautiful vista of two men hanging in chains in Kennington Common, with a distant view of St Paul's Cupola enveloped in a cloud of smoke';[42] and Jenner, too, lamented the unsavoury influence of the city:

> Where'er around I cast my wand'ring eyes,
> Long burning rows of fetid bricks arise,
> And nauseous dunghills swell in mould'ring heaps,
> Whilst the fat sow beneath their covert sleeps.
> I spy no verdant glade, no gushing rill,
> No fountain bubbling from the rocky hill,
> But stagnant pools adorn our dusty plains,
> Where half-starv'd cows wash down their meal of grains.
> No traces here of sweet simplicity,
> No lowing herd winds gently o'er the lea,
> No tuneful nymph, with cheerful roundelay,
> Attends to milk her kine at close of day,
> But droves of oxen through yon clouds appear,
> With noisy dogs and butchers in their rear . . .

There is plenty of evidence in his journalism that Goldsmith's temperament and political stance gave him a sympathy for those Londoners of 1766 who disliked the changes. Although he certainly patronised the emporia which aroused the indignation of the London Chronicle correspondent, and even gave his readers some not entirely impractical instructions on how to obtain credit from them,[44] he shared their suspicions of economic forces which had gathered momentum with bewildering speed in this period of rapid colonial and commercial expansion. There was no snobbery in his attitude. Like Johnson, who was at his most fierce when the simple pleasures of the poor were disparaged, Goldsmith had been too close to poverty himself to criticise people who found consolation from some of the nastiness of working-class life in a second-hand wig or in a cup of tea, however expensive. But from *The Citizen of the World* to *The Deserted Village* his position on his age's dangerous tendency towards luxury remained the same. What he perhaps failed to realise was that, without this new affluence, there would have been no middle class readership to cast an eye on his 'Chinese Letters' after studying the trade news in the *Public Ledger*, or to buy those popular histories for which he was to receive generous payment in the last years of his life. The success of such works signifies that the well-to-do tradesmen of Whitechapel with musical ambitions for their daughters sometimes also bought books.

*

The summer months were a slack period for Reynolds since by the end of June most of the people who could have afforded his prices had taken to the roads out of London and were now agonising over the siting of a beech grove on their country estate or perhaps, like Lord Harcourt of Nuneham Courtenay who had sat in Reynolds' painting chair eleven years ago, supervising the erection of a Grecian temple where until very recently an entire village had nestled round a mediaeval church.[45] There was no question of the sitter owning the finished portrait himself (he was to be installed with other members of the Johnson circle, also painted by Reynolds, in the house of a wealthy brewer at Streatham) but he was probably being accommodating to a friend by sitting in this dead season.

Reynolds' decision to remove all contemporary features from the portrait was unusual for him. He may have been consciously creating a record for posterity by portraying him timelessly, in a costume that he had worn at a masquerade in Soho Square; and this would also have been a tactful way of forestalling a man who was notorious for rigging himself up in flashy clothes. So, on Reynolds' canvas, Goldsmith becomes partly Hamlet, partly a Roman senator wrapped in a toga, partly a courtier of the reign of Charles I; and always, lurking in the dark eyes which another friend, Dr Glover, had seen to possess 'a melting softness . . . that was the genuine effect of his humanity',[46] is the possibility of an explosion of laughter which will take the slowwitted by surprise and be quite beyond the comprehension of the more stolid bystanders, who will congratulate themselves on discovering that the famous poet is a fool. By removing the curled and ribboned wig, the laced coat and the sword which, to a passer-by in the street, had once given him the appearance of an insect stuck on a pin, Reynolds both invested his friend with dignity and at the same time brought out the strain of almost child-like simplicity in him. For all the sombre draperies he is still the man who could steal away with a candle-stick from the company in George Colman's drawing-room to console the small boy who had been punished for smacking him across the face, and do conjuring tricks for him on the dining-room carpet.[47]

For two years, since the publication of a poem called *The Traveller*, Oliver Goldsmith had been famous. Lion-hunters sought him out in the taverns of Fleet Street, cadgers, especially if they were Irish like himself or men who could present literary credentials of one kind or another, tracked him down to his chambers at King's Bench Walk in the Temple. He was the subject of dozens of stories, many of them emanating from himself and many designed to show how thoroughly absurd he was, but his attempts to improve his image were rarely kept up for more than a few minutes at a time. Now, Reynolds was attempting to correct an impression which he knew to be misleading.

Goldsmith might have been forgiven, that afternoon on the rostrum, if the vertical furrow above his nose had deepened from a consciousness of being at the heart of London's literary and artistic life. This year had seen the publication not only of *The Vicar of Wakefield* but of French and German translations of *The Citizen of the World*,[48] the collected edition of a series of anonymous 'Chinese Letters' which had appeared in the *Public Ledger* in 1760 and 1761. The previous year an enviable cachet had been bestowed on him when he was invited by Reynolds and Johnson to become a founder member, with Burke and six others, of the club which assembled on Monday evenings in Gerrard Street. It was an honour for which David Garrick would have to wait another seven years.

The founding of The Club had marked a shift in the social orientation of London's literary and artistic life, for its leading members all came from lower middle class backgrounds. Johnson's father had been a none too successful provincial bookseller who on market days would travel from Lichfield to Uttoxeter to stand behind a stall. Reynolds was the son of an enlightened but badly paid Taunton schoolmaster, while Burke had grown up in the heart of commercial Dublin in a wine-merchant's house on Ormonde Quay and Goldsmith's father had been lucky to find a Church of Ireland living sufficiently poor not to have attracted a more influential churchman. These men were newcomers to London, as was demonstrated by Johnson's Staffordshire accent and by the brogue which neither Burke nor Goldsmith attempted to shed. Another member, Anthony Chamier was, like Garrick, of French Huguenot descent.

The prestige which this closely-knit group of men enjoyed illustrates a change in the literary scene since the time of Alexander Pope, who had died twenty-two years ago. Under the first two Hanoverian kings government policy had helped to give patronage a bad name. Robert Walpole had spent large sums of public money on buying support for the government but, rather than provide pensions or sinecures for writers of talent, he had sought the quick returns offered by the crude and often virulent journalism of his age. Pope's *Dunciad* and *Moral Essays* had in turn contributed to the undermining of private patronage, for they had not only given an invidious prominence to the struggling authors of Grub Street but had mocked their wealthy patrons, overlooking the fact that men of real talent like John Gay and Edward Young had sometimes received help from discriminating aristocrats. The would-be patron was inevitably discouraged by Pope's unfair attack on a man like the Earl of Halifax ('Bufo'), who had assisted Newton as well as Congreve and Addison, or by such satirical portraits as the young lord attended by his jockeys, huntsmen and poetasters in *The Dunciad*, As if anticipating the gap that his satire would create, Pope painted an heroic picture of the man of letters who had won his way through to financial independence:

> Not Fortune's Worshipper, nor Fashion's Fool,
> Not Lucre's Madman, nor Ambition's Tool,
> Not proud, nor servile, be one Poet's praise
> That, if he pleas'd, he pleas'd by manly ways . . .[49]

It is, of course, Pope's compliment to himself when, after ten years' hard work, his versions of the *Iliad* and the *Odyssey* had added prosperity to independence. This, he proclaimed, was the status to which in future all self-respecting authors should aspire, and when he himself sat in the Palladian summer-house at Cirencester Park or dined with Lord Bolingbroke at Dawley it was accepted that he was there on terms of equality.

Samuel Johnson's difficulties when he arrived in London as a failed schoolmaster in 1737 and the temporary solution he found by writing semi-fictitious 'parliamentary reports' for John Cave's *Gentleman's Magazine* reflect the climate of an interim period between the age when a writer was either a gentleman or a protégé and an age of publishers' advances and commissioned writing in which, in the 'sixties and 'seventies, Goldsmith had every opportunity of earning himself a respectable income. The links between the two are the magazines and the rising middle class audience which had been educated into buying them by the enormous prestige which accompanied the comparatively short runs of the *Tatler* and the *Spectator* between 1709 and 1712. By the 'thirties and 'forties, the number of weekly or bi-weekly journals compiled on the Addison/Steele plan with a mixture of social commentary, moral exhortation and, usually fictitious, 'letters from members of the public', had grown to such an extent that Cave seemed to be performing a public service when he announced that his new *Gentleman's Magazine* would be a compendium of the best pieces that could be found in the other journals of the day. The concept of literary property had still to be defined.

A new and specifically middle class identity can also be sensed behind the success of a writer like Samuel Richardson. His first novel, *Pamela*, had told the story of a lower middle class girl who through a combination of prudence, stubbornness and much proclaimed virtue succeeded in extracting an honourable proposal from Lord B——, the young rake who had tried to seduce her. Members of Lord B——'s class would hardly have approved of such a tale, but the prolonged success of *Pamela* in other spheres is illustrated by the recurrence of its plot in such popular works as the little illustrated books which John Newbery was persuading city folk to buy their children in the 'fifties and 'sixties. Significantly, Johnson praised Richardson (as the author of *Clarissa*) while disparaging the novels of Fielding. There is an echo of this judgment in the rapid decline in the popularity of Fielding's plays in the middle of the century and the prevailing taste for more sentenious works.

Many years before the publication of *The Deserted Village*, with its condemnation of landlords like Lord Harcourt, Goldsmith's writing had shown a strong anti-aristocratic bias. But the precedent had been created by Johnson in the great middle class Declaration of Independence, the Letter to Lord Chesterfield (written, ironically, after Chesterfield had given the forthcoming Dictionary a generous and anonymous puff in *The World*). Backed by a consortium of booksellers and with a team of Scots in his attic Johnson had toiled for eight years and now wished other observers than Lord Chesterfield to know that it was too late to think in terms of aristocratic patronage, which was easily bestowed but which did not always arrive at the right time. Johnson could, on occasions, be over-assertive about his hard-won independence and middle class identity. Making the acquaintance of Reynolds at the house of the Misses Cotterell near Cavendish Square and feeling that they were both being neglected in favour of the titled woman who had arrived after them, Johnson had mischievously assumed the honest working man and called across the room to Reynolds, 'How much do you think you and I could get in a week if we were to work as hard as we could?'.[50] On another occasion he criticised Reynolds for having remarked 'that nobody *wore* laced coats now; and that once everybody wore them': 'See now,' he commented afterwards to a friend, 'how absurd that is; as if the bulk of mankind consisted of fine gentlemen that came to him to sit for their pictures. If every man who wears a laced coat (that he can pay for) was extirpated, who would miss them?' For all this—and his own rather flamboyant scruffiness—he believed that lords should live up to their rôle and that Mrs Thrale should choose materials for her dresses that matched her affluent station in life. According to Mrs Thrale, he himself was not averse to being told that he had 'the notions [and] manners of a gentleman'.[52]

The only recorded contemporary reaction to the portrait which Reynolds was completing on this August afternoon of 1766 came from Reynolds' younger sister, Fanny, who ran his house for him and, in spite of her lively mind, moderate talent for painting and a spirit of initiative which led her to make some useful additions to her brother's collection in the course of a visit to a Paris saleroom, suffered the fate of other useful relations in being taken completely for granted. Snubbed in her efforts to enter her brother's world—

'They make other people laugh, and me cry,' he said quite unfairly about her paintings and tried to prevent her getting access to his paint-box—she nevertheless attempted to supervise his social life. When he returned from a visit to Blenheim with the news that he had received a frosty reception from the patrons who had graciously invited him to call on them, she quickly spotted what had gone wrong: her brother had gone straight into the presence of the Duke and Duchess without first removing his riding boots.[53] She was also highly dubious about a purchase which her brother was rumoured to have made from a retiring Lord Mayor, and shrank from driving about London in a coach gorgeously decorated with panels depicting the four seasons. (Reynolds apparently missed the point when he asked her if she would prefer to ride in a carriage like an apothecary's.) Fanny had strong feelings about her brother's friends. She revered Johnson and was loved and respected by him in return—she and not her brother was 'Renny'; but her attitude to Goldsmith was ambivalent, partly perhaps because the easy companionship and familiarity that existed between the two men made her a little jealous, and partly because, with his rambling stories which left one wondering when to laugh and his tendency to give untimely renderings of 'Death and the Lady' (singing the Lady's part in falsetto), he completely failed to reach her own level of decorum. She could see that in one sense the portrait of Goldsmith was true. It did not attempt to disguise features which, in her opinion, made him the ugliest man in London. But she could not understand the rather melancholy dignity with which he had been invested. Oliver Goldsmith's portrait, she told James Northcote, was 'a good likeness, but the most flattered picture my brother ever painted'.[54]

The paradox built into the portrait of 1766 is reflected in other contemporary reactions to Goldsmith, perhaps nowhere so strongly as in the account of him embedded in James Boswell's *Life of Johnson*. Boswell had returned in February from a two-and-half year visit to the continent and renewed his acquaintance with the writer whom he had first encountered in Johnson's company in the summer of 1763. Boswell had been twenty-three at that time, a clever and energetic young man who was determined both to capitalise on the advantage of being the Laird of Auchinlechs' elder son, and to overcome the disadvantages of a Calvinist upbringing.

His endeavours in the latter direction included a brief conversion to Roman Catholicism and a briefer affair with an 'actress' after a series of experiments in dark alley-ways off the Strand and in the starlit walks of St James's Park, of which he possessed one of the six thousand keys.[55] These two activities established a pattern which was to be fixed for many years to come. His philandering, as recorded in the journals discovered at Malahide Castle in 1940, often reads like a strenuous attempt to prove something to himself and frequently resulted in the same painful result as his encounter with the girl of Covent Garden; on the other hand a strange combination of intelligence and obtuseness gave him the courage to introduce himself to a series of authority figures who quickly suceeded the Roman Catholic church in his widely flung affections. What he sought from Johnson and, during his visit to Europe, from Rousseau and from General Gian Battista Paoli, was a reassurance that the greatness of mind and spirit which he believed he had detected in himself was not an illusion. 'I find myself an amiable pretty man of moderate abilities, but a soul truly noble, a soul which in reality sets me higher in the scale of being than if I had attained to the first honours which superior talents procure and been without such a soul.'[56] That was at Rome in the spring of 1765 two years after his vigils at Davies' bookshop in Russell Street, Covent Garden, had led to the long-hoped-for introduction to Johnson.[57] Having manfully swallowed Johnson's snubs he had soon been rewarded with the kind of recognition for which he craved: Johnson made jokes about Scots and Scotland, talked the young man down, shredding any ideas which he still had the courage to articulate within the steely jaws of a forensic examination which, in his later career as an advocate, Boswell must have frequently recalled. But the young Scot was more than content for, simply by entering the presence of greatness, he believed that the latent greatness in himself was being brought slowly to birth.

Johnson must have approved of Boswell's earnest desire to make something of himself. There was no complacency in him—unlike the young man who informed Johnson casually that he had 'lost all his Greek', and received the reply, 'I believe it happened at the same time, Sir, that I lost all my large estate in Yorkshire.[58] Whatever he thought about Boswell's dealings with the frail sisterhood of the Strand (for as he was regarded as a spiritual guide he is very

B*

likely to have known of them) he responded affectionately to the
young man's approaches and did him the honour of accompanying
him to Harwich to see him off at the beginning of his Grand Tour.

Heralded by a series of paragraphs which he had inserted in the
daily papers Boswell now returned bringing in his charge Rousseau's
ageing mistress, Thérèse LeVasseur. Having begun his Tour with
an emotional encounter with the author of *La Nouvelle Heloise* at
Geneva, Boswell now concluded it by sharing Thérèse's bed in a
series of inns on the road between Paris and Calais. He sincerely
wanted to hear more about the great man at first hand; but Thérèse
had alarmed him by establishing as her first priority a short course
in bedroom manners.[59] To be reunited with Johnson was the true
homecoming for Boswell. In spite of the fact that Johnson, hearing
of encounters on the continent with the exiled John Wilkes as well
as Rousseau, took strong exception to the company he had been
keeping, all the feelings of 1763 were revived, and it may have been
at this moment that the idea of the *Life* was conceived. Certainly by
the early 1770's it was taken for granted that he was to write it.[60]

It was inevitable that in the course of Boswell's five extended
visits to London between 1766 and 1774 he and Goldsmith should
often find themselves in one another's company. There were few
grounds for compatibility—least of all the streak of egotism which
could be observed in both men. Even worse from the point of view
of a constitutional hero-worshipper like Boswell was the absence of
opportunities for seeing the older man in anything resembling an
heroic light. The relationship was further complicated by the
jealousy which proximity to Johnson so often inspired—a jealousy
which made Mrs Thrale cool towards Reynolds and later hostile to
Boswell; which helped to produce an apparently universal dislike
of Johnson's friend Baretti (the linguist and political refugee who
found a home for a few years with the Thrales) and made Goldsmith
a popular target for sallies of wit and outbursts of exasperation as
well as the more damaging criticisms to be found in the pages of
Boswell and Mrs Thrale.

Boswell resented Goldsmith's nearness to Johnson and was
young and humourless enough to be at a loss as to what Johnson
could see in him. All these factors contributed to the predominantly
hostile portrait which is inserted in the *Life of Johnson* at Goldsmith's first eruption into the story.

Goldsmith, who in spite of a tendency to give money away to frauds and incorrigible loafers, was a fairly shrewd judge of character, seems to have understood this resentment and to have teased Boswell about it. The bar across the end of an evening with Johnson could be the door to the room of his blind dependent, Miss Williams, who would sit up at all hours of the night to make tea for him and his chosen friends. Boswell ran up against this custom near the beginning of his friendship with Johnson and was mortified to be left out of it. As he walked away with Johnson Goldsmith rubbed salt in the wound by calling back '*I* go to see Miss Williams'. Boswell had to wait twenty-eight years for his revenge, but the effect then of his bald verbatim account of the incident was damaging. As a corrective one needs to read carefully the sentence which concludes the episode and to sense the humourlessness of the man who could write it. 'It was not long before I obtained the same mark of distinction,' Boswell records with an unmistakable air of triumph and self-congratulation.[61]

Boswell's portrait of Goldsmith took Johnson's epitaph as its starting point:

'No man had the art of displaying with more advantage as a writer, whatever literary acquisition he made. "Nihil quod tetigit non ornavit." His mind resembled a fertile, but thin soil. There was a quick, but not strong vegetation, of whatever chanced to be thrown upon it. No deep root could be struck. The oak of the forest did not grow there: but the elegant shrubbery and the fragrant parterre appeared in gay succession. It has been generally circulated and believed that he was a mere fool in conversation; but, in truth, this has been greatly exaggerated. He had, no doubt, a more than common share of that hurry of ideas which we often find in his countrymen, and which sometimes produced a laughable confusion in expressing them. He was very much what the French call un étourdi, and from vanity and an eager desire of being conspicuous wherever he was, he frequently talked carelessly without knowledge of the subject, or even without thought. His person was short, his countenance coarse and vulgar, his deportment that of a scholar awkwardly affecting the easy gentleman. Those who were in any way distinguished, excited envy in him to so ridiculous an excess, that the instances of it are hardly credible. When accompanying two beautiful young ladies with their mother on a tour in France, he was seriously angry that more attention was paid to them than to him; and once at the exhibition of the Fantoccini in London, when those who sat next to him observed with what dexterity a puppet was made to toss a pike, he could not bear that it should have such praise, and exclaimed with some warmth, "Pshaw! I can do it better myself."

He, I am afraid had no settled system of any sort, so that his conduct must not be strictly scrutinized; but his affections were social and generous, and when he had money he gave it away very liberally. His desire of imaginary consequence predominated over his attention to truth. When he began to rise into notice, he said he had a brother who was Dean of Durham, a fiction so easily detected, that it is wonderful how he should have been so insonsiderate as to hazard it. He boasted to me at this time of the power of his pen in commanding money, which I believe was true in a certain degree, though in the instance he gave he was by no means correct. He told me that he had sold a novel, for four hundred pounds. This was his *Vicar of Wakefield*. But Johnson informed me, that he had made the bargain for Goldsmith, and the price was sixty pounds. 'And, Sir, (said he,) a sufficient price too, when it was sold; for then, the fame of Goldsmith had not been elevated, as it afterwards was, by his *Traveller*; and the bookseller had such faint hopes of profit by his bargain, that he kept the manuscript by him a long time, and did not publish it till after the *Traveller* had appeared. Then, to be sure, it was accidentally worth more money.[62]

There is enough praise in the opening section of the portrait to give an appearance of fairness, and when he presents 'greatly exaggerated' reports of his subject's 'foolish' conversation in order to sweep them away Boswell even poses as counsel for the defence. Having disarmed the reader, he introduces the major criticisms, that Goldsmith was vain, naive, foolish and dishonest—introducing, incidentally, at least one anecdote which reveals his inability to understand a certain straight-faced vein of humour in the expatriate Irishman.

Curiously, there is little in the pages that follow to substantiate this predominantly hostile picture, for Boswell's prodigious reputa-

tion as a biographer is based on his objectivity, and the writer who
presents faithfully the occasions when he was himself snubbed by
his hero also sets down moments when Goldsmith got the better of
Johnson in repartee, or when his quiet voice of common sense could
be heard through the thunder of one of those rearguard actions
which Johnson loved to fight. There are certainly passages when
Johnson is made to pass judgment on his friend (usually with strong
qualifications) but here it is sometimes difficult to escape the conclusion that Boswell, by playing devils' advocate, has set up a
situation in which Johnson is morally bound to be disparaging:

> Of our friend Goldsmith he said, 'Sir, he is so much afraid of
> being unnoticed, that he often talks merely lest you should forget
> that he is in the company.'
>
> BOSWELL: 'Yes, he stands forward.'
>
> JOHNSON: 'True, Sir; but if a man is to stand forward, he should
> wish to do it not in an awkward posture, not in rags, not so as that
> he shall only be exposed to ridicule.'
>
> BOSWELL: 'For my part, I like very well to hear honest Goldsmith
> talk away carelessly.'
>
> JOHNSON: 'Why yes, Sir; but he should not like to hear himself.'

Boswell spent several days in London in February '66 before
continuing his journey home to Scotland, and during this time he
renewed his acquaintance with the writer who in the two and a half
years since their last meeting had consolidated his position in the
literary world to which Boswell himself was at this moment aspiring.
In Johnson he observed a change: he was denying himself wine and
on the evening when Boswell and Goldsmith called on him together
at Johnson's Court he flatly refused to accompany them to the
Mitre, evidently preferring his own company at home—a remarkable
change for a man who had an habitual fear of solitude. Boswell
failed to see that Johnson was deeply depressed on this occasion
(although his detailed account of the visit reveals that Goldsmith
understood the mood and did his best to counteract it). He would
be back in Edinburgh when Johnson's nervous collapse occurred
and the entire episode would pass him by; but Goldsmith had
anticipated it this evening, scandalising Boswell as they walked
away down Fleet Street with the remark, 'Don't you think that

head's failed—wearing, eh?'[63] In the summer, the Thrales called on
Johnson to find him shut up in his room in a state of despondency
far more alarming than the depression that Boswell and Goldsmith
had witnessed in February. When Johnson began hysterically to
enumerate his own shortcomings, Henry Thrale clapped his hand
over his mouth to bring the confession to a forcible conclusion.[64] In
their alarm, the Thrales reacted promptly and generously, although
it was little more than a year since the Irish playwright Arthur
Murphy had introduced Johnson to them, and they had not been
married very long. They insisted on his returning with them to their
house at Streatham where a room was kept for him until Thrale's
death. For the next fifteen years he was either their guest or their
travelling companion on visits to Brighton and Wales, returning to
Johnson's Court only at weekends to deal with the hostilities and
recriminations amongst his pensioners there.[65]

Although there was often to be a place for him at the Thrales'
well-provided table, Goldsmith must have regretted Johnson's
departure this summer. They had known each other for five years,
having lived fairly close to one another in the Fleet Street area for
much of this time. At a crisis moment in 1762 Johnson had proved
himself to be a staunch friend and his intervention then had brought
the manuscript of *The Vicar of Wakefield* to light. Goldsmith, like
Boswell, had sought Johnson out and, in spite of the occasional
irreverence, he too seems to have set up the older man as a monument of goodness and wisdom in whose lee it was sometimes pleasant
to shelter. In return, Johnson treated Goldsmith with respect, even
if at times it was the respect which in another age would have been
accorded to the court jester, while his inscription for the monument
in Westminster Abbey records his deep appreciation of Goldsmith
as a writer. During his lifetime, his praise took a precise and qualified form that had the stamp of sincerity and, coming from such a
source, must have been immensely encouraging for the younger
man. His first play, *The Good-Natured Man*, was 'the best comedy
since *The Provoked Husband* (a play by Vanbrugh and Cibber which
had first been staged in 1728); *The Deserted Village* was 'a fine
performance' though containing, in Johnson's view, too many echoes
of *The Traveller*. *The Traveller* itself had received praise as warm as
he was able to give: 'There has not been so fine a poem since Pope's
time.'[66]

Johnson never suffered fools gladly, but even though Goldsmith's odd social style invoked feelings in him that fluctuated between bewilderment and exasperation his criticisms were usually good-humoured:

JOHNSON: It is amazing how little Goldsmith knows. He seldom comes where he is not more ignorant than any one else.

SIR JOSHUA REYNOLDS: Yet there is no man whose company is more liked.

JOHNSON: To be sure, Sir. When people find a man of the most distinguished abilities as a writer, their inferior while he is with them, it must be highly gratifying to them. What Goldsmith comically says of himself is very true—he always gets the better when he argues alone . . .[67]

If there had been occasions when Goldsmith was roughly silenced like so many other people who came into Johnson's ambit, Boswell would undoubtedly have fulfilled his duty and recorded them. But there is no hint of such an event until a public quarrel near the end of Goldsmith's life when it was he who attacked Johnson.

*

There was no Boswell to record the conversation in Reynold's studio on the afternoon of August 21st 1766, but it can be assumed that the atmosphere was relaxed and friendly. Mrs Thrale, hardly an admirer of either Reynolds or Goldsmith, noticed that they brought out the best in one another: '(Goldsmith) was while he lived the person Sir Joshua seemed to have most friendship for; he lent him money, loved his company, and a *little* lamented his death. Truth is, Doctor Goldsmith loved him in return, a favour he paid to but few';[68] and using the phraseology of an age which placed a premium on sentiment, Reynolds wrote two years after his friend's death: 'The author was intimately acquainted with Dr Goldsmith. They unbosomed their minds freely to each other . . .[69] They were both men who could only express in their art feelings for which they found no outlet in actuality. The coldness at which Mrs Thrale hints is not to be found in 'The Strawberry Girl' or the warmly glowing canvas of the courtesan Nelly O'Brien any more than in the depiction of Dr Primrose or of the exiled villagers in *The Deserted Village*, the poem which Goldsmith dedicated to Reynolds. Part of the understanding between them might have been a mutual recognition that they shared the same disability.

Reynolds' two portraits, the painting and the essay, are given a special validity by his wide experience of men and women and his own quietly impressive personality. The man who could switch off a tiresome dining companion simply by turning his ear-trumpet in the other direction—he had been deaf since painting in a damp draught in the Vatican as a young man—was not a person to be taken in by the garrulous prattler of Boswell's portrait. Though not well educated by the standards of his age, he was a man who strenuously attempted to enlarge his mind by enquiry and shrewd observation, with a strong intelligence and an originality which had immediately attracted Johnson at their first encounter and which can be felt in the essay probing behind the misleading surface, uniting apparent contradictions and allowing us to see Goldsmith not as the subject of a dozen or so stories (irrepressible or egregious according to taste) but as a credible human being.

Reynolds tackles the question of Goldsmith's obvious limitations at the outset, as if he had guessed in advance that they would feature large in future accounts and, a quarter of a century before the *Life of Johnson*, invalidates Boswell's literal interpretation of Goldsmith's behaviour with 'A great part of Dr Goldsmith's folly and absurdity proceeded from principle . . .': there is to be no solemn talk about the vain Irishman at Calais with the beautiful Horneck sisters. Another of Goldsmith's guiding principles was to shed any traits which might deter friends from seeking his company: 'He had a very strong desire, which I believe nobody will think very peculiar or culpable, to be liked, to have his company sought after by his friends. To this end, for it was a system, he abandoned his respectable character as a writer or a man of observation to that of a character which nobody was afraid of being humiliated in his presence' [*sic*]. Simple people who have approached him in awe depart again 'gratified to find so admirable a writer so much upon a level, or inferior to themselves . . .'. Having worked his way carefully into a quite indefensible position, he is at the centre of an excited ring of companions who are on their metal to challenge his outrageous paradoxes and to defend the comfortable opinions which, until now, society has sanctioned on their behalf. 'He often fought like a tiger, and like the tiger he fought when turned on his back. He risked every opinion which that moment came into his head . . . he made always a sort of bustle, and wherever he was there was no yawning. The conversation never stagnated or languished. The same company (that), the moment he had turned his back, were in open cry on his absurdity and folly, were still desirous of meeting him again next day . . . However this disposition to paradoxes might be sometimes troublesome, it often called out the rest of the company into conversation, and as has been often observed, wherever the Doctor was, the conversation was never known to languish'. In some of its features Reynolds' portrait anticipates another expatriate Irishman, George Bernard Shaw.

Reynolds accepts the charge of envy, but qualifies it: 'This odious quality . . . was not so disagreeable in him as it generally is in other people. It was so far from being of that black malignant kind which excites hatred and disgust, that it was, from its being so artless and obvious, only ridiculous'. His desire to dominate the conversation at inappropriate moments and by any means that came to hand (perhaps a more serious offence by eighteenth century standards of decorum than it would be considered today) is seen as a result of his acquiring fame suddenly and late and not knowing quite how to handle it: 'The Doctor came late into the great world. He had lived a great part of his life with mean people. All his old habits were against him . . .'. But this too is qualified for he is seen to have a natural tact: 'If he was sometimes foolish out of season, he never was what is worse—wise out of season. For instance, Dr Goldsmith never made common observations with the air and as if he had spoken oracles, or ever acquiesced in what others advanced, in order to conceal his own ignorance . . .'.

Reynolds' appreciation has the ring of truth. Was the other portrait, the painting destined for the dining-room wall at Streatham Park, 'flattered' as Fanny Reynolds suggested? Or had she simply failed to perceive qualities which lurked beneath an unprepossessing exterior? One of the points that her brother makes in his essay is that Goldsmith was not a success with women. They failed to appreciate his humour and as his object was always to make them laugh he was content, when all else failed, to let them laugh *at* him. Whether or not this counteracts the effect of Fanny's criticism, later

admirers sided with Reynolds rather than with his sister in their
view of Goldsmith. It was Goethe who at the end of his own life
recalled the profound effect that *The Vicar of Wakefield* had had
when read aloud to him in German when he was a student;[70] and
even in Goldsmith's lifetime the men whose good-natured mockery
of him received a sudden check in the perceptive pen-portraits of
Retaliation, or the readers who were sufficiently moved by *The
Deserted Village* to argue for or against the poem as a social document, had also seen, behind the gaucheness and the buffoonery, a
writer who could surprise and disturb.

TWO

The Dancing Boy

THE GOLDSMITHS of County Roscommon, Ireland, were the descendants of a Roman Catholic priest who in the second or third decade of the seventeenth century had renounced his orders, married and become a protestant minister within the Church of Ireland. John Goldsmith's brother, Francis, also a priest and living at Antwerp, kept to the old faith: John, whose conversion to protestantism seems to have been genuine, clung to his new creed even though to be an outspoken protestant in Connaught during the rebellion of 1641 was a hazardous vocation, and at one point he was only saved from death at the hands of a mob by the intervention of a Catholic friar. From the evidence he gave before a commission of enquiry into the sufferings of Protestants during the rebellion the picture emerges of a minister who took his ecclesiastical obligations seriously and used his considerable economic advantages as Rector of Burrishoole in the cause of winning converts:

... And because this deponent would the rather invite and draw the poor children of his parish to be catechised and instructed by him, as also the children of the richer sort, though papists, he did by all ways and gentle means seek to draw them unto him, by which way he brought many to be catechised every Sabbath day, and at other times ... And for the poorer sort, this deponent in the counties of Westmeath and Mayo gave the parents of the children some money, and lent them divers cows freely, sometimes by about twenty-two at once, for a good time together, and sometimes a milch cow for two years ... to suffer their children to come to him to be catechised and instructed in the grounds of the true Protestant religion.[1]

Nearly eighty years later, when John's great-grandson, Charles Goldsmith of Ballyoughter married Anne, the daughter of the Revd. Oliver Jones, the diocesan schoolmaster of Elphin, County Ros-

common, the Goldsmith family was completely identified with the
Church of Ireland which represented to them something between a
faith and a career. Charles was a younger son with few prospects
and no assets apart from an A.B. degree of Trinity College, Dublin.
He was twenty-eight and, following the family practice, had taken
orders, but no living had presented itself and the Joneses who lived
in one of the few substantial houses in the neighbourhood of a
dreary little provincial town were convinced that their daughter
was making a bad match.[2]

Mrs Jones was a strong-minded, enterprising woman who, once
it was clear that the young couple could not be dissuaded, did
everything she could to cushion Anne's descent into poverty. She
succeeded in persuading her brother, the Revd. Mr Green, Rector
of Kilkenny West in the neighbouring county of Westmeath, to
employ her son-in-law as a curate and even to share his house with
the young couple.[3] So Charles and Anne went to Mr Green at
Pallasmore, where he lived in a property rented from the Edgeworth
family, and Charles assumed responsibility for the church of
Forgney which could be seen from its windows, combining his not
very arduous pastoral duties with the farming of some fields on
which Mrs Jones had secured a lease, rather pointedly in her
daughter's name.[4] The first child, Margery, was born at Pallasmore.
Others followed: Catherine in 1721, Henry (and his sister Jane if
Forster was right in conjecturing that they were twins) between
1722 and 1724.[5]

Although a distance of forty miles now separated mother and
daughter the link between them was strong, for in spite of the
entry 'at Pallas' against the date November 10, 1728 in the family
bible, a tradition carefully preserved by the Jones cousins, maintained that Oliver Goldsmith was born at his grandmother's home,
that square, substantial but unpretentious farmhouse, Smith Hill.
Mrs Jones was now a widow and no doubt more than willing to
help her daughter through the last stages of her pregnancy, while
Anne, still without a home of her own, may have felt that her
mother's house was better suited to the occasion than her uncle's.
The young family at Pallasmore was probably left in the charge of
Elizabeth, a distant relative in her early thirties, who would later
teach young Oliver to read before leaving the Goldsmiths to get
married. At what stage Anne would have left the comforts of her

mother's home and returned to her family is a matter of conjecture but the Jones tradition had it that Oliver was 'nursed and reared' in his grandmother's house.[6]

Even in the eighteenth century a curate's income of £40 a year, together with whatever was brought in from the cultivation of Anne's forty acres, was very little for a family of two adults and four children (Margery having died) if they wished to preserve some vestiges of a middle class way of life. Fortunately, when Mr Green died two years after the birth of Oliver, Charles was chosen as Green's successor and, taking over the lease of a gentleman-farmer's residence a mile and a half away from his new church, he moved his family to the village of Lissoy. Their new home was a long, low house of five bays and two storeys with a central door in the Queen Anne style, set sixty yards back from the road behind a lawn bordered by clumps of ash. Stables, a dairy and farm buildings were attached. There were gardens and an orchard, and with the house Charles rented seventy acres of arable and pasture land at eight shillings an acre.[7]

The young Oliver grew up in a largely female environment while his brother was at school in Longford. Somewhere below such authorititative figures as his mother and his first teacher, cousin Elizabeth, there were two older sisters, to one of whom, Catherine, he was very much attached. When he first moved out into the world of school he was found to be a little diffident; but within the Lissoy household there had been plenty of stimulus for the imagination. Feminine discussions took place over the head of the boy who probably understood more than he was intended to, and in the kitchen he could listen to the dairymaid, Peggy Golden, singing *Johnny Armstrong's Last Goodnight*,[8] or to those travellers, half beggars, half wandering minstrels who drifted in to sit by the fire and tell strange tales. He may have had access to some thrillingly ramshackle collection of books like the one James Prior explored in a typical middle class household when gathering his Goldsmith material in the 1830s: '. . . the History of the Irish Rogues and Rapparees—Lives of the celebrated Pirates—History of Moll Flanders—of Jack the Bachelor (a notorious Smuggler), of Fair Rosamond and Jane Shore—of Donna Rozena, the Spanish Courtezan—the Life and Adventures of James Freney, a famous Irish Robber, and others of a similar description, then the principal books of amusement . . .' The boy who later as an undergraduate at Trinity would while away the dull moments of a Greek lecture by imagining that he was an M.P. and covering his lexicon with imitation frankings—'Free, Oliver Goldsmith'[9]—must have found a ready escape from the limitations of this uneducated female world by living out in his imagination the adventures of such delightfully dubious heroes. His own literary flair showed itself before he was eight. He was particularly attracted by verse, and Lissoy tradition still insists that he had the happy knack of encapsulating unusual incidents in rhyme and metre.*

Something of the atmosphere of the Lissoy household can be felt in *The Vicar of Wakefield* and in *The Citizen of the World* where Goldsmith's mouthpiece, the Man in Black, describes his own father and upbringing. Anyone who comes to the subject of parsonages via Trollope and the Victorians is probably inclined to treat too cautiously certain hints in these otherwise idealised accounts; but the racy letter with which Catherine answered Thomas Percy's enquiries recaptures the atmosphere of the Goldsmiths' home. The women of the family, forceful and lively characters but without education apart from being able to read and write, must have channelled a fair amount of energy into talk of romance and young men and, sometimes in the little boy's hearing, more direct allusions to sex. As John O'Donovan noticed when he collected material for an Ordnance Survey report on County Roscommon in the year of James Prior's biography, the Goldsmith clan had a reputation for being highly-sexed and for producing more than their fair share of children out of wedlock.[10] Receiving Catherine's quaint and breathless letter, the Revd. Thomas Percy may have come to a very similar conclusion:

> . . . there was company at his fathers at that time he was turned of seven they were attended at tea by a little boy who was desired to hand the Kettle—but the handle being to hot the boy took up the skirt of his coate to put between him & it but unfortunately the Ladys perceived some thing which made them Laugh immoderately whether from the akwardness of the turn or any

---

*Sitting in his father's church as a small boy, he is said to have noticed a rat descending one of the bell ropes and produced the couplet,
> A pious rat for want of stairs
> Came down the rope to say his prayers.

thing that might be seen there I cant say but the Doctor immeadietly perceived there cause of Laughter & informed his father who promised him a reward of Gingerbread to write some thing on it and as it was one of his earliest productions that can be recollected tho perhaps not fit for the Publick I shall insert it here

> Theseus did see as Poets say
> Dark Hell & its abysses
> But had not half so Sharp an Eye
> As our young Charming Misses
> For they cd through boys breeches peep
> And view what ere he had there
> It seemed to Blush & they all Laughd
> Because the face as all bare
> They laughed at that
> Which some times Else
> Might give them greatest pleasure
> How quickly the cd see the thing
> Which was their darling treasure[11]

The Revd. Charles Goldsmith who thought of this ingenious method of coming to the rescue of his puzzled, and perhaps humiliated, son (and may have helped him to polish his verses?) was clearly no Revd. Theobald Pontifex, and it is hardly surprising that his son's portrait should seem far more than a hundred years away from Samuel Butler's account of his Victorian father.

'My father, the younger son of a good family, was possessed of a small living in the church,' Goldsmith's Man in Black relates. 'His education was above his fortune, and his generosity greater than his education. Poor as he was, he had his flatterers still poorer than himself; for every dinner he gave them, the returned him an equivalent in praise; and this was all he wanted; the same ambition that actuates a monarch at the head of an army, influenced my father at the head of his table: he told the story of the ivy-tree, and that was laugh'd at; he repeated the jest of the two scholars and one pair of breeches, and the company laughed at that; but the story of Taffy in the sedan chair was sure to set the table in a roar; thus his pleasure encreased, in proportion to the pleasure he gave; he loved all the world, and he fancied all the world loved him.

'As his fortune was but small, he lived up to the very extent of it; he had no intentions of leaving his children money, for that was dross; he was resolved they should have learning; for learning he used to observe, was better than silver or gold. For this purpose he undertook to instruct us himself; and took as much pains to form our morals, as to improve our understanding. We were told that universal benevolence was what first cemented society; we were taught to consider all the wants of mankind as our own; to regard the *human face divine* with affection and esteem; he wound us up to be mere machines of pity, and rendered us incapable of withstanding the slightest impulse made either by real or fictitious distress; in a word, we were perfectly instructed in the art of *giving away* thousands, before we were taught the more necessary qualifications of *getting* a farthing.

'I can't avoid imagining, that, thus refined by his lessons out of all my suspicion, and divested of even all the little cunning which nature had given me, I resembled, upon my first entrance into the busy and insidious world, one of those gladiators who were exposed without armour in the amphitheatre at Rome. My father, however, who had only seen the world on one side, seemed to triumph in my superior discernment; though my whole stock of wisdom consisted in being able to talk like himself upon subjects that once were useful, because they were then topics of the busy world; but that now were utterly useless, because connected with the busy world no longer.'[12]

There is certainly no Butlerian savagery in this portrait of a lovable and genial man, but there is an undercurrent of irony nevertheless. The reader is presented with a Charles Goldsmith who has enthusiastically embraced the role which promotion conferred on him; but he is also invited to imagine the circumstances of such a family when its income is £40 a year as opposed to £200, or when the breadwinner dies in middle age leaving young sons unprovided for.

Such criticisms might fairly have been made by Anne Goldsmith who, at Lissoy, gave birth to three more sons, Maurice, Charles and John, between 1736 and 1740. It is unlikely that she did criticise. The household atmosphere that can be read between the lines of Charles' portrait does not provide much room for a nagging wife and, for all their faults, the mother figures in Goldsmith's works accept their husbands for what they are. But, married to men who at one level are completely unworldly and at another better educated and wiser than themselves, they dominate the domestic scene by constructing an empire around the inviolable island where their husbands content themselves (like prototypes of Jane Austen's Mr Bennett) with their good humour, their stories and certain deeply held beliefs as to how life should be conducted—which their families persistently undermine. These marriages of unsuitably matched couples are surprisingly happy, but the traits developed by the wives in the vacuum left by their husbands' quietism are in some ways unpleasant: they encourage their children to make fools of themselves and when confronted by results which might have been foreseen they promptly withdraw their support and affection. Livy Primrose, encouraged to flirt with a notorious rake, is disowned by her mother when it appears that she had been seduced by him, while her precocious little brother, Moses, who is applauded when he bores visitors with examples of his 'wit' is mercilessly scolded when he falls into the hands of a confidence trickster. It is Tony Lumpkin of course, who after his own mother has tearfully berated him for his treachery, coolly informs her that mothers of spoiled children must learn to live with their mistakes.

As the open-handed incumbent of Kilkenny West where only one family in ten would have belonged to his persuasion,[13] Charles Goldsmith was following in the footsteps of his great grandfather, though there are no echoes of John's proselytizing zeal. The landless Irishman of the mid-eighteenth century would have seen far fewer material advantages in the embracing of Protestantism than his counterpart a hundred years earlier. Since the introduction of an oppressive penal system after the rebellion of 1688–9 and the deliberate strangling of Irish trade, the economic blight fell equally on Roman Catholics and on Protestants like the Goldsmiths.

Catholic Ireland's support for James II had been answered by vigorous social and economic repression backed up by a legal code aimed at establishing a Protestant ascendancy. Though not all the laws against the practice of the Roman religion were enforceable— many being honoured more in the breach than in the observance by the time Goldsmith was growing up—the suppression of Irish trade was completely successful. A thriving woollen industry had been destroyed, and although there was some relenting in the 1730s when the production of coarse linen—a manufacture which, unlike the woollen, would not conflict with English interests—was half-heartedly encouraged, a total embargo was placed on Irish trade other than with England, the export of livestock and cattle produce (an essential part of the Irish economy) being completely forbidden.[14]

The social result of such policies was to deprive Ireland both of its natural leaders and of a mercantile/industrial middle class like that rapidly growing readership for which Goldsmith himself was to cater in the London of the 1760s. The hereditary Roman Catholic leaders had either lost their lands or been demoralised by a penal code which made frequent inroads upon their privacy and family life. The system actively encouraged Protestant informers and offered tempting financial rewards to an apostatizing wife or son. The Protestant landlords, who had in many cases succeeded them, found it more agreeable to live in England than amongst neighbours different in religion and background and so embarrassingly under a political cloud. Beneath them was a chain of tenants, sub-tenants and sub-sub-tenants, men who had nothing to contribute to the community and no social prestige to lose, but whose interest lay in doing as little as possible and keeping the screw of the rack turned tightly on the man underneath. At the end of the line were the labourer who received a patch of land for his own use in return for his services, and, superficially indistinguishable from him, the tenant-farmer who, far from being encouraged to introduce the new methods that were now increasing the efficiency of English farming, had no security of tenure and was penalised for any improvements he made by the increased value of the land when the time for the next Dutch auction (in which he too would have to compete) came round.[15] In such conditions there were no rewards for enterprise and initiative either in industry or agriculture.

Ireland was governed nominally by its Houses of Parliament in Dublin: in reality from London. In Lecky's phrase, the members of the Irish House of Commons were 'the minority of a minority' who found it expedient to accept the dictates of Westminster: they were sufficiently aware of political realities to realise that military protection might at some time be needed and, like Mrs Hardcastle, they had a treasure-chest in their keeping which contained very rich pickings in the shape of jobs and sinecures, government grants and church livings.

Whether it liked it or not the Church of Ireland, as the established church of the Protestant Ascendency, was inextricably involved with this system of organised corruption. Bishoprics and other rich livings became rewards either for direct political services or the services of one's kinsfolk; and once the Bishop was in possession of his large estate it was taken for granted that the income was his to divert into whatever channels he chose—which could well mean the pockets of a swarm of family dependents. A man like Archbishop Robinson at Armagh might turn himself to improving his lands and educating the peasantry, but at Elphin Isaac Weld found very few signs of the Bishop's attempting to spread the income of estates which, in the mid-seventeenth century had yielded the considerable sum of £1,500 per annum.[16] The account of Elphin given by this member of the Dublin Society in 1832 when conditions for growth were far more favourable than they had been during Charles Goldsmith's lifetime, makes depressing reading. The Church of Ireland cathedral and the Roman Catholic chapel (an innovation of the 1740s since before then the penal laws had deprived the Roman Catholic community of official places of worship) faced each other down the main street. Between them, Weld found 118 thatched cabins without windows or chimneys, many of them in 'abject' condition, their inhabitants 'ill-clad, squalid, haggard, listless, and idle; in every countenance discontent strongly marked, and, in some, an expression akin to despair.' Apart from the bishop's house, the deanery (once the home of Goldsmith's paternal grandmother) which had declined into a filthy inn, and the new diocesan school (replacing the building which Goldsmith had known), there were only '33 houses of 2 stories, thatched: 7 ditto slated' and '4 good houses of a better description partly built.' Although the Bishop of Elphin was easing the local employment problem by using more men than were actually needed to get in his harvest he was obviously presiding over a scene of desolation. Nor was a man in such a position necessarily as spiritually exalted—or even orthodox—as might reasonably have been expected. Deism was an increasingly fashionable creed in the eighteenth century and a bishop had been known publicly to deny the divinity of Christ.[17]

*

In the absence of men who—according to the social laws of the time—should have been leaders for reasons of either birth or economic standing, the pace was all too often set by the 'squireen'. Lecky, gives a vivid description of this class in his *History of Ireland*:

> Men who in England would have been modest and laborious farmers, in Ireland sublet their land at rack-rents, kept miserable packs of half-starved hounds, wandered about from fair to fair and from race to race in laced coats, gambling, fighting, drinking, swearing, ravishing, and sporting, parading everywhere their contempt for honest labour, giving a tone of recklessness to every society in which they moved.

Maria Edgeworth, born within a few miles of Lissoy the year after Goldsmith had sat for his portrait in Reynolds' studio, was later to give her impressions of this class and of the society which languished under its influence. But by this time, the squireen had already made his appearance in literature in the personage of Squire Thornhill, the villain of *The Vicar of Wakefield*. In that novel, the Primroses were saved in the best traditions of romance by a *deus ex machina* figure, Sir William Thornhill, who could well be taken either as an absentee Ascendency landlord returning at the climax of the story (as in reality they rarely did) to set his estates in order; or, in his disguise as the penniless and wandering Mr Burchell as one of the hereditary Irish leaders who, dispossessed of their land, were now drifting into obscurity.

At the other end of the social scale the labourer and the small tenant-farmer lived in the sub-human conditions which Edmund Burke described in 1748 in the newspaper which he conducted as an undergraduate at Trinity College:

> As for their food, it is notorious they seldom taste bread or meat; their diet in summer is potatoes and sour milk; in winter they are still worse; living on the same root only made palatable by a little salt, accompanied with water. Their clothes so ragged that they rather publish than conceal the wretchedness it was meant to hide. Nay it is no uncommon sight to see half a dozen children run quite naked out of a cabin scarcely distinguishable from a dunghill. You enter one of these cabins, or rather creep in, at a door of

hurdles plastered with dirt, of which the inhabitant is generally the fabricator; within side you see (if the smoke will permit you) the men, women, children, dogs and swine lying, promiscuously, for their opulence is such they cannot have a separate house for their cattle, as it would take too much from the garden, whose produce is their only support. Their furniture is much fitter to be lamented than described, such as a pot, a stool, a few wooden vessels, and a broken bottle. In this manner all the peasantry to a man live, and I appeal to anyone who knows the country for the justice of the picture.[18]

Lord Chesterfield, during his Lord Lieutenancy three years earlier had anticipated Burke's description. 'The poor people in Ireland,' he considered, 'are used worse than negroes by their lords and masters, and their deputies of deputies of deputies'.[19]

In a period of social and economic stagnation the Goldsmiths themselves were constantly threatened by loss of status, but during that brief spell of prosperity between 1730 and 1747 they probably did, as Oliver hinted, alleviate some of the more extreme cases of local suffering that came to their attention, particularly during famine years like 1740 and 1741. If Goldsmith himself is a typical representative of his family in this respect then their charity was impulsive, quixotic and badly organized. But there were other members of Charles' calling who brought some organizing capacity to their attempts to relieve distress. The Revd. Philip Skelton was so shocked to find a sick woman and her children trying to keep themselves alive by eating a mixture of sorrel and blood tapped from the cattle in her husband's keeping that he sold his theological books, imported grain from a neighbouring county and organised its distribution from his lodgings. (Nothing illustrates the iniquity of the Irish social system so clearly as Skelton's own career in the Church. It was said that in England the publication of his *Deism Revealed*, a book which won the respect of the man it had attacked, David Hume, would have brought him a bishopric. In Ireland the fact that he had no powerful connections and was the son of a small farmer could not be overlooked and he languished under a bishop—himself a deist—who finally went back on his promises and put his own nephew, straight from university, into the rectory to which Skelton had been attached for twenty years.)[20]

Men like Skelton and to a lesser extent Charles Goldsmith must take a great deal of the credit for the surprising degree of social harmony which was achieved in extremely unfavourable circumstances. In remote parts of the country common intellectual interests drew Roman Catholic priests and Protestant pastors together, and the simple people who wanted to provide a suitable breakfast for a priest who had celebrated Mass for them in a field or barn or ruined abbey would sometimes present themselves at the door of the local rectory to request the loan of a 'tea equipage'.[21] Perhaps Thomas Percy, in his later career as a Church of Ireland bishop, was acting under the posthumous influence of Goldsmith as well as Johnson when at Dromore he went out of his way to maintain good relations with both the Roman Catholic priest and the Unitarian minister. During a severe winter a joint service was arranged in the nonconformist meeting-house at which the Bishop's chaplain preached and the collection was taken up by the Roman Catholic priest and the two dissenting ministers who 'equally divided the pews amongst them and distributed the collection impartially amongst the poor of their four congregations'.[22] Goldsmith himself was to be a beneficiary of the good relations that could exist at local level between the two communities. As A. Lytton-Sells has suggested, he may have acquired the command of French which was to have a great influence on his literary career from priests who would have received their own theological training in France.

Although the 'Auburn' of *The Deserted Village* was a highly idealised portrait of the Lissoy he knew, some of its features can be detected amongst the accounts of poverty and depression in the descriptions left by eighteenth century travellers. Robert Bell shows that, for the poor, Sunday could be a holiday in every sense of the word:

... In the morning they went to their popish chapel, which was sometimes not sufficient to contain half the people: those, therefore, who could not gain admittance, prayed in the open air, near the doors of the chapel. As soon as service was over, the greater part of the congregation went home and dined; after which, during the summer season, they assembled in large bodies in some adjacent field, where the old sat in circles and entertained each other with stories, and the young danced to whatever music they could procure; and some of the young men exercised themselves with feats of bodily strength. Good humour and contentment always prevailed, as long as they drank no whiskey; but whenever that fiery spirit was introduced, intoxication and quarrels were the inevitable consequence.[23]

Goldsmith himself was fond of athletic pursuits. Being sturdily built he proved himself a good sportsman and was probably one of the first over the wall in those orchard-raiding expeditions which remained in the memory of his former schoolfellows. But although his diffidence had been shed as he embarked on his schooldays, the other, brooding, dreaming aspect of his character still existed—to be misread on occasions by an unsympathetic classmate who could see in such a withdrawal only signs that he was a 'blockhead'. He had already developed that faculty which could still be observed at the height of his career: of being able to retire into himself after bouts of noisy horse-play. It can be seen in Catherine's account of a party at the house of his uncle, John Goldsmith:

... one evening for a large Company of young people at his Uncles a young Gentleman playd the fiddle who thought him self a greater wit & humourist than any one Else did the Company insisted upon the Dr danceing a horn pipe which he refuse a long time but on the commands of his uncle he exibited he was then 9 years old and had lately had the small pox which left very deep red marks & he realy cut an ugly figure how ever he was a very good subject for the wit of our fiddleing Gentleman who Cryd out in rapture there was Esop how like Esop he was the very man by G, the D still danced for more than an hour till he fatagued our wit sufficiently who still kept on the Comparison of Esop with a very hearty Laugh at so bright a thought when the D stopt short & repeated these lines

> The Herald proclaimed out then saying
> See Esop Dancing & his Monkey playing

the Laugh turnd against our Wit & the D was Embreaced by his uncle & got some sweetmeats which was always his reward...[24]

Smallpox, contracted whilst attending his father's old school at Elphin, must have been a sad setback for a child who had been noticed only a few years earlier for his diffidence, but in the grim determination of the dancing boy there is a foretaste of that good-natured toughness—'he fought like the tiger . . .'—which Reynolds was later to observe.

His formal education had begun at the small school which his father was obliged to maintain in the village for the protestant families of the neighbourhood, and which was conducted by Thomas Byrne, a rather fierce retired quartermaster who punctuated his lessons with accounts of the campaigns of the Duke of Marl-borough in which he had seen service at the begining of the century. Catherine believed that there was a special bond between Byrne and Oliver, a suggestion which is borne out by Goldsmith's writing, especially in his plea for a more just treatment of veterans in *The Citizen of the World*.[25] After two years with Byrne he went at the age of eight to Elphin where he stayed in the Goldsmith family house at Ballyoughter. This arrangement continued until he was about eleven when he came home again and attended a school run by a clergyman in nearby Athlone, until the master's health failed and he became a boarder, probably in his thirteenth year, at a school kept by the Revd. Patrick Hughes at Edgeworthstown twenty miles to the north-east of Lissoy.

This was a lucky choice, for Hughes, like Thomas Byrne, had more than his acquired scholastic skills to share, and the boy who could retire into himself and give a convincing display of stupidity to an unsympathetic teacher flourished in the atmosphere of the Hughes' household, where he was evidently more than a vessel to be filled with the works of Virgil, Horace, Euclid and Herodotus. He was grateful to Hughes, as he later told Thomas Percy, for having 'conversed with him on a footing very different from that of master and scholar'.[26]

By the time he went to Edgeworthstown it was evident that Oliver was developing in the same direction as his brother Henry who, now seventeen, had just gone up to Trinity College Dublin where he was expected to distinguish himself and win a scholarship. But Charles, himself a younger son, was doubtful of the wisdom of pushing Oliver too far along this line. Henry would go into the church and eke out some kind of living for himself, but the pros-pects for a second cleric in the family might be dubious, and Charles could hardly have been blamed for being unable to envisage any prospects for a graduate of Trinity other than those offered by the family profession. The right course, in his view, was to find some opening in trade for this second son, possibly through an apprentice-ship, though this in itself was hardly a bright prospect in the Ireland of the mid-eighteenth century. But there was strong opposition. Anne Goldsmith, however narrow her own background and however much at sea she may have been with allusions to Theseus and Aesop, was convinced that she had reared a prodigy. The phrase 'liberal education' had lodged itself in her mind: Oliver must have a liberal education, like his brother, and this meant that he must proceed in two or three years' time to Dublin and to Trinity College.[27] Luckily, she had an ally on her husband's side of the family. The Revd. Thomas Contarine, who had been married to a sister of Charles Goldsmith was also an admirer of Oliver's and for some time had taken a friendly interest in him.

With two advocates to speak on his behalf, Oliver's academic future seemed assured. But at this stage the Goldsmith's fabled tendency to get themselves into trouble rose to the surface. Dates are hard to find in a country where records have often been lost or destroyed, and the Goldsmiths were too humble to preserve more than entries in a family bible and an occasional legal document: thus the exact sequence of events between 1742 and 1744 is obscure. The salient points are that, some time between these two dates (one authority suggests 1743),[28] Catherine gave birth to a daughter, and that in 1744 she was 'privately married' to Daniel Hodson, a member of one of the more affluent branches of another well-known Ros-common Church of Ireland family. As the marriage settlement shows, Daniel Hodson had been given massive encouragement to marry Catherine. Charles had made over to him £400 which he did not possess but which was to be met, in the absence of available capital, by diverting £20 a year (a large proportion of the income from the little Lissoy estate) into Hodson's pocket.[29] (He was little more than a boy, having been introduced into the house—presumably during the Trinity College vacation—as a pupil of Henry's.) The family's prospects had already been threatened by the fact that either from romantic impulse or necessity Henry, too, had married half way through his degree course at Trinity, and thus seriously diminished his already slender chances of a materially successful career in the Church.[30]

C

It was the Hodson settlement that had immediate consequences for Oliver. The following year he was due to take his place at Trinity, but now with a stroke of the pen Charles had impoverished his family and apparently deprived his second son of all hopes of that liberal education on which his wife had set her heart. In the face of this catastrophe it is likely that Mrs Goldsmith and Oliver turned for advice to Thomas Contarine.

*

In the same year that Charles Goldsmith had become the incumbent at Kilkenny West, Contarine had acquired the living of Oran, thirty miles away in County Roscommon, and built himself a house there. He was now sixty, and probably living alone as his only child, Jane, had been married for nine years. She and her husband, James Lawder Esq., lived about twenty miles to the north of Oran at Kilmore House, which had been created out of the ruins of a suppressed Augustinian monastery near Carrrick-on-Shannon by a bishop in the early seventeenth century.[31] Both the Lawders and Thomas Contarine were fond of Oliver and he seems to have been a frequent visitor at both houses, and to have gained access there to that other important liberalising influence: intelligently deployed money. Jane Lawder possessed a harpsichord, and sang: Oliver had taught himself to play the flute.[32] The atmosphere at his uncle's table where fellow-guests might be local historians or people who were beginning to take an interest in folk-lore, must have been very different from the breezy, jocular atmosphere of the dining-room at Lissoy.

Contarine, who as an undergraduate had been a friend of George Berkeley at Trinity College, anticipated the Ascendency of later generations in his tastes. He was the grandson of a Venetian aristocrat who, while in orders himself, had paid court to a nun, run away from Italy in her company and subsequently married her. He had settled in Ireland at the time of his second marriage to a relation of a provost of Trinity College and had taken his new wife's religion.[33] If Contarine was free from the prejudices of the more arrogant members of the ruling class this exotic background must have helped. One of his friends was Charles O'Conor—another ecumenical alliance—and their common interest was the indigenous culture of

Ireland, of which until 1738 the 'last of the bards', the blind Turlogh O'Carolan, about whom Goldsmith was to write and whom he had probably visited in the company of Contarine and O'Conor, was a living repository.[34] The Celtic name, Emlaghmore, which Contarine had given his house was one small sign of cultural liberation. At this stage of Goldsmith's life, Contarine with his interesting friends, his well-stocked garden, his books and music, must have seemed a figure-head of worldly authority and wisdom.

Contarine's resolution of the Goldsmiths' crisis was not entirely painless. There was more than one way of getting to Trinity College, he would have pointed out. He himself, like Charles Goldsmith and Henry, had gone as a pensioner, but for the promising boy with no money behind him (which was what Oliver had suddenly become) there was the prospect of a sizarship. In return for certain duties, which included waiting at high table and keeping the courtyards clean, his fees would be waived and at least one meal a day found for him by the College. Other living expenses could be made up by Oliver's relations and friends including, of course, Contarine. Sizars, he may have added, to salve his nephew's pride, were above-average students and were selected in the belief that after two years they would free themselves from their menial obligations by acquiring a scholarship.

At one level, both mother and son may have felt that the result of the appeal to Contarine had been disappointing, but there was good sense in such arguments. A liberal education was still within Oliver's reach, though not in the leisurely—and gentlemanly—terms in which they had been envisaging it. Oliver went to Dublin, took the stiff entrance tests which examined his knowledge of Homer, Virgil and Horace,[35] passed them, and on June 11, 1745, six weeks before the landing of Prince Charles Edward Stuart in Scotland and a month before Henry received his degree, he became officially an undergraduate member of Trinity College.

THREE

Fiction

TRINITY COLLEGE was a relatively small institution. By the 1770s the total student numbers were between three and four hundred, of whom seventy were scholars and thirty sizars. There were twenty-two fellows, the most senior of whom earned about £700 a year, a salary which reflected the considerable prestige of the College.[1] Richard Baldwin, a formidable man who had taken his academic responsibilities seriously, unlike his counterparts at Oxford and Cambridge, had been provost for twenty-eight years and was seventy-seven at the time of Goldsmith's entry. At Oxford Gibbon found that no notice was taken of his absence from tutorials and lectures, and Dr Johnson considered that by cutting a tutorial in order to go skating in Christ Church Meadow he had shown 'stark insensibility' rather than daring. But as can be seen from the few surviving records of Goldsmith's time there, absence from a lecture at Trinity College was met by an official reproof. The College kept four terms a year and undergraduates could proceed to their B.A. degree after eleven terms. Goldsmith, like Burke who had taken the entrance exam shortly before him, arrived very near the end of an academic year, but residence of only a few weeks was enough to qualify him to return the following October as a Senior, rather than a Junior Freshman. For a Senior Freshman the subject of the compulsory morning lecture in Hall (six days a week at 7.15 a.m.) was logic (which Goldsmith evidently hated). For a Junior Sophister, the following year, the subjects were physics, geography and astronomy, and for Senior Sophisters, ethics and metaphysics. There were Greek lectures three times a week, and catechetical lectures for Freshmen. Essays were written once a week, and undergraduates had regular tutorials.[2]

The position of the sizar was academically honourable but, in an institution where not all the criteria were academic, carried with it many of the disadvantages of second-class citizenship. In an age of cheap labour his duties appear to have been selected less for their real usefulness than as a visible reminder that he was in receipt of charity. When he cleaned Front Square or waited at high table on the fellows or on students whose noble birth was indicated by gowns trimmed with gold or silver lace, he was being pushed deliberately into a position of unenviable prominence. Out in the streets he could be identified by his red academic cap. Richard Murray, a sizar in his Junior Sophister year when Goldsmith entered the College, abolished the system when he himself became provost later in the century; one of his reasons was said to have been an incident at high table when a sizar emptied a dish of gravy over the head of a guest who had insulted him.[3]

The mixture of scholarship and rowdyism in accounts of Trinity College at this period fits the pattern of the times, though perhaps accentuated by local circumstances. Earlier in the century, before an act of parliament removed the obligation to attend Lenten services at St Patrick's Cathedral, Provost Baldwin himself had led his students into battle against the butcher-boys who laid in wait for them in the market place.[4] (Dublin life was occasionally disrupted altogether when these same butcher-boys and the 'Liberty-boys'—the tailors' apprentices—fought for the possession of the five bridges across the Liffey; and the bloods of Trinity were sometimes known to weight the sleeves of their gowns with their heavy room-keys and, having taken the precaution of bribing the Watch, to terrorise shop-keepers.)[5] Within the College, bullying was tolerated and the Trinity short way with bailiffs was notorious; if a bailiff did enter its unofficial 'liberties', he was liable to be stripped and held under the pump in Front Square. One unfortunate man was nailed to the pump by the ear—a refinement suggested to the tormentors by one of their most scholarly fellows, Theaker Wilder.[6]

Perhaps it was a sign of the Goldsmiths' idiosyncracy that, out of a score of possible tutors and on the basis of provincial loyalty, they should have selected this man to guide Oliver through his under-graduate career. He was to acquire a reputation for his vendettas against certain undergraduates and, in 1745, Oliver was his only personal student—a fact which may reflect this early-won reputation. He was twenty-eight when Goldsmith was placed under him and had been elected Fellow the previous year.[7]

A hundred miles away, in the Rector's house at Lissoy, it had seemed a good plan for Oliver to study under a scholar, equally brilliant in Mathematics and Greek, who came from the nearby town of Longford. But it was a mistake. Wilder's own high standard of academic discipline made him fiercely resentful of signs of inattention in his students, while his sadistic streak, combined with a probing intelligence, must have made those intimate tutorial sessions to which Oliver was now committed more of a penance than a privilege. At Edgeworthstown Goldsmith had won the confidence and respect of the sympathetic Mr Hughes; but the only picture that has survived of his academic performance at College suggests that under the hostile eye of Wilder he withdrew into himself and gave a passable imitation of stupidity. Wilder was attracted in a perverse way to whatever flaws he discovered in his students' characters, and when the subject under discussion was mathematics or physics it would have been fairly easy to confuse and humiliate Goldsmith in front of other students. But the man who was to be a founder-member of a slightly raffish club at Ballymahon and of the other Club that assembled at the Turks' Head, Gerrard Street, in the 'sixties, was not without weapons of his own and, if goaded, he could retaliate effectively. When Wilder tried to embarrass his pupil by demanding sarcastically in the course of a lecture, 'Where is *your* centre of gravity?', Goldsmith called his bluff and reduced the lecture-room to laughter by replying, reasonably enough, 'According to you it would appear to be in my arse.'[8]

Goldsmith was half-way through his Junior Sophister year when the news came from Lissoy that his father had died. The family was plunged at once into the miseries of bereavement and financial retrenchment. It soon became obvious that Charles' widow, with only the income of her Pallas fields to depend on, could not afford to keep up the tenancy of the Lissoy house, and this was taken over by the Hodsons. Anne moved into a cottage at Ballymahon, two miles away, with her three sons between seven and eleven and possibly her remaining unmarried daughter, Jane. She was not destitute, as we know from her purchases of such small luxuries as green tea from the shop next door, but Charles' death had left her with little money to spare for the incidental expenses of a son in Dublin. Uncle Contarine's contribution may have been increased now and Goldsmith found two expedients which fore-shadowed later developments in his career: he pawned his books, and he wrote ballads, for which he could earn 5/- apiece at 'the sign of the Reindeer' in Mountrath Street.[9] The talent for stringing verses together which he had discovered as a child—not the least Irish thing about him—now proved worthy of serious cultivation, for five shillings was the equivalent of an English labourer's wages for nearly a week. No examples have survived.

Within a few weeks of Charles' death events occurred which might well have found their way into one of those ballads. A group of Trinity students, including Goldsmith, were involved in a riot which had developed out of the 'pumping' of a bailiff. Their thoughts had evidently turned from the bailiff himself to his clients languishing in the Black Dog prison, and with a view to setting them free they had stormed the gates. A mob had quickly gathered and there had been fatalities when the warders defended themselves with firearms. Ten students were brought before the college authorities, five of whom, including Goldsmith, admitted their responsibility and consequently escaped being sent down. Although he received a public censure, Goldsmith's academic standing was not affected. The following year he missed the scholarship that a sizar was expected to win at this stage of the degree course but managed to scrape into seventeenth place for the award of nineteen exhibitions of about thirty shillings a year.[10]

Not for the last time in his life, it was the moment when there seemed to be some cause for self-congratulation that held most danger for Goldsmith. However morose he might seem on the occasions when fellow students found him lounging about the college gate, the award of an exhibition brought out the other, more convivial side of his personality, and his poorly furnished attic room in the corner of Library Quadrangle became the scene of festivities. As House 35 had a common wall with the Library itself it was probably not the ideal place for a party.[11] Oliver was playing into his tutor's hands, presenting him with an occasion on which he could administer a reproof in the most humiliating circumstances with at least the appearance of justice on his side. Wilder seized his opportunity and the party was brought to a sudden end, with the new exhibitioner sent sprawling to the floor in front of his guests.

*

For Goldsmith there were two kinds of fantasy: the creative fantasy which was later to be turned to account in poetry, drama and fiction of great quality; and the more private fantasy which offered a retreat when reality became too unpleasant. Goldsmith seems to have had a compartment in this area of his mind labelled 'Flight to Cork' and twice in his early life he made the mistake of allowing this pleasant fiction to become confused with fact.

The Cork fantasy had a theme that was well adapted to the Ireland of the eighteenth century: emigration. It was the dream of sailing to a new life, of finding a sphere of influence far away from a society which had so gravely underestimated the dreamer. He acted on it now, sold his books, and headed south down one of the excellent roads with which Ireland was already provided. Nothing else is known about the episode except that his money quickly ran out and that one day he had nothing to eat but a handful of grey peas offered him by a girl—'the most delicious repast he had ever tasted.'[12] Somehow he got a message to Henry, and it was the older brother who battened down the hatches on whatever remained of Oliver's daydreams, escorted him back to Dublin and negotiated a *modus vivendi* between him and Wilder. That he did all this with kindness as well as firmness can be seen from the glowing appreciation he received in the dedication of *The Traveller* and from the portrait of the struggling but saintly curate in *The Deserted Village*. But whatever impetus remained to Goldsmith's studies after the events of 1747–8 there are signs that his academic career had suffered from the interruption. In May 1748 he failed to satisfy the examiners in an end of term examination,[13] and it may have been at this point, as Catherine hints, that he withdrew temporarily from the College and went to live with Thomas Contarine, perhaps in preparation for re-sitting his exam a year later. In normal circumstances he would have been able to graduate in 1748, but evidently the college requirements were not met before 1749 and, whether or not he had been keeping residence during the interim, it was February 1750 when he received his bachelor's degree. In later years, after Percy had put himself forward as official biographer, Goldsmith was to blur the facts of the ending of his career at Trinity with the utmost mystification.

The fact that Goldsmith and Edmund Burke had to wait a dozen years or so before making each other's acquaintance as expatriates in London is less puzzling than might appear. They would almost certainly have known each other by name, for reasons that were creditable on one side and less so on the other after Goldsmith's public reprimand for his part in the Black Dog riot. Since, on average, a hundred students would have entered the college annually, two members of even the same year could quite conceivably get through their entire undergraduate course without ever having occasion to speak to each other. Burke had continued to live at home until he won a scholarship in June 1746;[14] and the difference between his aims and Goldsmith's as students is clearly defined by the constitutions of the debating club which Burke founded in his second year. It was to cater for 'the improvement of its members in the more refined, elegant and useful parts of literature, these seeming the most likely means for attaining the great end in view— the formation of our minds and manners for the functions of Civil Society'.[15] Even if Goldsmith, against all appearances, had set his mind on self-improvement, he would have disliked the idea that literature should be used so calculatingly: and whatever he felt about his recent public reprimand he may have come to the conclusion that it was priggish of a member of Burke's Society to deliver an oration, *after* the Black Dog riot, to dissuade members from taking part in an affray where 'the company ... (the vilest rabble) was sufficient to hinder such an attempt.'[16]

Inspiration for ballads was probably in short supply in Burke's Debating Club, though it might have been found in the warm interior of a Watch-house or one of those 'low prohibited gaming houses' of Jonah Barrington's memoirs, where Goldsmith may also have acquired his fatal partiality for cards. There must have been many occasions when he pocketed his red cap and, escaping from the usual student routes, sank himself in the town life of Dublin. It was on one excursion of this kind that he discovered the family whose plight moved him to return to his room to fetch his own blankets. The friend who called on him the next morning found that to keep himself warm Goldsmith had slit open his bedding and climbed in amongst the feathers.[17] In a city where the cathedral choir-boys went barefoot and where all the 30,000 beggars of Ireland would stand at some time or another outside the doors of a church or an assembly room to await the arrival or departure of more wealthy citizens, Goldsmith would have had plenty of opportunities to give expression to the feelings which his father had instilled in him.

C*

In Aungier Street he would have found Trinity in full force, for the Theatre Royal laboured under the disadvantage of being considered to have a special relationship with the undergraduates. In 1746 the new deputy-manager was surprised to find that forty or fifty college bloods would crowd into morning rehearsals, and only convinced the manager, Thomas Sheridan, of his naivety when he suggested that the reforms promised the previous year should include their removal.[18] Dublin could support three evening performances a week at this time and a strong Trinity College attendance might be expected, particularly if there was any possibility of incidents (when polite Dublin would rapidly vacate their places and make an early departure). Goldsmith was fortunate to be an undergraduate at a time when Sheridan was persuading the greatest actors of the age to undertake seasons in Dublin. In 1745 nervousness over the events in Scotland had been reflected, as in London, in poor houses; but Sheridan's first success on being appointed manager this year was to sign a contract with the young actor, David Garrick, whose Richard III had taken London by storm four years earlier.

Although it was an Irishman, Charles Macklin, who had first abandoned the chanting of the older generation of actors as represented by James Quin,[19] Garrick had really shown Londoners what could be achieved when, as an early critic put it, an actor 'neither whined nor bellowed', but modulated his voice naturally, seemed attentive to whatever was spoken on the stage, and never dropped his character at the end of a speech.[20] Sheridan evidently retained confidence in his own declamatory style, for he proposed that they should share the roles of Richard III and of Iago (against Spranger Barry's Othello) and alternate as the King and the Bastard in *King John*. As *The Citizen of the World* would prove, Goldsmith was a keen observer of theatrical styles and conventions, and now, as a seventeen-year-old from an obscure Irish village, he had access to a demonstration which must have aroused excitement in far more sophisticated theatre-goers than himself. Sheridan had also engaged the little blonde actress, George Anne Bellamy, the daughter of an Irish peer, who at the age of twenty-four was a leading member of Rich's company at Covent Garden. She played Constance in *King John*, after persuading her powerful Dublin friends to intervene with Garrick who thought her unsuitable for such a matronly part. The following season she appeared as Cleopatra in Dryden's *All for*

Love, as Portia (a performance which was modelled, she claimed, on the Irish Chief Justice) and as Juliet opposite Sheridan. In the '47–'48 season Henry Woodward appeared and Goldsmith may have had the opportunity, in the autumn of 1748, to see the most famous Shylock of the period, Charles Macklin. In this way Goldsmith was seeing for the first time, from gallery or pit, performers who would later appear in his own dramatic works and with whom in at least one case he would be closely associated.

During the '46–'47 season Burke and his friends, maintaining the Trinity College right to act as theatre-guardians, launched an attack against Sheridan who, like the London managers, was padding out his repertoire with the tepid and sententious works which were still so much in evidence twenty years later. Burke wanted 'Irish plays', but by this term he meant plays written by his friends (and a rejected play by a rogue journalist, Paul Hiffernan, who was one day to become a drain on Goldsmith's never bottomless financial resources) rather than histories of Deirdre and Conchubar, Cuchulain and Emer. The campaign was launched with maximum undergraduate self-importance. Although he praised Shakespeare and Ben Jonson, Burke condemned Wycherley, Farquhar, Vanbrugh and Congreve, who were bawdy, and had failed to enjoy Lee's *Orphan*, in spite of George Anne Bellamy. As for the audience, its faults could be 'reduced to these general heads; a taste for what is vicious, what is unnatural, and their customs of clapping, hissing etc. . . .'[21]

The eighteenth century audience could do worse than this. Two weeks before the appearance of the second number of Burke's magazine *The Reformer*, a performance of *Aesop* had been interrupted by Mr Kelly, a squireen from Galway who climbed over the spikes on to the stage, made his way into the dressing rooms and caused Mrs Bellamy to miss her cue by waylaying her in the corridor and planting wet kisses on the back of her neck. Admonished and replaced in the pit, Kelly purchased an orange which he aimed at Sheridan, managing to dent the iron of the false nose which he wore in the title rôle. An angry scene followed during which the crux of the debate was whether or not an actor could be a gentleman. Kelly was by no means the only member of the audience to be outraged when Sheridan said that he himself *was*. The next evening, a performance of *The Fair Penitent* was wrecked and, although Burke would probably have considered this no great loss, Trinity College threw its weight behind Sheridan, less out of conviction that his cause was just than from a desire to avenge a Trinity man who had been insulted by a Kelly supporter. Burke helped to drag Kelly and some of his friends out of their homes to keep an appointment at the College pump and, at a subsequent court hearing, when to everyone's surprise, Sheridan's claim to be a gentleman was upheld, Kelly received a three months' prison sentence for breach of the peace. This was remitted when Sheridan appealed on his behalf, in spite of the fact that Kelly's supporters had beaten up Charles Lucas, who during the original disturbance had begged the audience to give the play a fair hearing.[22] Lucas had perhaps already demonstrated that he was beneath consideration, having publicly declared the Dublin administration to be corrupt.

*

... after his Fathers Death he was taken a perticular notice of by his Uncle Contrine who wd have him persue his studdys & brought him to him self where he assisted him with his Mother till he took his degree he then wd have him read for orders & wd have given him Bread ...[23]

Catherine's hurried, elliptical style captures the graphic key-phrase. Contarine and the entire Goldsmith/Jones clan would have regarded the acquisition of a Trinity A.B. in February 1750 as Oliver's first step towards an income by way of the family profession. All the references to churchmen and the church in his writings indicate that Goldsmith himself would have had very different feelings. He had high standards, considered himself unworthy even to read Matins aloud to some ladies with whom he was travelling on the continent, loathed time-servers and lavished praise on men like his brother Henry who performed their obscure pastoral duties diligently and out of a sense of personal conviction. Certainly the act of taking orders would 'give him Bread': the snag for a man who always kept a sense of moral purpose even if he failed to live up to it, was that he had not the slightest sense of vocation. The phrase may have been sanctified by family use and would have been produced if Oliver had actually voiced his misgivings. But with no alternative plans for supporting himself, it would not have been easy to put his case to the clergyman who had contributed to his support over five years and whose house he had probably shared for considerable periods of time. In this situation he appears to have drifted. There was some desultory study under Contarine, but while Oliver may have assumed that this could continue indefinitely while he enjoyed the civilised atmosphere of Emlaghmore, the old prebendary's thoughts were turning towards the house at the top of Elphin's unprepossessing main street where Bishop Synge resided. Contarine, now sixty-six, evidently hoped that Oliver would be allowed to succeed him in the Oran living.[24] Finally, an interview was arranged. For this very reluctant candidate who had failed to communicate the message that he had neither desire nor aptitude for holy orders the visit to Elphin must have been something of a charade. His state of mind is perhaps reflected in the Man in Black's laconic account of his own difficulties in a similar situation, where moral misgivings are presented as a simple matter of taste:

> But in order to settle in life, my friends *advised* (for they always advise when they begin to despise us) they advised me, I say, to go into orders. To be obliged to wear a long wig, when I liked a short one, or a black coat, when I generally dressed in brown, I thought was such a restraint upon my liberty that I absolutely rejected the proposal. A priest in England, is not the same mortified creature with a bonze in China; with us, not he that fasts best, but eats best, is reckoned the best liver; yet I rejected a life of luxury, indolence, and ease, from no other consideration but that boyish one of dress.[25]

Ostensibly it was Goldsmith who was rejected. The 'tradition of the diocese', as Percy records, was that Goldsmith scandalised the Bishop (a kinsman of J. M. Synge) by presenting himself for interview in a pair of scarlet breeches. What have not survived are the attitudes that were allowed to come to the surface in the Bishop's study, whether confessional or listless, attitudes which were merely summed up by a careless appearance, and which produced the effect that was intended: to convince the Bishop of Goldsmith's unworthiness even by eighteenth century standards as a candidate for the ministry. Unfortunately he had also talked himself out of '£40 a year'.

Contarine overcame his disappointment and put his influence with the gentry of Roscommon at Oliver's disposal. A family called Flynn who lived near the county town were looking for a tutor for their son.[26] Oliver was suggested for the post and found acceptable; and he lived with the Flynns for about a year. The only information that has survived from this episode comes from Goldsmith himself and suggests that the engagement was terminated as a result of a quarrel when he found his employer cheating him at cards. Later accounts of his play suggest that although Goldsmith might well have been a good subject for a sharper, it is unlikely that he would ever have discovered that he was being cheated,[27] and a more probable explanation for his departure is that the Flynns objected to the tutor playing cards with their son when he ought to have been preparing him for his entrance exam at Trinity College. He now returned to his mother's cottage at Ballymahon without prospects and with only £30 and a horse to show for his year's tutoring.

*

For most of his life Oliver had been surrounded by people who within the wretched circumstances of the Irish social system had somehow 'got by' without too much discomfort, and at Oran and Kilmore there were hints of luxury and even culture. At Trinity College he had met young men whose liberal education would prepare them for little more than living off a private income in varying degrees of amiability, and nearer home there were people like his cousin Edward Mills and, from a neighbouring village, Robert Bryanton (he had been at school in Edgworthstown with him as well as at Trinity College) who, although not rich, appear never to have had to ask themselves how they could earn a living—a tricky question at this time and in this place. In the old house at Lissoy another young man, Daniel Hodson, would have been getting by fairly pleasantly, supervising his labourers, with few anxieties until the time came to provide for younger sons. Such an environment could not have provided much stimulus for thought to the new graduate who had somehow to make his way in a society which had been left to stagnate, and there were certainly few signs over the next two years that very much mental effort was devoted to the issue.

At Ballymahon life could be as pleasant in its way as at Oran and Kilmore. Oliver could be observed perched in the dormer window of his mother's cottage with his flute, or wandering along the banks of the river Inny, or taking part in village sports.[28] The echo of George Conway's ale-house in *She Stoops to Conquer* has to be treated with caution but Goldsmith, like Tony Lumpkin, appears to have presided over his own village club which included Hodson and Bryanton amongst its members.[29] In the play, Tony's drinking companions admired him for his 'gentility', just as some of the humbler patrons of George Conway's must have been impressed by the aura of Dublin College which Oliver now carried with him. But this young man lacked the prospect of £1,500 a year which in the play would be the destiny of the son of a gentleman who had 'kept the best horses, dogs and girls in the whole county'. Oliver was no squireen, either in tastes or in status, and the nostalgic letter he wrote to Bryanton at the time of his departure from Ireland shows that, like the members of Burke's debating club, they had little desire to associate with the class. 'The Gentlemen here are much better bred than among us; no such character here as our Foxhunter; and they have expressed great surprise when I informed them that some men of a thousand pound a year in Ireland spend their whole lives in running after a hare, drinking to be drunk, and getting every Girl with Child, that will let them . . .'.[30] Oliver had learned early in life how to get by with his more extravert neighbours, but a combination of poverty, distaste for what the squireen represented and an unexpected streak of puritanism made music, story-telling and simple buffoonery the staple diet of evenings at George Conway's, rather than the mayhem which Tony Lumpkin would have preferred. He was not a heavy drinker and for obvious reasons contented himself with comparatively humble sports like fives rather than those which required the upkeep of hounds and horses.[31] That he was welcomed at the Bryantons' house, where he admired the fine eyes and clear complexions of Bob's sisters shows that he was far from being the kind of young man whose society was acceptable at the ale-house but who had to be kept away from the women-folk at all costs.[32]

Although time could be made to pass pleasantly enough, there was still the question of the gap created by his disinclination to be either clergyman or tutor, and this may have been accompanied by a growing dissatisfaction with a provincial life which was philistine and narrow. As can be surmised from Goldsmith's letter to Dan Hodson from Edinburgh, Contarine and his friends were not typical: 'There are good company in Ireland? No; the conversation there is generally made up of a smutty toast or a baudy song. The vivacity supported by some humble cousin, who has just folly enough to earn his—dinner.—Then perhaps ther's more wit and learning among the Irish? Oh Lord! No! there has been more money spent in the encouragement of the Podareen mare there in one season, than given in rewards to learned men since the times of Usher.'[33]

A large part of the dissatisfaction that comes to the surface here was now being channelled into the old Cork fantasy—a dream which touched hands with what had become a bitter reality to many Irishmen, Protestant as well as Catholic: the necessity of emigrating. It is impossible to tell whether the Goldsmiths believed that they were saying goodbye to Oliver for the last time when the day came, but he did indeed set out from Ballymahon on his new horse with the apparent intention of finding an American boat at Cork.

Within a few weeks he was back at his mother's house, penniless, and riding a wretched little pony which sagged so dispiritedly in the middle that he had named it 'Fiddleback'. But if a fantasy of a rather different kind had allowed him to anticipate a rapturous family welcome for a son snatched from an untimely emigration he was quickly disillusioned. From between the lines of Catherine's letter emerges a collective decision on the part of the Goldsmiths to give Oliver a shaking.

A family conference was convened at Anne Goldsmith's cottage, and the young man who had listened as a child to story-tellers sheltering in the kitchen at Lissoy, and who was himself an admired performer at George Conway's, prepared himself for the expenditure of a great deal of creative energy. In the narrative which forms part of Catherine's letter to Percy, fact and fantasy appear to be indiscriminately mixed. The strictly factual part of the story was that Goldsmith, with his Trinity College credentials, his kinship with Isaac Goldsmith, the Dean of Cloyne, well mounted and with a few guineas in his pocket, reached the city of Cork and, possibly via tavern and gaming table, made the acquaintance of the local gentry. Enquiries revealed that a passage to America could be obtained on a ship now in harbour awaiting a favourable wind. Meanwhile as he amused and fêted his new friends (no doubt contributing to their winnings at the card-tables) his guineas drained away alarmingly. From this point the events which Catherine noted down have the air of fiction with all the identifiable advantages of fiction over intransigent fact.

Goldsmith misses the boat. The wind has veered unexpectedly but 'unfortunately the day the wind served he happened to be on a party in the Country with some friends & his friend the Captain never enquired after him . . .'.[34] Having sold his horse, purchased the deplorable Fiddleback and given one of his remaining two half-crowns to a woman with 'eight little clean children' whose husband has been arrested for debt, he takes stock of his situation, a hundred and twenty miles from home, and decides to call on an old Trinity acquaintance who lives in the neighbourhood. Since coming down, this young man has unfortunately developed strong traits of both hypochondria and miserliness. After listening to a long account of his host's illness, Goldsmith watches eagerly when the 'grim looking woman' who presides over the domestic arrangements comes in to lay the table. But dinner consists only of 'a very small bowl of Segoe a small poranger of bad sower milk & a peice of bad brown bread', to be followed by more bread and milk at 8 p.m. when his host retires to bed. The next morning, having refused Goldsmith a loan of money, the young man suggests lending him a horse, so that Fiddleback can be sold to defray his travelling expenses. When he asks to see this animal, Goldsmith is conducted to his host's bedroom where an oak stick is produced from under the bed. This is the promised 'horse'. Before the furious Goldsmith can put it to an obvious use a visitor is announced, 'a Gentleman dressed in mourning of a most pleasing aspect' who insists on taking the two men home to dine with him. Goldsmith is invited to stay with the Gentleman and his daughters for a few days and is well entertained— the Ladies brought the Dr. to the Gardens where the amused themselves playing a bouls and at Night they playd the Harpsicord and sung . . .'. On taking his leave he has difficulty in refusing the presents which his new friend is ready to shower on him—'the Counselor offerd him his purse and Insisted he shd take what he wanted also a Horse and Servant however he took three half Guineas but posotivly refusd the Counselors Horse.'

That Catherine, at least, was enthralled is clear from the way in which she recalled not only the story's details but even its 'literary' shape and climaxes twenty-five years after it had been told. Whether alarmed or not by his cool reception, Goldsmith has called all his narrative skills to his aid. The description of the frugal supper with its gradual build-up—the old woman 'with two plates and a spoon and Cloath which she laid on a table which renewed the Doctor's spirits'—and its prompt anti-climax on the host's vigorous invitation to eat—'he highly recommended a milk Diet for his part he was Confined to such Slops as this thrusting a spoonfull into the D mouth...' is a masterpiece of knock-about farce. The oaken 'horse' joke is just as deftly handled—' . . . pray Sr says the D shew me the horse you intend to lend me with that he brought hime to his bed Chamber which the D thought a strange pleace for a horse . . .'. *Pause for effect.*

But Goldsmith was obviously on guard against overdoing the comedy. The object of the story was to win sympathy as well as entertain, and in mid course—perhaps he was reacting to the expression on the listeners' faces—he attempted to take the harm out of the situation by grasping the nettle directly: '. . . in the morning he was resolved to borrow a Guinea & go of for his freinds living he did not like but when he mentiond his going of, why truly to be sure he had given his mother & freinds high offence at his foolish ramble that the longar he stayd from them the greater their anger must be, and that he would advize him by all means to go home with all expedition . . .'.

It is not perfect, and the captious might have seized on the inconsistency of the family's expecting his return; but psychologically it is right. And at the culmination of the story, with the wayfarer warmly received into the bosom of a stranger's family, Goldsmith's now rather desperate attempts to show how things would be in an ideal world can still be heard. Catherine remembered the more pathetic elements of this episode in the story without perhaps realising the skill that had gone into implanting the details in her memory: the Gentleman's black clothes on his first appearance are not mere circumstantial padding for later, when the harpsichord is played, 'the Dr Observed the Counselor drownd in Tears on hearing Ladys sing and p[lay] which he begd Mr Goldsmith wod excuse; since it had been their first time to play or sing since the Death of their Mother & his Wife . . .'.

Either deliberately, or because here, as elsewhere, she recalls facts less vividly than the fictitious details of a good story, Catherine blurs the sequel:

'And now Dr. Mother says he since I have struggeld so hard to come home to you why are you not better pleasd to see me, and pray says the Mother have you ever wrote a letter of thanks to that dear good man since you came home, no says the Dr. I have not then says the Mother you are an ungrateful Savage a Monster in short the whole boddy of his Friends which ware present up braid^{d} him for which he for a full half houre sat listning to with grate composure and after they had vented their Passion he begd they wod sit down and compos themselvs for what he told them was only to amuse them and that there was not one word in it; how ever he afterward assured me of its veracity'.

Between the lines, we can see that something has gone badly wrong. It is hardly credible that the family should have harangued Goldsmith so vigorously for his delay in writing to the Councillor: there had presumably been little time in which to do so. But it is quite possible that he was forced to listen 'for a full half houre' to complaints on another score, that Mrs Goldsmith (anticipating Mrs Hardcastle in the play) should have used terms like 'monster' and 'ungrateful savage', and that, whatever front Goldsmith managed to maintain up to the moment of breakdown and confession, he felt anything but 'grate composure' before this combined onslaught.

In the fantasist's scheme of things, any refusal to observe the rules of the game is an unforgivable offence: when he unlocks his store the listener must willingly suspend disbelief. His fictions are not only soothing to himself but are designed to liberate the recipient into an ideal world where every rough edge has been smoothed and every event, whether farcical, heroic or pathetic, is encountered in the superlative degree. A refusal to accept the fantasist's inner life is both churlish and wounding. Unfortunately Anne Goldsmith was in no mood for fiction. Angry and disappointed, she insinuated her questions cruelly into every crevice of the Fiddleback story until she had prised fantasist and fantasy apart. However badly he had behaved, Oliver might reasonably have expected that the mother who had once been so proud of him might have preferred him back at Ballymahon on even the most unsatisfactory terms rather than in permanent exile on the other side of the Atlantic; but he was forced at last to recognise the hardness of a woman whose one aim now was to confront her problematical son with facts: '. . . his Mother was much concerned at his folly & cd not be readily reconcild to him, but his Brother & Sisters so contrived to meet at his Mothers to bring on a reconciliation & after many cool repremands on her side She insisted on where he had been where he had spent his money horse linnen &c. as he brought nothing home but what was on his back . . .'

Anne Goldsmith had every excuse for being angry and bitter. She was a widow in her early fifties, no longer the mistress of the comfortably large house at Lissoy but living off whatever income could be derived from the leasehold of the fifty acres at Pallasmore which her mother had wisely secured in her name. At her cottage on the crossroads at Ballymahon she was bringing up three sons between the ages of fifteen and eleven. John, the youngest, was to die in childhood, possibly while Oliver was in Edinburgh two years later. Neither Maurice nor Charles showed any signs of the academic ability that Henry and Oliver had displayed, and as their standard of literacy remained closer to Catherine's than to Oliver's it is unlikely that they had received the educational advantages that had been bestowed on the older brothers. Henry and Catherine now had families of their own and there was little chance of the boys' receiving help from that direction. Now she was confronted by a son who, far from seeing the need to redeem the waning family fortunes, was apparently devoid of any sense of obligation. In return for all her past hopes and contrivances she was offered a story about a miser and a man in black.

To say that Goldsmith failed to 'see feelingly' a state of affairs that was all too obvious to his mother is to make a serious charge against him, but one which has to be qualified almost immediately with a plea of diminished responsibility. For better or worse the small boy whose high spirits had been punctuated by bouts of withdrawal and day-dreaming had developed into a man who was quite incapable of making a normal reaction to the circumstances he had created: he did not see that he had behaved badly, and felt instead that his mother had committed an unforgivable sin by withdrawing her affection from him in a moment of crisis. There is every indication that he brooded on it for the rest of his life. At another and deeper level of his personality he wrestled with a sense of guilt which was to become a driving force behind his art. He was ultimately to come to terms with the Ballymahon crisis in the very broad humour of a farcial comedy but at the time of his return from Cork on Fiddleback, and for many years afterwards, his mother's failure to welcome him was to wear a very different complexion. When Mrs Goldsmith died in 1770 he went into half-mourning and avoided Fanny Reynolds' enquiries by saying that a 'distant relative' had died. But by this time a man in full mourning had appeared for a second time in his fictional output. The first—the man in black in the Fiddleback story—is the ideal father-figure who behind the unpromising appearance and circumstances of the penniless traveller sees his true worth. The Man in Black who wanders, unexplained, through the pages of *The Citizen of the World* is, surprisingly, the habitually overdressed and flamboyant Oliver Goldsmith himself.

The Man in Black claimed, unaccountably, that his family despised him,[36] and this seems to have been the lesson that Goldsmith extracted from the half-hour grilling at his mother's cottage. It was not the best frame of mind in which to start again. After Dan and Catherine Hodson had taken pity on him, invited him to stay at the Lissoy house and helped to bring about a reconciliation between him and Contarine, who was perhaps still annoyed about the Flynn affair, there is a suggestion of limp passivity in his readiness to fall in with the family's new plan to make a lawyer of him. There was already one failed lawyer in the family: the Uncle John with whom he had lived as a schoolboy.[37] Oliver accepted the £50 which was raised to cover the expenses of travel to London and to launch him on a course of study at the Temple, but when he reached Dublin another fantasy overtook him—that of transforming his premium into a fortune at the gaming-tables. He encountered an old acquaintance, lost his money and once more appeared somewhere in the region of Ballymahon.[38] He may have returned to his mother, whose attitude by now had probably hardened into tight-lipped resignation. Even for the purposes of family debate he was rapidly running through the professions in which a degree might be useful. It is not clear whether the physician's calling was simply the next on the list, or if Goldsmith had at last got through to an idea in which day-dreaming and reality partly coincided. Catherine's narrative implies that, this time, some glimmerings of the enormity of the situation had penetrated Goldsmith's consciousness:— '[he] once more returned to his Mother a hart broken dejected being twas then he began to [repen]t of his past misconduct and if he was once more taken notice of [promised to] behave with more circumspection for the future, they then desired him he migh prepair for the studdy of physick and once More his Good Uncle was reconsild to him at lenth he was sent to Edinburg and in 1753 enterd that College . . .'. The medical school of Edinburgh was certainly better known than that of Dublin but, after all, this may by now have been less of a consideration with Contarine and the Goldsmiths than the desirability of placing the Irish Channel between themselves and Oliver.

FOUR

The Philosopher Who Carries
All His Goods About Him

A TORN manuscript preserved in the Huntingdon Library conveys the despondency that Goldsmith was to feel in the weeks following his arrival in Edinburgh in the autumn of 1752. He was writing to Dan Hodson:

> ... This country has little or nothin[g which I can] give an account of so instead of a D[escription of the] country you must be contented with [an account of the] manner in which I spend my Time, [during the] day I am obligd to attend the Publick L[ectures. At night] I am in my lodging. I have hardly an[y other s]ociety but a Folio book a skeleton my cat and my meagre landlady ...[1]

The spark of comedy flared for a moment, then failed; the letter halted to a conclusion with a reminder that Goldsmith's friends—'Exclusive of my Uncle'—had promised him fifteen guineas of which he had so far received only four.

Another to Hodson, written from London five years later, provides a clue to the air of constraint in this and the only other surviving letters (the three to Thomas Contarine) written to a member of the family circle over the next two years. He cannot forget his old friends he tells Hodson:

> ... whether I eat or starve, live in a first floor or four pair of stairs [   ] high, I still remember them with ardour, nay, my very country comes in for a share of my affection. Unaccountable fondness for country, this maladie du Pays, as the french call it. Unaccountable, that he should still have an affection for a place, who never received when in it above civil contempt, who never brought out of it, except his brogue and his blunders; surely my affection is equally ridiculous with the Scotchman's who refused to be cured of the itch, because it made him unco'thoughtful of his wife and bonny Inverary ...[2]

If his family's barely concealed contempt was still a memory so long after he had left Ireland, the burden of past defeats must have settled all the more heavily on the shoulders of the isolated new-comer in a raw northern city this winter of 1752.

A year later another letter, to Bob Bryanton (significantly, not a member of the family circle), gives a different picture and retro-spectively raises the suspicion of window-dressing in the family letters: but the man who was later to discover an anodyne against isolation and unhappiness in his music, his books and long hours of desk-work may also have found it in his medical studies during the early stage of his Edinburgh career. In Alexander Munro, the famous professor of anatomy who was now attracting pupils from as far away as Russia, Goldsmith had a teacher who could inspire enthusiasm.[3] He paid three guineas this October to enrol himself in the anatomy class, and was to invest another three in the same quarter the following year, in spite of there being by this time a long overdue account of £3. 15. 9¾d. to settle at the tailor's.[4] His en-thusiasm for his new studies is reflected at the beginning of 1753 in his joining the Edinburgh Medical Society. This was not expected of a first-year student. All the members of the medical faculty had studied at Leyden under Boerhaave, but in Goldsmith's estimation none of them had Munro's flair for teaching, and some of them had been presenting the same theoretical course for more than a quarter of a century. The practical side of the course, which consisted of doing the rounds of the Royal Infirmary with Professor Rutherford, was particularly disappointing. John Rutherford and his associate professor of the Theory and Practice of Medicine, Andrew Sinclair, 'say nothing but what we may find in the books laid before us,' Goldsmith tells Contarine, 'and speak that in so droneing and heavy a manner that their hearers are not many degrees in a better state than their Patients'.[5] Unfortunately, there is no record of what Professors Rutherford and Sinclair thought of their new student.

These teachers were poorly paid by Dublin standards. As opposed to Theaker Wilder's £700 a year, Alexander Munro's stipend as head of the faculty was less than £50 a year (the heads of the faculties of theology, arts and law were receiving £161, £113 and £200 respectively in the 1770s);[6] but materially Edinburgh was an impoverished city, even if not as provincial as Goldsmith, with the faint condescension of the man who has known the fine city of

Dublin, manages to suggest. The university was poorly housed and there was very little accommodation for students, who had to find lodgings in the town. This may have been a contributing factor to the isolation of Goldsmith's first few weeks. Once he had discovered his way round the cellar-clubs and the taverns where so much of the intellectual life of Edinburgh took place, it may equally have been a threat to his rather erratic powers of concentration. In one way, the Edinburgh system was attractive because there were few rules and—since only a small proportion of the students took a degree—no sense of working under outside pressure. But the exam system of Trinity College Dublin had been an inducement to work.

By January 1753 Goldsmith had evidently begun to enjoy life in Edinburgh. Outwardly, this dour and filthy city strung out like a fish's skeleton on its crag between the Castle and the palace of Holyrood House was an uncongenial place; but by now he must have familiarised himself with the narrow 'wynds' on either side of the High Street, where the flat-dwelling inhabitants of the city lived in fascinating and democratic confusion,[7] and begun to see that first impressions could be misleading. At first he had been startled to see 'a well dresd Dutchess issuing from a dirty close',[8] but he would soon have learned that she shared the same front-door as the cobbler in the cellar, and the same evil-smelling staircase as the attorney above her on the second floor, or the paviour on the tenth. With only 50,000 inhabitants Edinburgh could afford, after the initial coldness, to be a friendly place and, after that shaky start, the new medical student was drawn quickly into the life of the town.

A few years later in Glasgow, Mrs Bellamy lost most of her wardrobe and properties after a Calvinist preacher had inspired his flock to set fire to the stage on which she was to appear, and she had to play Lady Macbeth in white satin instead of the customary black velvet.[9] Goldsmith would have found the calvinist element equally strong in Edinburgh, but although the elders of the Kirk could impose heavy fines for sabbath-breaking (one of the most offensive results being that the contents of chamber-pots emptied out of the windows—by regulation—at 10 p.m. on Saturday night were not removed by the street-cleaners until 7 a.m. on Monday), most of the wynds with their oyster rooms and convivial clubs in candle-lit basements were well out of sight of the Lawnmarket and St Giles's Church. And in spite of a plethora of pulpit oratory against it there was an Assembly in one of those dark alleys, where the younger elements of Edinburgh society could gather on Thursday evenings between 4.0 and 11.0 and dance under the severely maternal eyes of Lord Mansfield's sister, Miss Nikky Murray, for half-a-crown.[10]

Miss Murray was a snob and is unlikely to have given Goldsmith a very warm welcome, in spite of his having secured an introduction to a good tailor and invested in an evening suit of 'rich Sky-Blew sattin', 'Blew Durant' and 'Sky-Blew Shalloon'.[11] (Perhaps following some mysterious inner dictate he had returned the following month and purchased another suit in 'Black Shalloon' and 'fine Priest's Grey-cloth'.) Although Miss Murray's badge of office 'a gold medal, with motto and device' was intended to be 'emblematical of charity and parental tenderness', it is all too likely that her interpretation of both qualities would have given high priority to the protection of well-born young ladies from encounters with penniless strangers like Goldsmith. He remarked to the man standing next to him that the rigid decorum (and segregation of the sexes in the pauses between dances) reminded him of the procession of the Roman matrons in honour of Ceres—a pleasantry which was greeted with a snub. But the evening was not a complete failure, for he struck up an acquaintance with the old man, the Lord Kirkudbright —his title was to be posthumously validated twenty-one years later— who stood selling white gloves at the top of the stairs. Goldsmith accepted defeat with good grace. At the end of a breezily satirical account of Edinburgh 'society' he confesses to Bryanton:

> But how ill my Bob does it become me to ridicule woman with whom I have scarce any correspondence. There are 'tis certain handsome women here and 'tis as certain they have handsome men to keep them company. An ugly and a poor man is society only for himself and such society the world lets me enjoy, in great abundance. Fortune has given you circumstances and Nature a person to look charming in the Eyes of the fair world nor do I envy my Dear Bob such blessings while I may sit down and [laugh at the wor]ld, and at myself—the most ridiculous object in it . . .[12]

Edinburgh, a city still under a cloud since the events of six years back, was teaching Goldsmith to accept his situation without being crushed by it—and without scurrying off into the safe retreat of fantasy. This resilient letter revealed that there were enough positive elements in his life here to compensate for his inability to attract the attention of the girls whose brogue fascinated him as they strode rather mannishly past on their three-inch heels. One of them was the proximity of other lively minds. Although very little is known about his life in Edinburgh, the rescue operations carried out on his behalf over the next four years in Newcastle-on-Tyne and London by his fellow students Laughlane Maclean, Fenn Sleigh and William Farr, prove that he was as much in demand as he had ever been at Ballymahon. However badly received at the Assembly Room, he would have had access to the many clubs which assumed the democracy of learning and wit and raised neither national nor social barriers. The previous two decades had witnessed a northern literary renaissance, and although the poet James Thomson had seen the need to take the London road, important projects were now on hand in Edinburgh itself. David Hume was writing the *History of England*—a work to which Goldsmith would one day be greatly indebted. Dr William Robertson's *History of Scotland* would appear five years after Hume's work, in 1759. (It was Robertson's *History* which Johnson compared unfavourably with Goldsmith's historical compilations, no doubt with the prime intention of teasing Boswell.)[13] Adam Smith's *Wealth of Nations* would also emerge from the Edinburgh Goldsmith knew: so would Dr James Beattie's *Essay on Truth*, a 'book of the year' which indirectly provoked Goldsmith's only recorded quarrel with Sir Joshua Reynolds.

He would have found himself at home in musical circles too. At the meetings of the Edinburgh Musical Society, he would have had the chance to hear a small baroque orchestra conducted from the harpsichord, sometimes by a gifted gentleman amateur; and although his own flute-playing was not in that category, he would have understood the prevailing enthusiasm for Scottish ballads, either the traditional, or new ballads set to old tunes by such Edinburgh ladies as Jean Elliot, Miss Oliphant of Gask and Lady Lindsay. He was no shy performer himself. The spontaneous rendering of an Irish ballad during an evening at a club in the company of fellow students, lawyers, physicians, lairds and aristocrats may have attracted invitations to private musical gatherings.

It was probably a combination of factors—his music, his readiness to embark on an Irish tale, perhaps also his assiduous application to the games of basset, loo and whist—that led to a series of appearances at the Duke of Hamilton's dinner-table. Although the informant is Goldsmith himself (adopting a brief and dismissive vein to show his uncle that he could take titles in his stride) this is probably not another fantasy. The Duke—'hot, debauched, extravagant' in Horace Walpole's opinion—was only four years older than Goldsmith and was far more accessible in a small town like Edinburgh than he would have been in London. His nineteen-year-old wife, Elizabeth, one of the great beauties of the age, was the daughter of John Gunning of Castlecoote, not very far away from Contarine at Oran. Goldsmith's daily appearance at an aristocrat's open table underlines the fact that he had made a reputation for himself in Edinburgh, but not perhaps on grounds consistent with being a diligent disciple of Alexander Munro: like a later expatriate from Ireland he was 'putting his art into his life', and it was his ability to keep the table amused, once proved, that assured him welcome on subsequent visits.

For two weeks he enjoyed a taste of that luxury which in his innermost being he could never bring himself to despise, but at the end of the fortnight he realised that, far from having put behind him the experience of waiting on young aristocrats at high table in the hall of Trinity College, he had simply become an unpaid entertainer. Promptly, if rather prematurely, he withdrew under the defensive shell of professional status. As he wrote to Contarine:

> I have spent more than a fortnight every second day at the Duke of Hamilton's, but it seems they like me more as a *jester* than as a companion; so I disdained so servile an employment; 'twas unworthy my calling as a physician . . .[16]

In later years his off-hand behaviour with even more influential noblemen than Hamilton would reveal the same lower middle class cautiousness.

*

In view of Contarine's past kindness, Goldsmith's three letters to him are strange compilations. The first, of May 8th, 1753, is little more than a series of comments on the Edinburgh professors, and acts only as a preface to the far more important postscript in which his uncle's allowance to him is discussed. The second, probably written in December 1753, is largely given over to an abstract discussion of the nature of an education in medicine, and gives his reasons for wanting to continue his studies in Paris. The third, written from Leyden, in May 1754, contains an elaborate story of the 'Fiddleback' kind, almost as circumstantial in its detail and equally probably untrue. The literary air is as evident in the first two letters as in the third.

> And now, dear Sir, let me here acknowledge the humility of the station in which you found me; let me tell how I was despised by most, and hateful to myself. Poverty, hopeless poverty, was my lot, and Melancholy was beginning to make me her own. When you—but I stop here, to inquire how your health goes on?...[17]

In this letter, however much he may seem to be putting on the style, it would be possible to give him the benefit of the doubt if he had not self-indulgently repeated himself in the postscript:

> ... Give my—how shall I express it? Give my earnest love to Mr and Mrs Lawder ...

The mannered anacolutha belong to the world of one of Dickens' most self-conceited characters. It is not altogether surprising that Jane Lawder should have made the decision to sever the last-remaining link with her cousin some time between the writing of this letter and of another addressed to herself, which she failed to answer, in August 1758. If Contarine himself did not resent the tone, Jane evidently did.

Contarine had arranged that credit should be available to his nephew on his arrival and throughout his stay in Edinburgh. The agreed annual sum was £10 and Contarine was to be informed whenever money was drawn.[18] It was not a large allowance, but would have gone a long way to meeting living expenses which Goldsmith had calculated on arrival to be £23 a year. (Dr Johnson, in fact, managed to live at a much cheaper rate when he visited Scotland twenty years later.) But other members of the family were also expected to contribute to his upkeep; and the best feature of Contarine's contribution was that, even after the Dublin fiasco, his nephew was trusted. In December 1753, he drew twice the agreed amount, assuming that this was justified by his imminent departure for the continent.[19]

Goldsmith never succeeded in grasping the link between the silver and copper specie which he jingled in his pocket or scattered about his rooms and their significance either in terms of working hours or of social prestige. Such a failing made him all the more attractive as a man but inevitably led to anxiety and unhappiness. By now it had probably vitiated his relationship with his patron, for the fact that Contarine and the Lawders lived in upper middle class comfort probably indicates not only that they were luckier than Oliver but that they did, very much, appreciate the significance of money. Contarine had by now put his hand in his pocket on several occasions, but so cautiously that he may deliberately have been reminding a young man who was a little too well endowed with imagination that he was no genie in an Arabian tale. He had not intervened to save Oliver from a sizar's life at Trinity and he had apparently been prepared to see him emigrate to America. He may have thought sincerely that Oliver must be taught to stand on his own feet: he may have felt even more strongly that money should stay in the family rather than be dissipated amongst the unreliable Goldsmiths. His will, in which he left Oliver £10, suggests that the latter impulse was stronger.*

For Oliver, the young man with a pronounced tendency to indulge in fantasies, it would have seemed reasonable that the folk of Emlaghmore and Kilmore House should do something fine for their less fortunate relative. But the departure from Ireland had been a shock to his system and the cold winter winds which blew down the Canongate must have brought the reminder that, materially, strict limits had been placed on Uncle Contarine's kindness. Inevitably there would have been moments when he was tempted to forget that this kindness had been real, and to give way to resentment that Contarine had failed to do even more for him—to guarantee, for example, his right to the pleasantly idle existence of so many young Irishmen of his time. To make things worse, Contarine was clearly included amongst those people who in Goldsmith's belief

---

*The Lawders' affluence brought tragedy rather than security. In 1779 James Lawder was murdered in front of his wife by drunken servants who had been speculating about the contents of an iron chest in his possession.[20]

had treated him contemptuously. He was far too sensitive not to detect any eagerness there might have been to get him out of Ireland, and now Contarine was compounding the crime by showing that he was sorry for his nephew. This message seems to have been conveyed to Oliver in a letter he received near the beginning of his stay in Edinburgh and the incriminating phrase is embedded in the rhetoric of his reply:

> My Dr Uncle
>
> In your letter (the only one I received from Kilmore) you call me the Philosopher who carries all his goods about him yet how can such a character fit me who have left behind in Ireland Every thing I think worth possesing freinds that I love and a society that pleasd while it instructed, who but must regret the Loss of such Enjoyments who but must regret his absence from Kilmore that Ever knew it as I did . . .[21]

The tone goes wrong, perhaps, as Goldsmith realises the full implications of the remark he has quoted. A facile rhetoric comes first to his rescue, to conceal his inability to say anything at all to Contarine and the letter is filled out to a moderately decent length with his guide to the Edinburgh medical faculty.

If Contarine and the Goldsmiths had made up their minds that Oliver's future mistakes must be perpetrated elsewhere, Contarine at least felt a little remorse after his departure. It was perhaps his doubt as to this highly irresponsible exile's future that prompted him to search for some rallying phrase and this Goldsmith had seized upon, at first perhaps gratefully as he embroidered it with rhetorical flourishes of his own, and then seeing not only pity but 'contempt' behind it. Whether reasonably or not it cancelled his obligation towards the older man. From now on, with the exception of a momentary return of the old feeling for his uncle when he is in Holland, he is the pensioner, writing bread-and-butter letters to a patron who must be kept equally well supplied with hints of studious application and with ornamental flourishes of gratitude.

*

Goldsmith had still not assuaged the thirst for travel which seems to have lain behind his attachment to the road to Cork. In the spring of 1753 he escaped from claustrophobic Edinburgh for a month and went on a tour of the Highlands. It was intended as a walking tour, but a troublesome corn forced him to hire a pony. His brief reference to this in the postscript of the first letter to Contarine indicates that he travelled alone. Unlike Boswell and Johnson twenty years later, he left no record of his journey through a country which had been forcibly 'pacified' less than a decade before; but nothing denotes him a late-Augustan so thoroughly as his comment on the Scottish landscape in the letter to Bryanton:

> Shall I tire you with a description of this unfruitful country? where I must lead you over their hills all brown with heath, or their valleys scarce able to feed a rabbet? ... every part of the country presents the same dismall landscape, no grove nor brook lend their musick to cheer the stranger, or make the inhabitants forget their poverty ...[22]

For the traveller who was to prefer the dykes and well-cultivated fields of Holland, not even the Scots heather could be purple.

A few months later he made the decision announced in the second letter to Contarine: to leave Edinburgh and continue his studies first at Paris and then at Leyden—both centres of medical learning; but before he could extricate himself from Edinburgh he tumbled into one of the financial crises which were to dog him to the end of his life. He had stood as guarantor to a fellow-student, Hugh Alexander Kennedy, who had run up a bill at the tailor's, and this bill was still unpaid. Whether this was an additional incentive to leave is not known; and the only clear fact to have survived the episode is that early in 1754 he was in Newcastle-on-Tyne, was arrested at the suit of the Edinburgh tailor, a Mr Barclay, and delivered from the hands of the bailiffs by his old Trinity College acquaintances and fellow medical students, Laughlane Maclean and Fenn Sleigh. Shortly afterwards he bought his passage on a ship travelling from Newcastle to La Brille, sixteen miles below Rotterdam. From here he made his way to Leyden.[23]

There was one unsatisfactory feature about this lucky escape. His rescuers were fellow-Irishmen who would enjoy describing the adventure in their letters home. Goldsmith, still anxious to preserve the appearance of the hard-working student, did not want his family to learn that he had at last seen the inside of a debtor's prison, and it was Contarine who was sacrificed in the need to obscure the truth of the episode. Convinced that some aspect of the Newcastle affair will get back to Counties Roscommon and Westmeath, he invents a story which cleverly incorporates a prison scene. From Edinburgh he has begun his journey to Paris (rather surprisingly in a ship bound for Bordeaux) but at Newcastle he and 'six agreeable passengers' (who turn out to be soldiers in the pay of France) are arrested by a 'Serjeant and twelve Grenadiers with their bayonets screwd'. A fortnight passes before Goldsmith's innocence is proved. (This was probably the exact term of his imprisonment at the suit of the Edinburgh tailor; and either to cover himself completely or, perhaps, remembering that even the slightest tincture of Jacobitism will do him no good if he ever returns to Trinity for a medical degree, he advises Contarine to 'keep all this secret or at least say it was for debt for if it were once known at the university I should hardly get a degree'.) As in the Fiddleback story, a stroke of pathos is now achieved with the revelation that his own life has been providentially spared, as the French ship sailed without him only to be 'wrecked at the mouth of the Graronne [*sic*] and every one of the crew was drownd. It happen'd the last great storm.'[24] He embarks instead for Rotterdam and writes—as the postmark proves—from Leyden.

*

His initial reaction to Holland was enthusiastic. For the first time he was setting foot outside the British Isles, and he was prepared to be enchanted by everything that came his way. The excitement was still fresh in his memory when he relived the experience in the Augustan couplets of *The Traveller*:

> To men of other minds my fancy flies,
> Embosom'd in the deep where Holland lies,
> Methinks her patient sons before me stand,
> Where the broad ocean leans against the land,
> And, sedulous to stop the coming tide,
> Lift the tall rampire's artificial pride.
> Onward methinks, and diligently slow
> The firm connected bulwark seems to grow;

Spreads its long arms amidst the watry roar,
Scoops out an empire, and usurps the shore.
While the pent ocean rising o'er the pile,
Sees an amphibious world beneath him smile.
The slow canal, the yellow blossom'd vale,
The willow tufted bank, the gliding sail,
The crowded mart, the cultivated plain,
A new creation rescu'd from his reign.[25]

He travelled up to Leyden in a covered horse-drawn barge in the company of some card-playing Englishmen, talkative Frenchmen and sleeping Dutchmen. For himself, he could only gaze at the unfolding new scene:

[I] was wholy Taken up in observing the face of the country, nothing can Equall its beauty. Wherever I turn my Eye fine houses elegant gardens statues grottoes vistas present themselvs but enter their Towns and you are charmd beyond description. No no[th]ing can be more clean [or beau]tifull.[26]

A reaction quickly set in. However much he envied their high degree of middle class comfort or admired their talent for languages, he found the Dutch far too phlegmatic for his taste. The more refined members of the bourgeoisie had the manners of Frenchmen without their liveliness of wit, and as for the 'downright Hollander' he was fair game for the satirical Irishman:

Upon a head of lank hair he wears a half cock'd Narrow leav'd hat lacd with black ribbon, no coat but seven waistcoats and nine pairs of breeches so that his hips reach almost up to his armpits. This well cloathd vegetable is now fit to see company or make love but what a pleasing creature is the object of his apetite why she wears a large friez cap with a deal of flanders lace and for every pair of breeches he carries she puts on two petticoats, is it not surprizing how things should ever come close enough to make it a match.[27]

The typical Dutchwoman was 'pale and fat', and walked 'as if she were stradling after a go-cart'. At the theatre, the young man who had known Dublin during the days of 'Garrick fever' inevitably felt superior to the sleepy Dutch audiences which could only be shaken out of their apathy by a prancing Harlequin.

The university, too, was a disappointment although like Edinburgh it had the advantage of being non-residential. The medical
faculty had not advanced since the days of the great Boerhaave,
under whom Goldsmith's Edinburgh teachers had studied; and
although he must have enjoyed the proximity of the botanical
garden that spring, he seems to have cast a rather jaundiced eye
round the octagonal anatomy hall where glass cases were crammed
with skeletons, stuffed animals, withered fruits, mummies, pickled
limbs and the anthropological flotsam which had arrived by courtesy
of the Dutch East Indies trade.[28] Using the privilege of the stranger,
he buttonholed the Chemistry professor one day and was treated to
an outburst of academic cynicism.

> ... he began by complaining, that all the English students,
> which formerly came to his university, now went intirely [to
> Edinburgh]; and the fact surprized him more, as Leyden was
> now as well as ever furnished with masters excellent in their
> respective professions. He concluded by asking, if the professors
> of Edinburgh were rich. I reply'd, that the salary of a professor
> there seldom amounted to more than thirty pounds a year. Poor
> men, says he. I heartily wish they were better provided for,
> until they become rich, we can have no expectation of English
> students at Leyden.[29]

Goldsmith's disenchantment with Holland seems to have confirmed him in political beliefs which he was to hold for the rest of
his life; for a coolly analytical eye forced him to look behind the
surface which, at first view, had delighted him: the neat gardens,
the grottoes, the cleanliness, the little domestic palaces full of fine
glass and pewter and paintings, out of which issued those same
'Hollanders' whom he had made fun of in his letter to Contarine. It
was a revelation for the expatriate from a country where the survival of the middle class was very much in doubt. Holland inspired
a complex feeling in which envy and admiration were mixed, but
the conscious reaction was to examine the foundations and the
effects of Dutch mercantile prosperity and to erect from his findings
a critique of colonialism which was to be one of his principal themes
as a writer. In the *Public Ledger* of July 1760 he would comment:

'When I compare the figure which the Dutch make in Europe

with that they assume in Asia, I am struck with surprize. In Asia I find them the great Lords of all the India seas; in Europe the timid inhabitants of a paltry state. No longer the sons of freedom, but of avarice; no longer asserters of their rights by courage, but by negociations; fawning on those who insult them, and crouching under the rod of every neighbouring power.[30]

But in criticising a rival colonial power in these terms, he was warning his English readership, in the fourth year of a war which was bringing in great territorial gains in India and North America, to be on guard against facile self-congratulation. The parable of the kingdom of Lao—also put into the mouth of his Chinese traveller—spells out the same message as to the dangers of expansionism combined with a neglect of things nearer home.[31] His stay in Holland reminded him of the existence of a moneyed class which could bend the laws and subject the populace to economic servitude:

> At gold's superior charms all freedom flies,
> The needy sell it, and the rich man buys[32]

This in turn strengthened his conviction that in his own country freedom could only be preserved if the balance was tilted against the squireen, the landlord and, behind them, the powerful Whig oligarchs who divided between themselves the offices, and rewards, of government.

But in the meantime Goldsmith was taking steps of his own to improve his slender income, and whatever the aristocratic members of Brook's and Almack's would have thought of his method, the thrifty Dutch merchants must have disapproved of it quite as much as he disapproved of theirs. The only episode to have survived from this period, other than those recorded obliquely in his writings, is Goldsmith's erupting one night into the room of a fellow-student, Thomas Ellis, with a pocketful of guineas which he had won at the gaming tables. Ellis evidently knew Goldsmith well enough to realise that this was not a typical result of an evening's whist. He strongly advised his friend to lock up the guineas and use them to defray his expenses during the completion of his medical studies. Unfortunately the fantasy of the gambler was stronger than Ellis's advice. Goldsmith returned to the tables to clinch his fortune, and lost everything. Ellis's account suggests that it was at this point that he decided to cut short his disappointing Dutch experience and leave Leyden on foot with his German flute, a clean shirt and a mere handful of small change in his pocket. On the point of departure, a fit of remorse seized him for his treatment of Contarine and the last of his money was impulsively laid out on the purchase of tulip bulbs for the garden at Emlaghmore.[33]

*

From the time of his departure from Leyden until his arrival at Dover in the late summer of 1756, very little is known about Goldsmith's whereabouts and activities. Even the date of his departure is a matter of conjecture: assuming that he did not set out for his long walk in the depths of winter, he left either in the autumn of 1754 or the spring of 1755. Perhaps he is more likely to have found tulip bulbs in the autumn.

When he visited his biographer-elect at Northumberland House in the spring of 1773 Goldsmith gave a panoramic view of his wanderings about Europe. Percy recorded this and added some biographical hints from *The Vicar of Wakefield*:

... He resolved to make the tour of Europe on foot, and to trust to Providence for his resources. He had observed in his *Enquiry into the Present State of Polite Literature in Europe*, Chapter XIII, that 'Countries wear very different appearances to travellers of different circumstances. A man, who is whirled through Europe in his post-chaise, and the pilgrim, who walks the grand tour on foot, will form very different conclusions, *Haud inexpertus loquor*.

He used to give an account of his own travels so nearly resembling those of the wanderer in his *Vicar of Wakefield*, that some of the following particulars are believed to belong to himself. 'I had some knowledge of music, and now turned what was once my amusement into a present means of subsistence. Whenever I approached a peasant's house towards night-fall, I played one of my most merry tunes, and that procured me not merely lodging but subsistence for the next day, I once or twice attempted to play to people of fashion, but they always thought my performance odious, and never rewarded me even with a trifle.'

His classical learning procured him also entertainment at the

monasteries, especially those of the Irish nation. And in some of
the foreign Universities and convents, upon certain days, theses
are maintained against any adventitious disputant; for which, if
the champion opposes with some dexterity, he may claim a
gratuity in money, a dinner, and a bed for the night. This afforded
another resource for our forlorn pilgrim. "Thus," says he ,"I
fought my way towards England, walked alone from city to city,
examined mankind more nearly, and, if I may so express it, saw
both sides of the picture."

In this manner he travelled through Flanders, and some parts
of France and Germany, till he arrived at Switzerland, . . .

It has been related by former Biographers, that at Geneva
Goldsmith was engaged to be travelling tutor, or companion to
a young Englishman, who, having been bred an attorney, had
succeeded to a large fortune from his uncle, a pawnbroker in
London; and who now resolved to improve himself by travel. It
is added, that through the sordid avarice of the pupil the tutor
was soon released from his charge. But it has, however, been
doubted by his intimate friends, whether this connection has not
rather been imagined from the adventure in the novel, than really
experienced by himself.

He then went to Padua in Italy, where he continued six months,
and if he ever took any medical degree it was probably in this
ancient school of medicine. Of Italy, he visited all the northern
part, and saw Venice, Verona and Florence. But losing his good
uncle and generous benefactor while he was in Italy, he was
obliged to travel on foot through France to England; still lodging
in convents, wherever he could find any of his own nation. He
landed at Dover about the breaking out of the war in 1756 . . .[34]

Goldsmith would have been gratified to see Percy rejecting the
findings of Dr Glover's brief memoir. The image of himself that he
had wanted to project that spring day at Northumberland House,
had no place for either travelling companions or peripatetic pupils.
Even after the lapse of nineteen years he was still building upon
Contarine's idea of the Wandering Scholar and he wanted Percy to
see him, in his mid-twenties, as a latter-day troubadour seeking
refuge amongst peasants whom he charmed with his flute and

priests or academics whose interest he aroused with his scholarship and skill in debate.

He may have been trying to perpetuate a fantasy which had been inspired by the death of Baron Holberg a few months before he left Holland. The place devoted to Holberg in the *Enquiry into the Present State of Polite Learning in Europe* reveals Goldsmith's interest in him, and he pays particular attention to the way in which Holberg, in the early years of the century before his writing had brought him honours and a title in Denmark, had kept himself alive during long tramps across Europe between Rome, Paris, Copenhagen and Oxford: 'A good voice, and a trifling skill in music, were the only finances he had to support an undertaking so extensive; so he travelled by day, and at night sung at the doors of peasant houses, to get himself a lodging.'[35] In a curious way, Goldsmith's certainty that Holberg's knowledge of music was 'trifling' shows the extent to which he was identifying himself in imagination with the Baron, for his own knowledge of the theory of music (as revealed by the French sculptor, Roubiliac, who discovered by means of a trick that he could not read music)[36] was indeed 'trifling', whereas Holberg's—as shown by his ability to teach—must have been considerably less so.*

If he had relied on his music to provide him with board and lodging as Holberg had done half a century earlier, he would have discovered, like other mid-century travellers, that there were plenty of peasants who were themselves skilled exponents of the German flute. He must also have found that universities with expatriate Irish students were not situated within easy reach of one another and were not prepared to entertain penniless strangers for longer than a

---

*Goldsmith probably knew Holberg from his writings as well as from the obituaries, as one of Holberg's best known works, a philosophical fantasy called *A Journey to the World Underground* had been translated into English and published in 1742 by B. Collins of Salisbury, under whose imprint *The Vicar of Wakefield* was later to appear. It is easy to imagine the delight that the humour and gentle philosophy of this Danish *Gulliver's Travels* would have given Goldsmith. One side of his personality would even have approved of the inclusion of frugality amongst the virtues that Holberg looked for in an ideal society. (The others are justice, tolerance and gentleness.) He would also have enjoyed the science-fiction. Holberg's traveller falls into the centre of the terrestrial sphere, where he executes a gravity-free space-walk together with his packed lunch which has gone into orbit round him.

night or two. Goldsmith's surviving at least one winter in spite of
these drawbacks suggests that his travels, as Dr Glover had hinted,
bore a closer resemblance to George Primrose's than to his own
idealised account.

George finds himself in Holland, as Goldsmith had done, with no
clear plans for the immediate future. He falls in with an Irish student
who has come from Louvain with the information that 'there were
not two men in his whole university who understood Greek'.
George resolves to go there himself to offer his services as a Greek
tutor, and having decided to begin his enquiries at the top, is told
by the 'Principal', 'I never learned Greek, and I don't find that I
have ever missed it. I have had a doctor's cap and gown without
Greek; I have ten thousand florins a year without Greek; I eat
heartily without Greek, and in short, . . . as I don't know Greek, I
do not believe there is any good in it.' After a Holberg episode, with
flute, George finds himself in Paris where having hungrily walked the
streets for four or five days, he meets a cousin who is acting as a
buyer of antiquities for a London dilettante. In spite of a lack of
qualifications for the task, the cousin has secured a position for
himself in the Paris art world by adhering strictly to two rules: 'the
one always to observe, that the picture might have been better if the
painter had taken more pains; and the other to praise the works of
Pietro Perugino'.

George is introduced to the English community and to the sale
rooms and stays with his cousin long enough to see him 'after giving
his opinion that the colouring of a picture was not mellow enough,
very deliberately take a brush with brown varnish, that was accidentally lying by, and rub it over the piece with great composure
before all the company, and then ask if he had not improved the
tints.' In Paris, George secures the post of 'governor' to the heir to a
West Indian fortune who is undertaking the Grand Tour before
beginning his apprenticeship to an attorney, and has already
acquired an appropriate obsession: '. . . all his questions on the
road were how money might be saved, which was the least expensive
course of travel, whether any thing could be bought that would turn
to account when disposed of again in London. Such curiosities on
the way as could be seen for nothing he was ready enough to look at;
but if the sight of them was to be paid for, he usually asserted that
he had been told they were not worth seeing. He never paid a bill,

that he would not observe, how amazingly expensive travelling was, and all this though he was not yet twenty-one.' At Leghorn the young miser, discovering that he can get a passage back to England that will save him the expense of a journey overland, dismisses George—who eventually makes his own way to London via the 'foreign universities and convents' which Goldsmith had mentioned to Percy.[37]

Significantly, although George claims to have been engaged as a 'governor' or travelling tutor, he is expected to know more about travel arrangements than about local customs or the history of art—perhaps fortunately, as he would have known very little about such things. There is a resemblance between the function George fulfils and that of the servant Smollett was obliged to engage on his visit to Paris in 1763:

> Nothing gives me such chagrin, as the necessity I am under to hire a *valet de place*, as my own servant does not speak the language. You cannot conceive with what eagerness and dexterity those rascally valets exert themselves in pillaging strangers. There is always one ready in waiting on your arrival, who begins by assisting your own servant to unload your baggage, and interests himself in your affairs with such artful officiousness, that you will find it difficult to shake him off, even though you were determined beforehand against hiring any such domestic. He produces recommendations from his former masters, and the people of the house vouch for his honesty. The truth is, those fellows are very handy, useful, and obliging; and so far honest, that they will not steal in the usual way. You may safely trust one of them to bring you a hundred loui'dores from your banker; but they fleece you without mercy in every other article of expense. They lay all your tradesmen under contribution; your taylor, barber, mantua-maker, milliner, perfumer, shoemaker, mercer, jeweller, hatter, traiteur, and wine-merchant; even the bourgeois who owns your coach, pays him twenty sols per day. His wages amount to twice as much; so that I imagine the fellow that serves me makes above ten shillings a day, besides his victuals, which, by the bye, he has no right to demand.[38]

Overcharging, as Smollett continually demonstrates throughout his disgruntled book, is often a tax imposed on strangers who have

D*

failed to equip themselves with a knowledge of languages. The faculty that Smollett's factotum and Goldsmith/George had in common and which made them so 'very handy' was that they spoke both English and French.

Dr Glover had access to details which are missing from *The Vicar of Wakefield*. His information was that Goldsmith had been ac-acquainted with *two* English travellers—the first was accompanied from Louvain to Berne and Geneva; the second (the 'miser') from Geneva to Marseilles. Although Glover borrows without acknowledgment from the text of the novel at this point, he clearly departs from it geographically, and says that the young man had been left not 'a West Indian fortune' but 'a considerable sum of money by his uncle Mr S——, formerly an eminent pawnbroker near Holborn.'[39] There is one inconsistency in Glover's account. The itinerary is prefaced, unthinkingly, with the words 'He travelled on foot most of his tour'. Glover, like Percy, had been given an embroidered account of Goldsmith's journey (and he too dutifully records the German flute, the dancing peasants, the universities and the convents). But in the give and take of an evening in a tavern Goldsmith was the kind of man who came clean. A few apt questions from Glover or other acquaintances would have elicited details which (to Goldsmith's way of thinking) had humiliating associations, very much as he had broken down in his mother's cottage and confessed that the Fiddleback story was an invention. The result is that, while Percy's account simply contains the fantasy, Glover's contradicts itself by blending fantasy with the bitter truth that, several years after having waited on the gentlemen commoners of Trinity College, Goldsmith was now seeing Europe by courtesy of other young men of means who employed him, not in a comparatively honourable capacity as bear-leader (as Adam Smith had been employed by the Duke of Buccleuch) but as an amateur courier. It is significant that facts which Goldsmith clearly regarded as too humiliating for his biography should have been embedded in his creative fiction.

Since 1753 Goldsmith had had the intention of going to Paris, but, unless his first employer made a detour to take in the French capital on his way from Louvain to Berne, it was probably 1756 before he arrived there. If George Primrose's experiences are a fair indication, he did not enjoy his visit to this city of 'venal hospitality'.

In George's view, 'the people of Paris are much fonder of strangers that have money, than of those who have wit'.[40] Goldsmith was still the outsider, without either the wealth, fame or social position which could have gained him acceptance. A decade later those acquaintances of his who, having some or all of these attributes, made their visits to Paris after the conclusion of Anglo-French hostilities, all had different stories to tell. Garrick, at the height of his career, was received rapturously both by the company of the Théatre Française and by the literary world; Horace Walpole—though he complained of having to wait upon elderly princesses who only wanted him to send them puppies—clearly revelled in his encounters with French aristocrats; Tobias Smollett, travelling for health reasons in the company of his wife and two ladies not very long after his release from a six-month spell in the King's Bench prison, rented a comfortable flat in the Faubourg St. Germain, engaged servants and travelled in well-equipped berlines, finally getting a successful book out of his irate encounters with grooms, coachmen and landladies.

Goldsmith's failure to write a travel book is regrettable, for this brief episode in *The Vicar of Wakefield* suggests that, even as an outsider walking the inhospitable streets, he observed some aspects of the Parisian scene as acutely as any of those other travellers. A letter which he wrote to one of the fellows at Trinity requesting a reference after he had arrived in England was remembered, long after it had been lost in a fire, as having been full of self-deflating humour on the subject of these continental travels.[41]

By the time Goldsmith left Calais for Dover he was carrying with him a document that would be better preserved. This was the poetic fragment out of which *The Traveller* would be developed ten years later. In the opening lines in which the poet projects himself as an exile alienated from the life around him and drawn irresistibly back in imagination to the places where he is no stranger, Goldsmith's Irish experience is gathered together round the figure of the man who on at least one occasion had rescued him from the effects of fantasy and compulsion:

> Remote, unfriended, melancholy, slow
> Or by the lazy Scheld, or wandering Po;
> Or onward, where the rude Carinthian boor

Against the houseless stranger shuts the door;
Or where Campania's plain forsaken lies,
A weary waste expanding to the skies,
Where'er I roam, whatever realms to see,
My heart untravell'd fondly turns to thee;
Still to my brother turns, with ceaseless pain,
And drags at each remove a lengthening chain.

Eternal blessings crown my earliest friend,
And round his dwelling guardian saints attend;
Blest be that spot, where chearful guests retire
To pause from toil, and trim their evening fire;
Blest that abode, where want and pain repair,
And every stranger finds a ready chair;
Blest be those feasts with simple plenty crown'd,
Where all the ruddy family around
Laugh at the jests or pranks that never fail,
Or sigh with pity at some mournful tale,
Or press the baschful stranger to his food,
And learn the luxury of doing good.

But me, not destin'd such delights to share,
My prime of life in wand'ring spent and care:
Impell'd, with steps unceasing, to pursue
Some fleeting good, that mocks me with the view;
That, like the circle bounding earth and skies,
Allures from far, yet, as I follow, flies;
My fortune leads to traverse realms alone,
And finds no spot of all the world my own.[42]

Amongst the homesickness and the self-pity there is a brief analysis of the problem which, after twice setting him on the road to Cork, had now brought him half-way round Europe. But instead of retreating from unpleasant reality into yet more daydreams, in this one tangible souvenir of recent wanderings secreted away in his portmanteau he has taken the first step that will turn him into a writer and, at the heart of a poem which will develop the theme of rootlessness, he has placed as a symbol of stability the one person who can be sincerely forgiven for having witnessed the humiliations of his last three years in Ireland: his brother Henry.

Whether these lines reflect a slowly maturing conviction or only the mood of the moment, it was towards the end of his travels that Goldsmith reached a firm decision: he would return to Ireland, possibly with the intention which had been in his mind two years previously, of obtaining a medical degree at his old college. He now wrote to his family through Dan Hodson, asking for money to be sent so that he could obtain a passage home. The letter reached its destination and money may have been collected, but whatever *poste restante* arrangements Goldsmith made, the reply failed to reach him.[43] It was only when all hopes of a welcome at home seemed to have faded that he made his way to London shortly before the outbreak of war in Europe on Frederick the Great's invasion of Saxony on August 29th, 1756.[44]

FIVE

Empiric

FOR AT least three years after his arrival in London Goldsmith was to regard himself as a frustrated physician, though the proportions of genuine bad luck and self-delusion in this attitude are debatable. In spite of Percy's pious hope that he might have obtained a medical degree at Padua he was almost certainly unqualified, but this alone was not an impediment in the London of the mid-eighteenth century. Technically only those men who had obtained a licence from the College of Physicians could practise in the London area and for this they would have needed to provide evidence of a medical qualification; but London was in reality flooded with 'empirics', some of them outright quacks and others, like Johnson's pensioner Robert Levett, knowledgeable amateurs who might have a large practice amongst the poor. 'Professional' medicine was very expensive. Even moderately well-to-do people must have been deterred by the physician's fee of one guinea a visit plus travelling expenses of fourteen shillings a mile:[1] in consequence much of the general practice fell into the hands of the apothecaries who combined the modern functions of dispensing chemist and district nurse. Smollett's Peregrine Pickle has to assure an apothecary that he can 'bleed and give a clyster, spread plaster and prepare a potion' before he is engaged as an assistant. If he was unsure of his diagnosis the apothecary could visit certain coffee-houses and receive a consultation from a physician who, in most cases, would never see the patient himself.[2]

Although the College of Physicians had little hope of enforcing its licensing laws, it was not easy even for a skilled amateur to establish himself in London. Between the licensed physicians, the apothecaries and the formidable quacks who filled the columns of the daily newspapers with praise of their nostrums he would have had to struggle hard to keep a precarious toe-hold. The unwelcoming scene which Goldsmith was to encounter is suggested by an advertisement which appeared in the *Public Advertiser* shortly before he arrived in the capital:

TO THE UNHEALTHY

My chief Care is, and has long been engaged in annihilating a fatal Crew of your Enemies, I mean Empiricks, who are daily laying Paper Baits to entrap you. I have daily fresh Reason to entreat you to dread them as you would a Pest. The Mind always suffers with the Body, and here it is evident; otherwise it would be impossible for sound Reason to be deluded by them. Lose no more Time, but let me give you Comfort in your Afflictions, and cheer up your despairing Thoughts . . .

'Mr J. O., Hospital Surgeon' hardly meets the expectations he raises, for the purpose of his announcement is to inform the public that his medicines for venereal diseases, to which 'most of the unhealthy People in this Metropolis originally owe their ill State of Body' are available on Mondays, Wednesdays and Fridays at his chambers in Scotland Yard.[3]

As a stranger in London without a decent suit and almost certainly without the threepence a day which would have entitled him to take his place in the discreet interior of a coffee-house, Goldsmith had little chance of lasting even a week as a (self-styled) physician. An urgent need of money forced him to offer his services to the apothecaries as an assistant rather than consultant, and before securing employment at a shop in Fish Hill Street close by the Monument he received his fair share of the snubs to which his shabby appearance and his Irish brogue entitled him.[4] A former Edinburgh student, Fenn Sleigh, was in London and it was probably on his encounter with this old acquaintance, now a qualified physician, that Goldsmith took a step which was to lead to many subsequent complications: he let it be known that in the course of his stay on the Continent he had acquired a medical degree. Evidently assuming that it was only the lack of a little capital that prevented Goldsmith from pursuing his calling, Sleigh lent him money. For a while, a new physician was to be observed on Bankside, the unfashionable area at the southern end of London Bridge.[5] He looked magnificent in a suit purchased from one of the second-hand dealers in Monmouth Street: the only drawback was the need to keep his tricorne firmly pinned against his chest, as the previous owner before parting with it had removed the star of one of the royal Orders revealing the unfaded cloth beneath.[6]

It was in a different suit, this time of 'rusty black' that Goldsmith was encountered by another Edinburgh acquaintance, William Farr. Whatever demands were made on his time in Bankside he had also found work as a proof-reader at Samuel Richardson's printing-house at Salisbury Court, Fleet Street.[7] While an exile's hunger for status might be read into his desire to act the physician it was perhaps his sense of humour as much as a need to convince Farr that he was doing well for himself that compelled him to display the pages of manuscript that now overflowed his pockets as his own first tragedy. After Goldsmith had consulted him about certain lines, obligingly dashing down whatever alterations his friend suggested, Farr went away deeply impressed to hear that Richardson himself had already given his views on the text, and clearly convinced that he had witnessed the birth of a new writer.[8] Even if his alternative career was proof-reading rather than writing Goldsmith was probably wise to diversify. The only impression of him as a physician to survive, in a story told about him by Reynolds, shows that however effectively he turned his experience of the medical faculties of Edinburgh and Leyden to conversational use, as a practitioner he failed to inspire confidence. In Reynolds' story the horrified apothecary to whom Goldsmith sent instructions simply refused to make up the prescription.[9]

Deliverance from make-believe, whether of a medical or literary nature, was to come from yet another Edinburgh student whose father, the Reverend Thomas Milner, a dissenting clergyman, ran an Academy for Boys. Dr Milner's health was failing and he was in immediate need of an assistant. Goldsmith accepted the post on the understanding that he was not committing himself to more than a temporary appointment and by the end of the year he was working as a schoolmaster in Peckham.[10]

At the close of the century, Hester Milner, who as a child witnessed some of the lighter moments of Goldsmith's stay with her family, wrote a brief, attractive account of it. She was one of those children—like the younger George Colman, Lord Clare's daughter, and the little girl who had once been his neighbour near the Old

Bailey, for whom Goldsmith's eruption on to the scene had been sheer delight: he made memorable things happen.

'There was a servant in the family', she remembered, 'who waited at table, cleaned shoes, etc. whose name was William; a weak but good-tempered young man. Goldsmith would now and then make himself merry at his expense, and poor William generally enjoyed the joke without any diminution of his own self-satisfaction.'

'William used to think, that in his way he was not to be outdone, and Goldsmith thought, one day, that he would make trial of him. Accordingly, having procured a piece of uncoloured Cheshire cheese, he rolled it up in the form of a candle, about an inch in length, and twisting a bit of white paper to the size of a wick, he thrust it into one of the ends, having blackened the extremity that it might have more the appearance of reality. He then put it in a candlestick over the fireplace in the kitchen, taking care that a bit of real candle, of equal size, should be placed by the side of it in another candlestick. The apparatus being thus prepared, in came William from his daily task; when Goldsmith immediately taking down the bit of candle of his own manufacture, challenged William in the following terms: "William, if you will eat yonder piece of candle" (pointing to what remained on the shelf), "I will eat *this* in my hand—but it must be done together, and I will begin!"—The challenge was accepted in the presence of the other servants in the kitchen, and Goldsmith immediately began gnawing his candle, making sad wry faces, but not flinching from his task. William beheld with astonishment the progress he was making in devouring it, however nauseous, but having no heart or stomach to touch his own. At last, when William saw that Goldsmith had devoured all but the last morsel, he, not willing to be outdone, opened his mouth, and flung his own piece down his throat in a moment. This sudden triumph over his antagonist made the kitchen ring with laughter. Some little time after, poor William could not help expressing his surprise to Goldsmith that he had not done as he did, swallowing so disagreeable a morsel all at once.—"Truly," replied Goldsmith, with great gravity, "my bit of candle was no other than a bit of very nice Cheshire cheese, and therefore William, I was unwilling to lose the relish of it!"'[11]

Goldsmith was still playing his flute, telling entertaining stories and getting through his money as quickly as he earned it. Sometimes it went to beggars and sometimes to buy sweets and apples for his pupils. When applying to Mrs Milner for an advance he submitted with good grace when she pointed out that he was as much in need of having his finances supervised as the boys.

Even when allowances are made for the effects of distance and nostalgia on Miss Milner's imagination, the Peckham experience seems to have been a cheerful one; and yet at least one of his contemporaries believed that it was something he afterwards preferred to forget.[12] In *The Vicar of Wakefield*, George Primrose considers a teaching career and is strongly advised against it by his cousin:

> But are you sure you are fit for a school? Let me examine you a little. Have you been bred apprentice to the business? No. Then you won't do for a school. Have you had the small-pox? No. Then you won't do for a school. Can you lie three in a bed? No. Then you will never do for a school. Have you got a good stomach? Yes. Then you will by no means do for a school. No, Sir, if you are for a genteel easy profession, bind yourself seven years as an apprentice to turn a cutler's wheel; but avoid a school by any means.[13]

However civilised the Academy by the standards of the times, Goldsmith was bound to be unhappy as a master. A captive audience of children automatically sits in judgment upon the presumptuous adult who has elected to impose his authority on them. Goldsmith had a need to be liked—he demonstrated it with the presents Miss Milner remembered—and at moments when his pupils ceased to be approachable individuals and became a censorious tribunal such a trait would not necessarily have told in his favour. There is a hint of such occasions even in Miss Milner's rose-tinted account:

> When amusing his younger companions during play hours with the flute, and expatiating on the pleasures derived from music, in addition to its advantages in society as a gentleman-like acquirement, a pert boy. looking at his situation and personal disadvantages with something of contempt, rudely replied to the effect that *he* surely could not consider himself a gentleman; an

offence which, though followed by instant chastisement, disconcerted and pained him extremely.

The memory of such slights was probably still alive when, at the height of his fame he met one of his former pupils in the City. This young man was accompanied by his new wife; and there seems to have been a mixture of quixotic humour and an unconscious desire to humiliate in Goldsmith's offer to buy him some apples—almost in the same breath as announcing that his engraved portrait was on sale in the print shops.[14]

The pert boy at Peckam had gone straight to the heart of Goldsmith's anxiety; at the age of twenty-eight, having failed to arm himself with a medical degree, he had nothing to show for his four years as an expatriate; his letter to his family had apparently been left unanswered; and he was now adrift in a city which was already full of Irish exiles, some of them, like Fenn Sleigh on the brink of distinguished careers, others who would eke out some kind of shabby-genteel existence with a mixture of charm and plausibility and, further down the social scale, those men whose physical strength gave them a near-monopoly of coal-heaving and the carrying of sedan-chairs.[15] An additional problem for Goldsmith was probably that as a member of the impoverished and threatened Irish middle class he was confronted in England by an equivalent group which showed every sign of enjoying the luxuries as well as the comforts of living. Without contaminating the roots of Goldsmith's personality the problem of acquiring status—rather late in life and in a strange city—would be responsible for many future mistakes. The first person to offer a solution to the problem was the publisher Ralph Griffiths, a Welshman of thirty seven who had come to London in his early twenties to work in a bookshop in Ludgate Street and who had by now achieved a prominent position in the literary world.

If Goldsmith's sense of humour was too well developed to allow his personality to be seriously affected by his search for security, ambition had given Ralph Griffiths some unattractive traits. His employer in the early 'forties, Jacob Robinson, had been a pioneer in the field of the literary review, his *History of the Works of the Learned*, which had run for six years and come to an end in 1743, having undertaken to provide commentaries on the publications of the day. Griffiths, the ex-watchmakers' apprentice from Shropshire, had been acute enough to see the importance of Robinson's review and in his early twenties his ambitions had coalesced round the possibility of a similar project, under his own editorship and on a much bigger scale, which would reflect his democratic and presbyterian views. The result was the *Monthly Review* which was launched in 1749. It established certain rules of conduct, including strict anonymity, and employed a small team of leading journalists, usually experts in particular disciplines such as theology, medicine, mathematics, physics and languages, together with a wide range of specialist consultants who made occasional contributions; and it was respected, if not feared, by the London publishers.

But Griffiths' success had only been purchased by a considerable outlay in belligerence, sharping and occasional brushes with the authorities. In the aftermath of Bonny Prince Charlie's invasion of England he had capitalised on the interest in the Jacobite cause following the panic that had gripped London in the summer of '45 by writing and publishing pamphlets whose topicality would ensure a ready sale. His first venture, after nine of the rebel lords had been beheaded on Tower Hill in July '46, was his *Letters and Papers Delivered by the Rebles at their Execution*; early in the following year appeared a poorly written tract, *Accanius, or the Young Adventurer, a true History Translated from a Manuscript Privately Handed About at Versailles* which presented Prince Charles Edward as the perfect romantic hero. These activities had come to the attention of the Duke of Newcastle but Griffiths had countered official displeasure with a mixture of candour and massive impertinence. The *Letters and Papers* could do no possible harm, he declared, because he had written them himself; *Ascanius* was simply a piece of devil's advocacy intended to be demolished in a sequel. It had presumably been a profitable undertaking, having gone through three impressions before the Duke's men intervened. Admittedly Griffiths had lost over the seizure of the *Letters and Papers*, for he wrote to the Duke demanding compensation, pointing out that he had a wife and family in Hoxton to support and that like many business people he had had a bad year in '45.[16]

But Griffiths' great opportunity had come at the end of 1748, A manuscript written by an impoverished gentleman who had left the service of the East India Company under a cloud found its way to his shop: it was called *The Memoirs of a Woman of Pleasure* (better known in Soho and paperback days as *Fanny Hill*). Griffiths may or may not have been one of the first to recognise its literary qualities: he certainly appreciated its commercial value—though this was not reflected in the £20 for which he persuaded John Cleland to surrender his rights in the work. Even by the standards of London's underground pornography trade it was a potent book and Griffiths took the precaution of issuing it under a false imprint.[17] Once again there was a brush with the Duke of Newcastle (whose messengers were met by the publisher himself, armed with a large hammer, when they came to search the warehouse in St Paul's Churchyard); but the outcome was entirely satisfactory for both writer and publisher. Cleland was summoned before the Privy Council for an official rebuke, but this was soon followed by a sweetener in the shape of a pension of £100 a year (possibly reflecting the coincidence that Lord Granville, the president of the council was, like Cleland, a former pupil of Westminster School). Griffiths continued to distribute the book both in its original and (under his own imprint) its expurgated forms and was believed to have pocketed a fortune of £10,000.[18] The début of *Fanny Hill* was followed within a year by the launching of the *Monthly Review*.

*

Ralph Griffiths was an unusual guest to encounter at the table of a dissenting clergyman in Peckham, but here Goldsmith met the publisher, and immediately attracted his attention. Griffiths' formal education had certainly not gone as far as that of the men he employed, but he had a flair for selecting people who would be useful to him. (A few years previously he had tried to secure the services of Philip Skelton when he visited London on the publication of *Deism Revealed*.)[19] Goldsmith could no doubt give a good account of himself in conversation, whether drawing on his old love of classical literature, throwing in whatever spices he had culled in the lecture rooms of Edinburgh and Leyden, and all too probably claiming a greater acquaintance than he actually possessed with the literatures of the countries in which he had recently travelled. Griffiths was impressed and Goldsmith was invited to fill a vacancy on the *Monthly*.

It was possibly the biggest step forward of his entire career. The salary was not lavish but £100 a year could have kept him in moderate comfort even if he rejected the board and lodging at the Griffiths' shop which was part of the contract.[20] As a schoolmaster he had probably received £20 a year, and the residential post at Peckham must have tied him down to a far greater extent than life with Mr and Mrs Griffiths, who required him to be at his desk from nine till two. When he installed himself under their roof in April and got to know his fellow reviewers his desire for status must also have been satisfied, at least for the moment, by the knowledge that he was working as part of a team of highly qualified specialists. It included Dr James Kirkpatrick (the senior member who did reviews of both medical books and general literature, especially the classics); the Revd. Dr William Rose, Griffiths' brother-in-law and co-founder of the Review, much esteemed by Johnson in spite of his presbyterianism; Dr James Grainger the poet; Dr Benjamin Dawson, another presbyterian divine who shared theology with Rose; and the American dramatist and political writer, James Ralph.[21] A less distinguished contributor, whom Goldsmith probably encountered since he shared the writing of the Monthly Catalogue with him in May, was Colley Cibber's boorish son, Theophilus: the newcomer seems to have been fascinated by the unrelieved disreputability of this man who was estranged from a beautiful and talented wife, the singer and actress Susannah Arne. The Monthly Catalogue, an appendix consisting of brief notes on the books which Griffiths considered too ephemeral for longer notice, was probably a chore imposed on unsuspecting newcomers. In May Goldsmith undertook the bulk of it; but a tacit recognition of his talent might be read into the much smaller proportion of Monthly Catalogue reviewing in his last four months as a full-time employee of the Review.

Goldsmith's first task on the Monthly was to lift a fifteen hundred word notice of a book by Paul Henri Mallet on Celtic Mythology from the previous autumn's number of the *Bibliothèque des Sciences at des Beaux Arts*.[22] No journalist of the age would have considered either Goldsmith or Griffiths to be unduly reprehensible in this instance, and Goldsmith learned a lesson which helped him to meet many a tight schedule in his later career as a columnist and popular historian. The opportunity to prove himself as critic came the following month with the publication of the theatrical success of the year, John Home's tragedy, *Douglas*. In spite of its reception at Covent Garden and David Hume's enthusiasm for 'the Scottish Shakespeare', Goldsmith found its situations unlifelike, its structure undramatic and its language lacking in poetic fire. Subsequent critics have agreed with him, though they may not always have expressed their views so elegantly. His quick dismissal of one of the academic talking-points of the age, the 'dramatic unities' of action, time and place, illustrates the remarkable confidence with which the unsuccessful doctor-cum-schoolmaster had taken his place in the Griffiths establishment:

> Theatrical lawgivers rather teach the ignorant where to censure, than the Poet how to write. If sublimity, sentiment, and passion, give warmth, and life, and expression to the whole, we can the more easily dispense with the rules of the Stagyrite; but if languor, affectation, and the false sublime, are substituted for these, an observance of all the precepts of the antients, will prove but a poor compensation.[23]

This authority was sustained, with a difference, in his brief notices of some of the more pretentious and catch-penny books that came his way in the following months. In his brief review of *The Fair Citizen; or the real Adventures of Miss Charlotte Bellmour. Written by herself*, he anticipates the methods of Dorothy Parker:

> As Miss Bellmour is now happily married, to the very agreeable Mr Frankly, we would not interrupt her present felicity, by any strictures upon her Authorship. But we must beg leave to offer her one hint, at parting, which she may profit from, if she does not too much mistake her talents; viz. that one good Pudding is worth fifty modern Romances.[24]

And, however much he approved of Jonas Hanway's vigorous efforts to improve the working conditions of children placed out in apprenticeships under the Poor Law regulations he was unable to suppress his sense of humour when he came to review the travel book which he produced this year:

> . . . he seems to reserve his powers till he comes to treat of TEA, against which he inveighs, through almost the whole of the second volume; assuming the Physician, Philosopher, and

Politician. To this plant he ascribes the scurvy, weakness of nerves, low spirits, lassitudes, melancholy, 'and twenty different disorders, which, in spite of the faculty, have yet no names, except the general one of nervous complaints.' Nay, (as the Author exclaims) our very nurses drink Tea! and, what is more deplorable still, they drink *run** Tea, that costs not above three or four shillings a pound! The Ladies spoil their teeth, and complexions, and the men have lost their stature and comeliness, by the use of this pernicious drug; our time is consumed in drinking it; our morals injured by the luxuries it induces; our fortunes impaired in procuring it; and the balance of trade turned against us by its importation. To remedy these evils, the Author, tho' he allows us to continue the use of our porcelane cups, and our sipping, would substitute in the place of tea, several very harmless herbs of our own growth, such as ground-ivy, penny-royal, hore-hound, trefoil, sorrel, not forgetting cowslip flowers, whose wine, he tells us, is a powerful soporific; and, truly, if this be the case, the infusion might have some good effects at many a tea-table.[25]

Although on the *Monthly* he picked up the bad habit of copious quotation, Goldsmith took his reviewing sufficiently seriously to reveal his own personality and opinions in what he wrote. A pamphlet criticising the inhuman and nonsensical treatment of debtors evokes a brisk paragraph in which the main points of the argument are forcefully summarised;[26] an American *History of New York* stimulates him to underline the chicanery, opportunism and hypocrisy that had taken root in the no longer virgin lands of colonial America;[27] and a book about the condition of Ireland gives him an opportunity to pillory 'a government which endeavours to enrich one part of its dominions by impoverishing another, and of chusing to have but one flourishing kingdom when it might be possessed of two.'[28]

The two important works that came his way during his time on the 'Monthly' were Burke's *Essay on the Sublime and the Beautiful* and the later *Odes* of Gray. Burke's essay was published anonymously by Robert Dodsley, and Goldsmith may not have realised that he was reviewing the work of one of his contemporaries at

*smuggled

Trinity College. Although he rejects some parts of Burke's thesis he gives it the sincerest form of flattery when he paraphrases it in one of his longest reviews.[29] Like Johnson, he was too deeply ensconced in the classical Augustan tradition to assimilate the poetic departures of Thomas Gray's later work. He did not like *The Bard*. In a closely reasoned article he suggests that the Pindaric ode is an unsuitable vehicle for English poetry, but, having said that, he concedes that as a master of the form, Gray has to be considered in the same class as Dryden.[30]

*

Within less than a year of his arrival in London Goldsmith had apparently found his métier and was speaking with authority from his place on the *Monthly Review*. That he should have surrendered it after a mere six months is not the least of the problems that are encountered in an attempt to trace his movements and understand his motives during these first three years in London.

Goldsmith's own version of what happened was that he grew tired of the 'thraldom' of working for Mr and Mrs Griffiths and resented their interference with his copy;[31] but the latter objection is suspect, coming from a man who at more than one stage of his later career showed that he had little concern for the fate of his writing once he had been paid for it. John Forster assumed that the Griffiths' ménage was a sweat-shop, thus overlooking Goldsmith's fairly distinguished colleagues besides the fact that it would be several years before he again had such secure employment. Goldsmith had not only found something he could do well: he had good working hours and a secure income on which with a little care he could have managed quite comfortably. Prices were stable in the middle of the century, and economic conditions in London in 1757 were not too dissimilar from those of 1737 when Johnson had arrived from Lichfield and, taking stock, decided that with some care and contrivance it was possible to keep up middle class appearances on £30 a year. (One lived in a garret for eighteen pence a week; made ample use of a coffee-house; and paid one's visits, once a week, on 'clean-shirt day'.[32]

There is a parallel between Goldsmith and Johnson himself at this stage in their respective careers. Both had arrived in London at the age of twenty-eight as unknown provincials who had achieved little other than a false start in life. Both had found employment in the world of literary journalism with energetic though not over-scrupulous businessmen far beneath them in talent and educational acquirements. In his first year on the *Gentleman's Magazine* Johnson made an effort to free himself from what must have begun to seem uncongenial work and return to schoolmastering in Shrop-shire: Pope made an attempt to help him over the matter of an academic qualification and luckily failed. Goldsmith, like Johnson, may have found the gap between the independence of scholarship and the need to sell his services to a man like Griffiths difficult to bridge: he resented being at the beck and call of such employers, particularly, one imagines, of Mrs Griffiths, in some accounts a shrewish woman, who took an active part in the running of the Review. When he displayed bundles of manuscript to William Farr and announced the completion of a tragedy, he may have been remembering that the young Samuel Johnson had arrived in London with the manuscript of a tragedy in his baggage.

Significantly, it is at this period of Goldsmith's life that several money-making or career-advancing projects are encountered, one of them wildly implausible and only one other coming to fruition. He had been told that a fund existed to send someone to Palestine to look at the lettering painted on a rock in the region of Mount Sinai which an Irish bishop, Dr Richard Pococke, had discovered on his travels. It did not occur to Goldsmith that before the grant was surrendered he might be expected to display a knowledge of either Arabic or Hebrew. The possibility of travel even further afield was raised by the factories of the East India Company where there were resident physicians. Percy was told that, at some stage in his dealings with Goldsmith, Dr Milner promised to use his influence with one of the East India directors, Robert Jones (who was elected in April, '57) to secure him such an appointment.[33]

As Katharine Balderston pointed out, Goldsmith was looking towards India at an unfortunate moment. In the early stages of the war Britain was suffering military reverses and although the public was kept in ignorance of the facts for almost a year, the French were in control of the Madras area—the Coast of Coromandel to which Goldsmith considered himself destined—from March '58 until February '59.[34] But the inability of the Company to ship a would-be physician out to Madras at this period does not in itself solve the riddle. There remains a puzzling gap between Goldsmith's obvious euphoria, as encountered in a batch of letters to Ireland in August '58 when he considers himself on the verge of departure for Coromandel (only wanting the money to buy his equipment) and a complete silence in the East India Company files on the subjects of both the medical appointment (for which evidence of a qualification might reasonably have been required) and of the Bond (a deposited sum of money) into which all travellers to India entered before they could embark. It is reasonably certain, however, that Goldsmith had already parted with £10 in the belief that this was an entrance fee to a lucrative Coromandel post as 'Physician and Surgeon' with good prospects for some private trading on the side.[35]

The recipient of that £10 is unlikely to have been either Dr Milner or Robert Jones Esq., who as a director of the Company was a mighty figure in the City of London. The man who pocketed Goldsmith's money in return for an empty promise has much more in common with 'Lofty' in his first play than with such eminently respectable folk. Lofty's air of preoccupation is enough to convince his victims that he is a man of influence, as demonstrated on his first entrance, when he simultaneously greets his hostess and pretends to issue directions to a servant off-stage:

LOFTY: And if the Venetian ambassador, or that teazing creature the Marquis, should call, I'm not at home. Dam'me, I'll be packhorse to none of them. My dear Madam, I have just snatched a moment—And if the expresses to his grace be ready, let them be sent off; they're of importance. Madam, I ask a thousand pardons.

MRS CROAKER: Sir, this honour ——

LOFTY: And Dubardieu! If the person calls about the commission, let him know that it is made out. As for Lord Cumbercourt's stale request, it can keep cold: you understand me. Madam, I ask ten thousand pardons.

MRS CROAKER: Sir, this honour ——

LOFTY: And, Dubardieu! If the man comes from the Cornish borough, you must do him: you must do him, I say. Madam I, ask ten thousand pardons. And if the Russian ambassador calls: but he will scarce call today, I believe. And now, Madam, I have just got time to express my happiness in having the honour of being permitted to profess myself your most obedient humble servant.

MRS CROAKER: Sir, the happiness and honour are all mine; and yet, I'm only robbing the public while I detain you.

LOFTY: Sink the public, Madam, when the fair are to be attended. Ah, could all my hours be so charmingly devouted! Sincerely, don't you pity us poor creatures in affairs? Thus it is; eternally solicited for places here, teized for pensions there, and courted every where. I know you pity me. Yes, I see you do . . .[36]

Amongst Lofty's ornamental flourishes is to be found the word *jaghire* which indicates that he is laying claim to influence with the East India Company as well as with government ministers.

However much Goldsmith was indebted to the French dramatist de Brueys for this character,[37] it is interesting to note that Lofty made his English début eight years before the production of *The Good-Natured Man* as 'Sir Imp Brazen, Knight' in an anonymous squib attacking Griffiths and his employees on the *Monthly Review*.[38] Besides dropping names as shamelessly as Lofty, Sir Imp indulges in pseudo-reminiscences about the political world of an earlier generation:

Damn it, what rare Work! what fine Sport I had in Sir R——t's Time! By —— I used to have at a Time attending on my Levée no less than two or three Dozen of fat, jolly Parsons, suing either for Sinecures or Bishopricks . . .

If the satirist was right in suggesting that the *Monthly Review* team contained such a 'smoke-seller' (and from his portraits of 'Rehoboam Gruffy', 'Mynheer Tanaquil Limmonad' and 'Martin Problem' it is possible to identify Griffiths himself and such reviewers of the early sixties as John Berkenhout and William Kenrick) he and Goldsmith might well have been drawn towards one another as manipulator and willing victim.[39]

*

The Coromandel episode is perhaps the most dramatic instance of Goldsmith's apparent need to demonstrate in what he did the very reverse of what he sincerely preached. The writer who warned his readers of the disastrous effects of 'luxury' would one day run up bills he could not pay, fit out a handsome apartment and buy silk underwear; the convinced anti-colonialist dreamed of becoming a nabob; on his death-bed, the 'man of science' would accept his apothecary's excellent arguments against the use of a patent medicine and then blindly but hopefully swallow yet another of the doses that helped to kill him. His alternating appearance in gaudily rich suits of green and gold, sky-blue or peach, and in unrelieved black, seem to have been an unconscious attempt to advertise the central weakness of his strange personality.

As his attitude to his brother and later to Dr Johnson and the publisher John Newbery proved, Goldsmith had the temperament of the hero-worshipper: whatever his own shortcomings, he needed to find outstanding qualities in his employers and superiors. It was intolerable for him to be in a subordinate position where there were no reasons for deference other than economic advantage, and in his departure from the Griffiths' household there is a faint echo of the Hamilton affair. His regular contributions ended in August. But however much he disliked the unscrupulous commercialism which had given Griffiths a bad reputation or to whatever extent the streak of Irish puritanism in him caused him to resent the dubious beginnings of the publishing house, the break with his employer was not yet complete. He had been commissioned to produce two translations—of Jean Marteilhe's account of his years as a prisoner in the galleys of Louis XIV (for which he was paid £20) and a life of Voltaire. In 1761 he also produced for Griffiths a work which has since been lost: the *Memoirs of My Lady B*. This was probably a re-hash of a French book of the same title published in 1760, and is unlikely to have been pornographic in spite of its name and stable— Griffiths was probably trying to repeat the success he had had with the *Memoirs of Letitia Pilkington*, a book which resolutely maintains the chaste fiction that courtesans were prized exclusively for their wit.

But in spite of the possibility of occasional free-lance work for Griffiths, he had sacrificed a secure position when he had nothing to put in its place other than his doubtful prospects as an unknown empiric and a fantasy about making a fortune in India. These were his circumstances when in the late autumn or early winter of 1757 his brother Charles, now a young man of twenty, found his way— all too probably unannounced—to Goldsmith's lodgings. Charles was able to reassure his brother that, even if no money had been received the previous year, the family had gone to some trouble to collect it.[41] But if he had imagined that Oliver would by now be in a position to give him a start in life he was quickly disillusioned. Goldsmith's uncertain prospects are reflected in Charles's decision to return to Ireland.[42]

At Peckham, Milner was now too ill to manage his school and Goldsmith may have returned there for a few months in 1758.[43] With or without the encouragement of a 'Sir Imp Brazen', through- out 1758 Goldsmith was still buoyant with Coromandel hopes, as unaware as the rest of the English public that Madras was now in the hands of the French. He had been informed that he must be ready to equip himself for his journey. 'I must pay 50 Lb for my passage ten pound for Sea stores, and the other incidental expenses of my equipment will amount to 60 or 70 Lb more,' he tells Dan Hodson in August.[44] To raise this money he was writing a book, and it is an indication of the confidence that his work for the *Monthly Review* had given him that it was to be nothing less than a survey of European learning and literature from classical times up to his own day. He had also had the idea of writing a series of essays in letter form on the model of Montesquieu's *Lettres Persanes* or the *Lettres Chinoises* which the Marquis d'Argens had published in 1739.[45] Confident that he would find a London publisher for his *Enquiry into the Present State of Polite Learning in Europe*, and knowing that if successful it would be pirated in Dublin, he wrote to a Dublin bookseller, Bradley, with a view to launching a separate Irish edition with the help of his friends, who would be asked to circulate subscription proposals.[46] It was then necessary to write to these friends—Dan Hodson, Edward Mills, Bob Bryanton and Dr Radcliffe of Trinity, together with his brother Henry—and inform them of the plans he had made on their behalf. At the prompting of his sister Catherine who must have sensed the coolness emanating from Kilmore House, he also wrote to his cousin, Jane Lawder. He knew by this time that it would be futile to write to her father who had become a victim of amnaesia and was not expected to live much longer.

Writing to people like Bryanton and his cousin Edward Mills when he had a favour to ask after years of silence was embarrassing, and he obviously squirmed as he sat at his table. Humour came to his rescue, rather too successfully in the letter to Bryanton. He begged his old friend not to miss the opportunity of helping the new Doctissimus Doctissimorum to enter the hall of fame. 'Think how Goldsmithius, or Gubblegurchius, or some such sound, as rough as a nutmeg-grater, will become me,' he tells him, and supplies his own biographical note: "Oliver Goldsmith flourished in the eighteenth and nineteenth centuries. He lived to be an hundred and three years old, [and in that] age may justly be styled the sun of [literature] and the Confucius of Europe".' But having prepared the ground, he is unable to bring his letter to its essential and proper conclusion and breaks off without mentioning the subscription at all: '... where the devil *is I*? Oh, Gods! Gods! here in a garret writing for bread, and expecting to be dunned for a milk score! However, dear Bob, whether in penury or affluence, serious or gay, I am ever wholly thine.'[47] The garret did not even have the advantage of a respectable address, and the surviving letters of 1758, with the exception of the one to the Hodsons, from which the address is missing, are written as from the Temple Exchange coffee-house at Temple Bar. In the outcome, both Mills and Jane Lawder ignored Goldsmith's appeal; and as no Irish edition appeared the other friends could have had little success in persuading fox-hunting gentlemen and supporters of the Padareen mare to back this particular outsider.

When writing to his brother-in-law about the post of physician and surgeon that awaited him in India he was probably deluding himself as much as trying to impress his family, but by the end of the year there had still been no return on his investment of £10, and his failure to get any firm promise from the acquaintance who rightly or wrongly claimed to have influence with the Company had produced a change of plan. Although still concealing the real state of affairs at Madras, the Directors were discreetly equipping warships. Goldsmith got wind of this and evidently decided that here was an opportunity to work his passage to India as a surgeon's mate. Before he could do so he had to get a licence and on December 21st he presented himself at the College of Surgeons for examination. No memory of the occasion has survived. Goldsmith preserved a total silence, and only the entrance under that date in the Company of Surgeons' Examinations book tells the story.[48]

Goldsmith was not applying for a Grand Diploma, for which he would have had to give proof of either a seven-year apprenticeship in surgery, or a period of regular attendance at university lectures together with a year's hospital experience. He was asking for a much humbler qualification which would entitle him to a place as medical assistant on a warship, ranking as first-, third-, or even fifth-rate according to the number of guns it carried: to be found incompetent to act even as surgeon's assistant on a fifth-rate warship (a post which would have called for little more than a knowledge of first-aid) must have brought the Coromandel dream crashing down in ruins.[49]

The warships sailed without Goldsmith and the euphoria of August dissolved into wintry depression. November 28th had been his thirtieth birthday—always a sobering moment—and had no doubt prompted him to take a gloomy retrospective view of himself and his circumstances. Henry, writing for advice as to how he should plan his eldest boy's future, touched off not only memories of the darker, more humiliating aspects of his life as a Trinity sizar but a self-pity (clearly intended to be visible behind the clown's mask) inspired by more recent disappointments. A positively zestful encouragement of his mood might be detected in his thinking of himself not simply as 'turned thirty' but as having entered his thirty-*first* year. (He then, either forgetfully or intentionally, adds a year to his actual age.) But the setback at Surgeon's Hall three weeks earlier is too fresh and painful to be described in a letter, though we feel its presence behind the naive desire to give a lying assurance that, in this direction, all is well:

> ... I have met with no disappointment with respect to my East India Voyage nor are my resolutions altered, tho' at the same time I must confess it gives me some pain to think I am almost beginning the world at the age of thirty one. Tho' I never had a day's sickness since I saw you yet I am not the strong active man you once knew me. You scarce can conceive how much eight years of disappointment anguish and study have worn me down. If I remember right you are seven or eight years older than me, and yet I dare venture to say that if a stranger saw us both he would pay me the honours of seniority. Imagine to yourself a pale

melancholy visage with two great wrinkles between the eye brows, with an eye disgustingly severe and a big wig, and you may have a perfect picture of my present appearance. On the other hand I conceive you as grown fat sleek and healthy, passing many an happy day among your own children or those who knew you a child. Since I knew what it was to be a man this is a pleasure I have not known. I have passed my days among a number of cool designing beings and have contracted all their suspicious manner, in my own behaviour. I should actually be as unfit for the society of my friends at home as I detest that which I am obliged to partake of here. I can now neither partake of the pleasure of a revel nor contribute to raise its jollity. I can neither laugh nor drink, have contracted an hesitating disagreeable manner of speaking, and a visage that looks illnature itself, in short I have thought myself into settled melancholly and an utter disgust of all that life brings with it. Whence this romantic turn that all our family are possessed with, whence this love for every place and every country but that in which we reside? For every occupation but our own, this desire of fortune and yet this eagerness to dissipate!

Even the answer to Henry's original enquiry is presented in negative terms:

Above all things let him never touch a romance, or novel, those paint beauty in colours more charming than nature, and describe happiness that man never tastes. How delusive, how destructive therefore are those pictures of consummate bliss, they teach the youthful mind to sigh after beauty and happiness which never existed, to despise the little good which fortune has mixed in our cup, by expecting more than she ever gave. And in general take the word of a man who has seen the world and studied human nature more by experience than precept, take my word for it I say that books teach us very little of the world. The greatest merit, and the most consummate virtue that ever grac'd humanity in a state of poverty would only serve to make the possessor ridiculous, they may distress but cannot relieve him. Avarice in the lower orders of mankind is true ambition, avarice is the only ladder the poor can use to preferment. Preach, then my dear Sir, to your son, not the excellence of human nature, nor the disrespect of

E

riches, but endeavour to teach him thrift and oeconomy. Let his poor wandering uncles example be placd in his eyes.[50]

However much alarm and despondency this letter gave rise to at Ballymore, where Henry was now living, it must have given some comfort to the writer. But before the end of the month Goldsmith was in trouble from which no easy rhetoric could rescue him.

Griffiths had probably exercised restraint when Goldsmith left his employment. For a man who had spent his youth exploring the mechanism of clocks rather than the syntax of Virgil and Cicero, Goldsmith represented scholarship and, even if the finer points of his English style had passed Griffiths by, he would have been reluctant to see the dilettante of Latin and Greek and the Natural Sciences disappearing altogether from the pages of the *Monthly Review*. He preferred to believe that at no expense to himself he was merely extending the leash. Some time in 1758 he sent Goldsmith four books, an anthropological and a linguistic study, both Oxford publications, and two new editions of classical texts. Probably at the same time he agreed to act as guarantor when Goldsmith ran up a bill at the tailor's, still no doubt in a state of August optimism. Goldsmith's four long reviews appeared in the *Monthly* for December, '58.[51]

Griffiths' publishing career had entered a difficult phase which would eventually result in, first, bankruptcy and then a remarkable recovery in which he regained control of the beloved Review, which he had by that time been forced to sell. The root of his problem was the appearance of the rival *Critical Review* a few months before Goldsmith's arrival in London. A seventeen-year-old monopoly was shattered and the *Critical* with its Tory political bias quickly gained a strong reputation. (When asked by George III for his opinion of their respective merits, Johnson had said that the *Monthly* could be relied on for thoroughness but that the *Critical* was the more brilliant.)[59]

It was perhaps unfortunate for Griffiths that, two months before Goldsmith joined the *Monthly*, Samuel Foote should have chosen to remind Drury Lane audiences, in a two-act farce called *The Author*, of the disreputable origins of his publishing house. Although, unlike Foote's 'Vamp', he had not lost his ears in the pillory, he could be identified by allusions to episodes which, as the publisher and editor of the *Monthly Review*, he would no doubt have preferred to be forgotten:

VAMP: . . . I don't deal in the sermon way, now; I lost money by the last I printed, for all 'twas wrote by a Methodist; but I believe, Sir, if they be'nt long, and have a good deal of Latin in 'em, I can get you a chap.

SPRIGHTLY: For what, Sir?

VAMP: The manuscript sermons you have wrote, and want to dispose of.

SPRIGHTLY: Sermons that I have wrote?

VAMP: Ay, ay, Master Cape has been telling me ——

SPRIGHTLY: He has; I am mightily oblig'd to him.

VAMP: Nay, nay, don't be afraid; I'll keep council, old Vamp had not kept a shop so long at the Turnstile, if he did not know how to be secret; why, in the year forty-five, when I was in the treasonable way, I never squeak'd; I never gave up but one author in my life, and he was dying of a consumption, so it never came to a trial.

SPRIGHTLY: Indeed!

VAMP: Never—look here [Shows the side of his head] crop'd close!—bare as a board!—and for nothing in the world but an innocent book of bawdy, as I hope for mercy: Oh! the laws are very hard, very severe upon us.[53]

By nature a choleric and violent man, Griffiths felt himself threatened and was in a mood to be vindictive towards anyone who crossed him. Unluckily for Goldsmith, he appears to have become convinced in January '59 that his ex-employee was both a 'traitor' and a 'sharper'. There were probably two distinct reasons for his anger. The warning signs of difficulties ahead for the *Monthly* must already have been evident by this time (in 1761 he would be forced to sell a quarter share of the review to Benjamin Collins of Salisbury)[54] and it was this January that two articles by Goldsmith appeared in the *Critical Review*.[55] It is not unlikely that Tobias Smollett, who was temperamentally a worthy opponent for Griffiths and had made some rough attacks on him and his wife, should have let it be known that Goldsmith had come over to the enemy camp.

This would have been bad enough but, in all innocence, Goldsmith had added insult to injury. Some time before the end of 1758 he had entered into a contract with Robert Dodsley at the Tully's Head Bookshop for the publication of the *Enquiry into the Present State of Polite Learning*. In book-trade terms this meant that he had by-passed Griffiths and a dozen other London publishers and submitted his manuscript to the chief representative of 'prestige' publishing in London.

Robert Dodsley had risen from the same social stratum as Griffiths. His father had been a schoolmaster in Mansfield and as a younger brother in a large family Robert had had to find a means of supporting himself. A good physique and a handsome face, as well perhaps as a taste for educated society, had caused him to enlist amongst that body of men who were chosen for the reflected glory which their presence in a well-cut livery could bestow on their employers. But the young footman from Nottinghamshire had a talent for writing verse and, once his employer had discovered him with pen and ink at the kitchen table, he was encouraged to publish first *Servitude* (with the help of Daniel Defoe) and then *The Muse in Livery*. Within a short time, two plays of his had been performed as afterpieces at Drury Lane, he had been brought to the attention of Pope and, with a gift from the latter added to the proceeds from his Drury Lane benefits, had opened a bookshop in the little court running at the back of St James's Street, opening into Pall Mall. With powerful backing from writers and statesmen he had prospered, and when he accepted Goldsmith's manuscript on the verge of his retirement at the age of fifty-four he had published many of the key works of the last quarter of a century, including Young's *Night Thoughts*, Akenside's *Pleasures of the Imagination*, Johnson's first poem, Gray's *Odes*, works by Horace Walpole and David Hume, and the early writings of Burke. He had been responsible for two moderately successful periodicals, in one of which—*The World*——Lord Chesterfield had issued his badly received puff for the Dictionary which Dodsley himself had urged the young Johnson to produce. He was now advising his brother James to risk his money on the first two volumes of Sterne's *Tristram Shandy*.[56]

Griffiths, as indicated by his friendship with Milner and Dr Rose and later with Josiah Wedgwood, had a longing for social acceptance and must have envied Dodsley's reputation for a delicate conscience as well as for the extremely distinguished clientèle of the Tully's Head. Still smarting from Foote's pointed references to the Jacobite pamphlets and the *Memoirs of a Woman of Pleasure*, it must have been galling to him that a 'literary understrapper' like Goldsmith should aspire to Dodsley's world. His revenge was petty but effective. The tailor's bill which Goldsmith had asked him to endorse was still unpaid and the new suit itself had been pawned together with the four books which Goldsmith had reviewed and which Griffiths regarded as his rather than the reviewer's property. Through the publisher the tailor now demanded the return of the unpaid-for clothes and, forwarding this demand to his ex-employee, Griffiths added to it a request for the return of the books, valued at twenty-three shillings (or four days' wages for a Monthly reviewer). Failing to get a satisfactory answer, he accused Goldsmith of theft and threatened him with legal action.

In spite of that attack on the treatment of debtors which Goldsmith had written and to which Griffiths had given the imprimatur, the reviewer himself was now, for the second time in his life, confronted with the prospect of imprisonment. There was no alternative other than to crawl to Griffiths as he had been intended to do. A less coarse and vindictive man might have been ashamed to elicit from a talented writer the kind of appeal which Goldsmith was now forced to make: but this was his humble request for a reprieve:

Sir,

I know of no misery but a gaol to which my own imprudencies and your letter seem to point. I have seen it inevitable this three or four weeks, and by heavens, request it as a favour, as a favour that may prevent somewhat more fatal. I have been some years struggling with a wretched being, with all that contempt which indigence brings with it, with all those strong passions which make contempt insupportable. What then has a gaol that is formidable, I shall at least have the society of wretches, and such is to me true society. I tell you again and again I am now neither able nor willing to pay you a farthing, but I will be punctual to any appointment you or the taylor shall make; thus far at least I do not act the sharper, had I been possessed of less good nature and native generosity I might surely now have been in better circumstances. I am guilty I own of meanessess which poverty

unavoidably brings with it, my reflections are filld with repentance
for my imprudence but not with any remorse for being a villain,
that may be a character you unjustly charge me with. Your books
I can assure you are neither pawn'd nor sold, but in the custody
of a friend from whom my necessities oblig'd me to borrow some
money, whatever becomes of my person, you shall have them in a
month. It is very possible both the reports you have heard and
your own suggestions may have brought you false information
with respect to my character, it is very possible that the man
whom you now regard with detestation may inwardly burn with
grateful resentment, it is very possible that upon a second perusal
of the letter I sent you, you may see the workings of a mind
strongly agitated with gratitude and jealousy, if such circumstances should appear at least spare invective 'till my book with
Mr Dodsley shall be publish'd, and then perhaps you may see the
bright side of a mind when my professions shall not appear the
dictates of necessity but of choice. You seem to think Doctor
Milner knew me not. Perhaps so; but he was a man I shall ever
honour; but I have friendship only with the dead! I ask pardon
for taking up so much time. Nor shall I add to it by any other
professions than that I am Sir your Humble servt.

Oliver Goldsmith

P.S. I shall expect impatiently the result of your resolutions.[57]

The threat of legal action was withdrawn in response to this appeal;
but Griffiths was still in a vengeful mood and would seize the first
opportunity to harm his former employee on his own literary ground.
    The book itself hardly merited the trouble which, directly or
indirectly, it was causing and would continue to cause in later years.
Even the *Critical Review*, for which Goldsmith was writing when it
appeared in April, had to admit that it was disappointing in spite of
the 'brilliancy of expression' with which the writer had clothed his
often borrowed ideas. But the reviewer was just in his praise as well
as his blame for, even where the *Enquiry* seemed to be literary
tourism at its most superficial, good and illuminating phrases had
been thrown out. Blank verse is a measure which the writers of
romances 'naturally hobble into' says the couplet-writing author;[58]
and there is an engaging account—the heartfelt plaint of a reviewer—
of the momentary despair of losing one's way in a tedious book:

... but woe to the reader, who not daunted at the immense distance between one great paste board and the other, opens the volume and explores his way through a region so extensive, but barren of entertainment. No unexpected landscape there to delight the imagination; no diversity of prospect to cheat the painful journey; he sees the wide extended desart lie before him; what is past only encreases his terror of what is to come.[59]

The Written Mountains and far-off Coromandel must have been very alluring at such moments.

When publication day arrived to find him working for the *Critical Review* rather than collecting his 20% at Madras, Goldsmith must have regretted his chapter on Criticism. Yet with its heartfelt allusion to his recent experiences on the *Monthly* it is the best in the book.

The finest sentiment, and the most weighty truth, may put on a pleasing face, and it is even virtuous to jest when serious advice might be disgusting. But instead of this, the most trifling performance among us now, assumes all the didactic stiffness of wisdom. The most diminutive son of fame, or of famine, has his *we* and his *us*, his *firstlys* and his *secondlys* as methodical, as if bound in cowhide, and closed with clasps of brass. Were these Monthly Reviews and Magazines frothy, pert, or absurd, they might find some pardon; but to be dull and dronish, is an encroachment on the prerogative of a folio.[60]

The chapter that follows, 'Of the Stage', adds little to his stature, doing no more than provide some embellishments to an author versus actor-manager dispute, aimed specifically at Garrick, which had erupted in the press the previous year. Its relevance to the principal thesis of the *Enquiry* is dubious and with its frequent borrowings from contemporary accounts of the stage may only have been included to swell the little book out to a decent size. Goldsmith would live to regret it. For no good reason he had picked a quarrel with an influential man whose support a few years later would have saved him endless frustration and anxiety. And yet it may well have been this chapter which sold the book to Robert Dodsley.

While Goldsmith was still squirming in the trap which Griffiths had set for him, Dodsley was enjoying his greatest dramatic success, the production of his tragedy *Cleone*, and presenting himself at the theatre every night to be reduced to tears by Mrs Bellamy's quietly effective interpretation of the title rôle. This was at Covent Garden and not at Garrick's theatre, Drury Lane. Garrick, until very recently a friend of Dodsley's, had had genuine doubts about a play which dwelt rather too exultantly on blood and calamity. This alone might have been enough to put his relationship with Dodsley under strain, but when he went out of his way to arrange a special attraction at his own theatre to coincide with Dodsley's first night, and to make sneering references to the coming production at Covent Garden, there was a complete rupture. Dodsley, not prepared to be magnanimous in triumph, wrote a cold reply to Garrick's letter of congratulation after a successful first performance. Garrick, accustomed to eliciting whatever response he wished from his applauding public, was caught off-balance and revealed the least pleasant side of his nature in a brief, angry note which sneered obliquely at the lowly beginnings that Dodsley had never attempted to conceal.[61]

In the final stages of this disintegrating friendship, Goldsmith's *Enquiry* with its parroted strictures on theatrical management found its way on to Dodsley's desk and he no doubt enjoyed seeing his former thick-eyebrowed friend in an uncharacteristically belittling context:

> . . . It were a matter of indifference to me, whether our heroines are in keeping, or our candle-snuffers burn their fingers, did not such make a great part of public care, and polite conversation. It is not these, but the age I would reproach: the vile complexion of the times, when those employ our most serious thoughts and seperate us into parties, whose business is only to amuse our idlest hours. I cannot help reproaching our meanness in this respect; for our stupidity, and our folly, will be remembered, when even the attitudes and eye brows of a favourite actor shall be forgotten.[62]

Garrick himself had a long memory. Even though he and Goldsmith had met each other socially before the problem of finding a theatrical home for *The Good-Natured Man* arose, it would become increasingly obvious that he was incapable of viewing with an open mind any play offered to him by a writer who had once affected to be less than dazzled by his art.

SIX

An Amphibious Creature

B Y THE spring of 1759 Goldsmith had had long enough to consider the effects of his bid for freedom on leaving Griffiths the previous year. He was in a despondent frame of mind. The thraldom of the *Monthly Review* had been replaced by the thraldom of the *Critical*, with the extra disadvantage that he now received payment according to the copy he produced rather than being provided with a guaranteed £2 a week, an office table and board-and-lodging. The only improvement was that for his editor, Tobias Smollett, he could feel a respect which Griffiths had not inspired. Smollett, who practised medicine in London in the 'forties, had published some verse and three novels before devoting himself to the profitable business of writing popular history. Behind Smollett was the printer, Alexander Hamilton, also a Scot, who was technically the owner of the Review. Goldsmith had a good working relationship with Hamilton, who was just as likely to rescue him from a bailiff as to bully him when his copy failed to reach the press on time. But he had already expressed his feelings about reviewing and, although his articles for the *Critical* have the same authority though not as much sprightliness as those he contributed to the *Monthly*, all his subsequent remarks about the business of criticism reveal that he had completely lost any liking he might once have had for this branch of letters.

He was also very short of money and was living at the seediest of his London lodgings, with the possible exception of his time on Bankside when he first arrived. This was Green Arbour Court, at the heart of a warren bounded by the Old Bailey, St Sepulchre's Church, the Fleet Market and the thirty-foot walls of the Fleet prison. Washington Irving, in the 1830's, was just in time to record his impressions of this courtyard of overcrowded and insanitary tenements before it was demolished:

> ... We came out upon Fleet-Market and traversing it, turned up a narrow street to the bottom of a long steep flight of stone

E*

steps, called Break-neck-stairs. These, he told me, led up to
Green-arbour-court . . .' At the top of the steps he found a small
square of tall and miserable houses, the very intestines of which
seemed turned inside out, to judge from the old garments and
frippery that fluttered from every window . . .[1]

When Thomas Percy came to see Goldsmith here, no doubt
before the court had degenerated into the outright slum which
Irving was to see seventy years later, there was to be a second
unexpected visitor:

> While they were conversing, someone gently rapped at the door,
> and being desired to come in, a poor ragged little girl of very
> decent behaviour, entered, who, dropping a curtsie, said, "My
> mama sends her compliments, and begs the favour of you to lend
> her a chamber-pot full of coals."[2]

Behind the mixture of farce and crushed gentility in the little girl's
request can be detected that lower middle class London world
which Dickens was to make so familiar.

Goldsmith responded readily to any sign of human suffering,
but it would be a mistake to think that it was always the world of
the proletarian poor that he had in mind when he contrasted the
real sufferings of poverty with the imaginary woes of cosseted
wealth. In the London of his time there was an army of people who
lived in the cellar doss-houses of St Giles', twenty to a room;
workmen who habitually slept on the bench in their underground
workshop; single, unattached people, particularly women who,
discriminated against by employers, sometimes starved to death in
deserted houses; and others who paid 6d a week to lie on straw in
small wooden sheds.[3] Then there were the migrant labourers,
particularly the Irish but also such groups as the women from
Shropshire and Wales who came to the suburbs each year to work
in the market gardens and make a living by undercutting London
labourers. He was aware of these evils and anticipated the rioting
which would frequently bring London to a standstill towards the
end of the next decade. Hard conditions produced harsh people he
believed. But poverty of the extreme kind was beyond his imaginative experience, and when he did try to write about it in an essay
which he called *A City Night-Piece* he sank at once into unconvincing
rhetoric.[4]

In Green Arbour he found the kind of poverty he already knew about—poverty calling for deception and contrivances in the interests of keeping one's self respect in wretched circumstances. The lives of small shopkeepers, skilled craftsmen and those 'genteel' people who through bad management or bad luck had come adrift from their class were exceedingly precarious.

His landlady, Mrs Butler, seems to have belonged to this class and it may be possible to detect the source of Goldsmith's evocative phrase 'the mask of sturdy contentment'[5] in Hogarth's portrait of her. Goldsmith loved to fill his room with the Butler children and their friends and to set them dancing with his flute. On a practical level he pawned his clothes when Daniel Butler was arrested for debt, and remained in touch with the family, helping them out with occasional presents, until he died.[6]

London had a floating population. Only a small proportion of Londoners owned the houses they lived in. The majority of middle class people lived in furnished rooms—a fact which, as Dorothy George points out, accounts for the frequent occurrence in cabinet makers' design books of beds masquerading as bookcases, tables and cupboards. Green Arbour Court, far too close for comfort to the centre of London's meat wholesale trade, was simply a drab version of typical lower middle class life in the middle of the eighteenth century; and here for a few months Goldsmith embarked on that 'amphibious' life which stretched from the crowded, washing-bedecked galleries of the tenement to the theatres and the coffee-houses of Covent Garden, St Martin's Lane and Fleet Street. A reviewer of books with a monthly deadline to meet might have been expected to resent the intimacies which revealed themselves on the occasion of Percy's visit. But in fact there is every sign that the discipline of Green Arbour was as positive in its effect on his personality as that of the *Monthly Review*. The writings which took shape in his mind while he reviewed the volumes supplied by Smollett and Hamilton are full of brisk reminders of the need to shake off daydreams, to reject the idea of some illusory happiness and to live in the present moment.

'Writers of every age,' he tells his readers in the autumn of this year, 'have endeavour'd to shew that pleasure is in us, and not in the objects offered for our amusement. If the soul be happily disposed, every thing becomes capable of affording entertainment, and distress will almost want a name. Every occurrence passes in review like the figures of a procession; some may be aukward, others ill dressed; but none but a fool is for this enraged with the master of the ceremonies.

'I remember to have once seen a slave in a fortification in Flanders, who appeared no way touched with his situation. He was maimed, deformed, and chained; obliged to toil from the appearance of day 'till night-fall, and condemned to this for life; yet, with all these circumstances of apparent wretchedness, he sung, would have danced, but that he wanted a leg, and appeared the merries, happiest man of all the garrison. What a practical philosopher was here; an happy constitution supplied philosophy, and though semingly destitute of wisdom, he was really wise.'[7]

In December he invents an Eastern Tale to prove that happiness lies in embracing life, however unsatisfactory, and rejecting the imagined utopias which would be insupportable in reality.[8] Between replenishing the chamber-pot with coals, meeting Hamilton's demands, and attempting to gain a footing in the literary life of the capital, there was evidently little time and energy left to pursue dreams of Coromandel and Sinai or even to continue the charade of being a physician. The wheels of Hamilton's press turned month by month, and Goldsmith's amused neighbours knew him well enough to appreciate the significance of the printer's visits. Loud words were heard on occasions, even the turning of a key in the lock, but by the time the two men emerged harmony had usually been restored and the overdue copy written.[9]

Shortly after the publication of the *Enquiry into the Present State of Polite Learning* in April, Hamilton had to bail Goldsmith out of a sponging-house into which he had been lured by a wily bailiff. A few months later the incident was worked into one of the 'Chinese Letters' that eventually became *The Citizen of the World*. The creditor had assumed quite wrongly that the publication of an octavo volume must have brought wealth to his client. The bailiff presented himself as the servant of a great man who was anxious to meet the new author and carried him away, not to the elegant quarter of St James's but to a less honourable address in the region of Carey Street.[10]

In spite of his unfashionable address Goldsmith kept up the appearance of gentility. Even if his clothes were a shade too bright he had had the right sort of education and although the Goldsmiths were not socially the stuff of which bishops were made his Church of Ireland antecedents gave him a kind of respectability. He had failed to achieve the rank of physician but there was nothing to prevent him from feeling at ease amongst the dilettanti of the Bedford and the amateur politicians of the Smyrna, or at the Italian opera which, with its high prices and the limited appeal of its castrati and Italian divas, had predominantly upper class patrons.

He was still in touch with at least one of his former *Monthly Review* colleagues, James Grainger, a poetry-writing physician who in February 1759 invited him to the Temple Exchange Coffee House and introduced him to the Revd. Thomas Percy, a tall ascetic-looking but quick-tempered young clergyman who acted as chaplain to the Earl of Sussex and had a passion for old manuscripts.[11] Five days later Goldsmith and Percy met again at Dodsley's bookshop, and on Saturday, March 3rd Percy spent the whole morning in Goldsmith's room at Green Arbour Court. Percy was a year younger than Goldsmith. Temperamentally there was a considerable distance between them but the new friendship would last until Goldsmith's death. The up-and-coming journalist was probably also a Sunday visitor at Monmouth House where, on this day, Tobias Smollett kept an open table for any of his contributors who were prepared to walk across the fields and marshes between Buckingham Gate and Chelsea in time for Sunday dinner. Smollett left a slightly patronising account of these occasions;[12] but Goldsmith would have been well received if only for his unfashionable Toryism—which was very dear to Smollett's heart. Goldsmith in turn admired his editor whom he spoke of in the same breath as Johnson[13] (before meeting the latter), and he was very probably indebted to Smollett before the end of the year for an introduction which was to be extremely useful in promoting his own career in journalism.

In this formative stage of his London life, however, it was probably the submerged half of the Green Arbour existence which was the more important. For while the wits and poetasters congregated in the arcades of Covent Garden, he was exploring less fashionable areas: the Robin Hood Inn in Butcher's Row near Temple Bar, the meeting place of some notable societies; Slaughter's Coffee House in St Martin's Lane, a good place to get into a political argument; Ashley's Punch House, where an elderly waiter had established his reputation as something of a pundit on foreign affairs; the Cyder Cellar in Maiden Lane; and on Saturdays the Broom out at Islington where a society of struggling authors had installed itself. Eating is always a problem for people who live in furnished rooms. Goldsmith is unlikely to have been able to afford either French cuisine at the St James's end of town or the more robust but also expensive fare at the Crown or the King's Arms in the City, and he was probably not yet familiar with such haunts of Dr Johnson as the Mitre in Fleet Street. When there was money in his pocket he no doubt joined the lawyers' clerks, upper servants, half-pay captains and other unsuccessful empirics whom George Colman had observed in chop-houses like Dolly's and Horseman's, or Betty's, where one could expect to be waited on by a pretty girl.[14] On difficult days he may have walked over to Moorfields— a good area for cheap cooks' shops—and may even have tried one of those 'farthing fries' which had horrified Johnson, as well as the less suspect sausages, black puddings and pies which were part of the lower middle class Londoner's staple diet.

Goldsmith found it far easier to make acquaintances than to lose them, and in the days of his fame members of the Johnson set were amused by his completely ineffectual attempts to avoid being patronised by an off-duty butcher or tallow-chandler.[15] They may have been members of the Robin Hood Society, a remarkable club which met at the inn in Butcher's Row to debate religion and metaphysics. As a young man just down from Oxford in 1754 George Colman had visited the Club, and although he had had to be slightly patronising about the artisans, small tradesmen and clerks who might surprise one by revealing a passion for Socrates or Lord Bolingbroke's *Patriot King*, he conceded that as a training ground in logic it was far in advance of either of the sleeping universities. It had a reputation for 'free thinking'—a blanket term which could cover anything from athesim, via deism, to a healthy desire to examine the basis of orthodox religious belief. A typical subject for debate might be 'Whether Lord Bolingbroke has not done greater service to mankind by his writings, than the Apostles or Evangelists', and one had not to be shocked if Socrates were preferred to all of them or if the apostles were 'unsainted' and referred to as 'plain Peter and plain Paul'.[16] Regrettably Goldsmith sacrificed his real feelings about the Club in the interests of broad comedy when he came to write about it later in the year;[17] but his fellow members recalled him as 'a good orator and candid disputant, with a clear head and an honest heart'.[18] Essentially middle of the road as he was in his religious convictions, it is reasonably certain that he argued on the side of the apostles, if not the angels.

Goldsmith's feeling of class identity with the world of Green Arbour is illustrated by the difference of tone between his account of the Robin Hood Society and that given in the *Connoisseur*, the magazine that Colman and his friend Bonnell Thornton had written on coming down from Oxford in 1754. Goldsmith's account of this and of other clubs is farcical but he himself is included in the joke and, even when he puts ungrammatical expressions into the mouth of Caleb Jeacocke, the butcher who was president of the society, there is no snobbish dissociation from the scene described. George Colman, however, the son of a diplomat and nephew of a statesman, William Pulteney, who had been made Earl of Bath, gives a report which is both detailed and patronising, a sociological study by a product of Westminster and Christ Church who feels that the natural order of things is threatened when he discovers that a workman is reading Plato.

However hard he struggled to lift himself out of Green Arbour Court Goldsmith never disowned his neighbours there. He saw both the comedy and pathos of their situation and recorded it in his journalism and in *The Vicar of Wakefield* as, at the end of the next decade, he was to record both these elements in the lives of the dispossessed villagers in his most famous poem. His comedy has kept its freshness because he was seeing these situations from within whilst Colman's essays, though often very amusing, are really period pieces. Goldsmith was writing about his own people and he never attempted to disguise it. The fact that a pig-butcher could hail the writer of *The Deserted Village* as 'Noll' across a crowded room at the Globe Tavern, to the undisguised delight of his literary friends, reveals the childlike innocence of the man who, on the debit side, bought furniture that would never be paid for and who had been on the point of betraying his convictions about imperialism by becoming a Coromandel nabob.

Even a casual study of incomes and prices in the eighteenth century reveals quite glaringly the reasons behind Goldsmith's entirely bourgeois aspirations. It takes an effort today to accept that the aristocrat who with tolerable equanimity could lose £10,000 in an evening's play at White's or Almack's, and the skilled Spital-fields silk-weaver, who in good times could earn ten shillings a week, inhabited the same planet. On purely economic grounds it was unlikely that the two could have any other relationship than that of servant and master. Within the middle class the situation was more fluid though the underlying economic disparities were just as glaring (as illustrated by Johnson's heartfelt relief, many years after he had become a national figure, on being offered a pension of £300 a year by Lord Bute). In the case of Colman and Goldsmith, the young man who inherited an income of nine hundred guineas from Lord Bath and the reviewer who was lucky to earn £2 a week had the same educational background, similar literary and artistic tastes, wore the same clothes and wigs and could have sat next to each other in the same coffee house, but at the end of the day Colman would return to a luxurious house in Soho Square and Goldsmith, no doubt concealing his address as many of his kind did, to the lice and flies and bad smells of his courtyard on the fringe of Smith-field.

If Goldsmith at this stage of his life seemed to be sinking, many of the other inhabitants of Green Arbour in a period of commercial expansion were undoubtedly coming up. Colman had been amused by the 'red-armed Belles' he met in the Park and by the trades-men's wives who were beginning to deck themselves on Sundays in silk frocks and paste jewellery, modelling their behaviour on what they saw and heard in the next alcove at Vauxhall.[19] A chair-carver in the Chippendale works, a jeweller at Pinchbeck's or a maker of optical instruments at Deard's in the Strand might be earning up to £3 or £4 a week and indulging in such luxuries as a silk waistcoat, a gold-laced hat or a tortoise-shell snuff-box; and Thomas Campbell on a visit to London in 1775 would visit the Chapter Coffee House, which had a subscription library, and describe how a tinsmith 'in his apron, and some of his saws under his arm, came in, sat down, and called for his glass of punch and the paper, both which he used with as much ease as a Lord'.[20] The expatriate Irishman, in the hot summer of 1759, having failed to heave himself up into the

1a Oliver Goldsmith
by Reynolds, 1766

1b Sir Joshua Reynolds,
Self Portrait, 1768

2a Green Arbour Court, with the opening onto Breakneck Stairs. Goldsmith lodged with the Butlers in the house on the right

2b A view of the fountain in the Middle Temple. The southern range of Brick court can be seen (foreshortened) in the background immediately above the child's hoop

3a Mrs Butler by Hogarth

3b Ralph Griffiths

3c Thomas Davies

3d William Kenrick

4 Samuel Johnson by Nollekens

medical profession, must have occasionally had an alarming sense of being overtaken. Perhaps this was good for him.

Goldsmith may have been tired of reviewing, but journalism didn't stop there. Johnson at this time was contributing a column to a not particularly distinguished weekly, the *Universal Chronicle*, his reputation as an essayist having been established at the beginning of the decade with his twice-weekly periodical, the *Rambler*. Between 1753 and 1755, Robert Dodsley had achieved a circulation of 2,500 with the *World*, which Edward Moore, a short-lived poet who had begun life as a linen draper, had been invited to edit. Between 1754 and 1756 George Colman and Bonnell Thornton had brought out the *Connoisseur* in weekly numbers, and had it reissued in book form in 1757. Goldsmith knew it well: it was one of the first books he had reviewed on the *Monthly*.[21] These writings sprang from the tradition which Addison and Steele had established at the beginning of the century, and for all the differences in tone between the rather vapid elegance of Chesterfield in the *World*, the self-conscious wit of the young Oxford men and the vigorous, flexible and deceptively light prose of Johnson's *Idler*, they had many common features. Like the *Tatler* and the *Spectator*, which had had an influence out of all proportion to their short runs, these columns tended to exhaust themselves within two or three years. Their writers accepted a responsibility as Addison and Steele had done for improving the moral tone of society, either through mildly satirical comment on the social scene or through the kind of appeal to reason and Christian morality of which Johnson was so powerful an exponent. Even Colman and Thornton felt compelled to take occasional excursions into the latter sphere and pillory gluttonous clergymen, debauched young aristocrats and ladies who had regrettably decided that it was unfashionable to sew in public.

This was a natural field for Goldsmith to enter. Reviewing had proved his authority and skill as a writer, and after three years' experience of London he was ready to set down what he had seen with all the freshness and detachment of an expatriate—if not outsider. He was also to reveal a need to edify and instruct that proved him to be indeed the son and brother of preachers, and well within the Addison-Johnson tradition. With this he brought a good working knowledge of the *Encyclopédie* and the writings of Mari-

vaux, Montesquieu and Voltaire. They were to be a valuable
standby whenever he was short of copy.

By the late summer he had made an arrangement with the
bookseller J. Wilkie in St Paul's Churchyard to compile a weekly
paper of thirty-two octavo pages, price 3d., to be sold on Saturdays.
The first number of the *Bee* appeared on October 6th. With another
bookseller, I. Pottinger, he made an agreement to contribute
essays to a journal called the *Busy Body* which was edited by a
fellow-expatriate and acquaintance, Edward Purdon. For this he
wrote ten pieces in two months and when it ceased publication at
the end of November, was invited to contribute to its successor,
the *Weekly Magazine*. As he was still contributing to the *Critical
Review*, this autumn was a period of intense literary activity. He
wrote about the stage, communicating his admiration for Mlle
Clairon (whom he had probably seen at the Théatre Française) and
for the great comedienne, Kitty Clive; about the sideshows at the
St Bartholomew Fair at Smithfield; education and the wretched
salaries allotted to teachers; about the need for legal reform; the
masters of English prose, amongst whom Dryden was prominently
placed; the jingoism unleashed by British successes in Canada;
and—in faintly disillusioned tones when he realised that the *Bee*
was not paying its way and would have to be discontinued—
about the book-trade. The fact that he could write with humour
about his poor sales suggests that he was in good spirits under the
intense pressure of producing several thousand words a week.
Comparing the performance of the *Bee*, at the beginning of the
fourth number, with that of rival journals he writes:

> Their fame is diffused in a very wide circle, that of some as far
> as Islington, and some yet farther still; while mine, I sincerely
> believe, has hardly travelled beyond the sound of Bow-bell; and
> while the works of others fly like unpinioned swans, I find my
> own move as heavily as a new-plucked goose.[22]

In the *Busy Body* for October 20th he shows himself to be
sympathetic to the mood of the French *philosophes* (who decried
the limitations of simple nationalism) by spelling out the realities
to citizens who after the reverses in Europe, Canada and India of
recent years had danced in the streets four nights previously on
receiving the news that Wolfe had captured Quebec. He anticipates

the political wrangles that were to come, when he urges moderation rather than the kind of vindictive peace terms which can only lead to further hostilities. 'Peace is the only triumph of victory' he claims. But an essay in which he presents himself walking through the crowded streets and having a squib tied to the tail of his wig is not entirely solemn. (It 'went off in a bounce' just as he entered George's coffee-house.)[23]

Goldsmith's strength as a journalist lay in his sympathy with the changing mood of his times, a mood that can be sensed in the writing of the *philosophes*, in a sermon preached in the Methodist tabernacle at Moorfields or in the diary of Thomas Turner, that Sussex grocer who recorded not only that he had been deeply affected when his wife read aloud to him 'that moving scene of the funeral of Miss Clarissa Harlowe', but also his concern that the Duke of Marlborough's landing on the French coast in 1757 might have brought disaster to 'many thousands of poor innocent wretches, that perhaps never did, nor thought of doing, any hurt to the British nation'.[24] It was typical of the former pupil of one of the first Duke of Marlborough's quartermasters that, within his first year of creative journalism, he should have drawn attention to the scandalous lack of provision for wounded and discharged servicemen, and commended the private individuals who had asserted themselves to improve the living conditions of the French prisoners of war in London.[25]

*

The year which saw Goldsmith's début as a columnist had been a difficult time for Hamilton and Smollett. The previous year Smollet had written a savage review of a pamphlet in which Admiral Knowles had attempted to explain the reasons for the failure of his expedition to Rochefort on the French coast in 1755. Knowles, Smollett wrote, was 'an admiral without conduct, an engineer without knowledge, an officer without resolution, and a man without veracity'.[26] Understandably this anonymous attack was considered slanderous; and in March Hamilton was indicted as its publisher. Smollett appealed to his friend John Wilkes, M.P., seeking help in having the indictment quashed, but Wilkes' intervention was unsuccessful. When the case came into court in October, Smollett confessed to being the author of the article. He was fined £100 and sentenced to three months' imprisonment in the King's Bench.[27] Since—like Leigh Hunt, incarcerated there on a similar charge half a century later—he was allowed his own room, furniture, books, outside catering and visits from friends, the sentence was less draconian than might at first appear. Friends rallied to his support. He was visited by Wilkes and David Garrick; his writers, including Goldsmith, had access to him; and he began work on a new book. One of the best-natured of the London booksellers boosted his morale by inviting him to edit a magazine. This was the *British Magazine*, which made its first appearance in January 1760, and the publisher was John Newbery who had a share in the *Universal Chronicle* and *Lloyd's Evening Post* and in the same month was to launch a daily paper, the *Public Ledger*, which survived until 1932. Whether or not they actually met for the first time within the walls of the King's Bench in St George's Fields, it was probably Smollett who introduced Goldsmith to Newbery, and the result of this meeting was an invitation to contribute regularly to the new paper. Goldsmith would have known that Newbery was connected with the *Universal Chronicle* and that one of the mainstays of this paper was the column which appeared over the sobriquet, 'The Idler'. To be invited to fill a rôle similar to Johnson's must have been encouraging enough for an anonymous reviewer. It also brought a constitutional hero-worshipper into close association with a new hero.

John Newbery was a publisher who inspired considerable affection in his writers. Goldsmith would make him appear briefly in *The Vicar of Wakefield* and Johnson wrote an attractive word-portrait of him in the *Idler* as the kind of businessman who is almost defeated by his inventiveness and energy.[28] 'Jack Whirler' is a man who always needs to be in two places at once and will invariably take up a new project before the last has been properly launched, arriving late for his meals and leaving early, finding it equally impossible to delegate responsibility and to keep an appointment on time. In spite of such shortcomings Newbery was highly successful and now at the peak of his career.

At the age of twenty-four he had been left a share in the *Reading Mercury and Oxford Gazette* on which he had worked for eight years, and shortly afterwards had married the widow of his employer and benefactor. She was six years older than himself and the mother of three children. In 1744 when Newbery was thirty-one they had moved to London and established themselves as booksellers in the shadow of St Paul's Cathedral.[29] Unlike Dodsley and Griffiths his interests were not exclusively literary. As Johnson's portrait suggested he was the kind of entrepreneur who remained alert to commercial openings wherever they appeared and could devote considerable energy to developing them. (Typically, in 1764, in conjunction with an apothecary and a linen-draper he took out a patent on a rotary intaglio method of printing cotton). He was not himself an originator of ideas but he had the knack of divining the drift of the times and in anticipating public demand.

While still living in Reading he had sensed a welcome change of atmosphere in the production of children's books in the small-scale publications of Thomas Boreman and Mary Cooper. His own venture, *The Little Pretty Pocket Book* contained amongst the baby-talk a hidden threat to Boreman that he was about to beat him at his own game of providing a substitute for the sometimes thrilling but rarely 'polite' chap-books which until now had been the chief vehicles of entertainment and pre-school education for children. Newbery's $2\frac{1}{2}''$ x $3''$ books with their flowered and gilt Dutch paper and little woodcuts really were pretty and made a genuine effort to re-enter the world of childhood. The educational benefits of a series called *The Circle of the Sciences*, which was launched on his arrival in London, were mixed: the early volumes which claimed to impart the skills of reading and writing overlooked too many basic educational principles to have been of much use as home-tutors but some of the volumes in the first principles of science reached a much higher standard.

The Newberys had chosen a bad time to transfer their business to London, but the recession of 1745 was an opportunity for this enterprising man to demonstrate both his business integrity and his skill as a survivor. Instead of taking refuge in bankruptcy like many of his contemporaries, he was able to assure his creditors of his intention to repay twenty shillings in the pound (a promise that was kept). Retrenchment involved relinquishing his share in the *Reading Mercury* and deferring plans for book production until the future. Instead, he concentrated for a few more years on an activity in which he was already experienced, the sale of patent medicines. The turning point in Newbery's career had been reached early in 1748 when he acquired the exclusive right to sell 'Fever Powders' which Dr Robert James of Lichfield had patented two years before.[30] They were to become the panacea of the second half of the eighteenth century and in the first sixteen years Newbery's receipts would have amounted to approximately £100,000.[31] By 1750 his financial position was already healthy enough to allow him to divert capital once more into independent book and magazine production.

In 1750 he had also embarked on a fruitful association with the poet Christopher Smart (who was later to marry his step-daughter Nancy Carnan). Together they produced the *Midwife*, a weekly saturnalia which contrasts startlingly with that other journal which came into being in the same year—and which the *Midwife* outlived—Johnson's *Rambler*. Its tone was established in the first number with an engraving which showed the garrulous and opinionated old woman herself sitting, with a pile of manuscripts before her, near a close-stool labelled 'The Jakes of Genius'. Smart's brand of enlightened absurdity had probably been aimed in the first place at students, lawyers' clerks and City apprentices, but before long the earthy and irreverent little journal had attracted a wider and more fashionable audience. Mrs Midnight detests doctors, is sceptical about marriage though she accepts that it is a necessary institution, despises literary critics, distrusts lawyers, is angered by the effects of superstition including the increase in the number of astrologers and palmists and the sufferings of an unfortunate woman at Tring who had been suspected of witchcraft and narrowly escaped being murdered by the villagers. In her most belligerent mood she advocates the setting up of a new government department, the Office of Annihilation (to be placed, of course, in the charge of the College of Physicians); in a lighter vein she recommends the cat-organ (in which the tails of carefully graded cats, placed in grooves, are struck by hammers) as a cheap alternative to the harpsichord. Thanks to Christopher Smart, M. Midnight also proved to be an accomplished writer of light verse, and the patrons of the chop-houses of Fleet Street, if not the admirers of Gray, would have sympathised with the clerk in *Verses written in a London Churchyard*, who seems as eager to eat the waitress as his twopenny Ordinary: 'Each sav'ry Dish to cit and fop / She bears, herself a nicer chop; / How far more elegant, to sop, / And feast on lovely Jenny.'[32]

At the end of the same year, under his own imprint, Newbery issued the first number of a very different journal—which was to consolidate his reputation as a children's publisher. The scope of this monthly was to 'attempt to mend the World, to render the Society of Man more amiable and to establish the Plainness, Simplicity, Virtue and Wisdom of the Golden Age so much celebrated by the Poets and Historians'. It cost 3d., was illustrated with clumsy copper plates, and its contents were strung together on the fiction that a group of children had formed themselves into a society for the promotion of knowledge and good behaviour: '. . . on the 20th of December 1750 . . . were then assembled a young Prince, several of the nobility, and a great many little gentlemen and ladies . . .'. That Newbery was in fact aiming at a public which was by no means sure of its gentility is illustrated in the sequel, and in the subject matter of the stories and poems which the children contribute. It is 'Master Meanwell' who is chosen to be the Speaker of this assembly. He modestly demurs on account of his relatively humble birth, but the Prince encourages him with the reminder: 'We are not met here to distinguish ourselves by birth and title, but for our mutual improvement . . . We have already had sufficient instances of your modesty and good manners . . .' Each little volume catered for an elastic readership whose age range lay between the five-year-old register of stories like *Little Tommy Trip and his Dog Jouler* to the adolescent concerns reflected in some of the verse and in stories like the *History of Florella*, which proved to be an unashamed condensation of Richardson's *Pamela* into a few hundred words. The happy outcome of Florella's problems is depicted in an engraving which must have given immense satisfaction to Newbery's readers: the virtuous City girl is found in a coach drawn by four horses in the drive of a rather top-heavy mansion—an apotheosis indeed for all members of her class who would have known that Green Arbour Court was only just round the corner.[33]

By the time Goldsmith met him at the end of the decade Newbery's business had gathered momentum, with the help of advertising which anticipated modern techniques including the 'true story' in the sale of medicines and 'free offers' to boost his children's books—which directly or indirectly also advertised one another. His publishing list was still modest: there appear to have been only nine titles in 1759 as opposed to Robert and James Dodsley's fifty-five.[34] He was concentrating on educational books and seems to have been aware that there was a demand for these amongst self-educated adults as well as children. In the first volume of *The Circle of Sciences* he had included copy-letters better designed for the young apprentice than for children and now, in publications like his *Pocket Dictionary* ('every word so accented, that there can be no uncertainty as to the Pronunciation') and Sam Boyse's book of myths retold, *A New Pantheon—For the Use of Those who would understand History, Poetry, Painting, Statuary, Coins, Medals etc.*, he was catering for people who were trying to improve themselves.

By this time Newbery had lost his *Midwife* collaborator in tragic circumstances. In 1756 in the fourth year of his marriage to Nancy Carnan, Christopher Smart had suffered a mental breakdown and was to spent the next seven years in confinement. His religious mania had taken a form which deprived him of any desire to return to his wife and daughters, who were Roman Catholics, and the family group was irretrievably broken up.[35]

*

The scheme that Goldsmith put to John Newbery at the end of 1759 was the series of 'Chinese Letters' that he had contemplated the previous summer. As in Montesquieu's *Lettres Persanes*, a foreigner was to write letters home describing the strange people and customs he had observed. Before Newbery met Goldsmith, he may have spotted the references to two of his writers in the issue of the *Bee* for Saturday, November 3rd. In the *Fame Machine* fantasy Goldsmith considers achievements of his contemporaries beginning with an account of his own rejection by the coachman waiting to admit the fortunate few to his waiting carriage: his own little journal is no passport to fame and when he has examined its pages the coachman 'loses all his former respect' for the stranger; others are put to an equally rigorous examination: Samuel Johnson is admitted, not for the *Dictionary* but for his *Rambler*; Hume is suspect because he is an atheist, but his *History of England* passes the test; while Smollett is disparaged as an historian and allowed to step into the coach only as a novelist.[36]

In agreeing to a scheme put to him by a virtually unknown writer who might make or break his new journal Newbery was shrewd enough to see that Goldsmith's unconventionality and freshness would establish the tone it needed—for the *Public Ledger* was exclusively a businessman's paper, and whereas the *World* and the *Connoisseur* might have been right for St James's and Covent Garden, something different was required in a daily paper that would be sold in the streets around the Royal Exchange. Later developments suggest that Goldsmith felt at ease with Newbery. This November he had a particular reason for being drawn to the protector of Mrs Midnight. Ralph Griffiths had waited until now to record the existence of Goldsmith's *Enquiry into the Present State of Polite Learning* in his Review and had set one of the nastier figures in London's book world, William Kenrick, to the task of denigrating it. This, Kenrick had done with characteristic gusto, condemning the book's style and (with more justice) its lack of originality. For good measure he repeated publicly the personal accusations Griffiths had made in private at the beginning of the year. Goldsmith would have been less than human if he hadn't drawn some comfort from the fact that a few years previously Kenrick himself had been mauled as 'Dr Kenderico', a hack with a notorious 'Itch of Scribbling', by Christopher Smart in the pages of the *Midwife*.

The quality of Goldsmith's writing for the *Public Ledger* over a period of twenty months from January 1760 to August 1761, and the close personal relationship of the writer and publisher until the latter's death in 1767 are a fair indication that they understood and liked each other. That Newbery was an extravert can be gathered from George Colman's account of him as well as Johnson's, and Goldsmith the expatriate Irishman, who evidently found English reserve and dull-eyed melancholy rather trying on occasions,[37] would have appreciated his geniality and freedom from inhibitions.

In an undergraduate paper, Colman had rather unkindly described an encounter with Mr and Mrs Newbery on a visit to their son Francis in Oxford, drawing attention to their provincial accents and *nouveau riche* outlook.[38] (Mrs Newbery is disappointed that there are no 'waxworks' in the University Museum but suggests installing in their garden at Islington a copy of the little lead statue of

Mercury at Christ Church, while Newbery puts his clever son through his paces before the assembled company and notices that there are many shelves waiting to be filled in the Radcliffe Camera.) Goldsmith could only have admired the spirit of enterprise which had brought the couple to London, like himself from a provincial backwater.

*

The facetious references to China and Confucius in his letter to Bryanton of August 1758 reveal that Goldsmith had been contemplating his 'Chinese Letters' for more than a year before the probable date of his meeting with Newbery. Since the late seventeenth century critics of society had found the persona of a wide-eyed foreign traveller a useful disguise—particularly in France where too ruthless an analysis of contemporary ills might have uncomfortable consequences for the writer. Montesquieu's *Lettres Persanes* had been imitated by Lord Lyttelton, and in 1757 Horace Walpole had recalled the Marquis d'Argens' *Lettres Chinoises* in his brief satire, *A Letter from Xo Ho, a Chinese Philosopher at London to his friend Lien Chi at Peking*, which in turn provided Goldsmith with half the name of his own traveller, 'Lien Chi Altangi'.

In the course of seventy years, interest in China had grown from enlightened curiosity to one of those popular cults which lose their original heat and significance as fast as they are diffused throughout society. This seems to have been partly a weary reaction to the recent European past, and partly a taste for the exotic which could find easy expression in novelettes and an orgy of interior and exterior decoration. To the thinking man at the end of the previous century, which had been shaken by fratricidal wars of religion, it was comforting to remember that there was a country on the other side of the world which had produced Confucius and which *might* offer an ideal alternative society. Accounts of this mysterious country had appeared in the writings of the French Jesuit missionaries, Le Comte and Du Halde (to whom Goldsmith would be indebted on the rare occasion when he took the trouble to find some circumstantial background for his own Philosopher).

In the England of the mid eighteenth century a general dissatisfaction with the conditions of society had manifested itself in

different ways. Practically-minded men and women had formed
themselves into committees for the establishment of a foundling
hospital, Sunday schools, refuges for ex-prostitutes and an
organisation to help the thousands of people who were imprisoned
for the non-payment of comparatively small debts. For the lazy, or
the sentimental, a romantic yearning for Utopia was perhaps a more
attractive option: it was comforting and not too taxing mentally to
direct one's thoughts to a country about which there was much to
learn but which might indeed be a seat of wisdom, enlightenment
and that 'reason' the century held so dear and found so difficult to
achieve. Not for the last time in the Western consciousness China—
blessedly inscrutable—was the land of promise towards which the
enlightened citizen in a moment of inspiration or a fit of the Hipps
could turn in imagination. Fashionable drawing-rooms provided
plenty of encouragement for the latter activity by way of porcelain
of 'the right pea-green' and figurines of pot-bellied oriental deities.
Nothing less than a popularisation of Rousseau and the cult of
nature sauvage would be needed to consign 'the pagods and' bramins
to the attic.

Journals of the 1750s like the *World* and the *Connoisseur* enjoyed
describing the follies of the Chinese vogue. The *Connoisseur* could
restrain itself when considering a fop's dressing-room with its
'various coloured sprigs of artificial flowers' and looking-glass
'inclosed in a whimsical frame of Chinese paling'[39] (perhaps a
product of Chippendale's workshop) but was clearly scandalised by
the realisation that a tallow-chandler of all people had erected a
Chinese bridge in the garden of his suburban retreat;[40] while the
World complained with cheerful exaggeration that in the country
'every gate to a cow-yard is in Ts and Zs'.[41] But fashion is not
easily discouraged. The Garricks continued to sleep in a Chinese
bed in a Chinese bedroom beside the Thames at Hampton, while
further downstream pagodas and temples stood in the Chinese
garden that William Chambers had created for the Princess of
Wales at Kew. The rich transformed themselves into mandarins for
a masquerade, and even Voltaire pandered to the prevailing taste
by writing a play in praise of oriental magnanimity, *L'Orphelin de la
Chine*.

In his Coromandel mood Goldsmith was prepared both to give
due credit to Confucius and to indulge his public with an oriental

tale. When inspiration ran low, as it did on occasions, he ruffled the tranquil surface of Lien Chi Altangi's life with alarming letters from his son. Hingpo in the course of eighteen months was to be captured by the Tartars, sold to a Persian slave-trader, to fall in love with a Christian slave (probably Johnson's Irene in disguise) to carry her off to Russia on the eve of enforced marriage to her master, lose her again while being pursued by pirates on the river Volga, and to be reunited with her in the City of London where she happily proved to be the niece of Lien Chi's friend, the Man in Black. But Goldsmith was too much a product of the Age of Reason to be capable of pursuing this vein for very long without breaking into laughter. He keeps up the Chinese identity of his Philosopher half-heartedly, enjoying it when he is able to squeeze some comedy out of comparative notions of beauty in Letter III and letting it go as soon as he is bored. The main virtue of Lien Chi Altangi is that he is an expatriate and the expatriate Goldsmith, no doubt misunderstood and underestimated by many literary Britons long before Boswell came on the scene, obviously enjoys the moments when Society in the full tide of its mania finds the travelling philosopher to be lamentably out of step. On one of these occasions he commits the solecism of describing his hostess's porcelain cups as *useful*:

Useful! sir, replied the lady; sure you mistake, they are of no use in the world. *What! are they not filled with an infusion of tea as in China? replied I.* Quite empty and useless upon my honour, Sir. *Then they are the most cumbrous and clumsy furniture in the world, as nothing is truly elegant but what unites use with beauty.* I protest, says the lady, I shall begin to suspect thee of being an actual barbarian. I suppose also you hold my two beautiful pagods in contempt. *What! cried I, has Fohi spread his gross superstitions here also? Pagods of all kinds are my aversion.* A Chinese, a traveller, and want taste! it surprises me. Pray, sir, examine the beauties of that Chinese temple which you see at the end of the garden. Is there any thing in China more beautiful? *Where I stand I see nothing, madam, at the end of the garden that may not as well be called an Egyptian pyramid as a Chinese temple, for that little building in view is as like the one as t'other.* What! Sir, is not that a Chinese temple? you must surely be mistaken.

Mr Freeze, who designed it, calls it one, and nobody disputes his pretensions to taste . . .[42]

Lien Chi Altangi is a disappointment to society—as Goldsmith was so often to be in the days of his fame when the curious came to see a great man and departed in all the satisfaction of concluding that he was if anything a little more foolish than themselves:

This gentleman's conversation (says one of the ladies, who was a great reader) is like our own, mere chit chat and common sense; there is nothing like sense in the true eastern style, where nothing more is required but sublimity. Oh for a history of Aboulfaouris, the grand voyager, of genii, magicians, rocks, bags of bullets, giants, and enchanters, where all is great, obscure, magnificent, and unintelligible.[43]

The twice-weekly column in Newbery's paper, for which he was to be paid £100 a year,[44] was Goldsmith's big chance. Five days after his introductory letter of January 24th he was beginning to show every sign of confidence. He is describing a man of fashion:

. . . to make the picture more perfectly striking, conceive the tail of some beast, a greyhound's tail, or a pig's tail for instance, appended to the back of the head, and reaching down to that place where tails in other animals are seen to begin; thus betailed and bepowdered, the man of taste fancies he improves in beauty, dresses up his hard-featured face in smiles, and attempt to look hideously tender. Thus equipped, he is qualified to make love, and hopes for success more from the powder on the outside of his head, than the sentiments within.

This is followed by a nostalgic paragraph as Lien Chi dwells lovingly on the beauties he has left behind him:

How very broad their faces; how very short their noses; how very little their eyes; how very thin their lips; how very black their teeth; the snow on the tops of Bao is not fairer than their cheeks; and their eye-brows are as small as the line by the pencil of Quamsi.[45]

Two days later, there is an incisive analysis of the English character ('their gayest conversations have something too wise for innocent relaxation') and an anecdote which, by suggesting that it is a little soon for England to be advertising itself as the land of liberty, makes an effective thrust against cant.[46] One of the shortcomings of the English in Goldsmith's opinion was that they 'seem fonder of gaining the esteem than the love of those they converse with'; and perhaps one of the reasons for the enduring charm of these little essays is that, even when he is discussing the ills of society or recommending a recipe for the good life, he never forgets that he is conversing with an audience which he would rather please than impress. There is a stylistic lightness and flexibility which admits the possibility of surprise: although he admired the *Rambler*, he never attempted to imitate the resounding but predictable rhythm of Johnson's early style. Even if in company he was to measure himself against the intellectual standards that Johnson set, when he had a pen in his hand he knew instinctively that he lacked the massive intellectual stature of the Doctor, and that his own forte was good-natured reflection, enlivened by humour and accurate reportage. Where Johnson might have thundered against the Dean and Chapter of Westminster Abbey for allowing the verger to solicit tips, Goldsmith makes his point simply by introducing us to the verger:

> This armour, said he, belonged to general Monk. *Very surprising, that a general should wear armour*. And pray, added he, observe this cap, this is general Monk's cap. *Very strange, indeed, very strange, that a general should have a cap also! Pray friend what might this cap have cost originally*? That, Sir, says he, I don't know, but this cap is all the wages I have for my trouble. *A very small recompence, truly, said I*. Not so very small, replied he, for every gentleman puts some money into it . . .[47]

In the *Bee*, Goldsmith had composed an imaginary letter from an English traveller who found himself in Cracow in the course of his European wanderings, always in search of a happiness that eluded him, 'still expecting ease every where but where I am'. He writes to a friend: 'It is now seven years since I saw the face of a single creature who cared a farthing whether I was dead or alive. Secluded from all the comforts of confidence, friendship, or society, I feel the solitude of an hermit, but not his ease.'[48] The traveller

in this instance is quite clearly Goldsmith himself, and although
there are no such overt appeals for sympathy in the 'Chinese Letters',
it is the isolation of the unattached expatriate's life which gives
them their special quality: he adopts the stance of the man who is
on the fringe of the life he observes even when he happens to be the
centre of attention, or who is invariably the passive object of a
confidence trick, joke, or accident.

However much dictated by his circumstances, such awareness of
self is none the less egoistical. But here the discipline of two dead-
lines a week effectively counterbalanced a natural tendency. If the
'Chinese Letters' create a strong impression of Goldsmith's
personality and interests, it is because he had no time to be self-
conscious. In these circumstances and amidst such recurring
themes as contemporary culture (especially the world of books), the
social structure of England, the need for reforms, and the practice
of religion, it is interesting that in the 'Chinese Letters' a preoccupation with the need for a change of heart both individual and
national should be felt so strongly.

With his intimate knowledge of the writings of the French
philosophes it was hardly surprising that Goldsmith should take up
the theme of man's quest for happiness. But its particular urgency
for him is unmistakable, and leads in Letter 90 (of December
17th, 1760) to an oblique but moving consideration of the nature of
evil—a theme, which as Voltaire unforgettably illustrated, the
eighteenth century was inclined to handle rather glibly. The essay
was inspired by a book by Joseph Cox, *A Faithful Narrative of the
Most Wicked and Inhuman Transactions of that Bloody-minded
Gang of Thief-takers alias Thief-makers ... Shewing the Diabolical
Arts by Them Practised, to Get Innocent Persons Convicted for
Robberies, and to Share amongst Themselves the Rewards Paid for
Such Convictions.* Cox's exposé produces a feeling of outrage in
Goldsmith. Yet the cruelty and hypocrisy described in it remain
beyond his comprehension: in itself the bitter exclamation 'Yet
these are men!' does not go very far towards assimilating the experience of evil. But his treatment of the subject reveals a lot about the
man and about the reasons for his success as an essayist, while
reminding us of the qualities that Reynolds had described: 'If he
was sometimes foolish out of season, he never was what is worse,
wise out of season'. A Pangloss—or that bête noire of Johnson's,

Soame Jenyns*—might be wise out of season and explain away the imperfections of the universe; but Goldsmith knows when to accept defeat. The Man in Black, Goldsmith's persona here as in other letters, has been discovered playing the flute, rather badly. He explains to Lien Chi Altangi that it is the only way he knows to banish the fit of spleen to which he succumbed on reading about the thief-takers, and the letter which began with a comic review of English types battling with attacks of depression now ends on a note which is also not far removed from comedy:

> This was an instance of such complicated guilt and hypocrisy, that I threw down the book in an agony of rage, and began to think with malice of all the human kind. I sate silent for some minutes, and soon perceiving the ticking of my watch beginning to grow noisy and troublesome, I quickly placed it out of hearing; and strove to resume my serenity. But the watchman soon gave me a second alarm. I had scarcely recovered from this, when my peace was assaulted by the wind at my window; and when that ceased to blow, I listened for death-watches in the wainscot. I now found my whole system discomposed, I strove to find a resource in philosophy and reason; but what could I oppose, or where direct my blow, when I could see no enemy to combat. I saw no misery approaching, nor knew any I had to fear, yet still I was miserable. Morning came, I sought for tranquility in dissipation, sauntered from one place of public resort to another, but found myself disagreeable to my acquaintance, and ridiculous to others. I tried at different times dancing, fencing, and riding, I solved geometrical problems, shaped tobacco-stoppers, wrote verses and cut paper. At last I placed my affections on music, and find, that earnest employment if it cannot cure, at least will palliate every anxiety.[49]

Flute-playing is hardly an answer to the problem raised by Cox's book and Goldsmith knows this; but by describing the ineffectuality of the Man in Black at such a moment he is taking a clear look not only at himself but at the human condition.

Goldsmith's use of the word 'dissipation' is curious, for it is

*In 1756 Johnson made withering observations on Jenyns' facile *Inquiry into the Origin of Evil* in *The Literary Review*.

clearly not intended to suggest the gambling, drinking and whoring which, rather than any milder forms of occupational therapy, it has since come to denote. Nor is it in any sense a pejorative term albeit that he is mocking his own helplessness. The positive need for 'dissipation' had been stressed in previous letters, where it is represented as the only safeguard against on the one hand a nostalgic longing for an idealised past and on the other, daydreams about unrealisable happiness. Dissipation is a means of 'seizing the present' and unhappiness the inevitable result of its neglect. Dissipation may still in one sense denote the idle pursuit of pleasure —'The man of pleasure pursues dissipation by profession'; but, in Goldsmith's usage, 'the man of business pursues it not less, as every voluntary labour he undergoes is only dissipation in disguise. The philosopher himself, even while he reasons upon the subject, does it unknowingly with a view of dissipating the thoughts of what he was, or what he must be'. Goldsmith is too much of a puritan to be able to accept sensual gratification as a guide-line in life, and he rational-ises his feeling by claiming that this path leads inexorably back to the Time-snared path of Past and Future. 'Happiness is con-stitutional,' he decides—not over-optimistically—and 'Philosophy can add to our happiness in no other manner, but by diminishing our misery'; but the *philosophe* has chosen the best path because 'the concerns of others make his whole study, and that study is his pleasure; and this pleasure is continuing in its nature because it can be changed at will, leaving but few of those anxious intervals which are employed in remembrance or anticipation'.[50] The application to Goldsmith the fantasist both in its negative and positive aspects is obvious: as a twice-weekly contributor to Newbery's trade journal he was both *philosophe* and journalist, and here he was congratulating himself, less than a year after the beginning of his career as a creative writer, on having found an answer to the problem which had first been held up for inspection at a family conference nine years before.

*

Johnson's inscription for Goldsmith's memorial tablet in West-minster Abbey speaks of him as a 'Poet, Naturalist, Historian, who left scarcely any kind of writing untouched, and touched nothing

F

that he did not adorn'. Thus one of Goldsmith's most emphatic admirers recorded in all the dignity of its original Latin what he was to repeat several times in private. Boswell, however, was quick to find a double meaning and his contemporaries, as familiar with Goldsmith's literary habits as with Johnson's sterling veracity, must also have asked themselves if the Doctor's phrase hadn't contained more analysis than rhetoric. '. . . touched nothing that he did not adorn' is liable to more than one interpretation when applied to an eighteenth century journalist with a fresh batch of copy to find every third or fourth day. Plagiarism or unacknowledged borrowing, as people in the book trade would have preferred to call it, was a common practice in this period. Goldsmith's essays were frequently reprinted above other names, as he pointed out in the witty preface to the Collected Edition of 1765:

> . . . though they have past pretty silently into the world, I can by no means complain of their circulation. The magazines and papers of the day, have, indeed, been liberal enough in this respect. Most of these essays have been regularly reprinted twice or thrice a year, and conveyed to the public through the kennel* of some engaging compilation. If there be a pride in multiplied editions, I have seen some of my labours sixteen times reprinted, and claimed by different parents as their own. I have seen them flourished at the beginning with praise, and signed at the end with the names of Philautos, Philalethes, Philalutheros, and Philanthropos. These gentlemen have kindly stood sponsors to my productions, and to flatter me more, have always taken my errors on themselves.[51]

His own unacknowledged borrowings, which have been traced in a sizeable proportion, though not necessarily the best, of the 'Chinese Letters', always took the form of translation and intelligent adaptation of French writers, especially the Marquis d'Argens, Montesquieu and Marivaux (whose *Spectateur Francais* of the years 1722 and 1723 had been a conscious attempt to emulate Addison and Steele). If Goldsmith's journalistic practice was typical of his age it was none the less true that he really did adorn the unconsidered trifles that came into his nimble fingers. Comparisons invariably

---

*Before the time of the urban improvements, the kennel was the gutter which ran down the middle of the street.

reveal his flair for imbuing the original with his own personality and wit. In Marivaux's sketch, the *indigent philosophe* describes the difficulties he faced when he decided that the time had come to part company with the army: 'I was very tired of army life; but as I was well built, strong and muscular, my captain was decidedly against my leaving ...'. Goldsmith, however indebted to this French source in *The Adventures of a Strolling Player*, makes the episode dramatic with a single phrase: 'The life of a soldier soon, therefore, gave me the spleen; I asked leave to quit the service; but as I was tall and strong, my captain *thanked me for my kind intention*, and said, because he had a regard for me, we should not part'.[53] In the 'Chinese Letter' of September 15th 1760, he draws on Montesquieu's *Lettres Persanes* to discuss the negative influence on the arts of men with more money than discernment. Montesquieu had described an encounter with such a patron: 'The other day I found myself in a place where I saw a man who was very pleased with himself. In a quarter of an hour, he decided three questions of morality, four historical problems and five matters of scientific fact.' Goldsmith refers the episode to a specific situation and whets the reader's appetite for the conversation to follow with his brisk introduction: 'I was yesterday invited by a gentleman to dinner, who promised that our entertainment should consist of an haunch of venison, a turtle, and a great man. I came, according to appointment. The venison was fine, the turtle good, but the great man insupportable...'.[54] Here the individual tone of the writing with its anticipation of George Bernard Shaw reveals that the task of 'adorning' can in itself be creative.

*

William Cooke in his biographical sketch in the *European Magazine* for 1793 states that Goldsmith left Green Arbour Court for new lodgings in Wine Office Court, Fleet Street, where *The Vicar of Wakefield* was to be written, shortly after his meeting with Newbery. This is probably correct as Goldsmith was the kind of man who would build upon the smallest advantage. Although he would keep an eye on the Butlers until the end of his life he had no intention of sinking with them socially if he could avoid it. In the course of the *Public Ledger* contributions after August 1760 there are several small indications that he is in better circumstances. These include Lien Chi's references to a landlady of a rather different type from Mrs Butler. In August it is her early morning irruption into the writer's bedroom with a story about the dreadful havoc caused by a mad dog which inspires one of the more famous essays—'. . . A mad dog down in the country, she assured me, had bit a farmer, who soon becoming mad ran into his own yard, and bit a fine brindled cow; the cow quickly became as mad as the man, began to foam at the mouth, and raising herself up, walked about on her hind legs, sometimes barking like a dog, and sometimes attempting to talk like the farmer.'[55] However much inspired fiction there may be here it is recognisably the same woman who is mentioned on the 3rd of December when she invades Lien Chi's room again to show him a diary which has been left behind by a previous literary tenant.[56] Two months earlier, Goldsmith had publicly congratulated himself on circumstances which seem very far removed from the shabbiness of Green Arbour. In a 'Chinese Letter' retailing the miseries endured by professional writers in the past he concludes on an optimistic note:

> At present the few poets of England no longer depend on the Great for subsistence, they have now no other patrons but the good public, and the public collectively considered, is a good and generous master. It is indeed, too frequently mistaken as to the merits of every candidate for favour; but to make amends, it is never mistaken long.[57]

The final paragraph consigns the proverbial garret to oblivion: 'The ridicule therefore of living in a garret, might have been wit in the last age, but continues such no longer, because no longer true'. When he finds further cause for self-congratulation in the fact that 'He may now venture to appear in company with just such cloaths as other men generally wear' all doubts as to the personal application of these remarks vanish. As a result of his own considerable efforts over the preceding ten months, Goldsmith had at least by August 1760 gone up in the world and found rooms on a rather different basis from his tenancy in Green Arbour Court. Here in the place of the little girl with the chamber-pot is a landlady with social pretensions who has set out to cultivate the acquaintance of her literary gent. She had had other lodgers who were writers—perhaps this was Goldsmith's introduction to her—and she took a proprietorial interest in her new tenant's work. She herself was to have some impact on it—though not of the kind to inspire any gratitude on the part of posterity.

The contributions to newspapers and journals continued throughout 1761. Predictably, after a whole year of Chinese Letters, there was a slackening off in this quarter. Between March and May there were only three letters per month, in June none, in July one, and in August two including the letter of August 14th which described the reunion of the young lovers and allowed Lien Chi to take formal leave of his public.[58] Essays unconnected with this name continued to appear in the *Public Ledger* until the end of September. Goldsmith had also made contributions to the *Royal Magazine* (published by a business associate of Newbery's), the *British Magazine* which appeared for the first time on Smollett's release from the King's Bench in February, and a journal edited by 'The Honourable Mrs Caroline Stanhope', the *Ladies' Magazine*, for which he wrote essays in September, October and December 1760 and in which the *Life of Voltaire*, usually attributed to him but very probably an adaptation of an untraced French memoir on which Griffiths had set him to work in 1757, was serialised in ten instalments. If Percy was correct in believing that Goldsmith himself was the editor of the *Ladies' Magazine*, then the remuneration granted to 'the Honourable Mrs Caroline Stanhope' was at least partly responsible for the bumptious tone of the letter which had bidden farewell to garrets.

The 'Chinese Letters' helped to launch the *Public Ledger* on its long career, and there are several indications that they also raised Goldsmith's literary credit. Although his column appeared anonymously he was becoming known and beginning to meet some of his more famous contemporaries. In 1760 he encountered Garrick, whose thick eyebrows he had treated with something less than reverence the previous year. The secretaryship of the Society of Arts was about to become vacant and, perhaps seeing this as a solution to problems of status as well as finance, Goldsmith called on Garrick and asked him for his vote in the coming election. To the actor-manager whose feelings had been wounded by the criticisms expressed in the *Enquiry into the Present State of Polite Learning*, the request must have seemed audacious. He replied huffily that as

Goldsmith had 'taken pains to deprive him of his assistance by an unprovoked attack upon his management of the theatre' it was 'impossible he could lay claim to any recommendation from him'. Goldsmith with the instinctive grace of a man in whom sincerity and naivety were often interchangeable, answered that he 'had spoken his mind, and believed what he said was very right, and took his leave'.[59]

Unfortunately, virtually nothing is known about his acquaintance with William Hogarth, although it is to the painter that we are indebted for the single visual record of the submerged, shabby-genteel life of Green Arbour Court, the portrait of 'Goldsmith's Hostess, Mrs Butler'.[60] Hogarth was a disillusioned man and nearly at the end of his life. Disappointed by the comparative absence of interest in his own paintings at a time when only portraitists could hope to survive in a market flooded with often dubious old masters, he was devoting himself again exclusively to engraving. This brought him a comfortable income on top of the £200 per annum which he received as 'Serjeant Painter of all his Majesty's works'. He had recently had the mortifying experience of being commissioned to paint a conversation piece and to find his wealthy 'patron', Sir Richard Grosvenor, swiftly wriggling out of the arrangement when the painting proved not to his taste, Hogarth's fierce pride prompting him to release Grosvenor from his obligations.[61] It is easy to see that the painter and the writer, one near the end of his career and the other at the beginning, had many common interests. Goldsmith did not share the vision which produced the horrific and grotesque elements in Hogarth's work, but he had the same keenness of observation and a desire to celebrate what was happening around him irrespective of preconceived social attitudes. The lower middle class world which is recorded incidentally in the essays of 1760 and 1761 and in *The Vicar of Wakefield* is one which can be encountered again in a different medium in Hogarth's 'Shrimp Girl' or the group-portrait of his servants. With his recent experience of Sir Richard Grosvenor in mind Hogarth would have approved of the stance Goldsmith was adopting towards the undiscriminating patron and would-be dilettante. With the Tory political views that Goldsmith revealed in the 'Chinese Letters' he was completely in sympathy. His entry into the public debate over the signing of the

peace treaty was to involve him in a bitter quarrel with Wilkes—
who as a friend of Smollett as well as the painter may have been
the link between Goldsmith and Hogarth.

A much better documented friendship began on May 31st, 1761,
when Goldsmith invited Samuel Johnson to supper. Their common
friend, the Revd. Thomas Percy, was back in London this summer
and the entries in his diary suggest that it was he who brought the
two men together:

25 May	Dined and Tea with Goldsmith
26 May	Dined with Mr Johnson at Miss Williams' and stayed the evening. (Miss Williams' maid 1s. 0d.)
27 May	Breakfast with Mr Garrick at Rehearsal of Lear
Wed. 3 June	Evening at Goldsmith's
Sat. 6 June	Called on Goldsmith.[62]

On the evening of May 31st Percy called for Johnson and escorted
him to Wine Office Court:

As they went together [Percy] was much struck with the studied
neatness of Johnson's dress: he had on a new suit of clothes,
a new wig nicely powdered, and everything about him so perfectly dissimilar from his usual habits and appearance, that
his companion could not help enquiring the cause of this singular
transformation. "Why sir," said Johnson, "I hear that Goldsmith
who is a very great sloven, justifies his disregard of cleanliness and
decency, by quoting my practice, and I am desirous this night to
show a better example."[63]

The anecdote, of course, conceals another joke—against Johnson.
He had been misinformed about Goldsmith who, even if his suits
were unpaid for or had once clothed someone else could by no means
be described as a sloven. Johnson, too, was in for a surprise.

With or without Percy's help in carrying an invitation and getting
him over the awkwardness of the first encounter, Goldsmith was
showing considerable courage in making the first approach to a man
who while admitted to be a literary lion was frequently described as
a bear, too, by those who had seen him at close quarters. Mrs Thrale
suggests the impression he would have made on someone meeting
him for the first time:

His features were strongly marked, and his countenance particularly rugged; though the original complexion had certainly been fair, a circumstance somewhat unusual: his sight was near, and otherwise imperfect; yet his eyes, though of a light-grey colour, were so wild, so piercing, and at times so fierce, that fear was I believe the first emotion in the hearts of all his beholders.[64]

Boswell, in May 1763, found him 'a man of a most dreadful appearance. He is a very big man, is troubled with sore eyes, the palsy, and the king's evil. He is very slovenly in his dress and speaks with a most uncouth voice . . .'[65] In addition to these disabilities he had a nervous tic which made it impossible for him to cross the room without pausing and then taking a violent jump. This might be only a prelude to terrors to come. Old friends were treated roughly if their remarks showed signs of irrationality. Bennet Langton's mother, playing the hostess and asking Johnson if he didn't agree that her grotto would make 'a pretty cool habitation in summer?' received the appropriately cool answer, 'I think it would, Madam— for a toad',[66] and a stranger happening to make a foolish remark at a dinner party might find himself silenced by some alarmingly candid reflections.

With the support of his complaisant landlady, Goldsmith may have been lion-hunting on the evening of May 31st. But he had sounder motives than this for wanting to do homage to Johnson. For a start they had both written newspaper columns for John Newbery and in many ways Goldsmith would have regarded Johnson as the most prominent exponent of the literary attitudes to which he himself subscribed. Johnson had written the *Life of Pope* and in his essays and in *Rasselas*, that apotheosis of the 'oriental tale' which Dodsley had published in the same month as Goldsmith's book, he had given dignified, robust expression both to the congenital pessimism of the classical age and to its stolid insistence on clarity, tolerance and good sense. In poetry as well as prose he was preoccupied with man in relation to society and, like Goldsmith, was out of sympathy with the writers who were the heralds of cultural change. An innate tendency to fear the effect of solitary musings in a churchyard or of that fit of self-destructive enthusiasm which had seized a Welsh Bard made it as difficult for him as for Goldsmith to evaluate Gray's achievement, and a friend's comments on Sterne had been the occasion of one of the famous snubs:

On Miss Monkton's insisting, one evening, that Sterne's writings were very pathetic, Johnson bluntly denied it. 'I am sure,' she rejoined, 'they have affected me.' 'Why,' said Johnson, smiling and rolling himself about, 'that is because, dearest, you're a dunce.'[67]

Goldsmith, like Johnson, had breathed the atmosphere of the Augustan age, of which Johnson would prove to be the last great figure. Little more than three weeks before this meeting one of the 'Chinese Letters' had rejected the romantic *nature sauvage* philosophy which in 1755 Rousseau had promulgated in the *Discours sur L'Origine de L'Inégalité Parmi les Hommes*: his scepticism expressed itself in the suggestion that an ignorant being was more likely to be a creature of over-bearing pride than an uncorrupt fountain-head of virtue and truth.[68] He had no feeling for Nature in the Wordsworthian sense and would have heartily approved when Johnson asked the poet William Shenstone if there was anything to *eat* in the softly murmuring streams of which he was so fond.[69]

Like Johnson but perhaps for less creditable reasons, Goldsmith failed to appreciate the brilliance of the first two volumes of *Tristram Shandy* which James Dodsley had published in January 1760. Perhaps quite genuinely shocked that a man in holy orders should have produced a work which celebrated a lingering flirtation with the bawdy, he had written a sharp, outspoken attack on 'fashionable Pruriency' in the *Public Ledger* for 30th June, 1760.[30] When he concluded with a reference to an author who 'must speak of himself and his chapters, and his manner, and what he would be at, and his own importance, and his mother's importance with the most unpitying prolixity', he at once identified the object of his attack and revealed his failure to respond to the book's humour. Sterne's brilliant study of alienation had been received rapturously by an audience which was delighted to find that 'sentiment' could also be funny.

There was more than straightforward envy in Goldsmith's attitude. However fine a writer, Laurence Sterne was a poor churchman and it was the church which kept him in comfort, asking for little in return, while he wrote. This must have been extremely offensive to the man whose frequent pleas for sincere communica-

F*

tion from the pulpit sprang from a strain of Christian evangelism[71] and who so much admired the brother whose own work in the church was still receiving a very poor financial reward. But inevitably there was envy too—envy which seriously distorted his critical judgment. The fashionable world of St James's which kept Johnson (and Goldsmith) at arm's length—'Great men do not like to have their mouths stopped', Johnson had replied when asked why this was so[72]—had greeted Yorick with acclaim when he arrived from York to reside for a few weeks in Pall Mall. Joshua Reynolds had been commissioned to take his portrait. In a highly stratified society, Sterne's fashionable London address clearly announced a certain distance between him and the writers of Fleet Street in terms of class as well as material reward.

Although there was no Boswell to record it, the evening at Wine Office Court was clearly a success. Johnson, who rarely initiated either a friendship or a conversation, loved company and particularly appreciated a captive audience. The friendship that ensued lasted until Goldsmith died and the occasions on which the two writers indulged in verbal fencing-matches would provide Boswell with some of his liveliest material. At a deeper level than the cultural, Goldsmith would have been drawn to a man who was known to have accepted the moral imperatives of Christianity as personally binding. Where Goldsmith had given away his blankets or found a hard luck story irresistible Johnson had filled his house in Gough Square with a group of quarrelling dependents and—when lack of money forced him to move in 1759 to lodgings at Gray's Inn, and shortly afterwards at 1 Inner Temple Lane—to make sure that they were suitably rehoused. Like Goldsmith, he had seen destitution and deformity in the streets of London and felt them—in Goldsmith's phrase—'shooting icicles to his heart',[73] and he never allowed people to speak lightly about poverty or to mock the makeshift contrivances of shabby gentility in his presence. When Mrs Thrale made a sarcastic reference to 'Porridge Island' (a street behind St Martin's in the Fields where there were many cook-shops) she was reminded: 'Hundreds of your fellow-creatures, dear Lady, turn another way, that they may not be tempted by the luxuries of Porridge Island to wish for gratifications they are not able to obtain.'[74] He would have been the last to condemn Goldsmith's rather haphazard benefactions. It made no difference if the money was spent on gin and tobacco: 'Why should they be denied such sweeteners of their existence? It is surely savage to refuse them every possible avenue to pleasure, reckoned too coarse for our own acceptance.'[75]

Goldsmith had thought carefully about his own religious beliefs. Although he lacked both the intellectual and moral stature of Johnson, and although a streak of narrowness showed itself whenever he passed on the prevailing mid-century opinions on Roman Catholics or dangerously 'enthusiastic' Methodists, Christianity had a central place in his philosophy of life. When mentioned in this context the 'dissipation' which was to release him from the treadmill of time has an affinity to the contemplative's abandonment to the present moment and owes something to the gospel directive to 'lose one's life to save it.' Goldsmith knew enough about Johnson before he issued his invitation to feel that here was the moral force he had failed to discover as he did the rounds of London's churches. He needed to attach himself to such a man.

Johnson was fifty-two when he met Goldsmith and, in Boswell's account, at one of those low-ebb moments in his life like the one which preceded the breakdown of 1766. The burst of energy which had produced *Rasselas* in a week shortly after his mother's death in January, 1759, had been followed by a long period of lethargy and despondency in which he produced nothing except an introduction to one of Newbery's publications, Rolt's *Dictionary of Trade and Commerce*. Work on the projected edition of Shakespeare appeared to be at a standstill and the money brought in by the subscriptions had been spent. The *Dictionary* had not enriched him, most of the 'profit' having been swallowed up in the cost of producing it. Boswell admits that in 1761 Johnson 'certainly was . . . not active'; and that by Easter he had fallen into one of his dangerously introspective states of mind: 'for, in his scrupulous examination of himself on Easter eve, he laments, in his too vigorous mode of censuring his own conduct, that his life, since the communion of the preceding Easter, had been "dissipated and useless" '.[76] (Clearly Johnson was not using the word in Goldsmith's positive sense.) There are many signs of despondency in the letter which he wrote to Joseph Baretti in Milan ten days after his visit to Wine Office Court. Whether or not Goldsmith had discussed his philosophy of 'dissipation' that Sunday evening, Johnson is referring to something very like it when he writes 'Surely life, if it be not long, is tedious, since we are forced to call in the assistance of so many trifles to rid us of our time, of that time which never can return.'[77]

Percy may have been concerned about Johnson's mood and may even have felt that he was doing Johnson rather than Goldsmith a service by bringing them together for, if Johnson placed Truth first in his order of priorities, Humour was not far behind. As Mrs Thrale recalled: 'He used to say, "that the size of a man's understanding might always be justly measured by his mirth"; and his own was never contemptible. He would laugh at a stroke of genuine humour, or sudden sally or odd absurdity, as heartily and freely as I ever yet saw any man; and though the jest was often such as few felt besides himself, yet his laugh was irresistible, and was observed immediately to produce that of the company, not merely from the notion that it was proper to laugh when he did, but purely out of want of power to forbear it'.[78] Although Mrs Thrale was to have strong reservations about Goldsmith she would have no difficulty in accounting for the success of the supper party of May 31st, 1761 in his lodgings at Wine Office Court.

SEVEN

Goose-Pie and Gooseberries

SIX WEEKS before his supper-party for Johnson, Goldsmith had been a detached and faintly contemptuous observer of a nine days' wonder that attracted considerable attention in the press. A clever and dissolute young curate of St John's, Westminster, who had been drawn into financial difficulties by philandering and a taste for gold braid and ruffles, capitalised on his love of the theatre by publishing a poem in the manner of Pope which, as a prelude to a eulogy of David Garrick, analysed the professional shortcomings of leading actors and actresses. To the subsequent embarrassment of Smollett, who had had a play successfully produced by Garrick and wanted to remain on good terms with him, the *Critical* reviewer was hard on the poem:

> The whole drift of the performance seems to be plainly and indisputably this: first to throw all the players, like so many faggots, into a pile, and set fire to them by way of sacrifice to the modern Roscius; and secondly, to do the same by all the wits and poets of the age, in compliment to Messrs Lloyd and Colman, the heroes of the piece.[1]

Guessing that the poem had been written by one of 'the new triumvirate of wits, who never let an opportunity slip of singing their own praises' (i.e. Colman, Charles Churchill—the actual author of *The Rosciad*—and their former companion at Westminster School, Robert Lloyd) he came to the conclusion that the poem was Lloyd's. This sparked off a discussion in which Churchill and Lloyd eagerly participated and in April a second edition of the poem appeared with the real author's name.

Despite Churchill's keenness of observation and witty handling of the Augustan couplet, it is difficult to repress memories of the Aungier Street *fracas* when Goldsmith was a student of Trinity College Dublin: like Mr Kelly from Galway, Churchill had assumed that actors, since they could never be gentlemen, were anyone's fair game.

Although Goldsmith's disparagement of a successful fellow-writer might seem suspect, the unusually heavy irony of the 'Chinese Letter' of April 14th conveys a genuine feeling of impatience that the literary tradition to which the satires of Dryden and Pope belonged should now be represented by a work as fundamentally devoid of ideas as *The Rosciad*:

> An important literary debate at present engrosses the attention of the town. It is carried on with sharpness, and a proper share of . . . epigrammatical fury. An author, it seems has taken an aversion to the faces of several players; and has written verses to prove his dislike; the players fall upon the author and assure the town he must be dull, and their faces must be good, because he wants a dinner; a critic comes to the poet's assistance, asserting, that the verses were perfectly original, and so smart that he could never have written them without the assistance of friends; the friends upon this arraign the critic, and plainly prove the verses to be all the author's own. So at it they are all four together by the ears, the friends at the critic, the critic at the players, the players at the author, and the author at the players again. It is impossible to determine how this many sided contest will end, or which party to adhere to. The town, without siding with any, views the combat in suspense, like the fabled hero of antiquity, who beheld the earth-born brothers give and receive mutual wounds, and fall by indiscriminate destruction.[2]

An anecdote of Cooke's suggests that Robert Lloyd had introduced himself to Goldsmith at the Chapter Coffee House and tricked him into settling his outstanding account with the manager. If this is so, the young ex-schoolmaster could hardly have objected to the mild reference to himself in this same letter—though he would respond by giving a bad review to one of Goldsmith's publications in the magazine he edited. Churchill, whose sales had benefitted from the 'debate' of 1761, was soon to become involved through a fellow-member of the Hell-Fire Club in the early stages of a far more venomous dispute which would continue to engross the nation long after his and Lloyd's deaths in 1764. Again, he and Goldsmith would be on different sides.

On Quebec Night in 1759, Goldsmith had given expression to a growing popular desire for an end to the war which had begun in 1756. This war still dragged on in spite of intermittent peace talks with the French. It had begun with European reverses for Britain and under the direction of a great war minister, the elder Pitt, had led to spectacular successes in India, Canada and the West Indies. It was also fiercely expensive. In 1761 the national budget was £19½ million as opposed to the 1755 figure of £4 million. Goldsmith, who could see only danger in colonial aggrandisement, would have been gratified to learn at the beginning of the year that peace talks had been resumed at Augsburg. Two years earlier he had written: 'a peace bought too dear can never last long, it is the part therefore of a victorious people to give up something of its advantages, and to soften their enemies' dishonour with such terms as may keep them content with their situation'; and in the same essay he repeated his warnings against expansionism:

To enlarge our territories, therefore in America, should not be the aim of our ministry, but to secure those we are already in possession of: Aye, but perhaps an opponent will say, if we people those countries, we shall have more tobacco, more hemp, and we shall be able to procure prodigious quantities of raw silk! Away then with thousands of our best and most useful inhabitants, that we may be furnished with tobacco and raw silk; send our honest tradesmen and brave soldiers to people those desolate regions, that our merchants may furnish Europe with tobacco and raw silk. Though I have seen such sordid opinions broached from the press, yet I hope our present glorious ministry will not comply with the mercenary or the vulgar in this repect; we are a commercial nation, it is true, but that is our smallest glory; we have excelled in arts and arms, Europe owns our superiority; let us not then sacrifice every consideration to commerce alone, and while we have of late carried on such a glorious war, let us not conclude a peace dictated by avarice or mistaken policy.[3]

By September this convinced European knew that hopes of a peace treaty had collapsed. Pitt suspected France of negotiating secretly with Spain, a country not overtly involved in the war. The talks were discontinued, but the general scepticism at home which greeted Pitt's subsequently justified suspicions led to his resignation the following month. It was the first hiatus in the ministerial game of musical chairs which was to be played with vigour during the early years of the new reign.

George III had succeeded to the throne as a youthful idealist of twenty-two in October 1760, hating everything associated with his grandfather, George II, and fastening his hopes for a less corrupt future on his adviser and friend, Lord Bute. An honest but shy and rigid man of forty-seven, Bute had neither the taste for, nor the experience of politics which would have allowed him successfully to fill the rôle in which the King, with a rather pathetic faith in his ability to cleanse a political Augean stable, had cast him. The resignation of Pitt in October '61 and of Newcastle in May '62 were a result of mutual suspicions, a fear of being held politically responsible for a peace treaty whose terms might prove to be unpopular, genuine divergences of opinion about Britain's European policy, and personal vanity which produced the kind of manoevrings which were perhaps more familiar in the setting of the opera house in the Haymarket.

By May '62 Bute found himself installed as First Lord of the Treasury and first minister, with little hope of winning the co-operation of the two men who were still considered to be politically indispensable. From the outset, the new Ministry was under attack. Pitt, alternately statesman and demagogue, could be sure of arousing feeling against Bute amongst his mercantile friends, and his brother-in-law, Lord Temple, set up an anti-government journal, the *Monitor*, which he entrusted to the editorship of John Wilkes. Bute armed himself in turn with the *True Briton*, choosing a fellow Scot, Tobias Smollett, as editor.

In spite of all the noise directed against the new ministry it was plain by the end of the year that it commanded a fair amount of support up and down the country. Preliminary negotiations with France were concluded in October, and in December, in spite of the opposition of Pitt and the Newcastle faction, the House of Commons gave massive support to the Peace.

At a time when there was a possibility of financial gain from writing in support of the Ministry, Goldsmith remained detached from the pamphleteering and the private squabbles that were beginning to develop—just as he had stood back from the more obvious absurdities of the *Rosciad* 'debate' the year before. But

Bute's appointment as Minister—and more especially his securing of a pension for Johnson this July—had already left its mark on his mind. Once again he surrendered to those daydreams of exotic places which were always threatening to bring his normal mental processes to a standstill. Encouraged by the rise to power of a man who had the literary interests appropriate to a son-in-law of Lady Mary Wortley Montagu, Goldsmith managed to persuade himself that in the First Lord of the Treasury he had at last found an honourable and impartial patron. His researches for the 'Chinese Letters', however meagre, had made him curious about 'the most eastern parts of Asia' and his reading of the *Encyclopédie*, together with his own commonsense and open-mindedness, convinced him that Europe had much to learn. 'The only difficulty,' as he had already declared in the 'Chinese Letter' of February 27th, 1761, 'would remain in choosing a proper person, for so arduous an enterprise. He should be a man of a philosophical turn, one apt to deduce consequences of general utility from particular occurrences, neither swollen with pride, nor hardened by prejudice, neither wedded to one particular system, nor instructed only in one particular science; neither wholly a botanist, nor quite an antiquarian; his mind should be tinctured with miscellaneous knowledge, and his manners humanized by an intercourse with men. He should be in some measure, an enthusiast to the design; fond of travelling from a rapid imagination, and an innate love of change, furnished with a body capable of sustaining every fatigue, and an heart not easily terrified at danger.'[4] Satisfied that he had found these qualities in himself, Goldsmith sent a memorial to Bute offering his own services in the capacity of philosophical traveller in return for a government grant.[5] This initiative was not quite as quixotic as might appear, for the spirit of Enquiry was already hovering over Buckingham House where the young King was an enthusiastic amateur scientist. Fortunately, Goldsmith's request to be exiled to the Far East was either overlooked or refused, and he remained in England to see those business associates and friends of his who actively supported Bute and the Peace of Paris becoming increasingly embroiled in the pamphlet campagin which Wilkes was now conducting with the help of Churchill. Still encouraged by Lord Temple, Wilkes had set up the *North Briton* in opposition to Smollett's *True Briton*. In the autumn of '62 their aim was to discredit the provisional treaty by first discrediting Bute (and such friends of the government as William Hogarth who had published an allegorical engraving in favour of the peace and against the fire-raising activities of Pitt in the City)*.[6] The climax of the anti-Bute campaign was reached in April the following year. The signing of the Peace the previous month had not produced the economic miracle that had been popularly expected and, after the imposition of the excise tax on cider, London was gripped by rioting. The pamphleteers fanned the flames—which died down as suddenly as the original combusion; but Bute resigned, having altogether lost his taste for politics. Subsequently the illegal arrest of Wilkes initiated that chain of events which acted as a curtain-raiser to the Wilkes and Liberty campaign at the end of the decade.

Goldsmith's attitude to these events was to be made clear later. But while other expatriate Irish journalists like Hugh Kelly and Paul Hiffernan had profited by writing for the opposition, he seemed in this year to have deliberately let slip the chance to add to his income by entering the battle on the other side under the command of Smollett. His political views were none the less strong and consistent. He was a committed monarchist in the sense that he wanted to see the power of the state, under the safeguards of the law, concentrated in the hands of an hereditary ruler rather than dispersed amongst groups of wealthy landowners—which George III had some cause to regard as troublesome 'factions'. In Goldsmith's political philosophy, the monarch was the protector of individual liberties against those whose wealth and freedom of action was a constant threat to the freedom of others. In a century when a rich grocer could set himself up to trade in justice as one of the notorious Middlesex magistrates, or a land-owning Justice of the Peace become a law unto himself, there was a lot to be said for Goldsmith's attitude, however much it may have been bound up with his need for a hero or a father-figure. 'The constitution of England is at present possessed of the strength of its native oak, and the flexibility of the bending tamarisk,' he had written in one of the 'Chinese Letters' in the last months of the reign of George II (that monarch who had professed such a hatred of 'bainting and boetry'); 'but should the people at any time with a mistaken zeal, pant after an imaginary freedom, and fancy that abridging monarchy was

*See Plate 5.

encreasing their privileges, they would be very much mistaken, since every jewel plucked from the crown of majesty would only be made use of as a bribe to corruption; it might enrich the few who shared it among them, but would in fact impoverish the public.'[7]

Although he had remained aloof from the pamphlet war, he later expressed the view that it was the duty of honest men to 'assist the weaker side of our constitution, that sacred power that has for some years been every day declining and losing its due share of influence in the state'.[8] And although, as the 'Chinese Letters' illustrate, he was under no illusions as to the serious limits of 'liberty' in England, both legal and economic, at the height of the first round of the Wilkes controversy, in June, '62, he re-minded the readers of *Lloyd's Evening Post* that it was often in the much-vaunted refuges of civil liberties that the reality was most elusive:

> Wherever we turn we shall find those governments that have pursued foreign commerce with too much assiduity at length becoming Aristocratical; and the immense property, thus necessarily acquired by some, has swallowed up the liberties of all. Venice, Genoa, and Holland, are little better at present than retreats for tyrants and prisons for slaves. The Great, indeed, boast of their liberties there, and they have liberty. The poor boast of liberty too; but alas, they groan under the most rigorous oppression.[9]

There were good reasons, apart from a desire to keep well clear of a scurrilous political squabble, for Goldsmith's apparent reluct-ance to contribute to the polemics of 1762; it was another very busy time in his literary career. In January and February he was con-tributing to *Lloyd's Evening Post*, a newspaper in which Newbery had a part share. In the first half of the year he translated four and a half volumes of Plutarch's *Lives* and in October his biography of Richard Nash, the 'King of Bath', was published. Both these works were for Newbery, and the latter sprang out of a visit to Bath in the early summer after an illness which had confined him to his room for three weeks. (Perhaps he had recalled the reviews on the subject of spas which Sir Tanfield Leman had contributed to the *Monthly* during the summer of '57) By October he had also sold a novel for £60 to Newbery and two of his business associates. This was *The Vicar of Wakefield.**

*

Evidently working under some pressure in July 1760 Goldsmith had dashed down a little story to provide some background for the 'Beautiful Captive' with whom Lien Chi's son was now on his way to Moscow.[10] The more serious purpose, of course, was to fill another column in Newbery's *Public Ledger*; and the following week when Smollett in turn demanded his copy for the *British Magazine*, Goldsmith produced a variant of the same story which was now set rather vaguely in the north of England and called *The History of Miss Stanton*.[11] The common features of both tales were a father and daughter whose happy privacy was invaded by a rake, who would eventually fight a duel with the father after paying unscrupulous attention to the girl. The first version had ended with the Beautiful Captive's father dying on the duelling ground in the arms of a daughter whom he quite wrongly believed to have 'forgotten her own honour and stained his'. A dramatic tableau concluded the scene: 'I called out upon the dead body that lay stretched before me, and in the agony of my heart asked why he could have left me thus? Why, my dear, my only Pappa, why could you ruin me thus, and yourself for ever! O pity, and return, since there is none but you to comfort me.' In the second version Goldsmith acted on the hint conveyed in the Beautiful Captive's lament. The Revd. Mr Stanton merely feigns death and, when Mr Dawson (this time a completely successful seducer) evinces signs of re-

*No really satisfactory explanation has been offered for Goldsmith's apparently arbitrary choice of Wakefield in his title, though it inevitably gave rise to a tradition that he had visited Yorkshire. He need not have travelled far from Fleet Street, however, to be put in mind of that town. At King's Cross, close to the junction of the Gray's Inn Road with the 'New Road' to Islington (i.e. the Euston and Pentonville roads) stands a public house. The Pindar of Wakefield. It was once a landmark: Bagnigge House, a well known tea-garden in the mid-eighteenth century, advertised itself as being 'near the Pindar a Wakefield' and after 1762 Goldsmith must have passed near it frequently on his way to and from Islington. He may have felt some enthusiasm for the Pindar himself. 'George-a-Green, Pound Keeper' was a folk hero of the Plantagenet period who on one occasion defied a tax-collector on behalf of the town.

pentance, he sits up again and clinches a bargain on his daughter's behalf:

> Though Mr Dawson was before untouched with the infamy he had brought upon virtuous innocence, yet he had not an heart of stone; and bursting into anguish, flew to the lovely mourner, and offered that moment to repair his foul offences by matrimony. The old man, who had only pretended to be dead, now rising up, claimed the performance of his promise; and the other had too much honour to refuse. They were immediately conducted to church, where they were married, and now live exemplary instances of conjugal love and felicity.[12]

For all the absurdity of *The History of Miss Stanton* it is impossible to ignore the links between it and Goldsmith's novel. The hospitable Mr Stanton is recognisably Dr Primrose, the impressionable Fanny, Olivia, and Mr Dawson, Squire Thornhill. Like the philandering squire of the Stanton Tale, the *deus ex machina* of the novel, the Squire's uncle, Sir William Thornhill, is in disguise for most of the story; there is a feigned death (Olivia rather than her father); and the squire only avoids fighting a duel with George, the Vicar's son, by having him arrested. Like *The History of Miss Stanton*, *The Vicar of Wakefield* has a happy ending, as the 'bogus' marriage which the squire has arranged proves to be valid after all—though for Olivia there is much less emphasis on that unlikely 'conjugal love and felicity' which Miss Stanton is promised.

Goldsmith's ability to write fiction had already been demonstrated, not by the absurd *History of Miss Stanton* or the oriental wanderings of Hingpo but in the scenes from lower middle class life which had occasionally appeared in the 'Chinese Letters'. The man who had once kept his sister enthralled with the story of Fiddleback had found in the course of his journalism that he had the knack of inventing farcical situations, life-like dialogue and recognisable types. Predictably, he drew heavily on the Green Arbour world which he had recently left behind. Two of his best known creations, Beau Tibbs and his wife, desperately trying to keep up appearances in their skimped and tarnished finery, belong to this setting. In the Chinese traveller's account of the humiliation endured by the Beau as he tries to cut a figure in the Mall, there is an anticipation of George Grossmith, but without the latent cruelty which is always present in *The Diary of a Nobody*:

> When we were got to the end of our procession, *blast me*, cries he, with an air of vivacity, *I never saw the park so thin in my life before; there's no company at all to day. Not a single face to be seen.* No company, interrupted I peevishly; no company where there is such a crowd; why man, there's too much. What are the thousands that have been laughing at us but company! *Lord, my dear,* returned he, with the utmost good humour, *you seem immensely chagrined; but, blast me, when the world laughs at me, I laugh at the world, and so we are even.*[13]

Goldsmith, who was perfectly familiar with the disadvantages of secondhand clothes, clearly admires the Beau's courage. For a moment there is an anticipation of the very tone of *The Vicar of Wakefield* when Lien Chi, this time only partly aware of the Beau's sufferings, describes the problem of finding a good box at Vauxhall:

> Mr and Mrs Tibbs would sit in none but a genteel box, a box where they might see and be seen, one, as they expressed it, in the very focus of public view; but such a box was not easy to be obtained, for tho' we were perfectly convinced of our own gentility, and the gentility of our appearance, yet we found it a difficult matter to persuade the keepers of the boxes to be of our opinion; they chose to reserve genteel boxes for what they judged more genteel company.[14]

Although he used the fictional element sparingly in the 'Chinese Letters', Goldsmith seemed to acknowledge its importance (and no doubt its popularity) when he came to wind up the series on August 14th 1761. Hingpo and the Beautiful Captive received rather perfunctory treatment but a prominent place was given to the disintegrating relationship between the Man in Black and the pawnbroker's widow who had made her first over-dressed appearance in the Vauxhall episode. This picture of 'antiquated passion' (the Man in Black 'helped her plate, chimed her glass, and jogging her knees and her elbow . . . whispered something arch in her ear, on which, she patted his cheek . . .') quickly gives place to an irreversible quarrel over the correct way to carve a turkey.[15]

The bulk of the 'Chinese Letters' appeared in the *Public Ledger* in 1760. Out of a total of 116, only twenty were published between January and August 1761. Apart from these, the handful of essays in the *Public Ledger* outside the Chinese sequence and the *Life of Voltaire* (which had been advertised by Ralph Griffiths as long ago as 1759 and must have existed in manuscript before 1761), there is no other record of literary activity for this year. As 1762 was to be as productive as 1760 in spite of delays caused by illness and convalescence, 1761 suggests itself as the year in which Goldsmith began to develop the embryo which had been conceived the previous summer. As there was something to show Newbery by the autumn of the next year, it is probable that he made a good start on it during this relatively slack period. Contemporaries like Thomas Percy and William Cooke were satisfied that Goldsmith's novel was written in Wine Office Court.

The reasons for embarking on a novel were probably in the first place monetary. Even if the firm of Dodsley hadn't been involved in its publication, the great success of *Tristram Shandy* would have been observed the previous year by Goldsmith as by the rest of literary London. He had taken note, and now began writing his own novel in the belief that it would 'make his fortune'.[16] His later experiences in the writing of plays suggests that the finding of a plot may have been the most difficult part of the enterprise. For all his tall stories, he was not inventive when it came to setting down the outline of a story on paper. Nor would he have taken much comfort from the slowly evolving joke of Sterne's book, that considerations of plot could be deferred again and again to some imagined moment in the always receding future. It was only Sterne's commercial success that Goldsmith wished to emulate. The choice of the Miss Stanton tale with its vague social setting, its stage villain and its theatrical climax may reflect both an absence of the architectonic gift from Goldsmith's creative faculty and an over-cynical assessment of the kind of story the mid-century reader would enjoy—a cynicism suggested by his letter to Henry two years before when novels were spoken of in the same breath as those romances which 'paint beauty in colours more charming than nature, and describe happiness that man never tastes'.[17] Nothing in these unpromising circumstances gave any hint of the imaginative energy that would be unleashed as soon as he began to write.

It was nearly ten years since Goldsmith had left Ireland—a long enough period to create a sense of perspective and lend the charm of distance if not to salve the wounds to which his hyper-sensitive nature laid him open. Some of those wounds had been exposed, in passing, in the autobiographical 'Man in Black' sections of the 'Chinese Letters' and, underlying even the breezy portrait of Charles Goldsmith, there had been a strand of irony. Now the 'Miss Stanton' framework gave him the opportunity to explore the Lissoy experience at a depth well below the level of that irony, and to regain access to the joys and comedy and pathos of the family situation as well as the darker side that he could never bring himself to forget. Above all it brought him a creative understanding of his father. Charles Goldsmith was approached no longer analytically but from within, and as his son embarked on the task of learning what it was like to look at the world through his father's eyes, he discovered beneath the curious mixture of naivety and extravert humour, which he had already portrayed, those qualities of tolerance, gentleness and quiet strength which had probably made him the focal point of harmony within the family.

The biographer who refused to read the family life of the Gold-smiths into the account of the Primrose family would have to be made of stern stuff. Like the Goldsmith family, the Primroses fall into two age groups with a detached child in the middle— George, Olivia and Sophia are grown up when the two little boys are still small enough to be treated to gingerbread and held by the hand, and Moses is a precocious twelve or thirteen; and like the Goldsmith family after the death of Charles, the Primroses undergo a rapid change of fortune, finding refuge in a cottage. When the Vicar claims, amongst a string of other virtues enumerated in the first chapter, that his children are *credulous*, the reader should be in no doubt at all that he is in Lissoy rather than the north of England. The first seventeen chapters of the novel, full of picturesque detail, provide an often very funny sketch of family life. The outstanding character is the Vicar himself. Using him as the narrative voice, Goldsmith creates a well-rounded portrait of a man who is com-pletely lifelike in his apparent self-contradictions: shrewd on many issues, startlingly naive on others; sincerely religious and yet worldly and cautious when his younger daughter seems to be becoming too fond of a penniless stranger; a figure of authority who rallies his

family round him in adversity, organises a gruelling routine for
them all on the little farm to which they retreat when they lose their
money—and is utterly disregarded on the vital issue of whether or
not Olivia should be allowed to receive attentions from the notorious
Squire Thornhill.

In these chapters it is never quite clear which way the Vicar is
going to jump. His description of his wife in the first paragraph
keeps the reader guessing from the start. How aware is he of the
number of qualifications he has added to the list of virtues?

> To do her justice, she was a good-natured woman; and as for
> breeding, there were few country ladies who could shew more.
> She could read any English book without much spelling, but for
> pickling, preserving, and cookery, none could excel her. She
> prided herself also upon being an excellent contriver in house-
> keeping; tho' I could never find that we grew richer with all her
> contrivances. However . . .[18]

If there is some quiet irony in this, it would be churlish to read anything more than a glorious demonstration of simplicity into the
account of the epitaph which he has already composed in rather
premature memory of Deborah:

> I wrote a similar epitaph for my wife, though still living, in
> which I extolled her prudence, economy, and obedience till
> death; and having got it copied fair, with an elegant frame, it was
> placed over the chimney-piece, where it answered several very
> useful purposes. It admonished my wife of her duty to me, and my
> fidelity to her; it inspired her with a passion for fame, and
> constantly put her in mind of her end;

and when a few paragraphs later he is found presenting his tracts on
the evils of the re-marriage of clergymen to his son's prospective
father-in-law, a septuagenarian divine who (unknown to Primrose)
is courting a fourth wife, the picture of his splendid unworldliness is
complete. But authority and occasionally breath-taking candour are
not far away. Giving advice to his eldest son, George, who sets out
for London in the hope of redeeming the family fortunes, he
acquires the dignity of the scriptures he quotes; and observing the
behaviour of his beloved Livy with Squire Thornhill he tells us that

she 'acted the coquet to perfection, if that might be called acting which was her real character . . .'

The atmosphere of these chapters is distinctive but hard to define. Even though it would be mistaken to talk in terms of ambivalence, the Vicar's idiosyncratic brand of narrative 'pluralism' makes it difficult to read this part of the book as a straightforward plea for cheerful frugality and goodwill; and yet it is impossible to believe that readers who have seen it as an idyll of family life are completely wrong. If the Vicar recognises that Livy is a little coquette, he also sets out on foot in an attempt to rescue her when she elopes with Thornhill and greets her with rapturous forgiveness before she has had time to offer a word of explanation. He has foreseen the end to which the concoction of face-washes in the cottage kitchen is leading, and has even surreptitiously upset them over the floor with a twitch of his foot, but there is no hint of moralising after the event. *The Vicar of Wakefield* could be seen as a novel of acceptance: its personages accept each other as they are and accept the acts of fate that overtake them. Uncomplainingly they adapt themselves to new conditions, whether in the cottage which they enliven with cheerful co-operation, story-telling and ballads, or the prison where the Vicar, far from sinking into despair, sets to work to improve the conditions of men whose situation he immediately recognises as worse than his own. If it has a message it is probably that family life is made possible by a combination of tolerance and (merciful) short-sightedness.

Primrose's wife, Deborah, amply illustrates this theme. The novel begins with the Vicar's assertion that he has chosen her 'as she did her wedding gown, not for a fine glossy surface, but such qualities as would wear well', and ends with a scene of family celebration in which he affectionately records that her only disappointment, a result of George's seating arrangements at the wedding-breakfast, has been not 'to have had the pleasure of sitting at the head of the table and carving all the meat for all the company'. In view of the list of near-disasters that can by this time be laid at her door, it might be asked privately if she has really earned herself such a place. Having discovered that their new landlord is 'particularly remarkable for his attachment to the fair sex' and that there was 'scarce a farmer's daughter within ten miles round but what had found him successful and faithless', Deborah

brightens up considerably; and at the conclusion of his first visit to
their cottage, on which he has devoted much of his attention to
Olivia, she at once congratulates herself: 'I'll fairly own, that it was
I that instructed my girls to encourage our landlord's addresses. I
had always some ambition, and you now see that I was right; for
who knows how this may end?' ('Ay, who knows that indeed,'
answers the Vicar 'with a groan'.) Deborah gradually proves
herself to be a vulgarian of the first order. Her best gown is made of
'crimson paduasoy', she is a connoisseur of spiced ale, and she is
easily deceived when the Squire's women masquerade as Lady
Blarney and Miss Carolina Wilhelmina Amelia Skeggs. At moments
of crisis she can be relied upon to let the family down. When Moses
returns from market having been persuaded to exchange the colt
for a gross of green spectacles, and when the penitent Olivia is
brought home by the Vicar, they both receive a hostile reception.
Livy is greeted with cold sarcasm: ' "Ah, madam," cried her mother,
"this is but a poor place you are come to after so much finery. My
daughter Sophy and I can afford but little entertainment to persons
who have kept company only with people of distinction" '. Nor
are the lives of her children completely safe in her hands: when the
cottage bursts rather inartistically into flames just as the Vicar
approaches it at the end of his travels, Deborah rushes out in
horror, but it is Primrose who remembers that their two little boys
must still be inside; and at the end of the book George narrowly
escapes a capital sentence after Deborah has urged him to challenge
Thornhill to a duel. But to list such shortcomings is in a way to
distort the effect of the book. Thanks to the narrative form Goldsmith has adopted it is the character of Primrose himself which
dictates what the story's atmosphere will be, and his failure to
analyse Deborah's deficiencies gives the novel its patina of serenity
and tolerance.

It is difficult to resist the idea that Goldsmith's imagination took
him by surprise in the course of the year 1761. The *Beautiful
Captive/Miss Stanton* tale, which might have been expected to
produce at best a novelette, unlocked his imaginative faculties and
gave him the opportunity to create at least two fully realised
characters, a convincing family situation, and a wealth of amusing
detail from the songs to be heard by the kitchen fire (like the
Goldsmiths at Lissoy, the Primroses enjoyed the ballad of *Johnny*

Armstrong's Last Goodnight) to the problems created in the attempt
to get three ladies to church in style on two decrepit farm-horses and
one saddle. But the faculty which had produced the embryo,
perhaps to assuage an impatient printer, and that which had now
released a quite disproportionate amount of creative activity were
too far removed from one another not to create a problem for the
writer who had to tether this creativity to the exigences of a trite
plot. If Goldsmith had begun his novel with the vague idea that it
would culminate in the dramatic scene sketched out in *The History
of Miss Stanton*, he must have begun to have grave doubts as to the
wisdom of this plan long before he reached the point at which
Olivia absconded with her Squire. The store of memory to which
the work of embodying the Miss Stanton story gave him access
contained many surprising insights but no grand theatrical effects.
In the character of the father, in the sense of comedy produced by
the genial atmosphere of life in the cottage, and in the ironies of
the first-person narrative, 'Miss Stanton' had been left far behind.
It seems probable that the first seventeen chapters leading up to the
crisis of Livy's disappearance were written with comparatively
little thought as to the atmosphere which the betrayals at the heart
of the story would produce; and it must soon have become evident,
once the character of the Vicar had taken control of the author and
of the book, that the dénouement of the original tale was now out
of the question. This convincingly Christian gentleman, unlike
Mr Stanton, could never take the law into his own hands and
challenge the wicked squire to a duel.

*

In the January and February of 1762 a series of essays contributed
to *Lloyd's Evening Post* reveal that Goldsmith was in a depressed
frame of mind. They appeared under the heading *The Indigent
Philosopher*, a title which he had borrowed from Marivaux. Three
of the five express in varying ways a good deal of disillusionment
with the business of writing—particularly of writing for journals
and newspapers. The first is the most personal in tone, suggesting
wearily a sense of isolation, of talking into a vacuum, and of trying to
proceed in the opposite direction from everyone else. 'How cold a
reception must every effort receive,' he complains, 'that comes . . .

endeavouring to regulate the passions, in a place where almost every paragraph tends to excite them'. He may be thinking of the twenty-three year old Hugh Kelly who had come to London from Dublin in 1760 and was now writing political pamphlets for Pottinger when he reflects: 'It is not every Gentleman who can forego, like me, the common and vendible topicks of government abuse, on which I could descant with elegance, in order to select general follies, on which topick it is probable I may be generally disregarded.' The rider seems to convey a sudden gush of despondency which is felt again in the bitter concluding paragraph:

> For all this, as I said in the beginning, I expect to be paid; and this I dare aver, that the reader will remember my advice, longer than I shall keep his money; for coin of all sizes has a surprizing facility of slipping from me. Let the reader then only permit me to eat, and I will endeavour to encrease his pleasures; his eatables and my philosophy will make a tolerable harmony together. A rich Fool, and an *indigent Philosopher*, are made for each other's support; they fit like ball and socket; but this I insist on, that, if the Publick continue to keep me much longer in *indigence*, they shall see but very little more of my *philosophy*.[20]

This is raw, self-pitying, and very much a lapse from the standard of literary courtesy which Addison and Steele had set at the beginning of the century. But the cry for help is unmistakable and in the third essay the long list of current journals cited by Goldsmith creates the impression that he is drowning in a sea of ink. His account of them (including papers to which he himself had contributed) strikes the same cynical note that has been heard in the earlier essay, and makes a sharp contrast with the mood which had inspired his cheerful acceptance of poor sales for the *Bee* two years previously:

> This was a fine picture of the state of genius at that time; no pert ribaldry through the whole; all serious, chaste, temperate compilations, calculated to instruct mankind in the changes of the weather, and to amuse them with eastern tales, replete with grave essays upon the cultivation of madder and hemp. The smallness of the type, however, shut out two classes of readers to whom they might have been otherwise very serviceable,

children learning to read, and old women who read with spectacles.'[21]

This is followed by the satirical *Specimen of a Magazine* entitled, appropriately enough it might be felt by now, *The Infernal Magazine*. It includes some *Rules for Behaviour, drawn up by the Indigent Philosopher*:

> If you be a rich man, you may enter the room with three loud hems, march deliberately up to the chimney, and turn your back to the fire. If you be a poor man, I would advise you to shrink into the room as fast as you can, and place yourself as usual upon the corner of some chair in a corner ... Don't laugh much in publick, the spectators that are not as merry as you will hate you, either because they envy your happiness, or fancy themselves the subject of your mirth.[22]

Perhaps the Philosopher comes closest to the heart of Goldsmith's despondency in his request for the freedom to 'write bad prose'.

These essays are strange productions for a man who, if the 1761 dating for the bulk of *The Vicar of Wakefield* is correct, had just produced or was in the middle of producing his finest work. But if this work had encountered a major obstacle, or if the writer was temporarily exhausted by the effort of imagination involved in recreating the life of Lissoy, then it would be perfectly understandable; and if by this time, or during the early part of 1762, the novel had been actually abandoned, the decision in the course of the year to ask Lord Bute to send him to Asia could be seen in the same light as his setting out on the road to Cork when life at Trinity College became unpleasant. To a frustrated and momentarily despondent writer of Goldsmith's temperament an intractable novel would have seemed something to escape from just as an intractable tutor had done to the humiliated undergraduate. The signs are that by the end of 1761 Goldsmith had outwritten himself without completing his book, although he had devoted time and energy to it which might have been given to more profitable pursuits. Now he was in financial difficulties; and confronted by the artistic problem presented by the gap between his account of the Primrose family and the novelettish plot to which he had committed himself, he lost faith in his novel and very probably abandoned it. It was necessary to make some money, and Newbery was at hand either to make or receive suggestions. At the beginning of 1762 Goldsmith returned to journalism with his *Lloyd's Evening Post* essays and also began work on the translation of Plutarch, managing to complete four and a half of Newbery's seven volumes before being overtaken by illness. Whilst recuperating in Bath, he became interested in the life of Richard Nash who had died the previous year and suggested himself as Nash's biographer to Newbery, who agreed. A solution to his continuing financial difficulties was also sought by means of the memorandum to Lord Bute. When this failed to produce the desired result it became clear that he must undertake yet more work for Newbery. With the *Life of Nash* quickly written and now ready for publication (it came out in October) he took a step which would lead ultimately to the mortgaging of his literary career.

Goldsmith's appearances in the lecture halls of Edinburgh and Leyden and at the Edinburgh Medical Society had reflected a genuine interest in the natural sciences. He was particularly drawn to anatomy and botany.[23] Even though the evidence of his abortive medical career suggests that he never applied himself very earnestly to his studies, he had shown at least the zeal of the intelligent dilettante of his age. Now he was earning his advances from a firm which had a special interest in popular science and, for the writer who in the *Lloyd's Evening Post* essays was showing every sign of being sick of the literary journalism of his day and who may have got badly stuck with the novel that was to 'make his fortune', the prospect of diversifying and turning his other interests to account must have been attractive. Although Newbery had qualified science writers like Benjamin Martin and Dr Brookes to call upon, he was evidently persuaded that Goldsmith was well suited to such work. The result was an agreement which, in return for an advance of £60, committed Goldsmith to producing a *Survey of Experimental Philosophy*.[24] He had embarked on a course which in the end would certainly improve his income but, as far as his career as a creative writer was concerned, at a very considerable cost.

In the course of the year a difficult situation had arisen at Wine Office Court. Forster believed that the landlady who had been so anxious to set Goldsmith's tenancy on a familiar and intimate footing the year before was a relative of Newbery's. This is corro-

borated by the appearance of the name Prudence Carnan amongst
the residents of Wine Office Court who were assessed for rates this
year:[25] Mrs Carnan would have been not a relative of Newbery
himself but an in-law of his benefactor and former employer. The
lady was a milliner and living with her was a marriageable daughter.
Goldsmith was unwary. At Peckham and at Green Arbour Court
he had established a cordial and lively relationship with the families
who had opened their doors to him. There had been leg pulling,
songs, extempore dances for the young people and, if his letters to
the Bindley brothers[26] and his relationship with the Hornecks in
later years are any indication, probably a lot of chatter, punning and
private jokes good, bad and indifferent. But in Wine Office Court
he had encountered a 'smart girl' (as she was later described) who
was more than prepared to look for a deeper significance behind the
lodger's geniality. Her age is unknown, but it may well have been
an age at which both mother and daughter considered marriage
desirable, and the Dr Oliver Goldsmith who received visits from
Samuel Johnson and the Earl of Sussex's chaplain was considered
a reasonable catch, even if he was sometimes late with the rent.

It was perhaps no accident that Goldsmith should have chosen to
write the life of the man who had introduced the gaming tables to
Bath, or that Dr Primrose should be found throwing dice in the
second chapter of the novel; by the end of the year, even if he had
read the warning signs in Wine Office Court, Goldsmith's financial
difficulties were such that the obvious solution to the problem of the
landlady's daughter was momentarily beyond his reach. Fatally, he
allowed things to drift. The friendly informality of the early days of
his tenancy had probably induced a dangerous carelessness with
regard to rent-day and he was now very much in arrears. Both
mother and daughter were becoming restive, and eventually the
storm broke. As Goldsmith must have described it afterwards, it was
very difficult to make out whether he was being asked to pay the
rent or to commit himself to instant matrimony with the smart
girl.[27] Whether or not he appreciated the strength of feeling behind
the confused outburst, he may have gained a sense of false security
from the lull that followed the storm, for he was taken completely
by surprise when he woke up one morning to discover that the
bailiffs had been summoned. His landlady was now obdurate. The
only concession wrung from her was that a message could be

delivered to a friend. He turned instinctively to Johnson, now living four hundred yards away across Fleet Street and demonstrably a tower of strength and wisdom.

Johnson responded with one of Bute's guineas and the message that he would follow it as soon as he was dressed. Goldsmith accepted the guinea and either with the intention of drinking himself into a state of happy release or of demonstrating his contempt for his landlady's draconian measures, insisted that part of it should be spent immediately on a bottle of Madeira. By the time Johnson presented himself at the house in Wine Office Court the bottle was on the table and Goldsmith was beginning to lose what little grasp he had of the realities of his situation.

Johnson was predictably authoritative, incisive and reasonable. He firmly replaced the cork and proceeded to examine his friend on the state of his finances—how much he owed and what prospects he had of meeting his debts. As Goldsmith gave him details, however vague, of the recent advances from Newbery and of work undertaken yet hardly begun, the situation must have appeared increasingly desperate. Perhaps Goldsmith was sobered by the Doctor's reactions. There was only one piece of property whose value—whatever that was—had still to be realised. With reluctance he produced his intransigent novel (possibly concealing its lack of a conclusion) and Johnson, beginning to turn over its pages there and then, became the first person to see *The Vicar of Wakefield*. Recognising its worth and realising that, with the weight of his approval behind it, Newbery was unlikely to refuse an advance, he bore it away to St Paul's Churchyard.[28]

In May this year Newbery had acknowledged Goldsmith's success as a journalist by bringing out a collected edition of the 'Chinese Letters' under the title *The Citizen of the World*. But he was not interested in publishing novels—there is only one other surviving example in his list[29]—and his response to Johnson's suggestion that he should immediately put down an advance on Goldsmith's manuscript was cautious. He appears to have sent his desperate author £20 for a third share in it and promised to use his interest with other publishers to secure the sale of the other two thirds. (In due course this would lead to the one clearly substantiated date, apart from its actual publication in 1766, that can be attached to *The Vicar of Wakefield*: the sale of a third share in

G

the book to Benjamin Collins of Salisbury in October 1762.)[30]

So the domestic crisis of 1762 was resolved. Newbery, perhaps embarrassed now by his connection with Wine Office Court and realising that it was in his own interest to save his authors from distractions, conceived a plan for keeping him out of further trouble. He introduced him to a Miss Fleming, the occupant of Canonbury House at Islington, from whom he rented an apartment, and proposed that Goldsmith should lodge with her, all his expenses down to an occasional glass of sassafras to be met by himself and off-set against further advances. It was very much the kind of arrangement that Mrs Milner, at the Peckham school, must have had in mind when she discovered that the young master was as much in need of financial supervision as his boys. At the end of December Goldsmith took himself off to Islington, that pleasant and airy hill-top suburb, with its fairground booths, tea-gardens and pump-room within forty minutes' walk of Fleet Street.

Here Goldsmith could apply himself to the task of bringing *The Vicar of Wakefield*, most probably interrupted at the end of chapter seventeen when the Vicar sets out in search of his daughter Livy, to a conclusion.* Something of his relief at having been spirited away from Wine Office Court, and an acknowledgment of the fact that his novel is now earmarked as a Newbery publication, can be felt in chapter eighteen where John Newbery himself makes an appearance. Five hundred words after setting out on his journey Dr Primrose is taken ill and it is the timely arrival of the bookseller that relieves him from the embarrassment of not being able to pay his bill at the alehouse where he has found refuge:

> I languished here for near three weeks; but at last my con-
> stitution prevailed, though I was unprovided with money to
> defray the expences of my entertainment. It is possible the
> anxiety from this last circumstance alone might have brought on
> a relapse, had I not been supplied by a traveller, who stopt to take
> a cursory refreshment. This person was no other than the
> philanthropic bookseller in St Paul's church-yard, who has
> written so many little books for children: he called himself their
> friend; but he was the friend of all mankind. He was no sooner

*The dating of *The Vicar of Wakefied* is discussed at greater length in the Appendix, page 363.

alighted, but he was in haste to be gone; for he was ever on business of the utmost importance, and was at that time actually compiling materials for the history of one Mr Thomas Trip. I immediately recollected this good-natured man's red pimpled face; for he had published for me against the Deuterogamists of the age, and from him I borrowed a few pieces, to be paid at my return . . .

If there was a similarity between this episode and the story of the Good Samaritan it is understandable since Newbery advertised the sale of Dr James's Fever Powders (hardly given away at 2s. 6d. for two)[31] with an engraving of the New Testament story. Goldsmith was also borrowing an idea from other Newbery books by inserting a puff for the firm within his own text. Though perhaps an artistic blemish, it was almost certainly a gesture of gratitude rather than of sycophancy.

Having made his flourish in Newbery's direction, there was still the problem of concluding a novel which, with the elopement that had been an essential feature of the *Miss Stanton* scheme, had run into a major snag. Although the presence of the mysterious Mr Burchell and his interest in the second daughter, Sophia, had considerable promise, the spontaneous development of the Vicar into a rather different character from the clergyman in the short story was still threatening to create a large hole in that neat but silly plot. Goldsmith's Vicar was no duellist, but if he was to be denied means of retaliation against young Squire Thornill there was a real danger that he might become far too passive a figure to bring the story to a strong conclusion. To a man who loved the theatre and theatrical effects the loss of Olivia's big scene must also have caused regrets.

A writer who had worked under the editorship of Smollett had one obvious solution at his command: the departure of Dr Primrose in search of the erring Livy could be the signal for a string of picaresque episodes in the tradition of Roderick Random or Peregrine Pickle (or Parson Adams and Tom Jones before them). But where episodes like the amusing Ephraim Jenkinson interlude of chapter fourteen might have been expected, Primrose's only encounter of any note apart from those with people already mentioned in the story appears to be inserted to give him an opportunity to preach. In the spring of 1763 the press campaign against Bute,

engineered by Pitt and Temple through Wilkes' *North Briton*, was
reaching its climax and 'Mr Wilkinson', the butler who masquerades
as the master and entertains Primrose in a country house, is a
character hardly distinguishable from the political ideas he is made
to voice—the opinions of the men who had chosen Wilkes as their
mouthpiece.

Primrose's Tory 'sermon' which comprises the bulk of the
Wilkinson episode presents in an expanded form the defence of
monarchy that Goldsmith had already made as a journalist; and in
fact it was to the world of journalism, of the occasional essays and of
the 'Chinese Letters' rather than to that of the picaresque novel that
he turned in his attempt to resolve the structural problem of his
novel. Although the voice of Dr Primrose undergoes a subtle
change, the first person narrative is enough to provide the necessary
continuity but, even when this has been admitted, the remaining
chapters of the book are plainly composed along the lines of a
sequence of 'Chinese Letters', with a mixture of politics, inter-
polated narrative (George's long account of his travels and adventures), philosophical reflection on the best way to conduct one's
life (as in that other sermon on the consoling power of religion
which, as chapter twenty-nine, is visibly detachable from the rest of
the book) and analyses of contemporary ills (as in the Vicar's
advocacy of penal reform). Far from noticing the gap created by the
omission of the climactic duel scene, the reader finds his attention
engaged by a variety of skilfully introduced distractions until the
time comes for the reappearance of the Thornhills, uncle and
nephew, for the strands to be unravelled and wedding-bells rung.

*

'But the stamina's good, the stamina's good!' Goldsmith exclaimed
when, a few years later as he was recovering from an illness, friends
commented on his pallor.[32] Unfortunately, his artistic stamina, as
revealed in the composition of *The Vicar of Wakefield* and subsequent
works, often failed to match his inspiration. The irrepressible
humour, the originality of vision and the natural charm of his
writing, whether in the form of Augustan verse or a newspaper
article, were accompanied by carelessness with regard to structure
(and even consistency of plot) and a tendency to give up when his

material seemed to resist his efforts to get it into shape. Although his contributions were fractional it would nevertheless have to go on record that Johnson had finished both Goldsmith's major poems for him. The difficulty was partly financial. In Mrs Thrale's version of the Bottle of Madeira story, Goldsmith at the time of the domestic crisis in Wine Office Court was 'fretting over a novel which when done was to be his whole fortune; but he could not get it done for distraction' and, apart from the troubled domestic scene and the artistic problem at the heart of the book, the distraction must have included the pressing need to make some money. This can be felt in a conversation about *The Vicar of Wakefield* between Goldsmith and his Edinburgh friend Dr William Farr[33] which Percy recorded in his *Memoir*:

> 'Dr Goldsmith, speaking to his medical friend, ... asked him his opinion of this fascinating performance. "I spoke of it," said his friend, "in the warm terms I thought it deserved, pointing out however certain parts which I wished, had he had more time for the purpose, had been altered or corrected. Goldsmith concurred with me in my remarks, but added that it was not from want of time it had not been done, as Newbery kept it by him in manuscript two years before he published it; he gave me, I think he said, 60l. for the copy, and had I made it ever so perfect or correct, I should not have had a shilling more."

Dr Farr's anecdote has the ring of truth. At one level of his personality Goldsmith had little confidence in either himself or his writing. At a reception, an impertinent girl could make him retreat in confusion by quoting his own line at him: 'The loud laugh that speaks the vacant mind' (one is reminded of Oscar Wilde being crudely suppressed by a stranger at the next table in the Café de Paris); and during the rehearsals of *She Stoops to Conquer* he would listen humbly while a casual acquaintance told him what was wrong with his play.[35] In this instance Goldsmith seems to have accepted Farr's criticism without argument and to have thoughtlessly thrown out a remark which could only damage his reputation as a writer. But the admission is credible. Once an agreement had been reached with Newbery, the book which had been a matter of artistic concern to him before the summer of 1762 became simply a marketable property. He had lost interest and, once his £60 was assured, he was inclined to let the novel go and apply himself to the task of earning the next advance.

It is impossible to tell whether Goldsmith could have found a way of bringing his novel to an end without abandoning the delicate ironies and humour of the first seventeen chapters. Once the manuscript had been shown to Johnson and carried off to Newbery its ecological climate as far as Goldsmith was concerned had been contaminated. Later in the century the unexpected arrival of 'a person from Porlock' brought Coleridge's *Kubla Khan* to a premature conclusion. For anyone who believes that, left to himself, Goldsmith might have got his second wind and re-inhabited the elusive persona of Dr Primrose, the intervention of a Wine Office Court landlady in the autumn of 1762 will assume the dimensions of just such a disaster.

Newbery's lack of enthusiasm for the novel, demonstrated in 1762 by his venturing only a third share in it, must have communicated itself to Goldsmith, giving him yet another reason for carelessness in bringing it to a conclusion. The possibility must also be considered that Newbery's comments and advice about the chapters Johnson had taken to him may have had their influence on the tone of those still to come. It is unlikely that the publisher of the *Midwife* should have failed to respond to their humour, but as he now had several devotional works on his list and, since 1760, the first religious magazine in England, the *Christian's Magazine* under the editorship of a worldly clergyman, Dr William Dodd, he might have had doubts as to the wisdom of allowing a novel which occasionally appeared to make fun of a minister of religion to come out under his own imprint. Even in 1750 his nervousness that the issue of the *Midwife* might be detrimental to his children's books had shown itself in the decision to issue the former in the name of his stepson, Thomas Carnan. If he felt that *The Vicar of Wakefield* presented a similar problem this was resolved in very much the same fashion, for it appeared under the joint imprint of B. Collins of Salisbury and F. Newbery—i.e. Francis Newbery, a nephew of John's who had separate premises near his own.

It would be interesting to know whether Dr William Dodd, as clergyman-in-residence at Newbery's firm, was consulted after the manuscript of an incomplete novel had come into Newbery's hands. It is at least a possibility, in the light of the change of atmosphere and the frequency of the sermons, that some such adviser warned Newbery of the need to have the tone of a novel about a clergyman improved, and perhaps to make Dr Primrose more overtly aware of his status as a clergyman. Newbery would have communicated such advice to Goldsmith, and Goldsmith, with ample journalistic practice, would have supplied the necessary and unexceptionable sentiments to go into the Vicar's mouth. Eleven years after the publication of *The Vicar of Wakefield* Dr Dodd was found guilty of having forged a cheque in the Earl of Chesterfield's name, and sentenced to death. In a desperate attempt to rally popular sympathy and gain a reprieve, Johnson wrote a sermon for the unfortunate man to deliver in Newgate.[36] But the authorities were obdurate and, unlike Dr Primrose who after preaching to his fellow captives, leaves the prison a free man to attend the double wedding of the last chapter, William Dodd left Newgate only for the ride to Tyburn.

*

The reviewers of both the *Monthly* and the *Critical* used the word 'singular' in their account of Goldsmith's book when it was at last published in 1766. They had enjoyed it in varying degrees. Predictably, the *Critical* was the more enthusiastic in its response to 'genuine touches of nature, easy strokes of humour, pathetic pictures of domestic happiness and domestic distress'; but in his concluding remarks the reviewer seems to agree with the *Monthly* that here was an author 'capable of . . . strangely underwriting himself'. He then indicates where the novel's principal flaw is to be found: 'But pray, Dr Goldsmith, was it necessary to bring the concluding calamities so thick upon your venerable friend; or in your impatience to get to the end of your task, was you not rather disposed to hurry the catastrophe?' But the same reviewer has freely acknowledged the novel's charm and the presence in it of an art that conceals art: 'He appears to tell his story with so much ease and artlessness, that one is almost tempted to think, one could have told it every bit as well without the least study; yet so difficult is it to hit off this mode of composition with any degree of mastery, that he who should try would probably find himself deceived . . .'.[37]

The public agreed with the *Critical Review*'s enthusiasm. The first edition of March 27th was followed at the end of May and again in August by editions of a thousand copies each. Unauthorised editions in Ireland and London quickly followed.[38] It was to become one of the most frequently reprinted novels of the eighteenth and nineteenth centuries. In the face of such massive acclaim, including the implied enthusiasm of Henry James who quotes Goldsmith's book twice in that most sophisticated of novels, *The Ambassadors*, it is perhaps grudging to talk in terms of artistic problems. But to suggest that the concluding chapters issue from a different faculty of their creator's mind is not to claim a total loss of power. Coleridge's distinction between the imagination and the fancy is applicable here. If the first seventeen chapters of the book are under the controlling influence of the imagination, in the last third the story is released into the fairy-tale world of fancy—to which by temperament Goldsmith always had much easier access. Here he was no longer bound by the need to tether invention to reality. The humour and irony fall away, and at the very moment when in terms of the plot Dr Primrose meets most resistance from his environment, he meets least from the now almost dormant critical faculty of his inventor. In the midst of Job-like adversities he is serene. 'Observe this bed of straw, and unsheltering roof,' he tells Moses; 'those mouldering walls, and humid floor; my wretched body thus disabled by fire, and my children weeping round me for bread; you have come home, my child, to all this, yet here, even here, you see a man that would not for a thousand worlds exchange situations.' With all the primitive symbolism of the fairy story Goldsmith inflicts ordeal by ice on top of the ordeal by fire: in a high fever, Primrose is conducted to prison through the snow. But in captivity he has the power to comfort his family, inspire repentance on the part of Ephraim Jenkinson and convert many of his fellow prisoners. Though it may be felt that there is some degree of imaginative failure here, the faculty that channelled so much energy into Goldsmith's daydreams is deeply engaged. At the analytical level the reviewer on the Monthly felt that perhaps he should not have enjoyed this novel as much as he did. Its author, he says, 'finds such resources in his own extraordinary natural talents, as may, in the judgement of many readers, in a great measure, compensate for his limited knowledge of men, manners, and characters, as they really appear in the living world.'[39] If these strictures were applied to Goldsmith himself and to his achievement as a whole it would be necessary to protest; but if they refer only to the last third of *The Vicar of Wakefield* they seem apposite.

Examined critically, Goldsmith's novel is indeed 'singular'—as singular as *Northanger Abbey* would have been if it had been abandoned at the moment when Catharine Morland discovered the slip of paper in the Tilneys' ebony cabinet and brought to a conclusion by 'Monk' Lewis. But *The Vicar of Wakefield* has outlived its age not because it rewards analysis but because Goldsmith himself, critically or uncritically, believes in the goodness of the hero he has created and in the power of such goodness to survive both ordeal by fire and ordeal by family, and ultimately to gather all the stray ends of life within its own inviolable sphere. On one level it is a simplistic vision; on another it is profound in the manner of 'primitive' art. The figures in a painting by L. S. Lowry have their obvious relation to the figures in a child's drawing, but within their gauntly simplified landscapes they have the power to speak to us.

EIGHT

Comedy of Humours

GOLDSMITH MOVED to his new quarters in Islington at Christmas 1762. The solution that John Newbery had worked out to put an end to his author's financial difficulties was quite simply that he should become Goldsmith's banker and that Miss Elizabeth Fleming should supervise every aspect of his life from his bedtime drink to the repair of his stockings and shirts. She had authority to make small loans—10d for example on May 24th 1764; 1s. 2d. on June 9th. The accounts were to be presented quarterly to Newbery after having been checked and signed by Goldsmith, and to be offset against literary earnings. The records available for James Prior's inspection in the eighteen-thirties showed that at the end of his first nine months at Islington Goldsmith was committed to reimbursing Newbery with literary property to the value of £48, having overdrawn this year to this extent on advances as well as on Miss Fleming's account and on drafts for the payment of tailors' bills which had been presented to Newbery. Allowing for an outstanding debt of £14. 19s. which had been owing to the publisher since the previous year, Goldsmith had so far overdrawn to the extent of £33. He had been charged a fair rent of 12s. 6d. a month for his room and £4. 2s. 6d. a month for board. Throughout this first year, Miss Fleming seems to have been instructed to err on the side of liberality, as her accounts indicate that an occasional guest had been invited to stay for dinner at no extra charge.[1]

At weekends the Newberys migrated to Canonbury from the shop at the northern corner of Ludgate Hill and St Paul's Churchyard accompanied by their teenage daughter and, during holidays from Merchant Taylor's School, by their talented son. Francis Newbery had a keen interest in literature and music and was a frequent visitor to the room in the upper storeys of the house where Goldsmith 'often read to him passages from the works he had in hand, particularly some favourite portions of *The Traveller*, and stanzas from his beautiful tale of *The Hermit* introduced into *The*

Vicar of Wakefield'.[2] Unlike William Cooke, Francis omitted to mention in his autobiographical sketch that Goldsmith read in so slovenly a manner 'that it was sometimes difficult to distinguish his poetry from his prose'.

The arrangements made for Goldsmith's retirement to Islington had confirmed his status as Newbery's leading writer. He was living above the rooms which Nancy Smart had recently vacated on her departure for Dublin. His awareness of the family tragedy that had taken place was reflected in the time he devoted to amusing Smart's two little girls (left behind in the care of Miss Fleming) as well as in his attempts to launch a subscription for his brother writer.[3] Newbery was determined to take care of Smart's successor. As far as advance and overdrafts were concerned he seems to have realised that it was too late even for Miss Fleming to turn Goldsmith into a more competent manager: consequently the rein was comfortably loose. But on the other hand there is nothing to suggest that the publisher was aware that he was monopolising the talents of one of the most gifted writers of his generation. Materially there was still little to choose between his régime and that offered by Ralph Griffiths six years earlier. Griffiths had guaranteed £100 a year plus board and lodging. The advance of £60 which Goldsmith was given for his *Survey of Experimental Philosophy* would have represented a maximum of seven months' work in Griffiths' reckoning, and it is probable that Goldsmith needed much longer to complete this compilation for Newbery. However, he embarked on a study of French scientific works, and had the opportunity of further off-setting Miss Fleming's quarterly account by producing prefaces— at three guineas a time—to four volumes of Brookes' *Natural History* which Newbery published in 1763.[4] His other major project at this time—apart from the completion of *The Vicar of Wakefield*—was the *History of England* designed for young people, to be published anonymously by Newbery in the summer of 1764.[5]

If nostalgic references in such essays as *A Reverie at the Boar's-head-tavern in Eastcheap* are an indication, Goldsmith would have found Canonbury House a pleasant place for the heavy programme of reading to which he had committed himself in the execution of these projects. The oldest part of the house contained some hand-some rooms with Elizabethan panelling and plaster work and on the wall at the top of the staircase a seventeenth century decorator had offered encouragement to would-be historians in the form of a list of the royal succession from William the Conqueror to Charles I. It was wildly inaccurate but in this and in the motto he would have discerned amongst the plaster work in one of the state rooms, SPES CERTA SUPRA, Goldsmith probably sensed a more genial household god than he had known in the dark and narrow little courtyard off Fleet Street. There was a garden, and not far away on the banks of the New River canal there were taverns and tea gardens which on Sundays drew crowds of Londoners up the hill to enjoy the fresher air and the wide views across the smoky city.[6] Newbery had probably reasoned that Goldsmith would be at one remove from the temptation of the whist and hazard tables without feeling irretrievably cut off from the life of the capital.

Since 1757 there had been an alternative route to Islington for visitors and commuters—the New Road* which came over the fields and up the hill from the new London which was spreading westwards and northwards.[7] Doubtless it was this route which Goldsmith took on the Monday evenings of his second year at the Tower, having been invited to become a member of a newly established club which early in 1764 began to meet in a private room at the Turk's Head Tavern, Gerrard Street, between Leicester and Soho Squares.

The prime mover of what came to be known simply as 'The Club' was Reynolds, with whom Goldsmith perhaps had a nodding acquaintance at this time:[8] its lynch-pin was Samuel Johnson, and nothing illustrates the strength of the bond between Johnson and Goldsmith so strikingly as this extremely flattering invitation. He had been given precedence over men like Percy and Garrick who had known Johnson longer. (Percy had to wait until 1768 for his invitation and Garrick until 1773).[9]

Reynolds had known Johnson for a decade. On holiday in his native Devon he had picked up the *Life of Savage* intending to leaf through the pages and found himself compelled to read it to the end standing with one arm propped numbly against the mantelpiece.[10] Later, when he and Johnson met by chance at the house of their common acquaintances, the Misses Cotterell of Castle Street, Cavendish Square, it was Johnson's turn to be impressed. Reynolds was not a brilliant talker like Johnson, but his quiet interjections

*Now the Euston and Pentonville Roads.

were considered thoughtful and original. On this occasion the Cotterell sisters were shocked to be informed, as they lamented the death of a friend who had been their benefactor, that they had 'the comfort of being relieved from a burden of gratitude'; but Johnson approved of Reynolds' observation, walked home with him and spent the evening in his company.[11]

The early stages of the lifelong friendship that followed had been difficult at times. Reynolds' understanding of Johnson's terror of being left alone[12] was acquired the hard way. His new friend made frequent calls and would often linger on into the small hours as though incapable of uprooting himself again. Johnson's mornings began shortly before noon, but Reynolds was an early riser, a man of routine who loved his work and was in the habit of spending an hour alone in his studio, making sketches or experimenting with his colours before the first sitter arrived at 11 a.m.[13] Even if his sister, Fanny, who was to become one of Johnson's favourites, seemed to be quite happy pouring endless cups of tea for this eminent visitor, Reynolds' patience sometimes snapped: on one occasion, finding Johnson installed in his drawing room, he had seized his hat and left the house.[14] The Club was Reynolds' attempt to provide Johnson with the sounding-board his dialectic talents demanded—and as a stage manager he was brilliantly successful. He would have known that a small group of men had gathered round Johnson at the King's Head in Ivy Lane in the late 1740s, and this was probably the topic he raised by the fireside at 47 Leicester Square in the winter of '63/'64 as a prelude to the suggestion that that club should have a successor. Reynolds' circumstances were very different from Johnson's: he was a rich man whereas Johnson had only very recently been rescued from comparative poverty; he had a luxurious house, a team of servants and either his sister or his nieces in attendance as housekeepers, and so could give frequent dinner-parties, whereas Johnson was now living in cramped accommodation at 1 Inner Temple Lane. Reynolds had clearly decided on complete self-effacement. Of the seven other Club members who had been gathered together by the end of the year, only one, the civil servant Anthony Chamier, seems to have been primarily in Reynolds' rather than in Johnson's ambit at this time. Two of the Club's first members had belonged to the Ivy Lane club: they were John Hawkins, a lawyer and Middlesex magistrate, and Samuel Dyer, a fellow of the Royal Society. Dyer was a man of considerable intellectual gifts but in spite of being disinherited he had obstinately rejected his friends' advice and refused to forge a successful career for himself. The two youngest members, Bennet Langton and Topham Beauclerk, belonged to the Oxford world with which Johnson maintained close links. Edmund Burke, keenly interested in the visual arts and the author of a celebrated essay on aesthetics, was probably the sole member of the Club who, in 1764, was equally well known to Johnson and Reynolds.

However much discussion of personalities went on at 47 Leicester Square, in an age when the tavern was a place of assembly for men at every level of society the two friends would have been in complete agreement about the definition of the word 'club'. Reynolds belonged to a Thursday dining club at the Star and Garter in Pall Mall and another which met on Saturdays at the Crown and Anchor.[15] Later in the decade James Boswell joined a group of Benjamin Franklin's London friends who met fortnightly at the St Paul's coffee-house as 'The Honest Whigs' (a name which would have inspired derision in both Johnson and Goldsmith). It is probably safe to take Boswell's description as typical of the activities of such a club:

> We have wine and punch upon the table. Some of us smoke a pipe, conversation goes on pretty formally, sometimes sensibly and sometimes furiously. At nine there is a side-board with Welsh rabbits and apple-puffs, porter and beer. Our reckoning is about 18d. a head.[16]

No doubt out of deference for Johnson and his unusual daily routine, the Turk's Head club assembled at the rather late hour of nine; 'supper'—which was taken seriously, a menu being studied on arrival—was over by 11.0, and the talk went on into the small hours of the morning.[17]

The Reynolds-Johnson Club appointed a chairman each evening and, on occasions at least, decided in advance what the topic of conversation or debate should be (in the early 'seventies, for example, they can be found devoting evenings to the problem of the Chatterton forgeries).[18] Neither Reynolds nor Johnson wished to burden its members with rules and the principal consideration was to be that they 'should be men of such talents, and so well known to each other, that any two of them, if they should not happen to be joined by more, might be good company to each other.'[19] Reynolds had probably already considered a setting for the prospective Monday meetings. The Turk's Head in Gerrard Street had been known to him at least since 1759 when he had gone there to attend the meeting that launched the first annual exhibition of paintings in London and, subsequently, the Royal Academy.[20] It was in the tavern's first-floor* room communicating with a back-parlour by means of folding doors that the Club met for the first nineteen years[21] of its existence.

Although it came to be talked of as 'The Literary Club'—the soubriquet was bestowed by Mrs Montague, a wealthy intellectual who in the early years had tried to take it under her wing by inviting all the members to an annual dinner at her house—its composition and interests were more varied than that title suggests. Johnson was primarily a man of letters but at various times his friends were confident that he might embark on a career as a member of parliament or as a barrister; and like many educated men of his time he was interested in the natural sciences, particularly medicine. Certain members of the club were probably invited to participate on the grounds that they would meet Johnson on the level of one or more of these interests. The law was represented by Hawkins and, after 1768, by Robert Chambers (who became the Vinerian professor of Law at Oxford at the age of twenty-five); government—though members were not allowed to discuss the politics of the day[22]—by Burke and by Anthony Chamier (the thirty-nine-year-old civil servant with a taste for opera and for flirting with the young Burney sisters, who had made a fortune on the stock-exchange). Medicine was ably catered for by Burke's father-in-law, Dr Christopher Nugent, who had recently arrived in London from Bath, where his successful treatment of a servant girl for hydrophobia had led to his publication of a treatise on the subject. At a possibly more amateur level, Bennet Langton might have been expected to respond to Johnson's interest in ecclesiastical history; while Topham Beauclerk, besides being a suave and witty member of the *jeunesse dorée*, was something of a bibliophile. These two young

*9 Gerrard Street became a private residence again in 1773[21]. The creator of 'Lien Chi Atlangi' would no doubt have been charmed to discover that by the year 1976 the room had been turned into a Chinese bookshop.

men who had been friends at Trinity College, Oxford, were admitted because of their closeness to Johnson rather than for having
taken their stand on any specific intellectual or professional platform. English-born and heirs to landed wealth they were the
exceptions in a group which was predominantly middle class with a
strong expatriate strain. Dyer was the son of a London jeweller,
Hawkins of a carpenter who had become a surveyor, and Chambers
was the son of a Newcastle attorney; Chamier was the grandson of
a Huguenot immigrant; Burke, Nugent and Goldsmith were
Irish.

Although Johnson liked to boast about the mixture of talents
represented by the Club (he and Boswell amused themselves by
imagining it transferred to a large house at St Andrew's where it
would become a ready-made university, each member in his
appropriate room),[23] 'clubbability' as well as talent was considered
a desirable criterion of membership. There was a skilfully contrived
balance between the highly articulate, brilliant and sometimes
explosive members (like Johnson himself, Burke and, on a different
level, Beauclerk) and those who had social gifts of a more passive
kind—the urbanity of Chamier, the quiet rectitude of Chambers
(whose failure to enrich himself in twenty-five years of service as an
Indian Judge was to be an impressive demonstration of virtue) or the
patience of Samuel Dyer who was always prepared to make in-
telligible to others the learning which he had so lamentably failed to
make of service to himself. It says much for Reynolds' tact and
judgment that there was only one casualty. John Hawkins was an
authority on music and a good man in a crisis but, in the words of his
oldest friend, Johnson—himself perhaps something of an authority
in such matters—he had 'a tendency to savageness that cannot
easily be defended'.[24] At one of the Club's early meetings Hawkins
was so offensive to Burke that the other members closed ranks and
prompted his retirement.[25]

How did Oliver Goldsmith fit into this group? Certain views of
his personality that have been current at one time or another are
difficult to reconcile with his inclusion in it. One is that he was
impelled to force himself into the presence of the famous. But no-
one could force his way into this highly exclusive and self-
prepetuating Club. (Johnson was scornful when Garrick's 'I'll be of
you' was repeated to him.)[26] Garrick's own view of Goldsmith, that

he 'wrote like an angel but talk'd like poor Poll' is at least qualified by the decision of Reynolds and Johnson to include him in a company of highly articulate men. Boswell's picture of the vain, humourless and self-important little Irishman is incompatible with the fact that his company was found acceptable by men like Reynolds, Langton, Chamier and Dyer who were all praised by their contemporaries for their sweetness of disposition, their good manners and evident clubbability. Neither did Goldsmith have fame on his side when the Club was founded. As with other members—particularly Burke who was merely private secretary to an undistinguished M.P.—this lay in the future. As yet he was simply a journalist who had conducted a column in a Newbery paper and whose company Johnson enjoyed.

Goldsmith, therefore, became a founder member of the Club on the strength of his personality and on the recommendation of the man for whose pleasure it had been brought together. Although, in Reynolds' account, he had 'come late into the great world' and 'lived a great part of his life with mean people', phrases which signify that the ugly pock-marked man with the brogue and a tendency to overdress seemed at first startlingly out of place in this company, he was considered as indispensable to Reynolds' project as a man like Burke whose mind was arguably an even keener instrument than Johnson's. Foolishness of any kind in his own sex aroused a latent cruelty in Johnson. Even Fanny Reynolds had to remonstrate with him after he had humiliated a fellow-guest in front of his wife at Reynolds' dinner-table.[27] Both Boswell and Mrs Thrale at times create the impression that he viewed social gatherings as a bear-baiting in which the bear was always victorious. Goldsmith, in Reynolds' account, was a man who 'always took care to stand forward and draw the attention of the company upon himself' and who 'talked without knowledge, not so much for the sake of shining as [from] an impatience of neglect by being left out of the conversation.' Yet even an unsympathetic Boswell can provide only one example of the kind of social disaster which these conditions seem to dictate, and on that occasion it was Goldsmith, a sick man with only a few months to live, who went out of his way to provoke Johnson's wrath.

Goldsmith was evidently not considered a foolish garrulous fellow who had to be silenced at the first opportunity. But he may very well have been the Fool, the licensed fool of a Shakespeare play who is allowed the reflections, at once acute and ingenuous, that no-one else can make. That this was the rôle in which he found himself cast on the Monday evenings when he came down to Gerrard Street from Islington is borne out by Reynolds in his reconstruction of one of those moments when all eyes were turned on Goldsmith:

The following happened once in a large company, which may serve as an instance to characterise the Doctor's manner. Somebody said that one of Mr Garrick's excellencies, amongst many others, was his powers in telling a story. This being universally agreed to, excited the Doctor's envy.

"I do not see what difficulty there can be in telling a story well. I would undertake to tell a story as well as Mr Garrick, and I will tell you one now, and I will do my best. There lived a cobbler— some do laugh at this story and some do not; however, the story is this—there lived a cobbler in a stall. This stall was opposite our house, so I knew him very well. This cobbler a bailie came after, for I must tell you he was a very low fellow."

("But you was acquainted with him, you say. He used to be often at your house.")

"Ay, he used to come over to fetch our shoes when they wanted mending, but not as an acquaintance. I always kept the best company."

("Go on with your story, Doctor.")

"This cobbler was afraid of being arrested. — — Why, the very best company used to come to our house. Squire Thomson used to dine with us, who was one of the first men in the country. I remember his coach and six, which we used to see come galloping down the hill, and then my mother, who was a little woman, was quite hid at the head of the table behind a great sirloin of beef. You could but just see the top of her head."

("Well, but go on, Doctor Goldsmith, with your story.")

"When the bailie came to, and knocked at the door of the cobbler's stall in order to have it opened, the cobbler, being aware, answered in the voice of a child (here the Doctor changes his voice), 'Put in your finger into the hole and lift up the latch,' which as soon as he had done, the cobbler with his knife cut the finger off, and still speaking in the child's voice, 'Put in the other finger, Sir, if you please.' "[28]

Perhaps failing to realise that their sense of humour was often less well developed than his own, Goldsmith gave his friends a hard time. On holiday in France at a later period with Mrs Horneck and her daughters he would pretend to be extremely annoyed that a crowd outside the hotel at Calais was more interested in the beautiful girls than in him. "I can assure you, ladies," he protested, "it is not always with me as at present, for there are times and places where I am also the object of admiration," and at least one of them—Mary—was convinced that she had witnessed an awe-inspiring exhibition of adult petulance.[29] It will have been noticed that even Reynolds, introducing his appreciative reconstruction of Goldsmith's shaggy-dog vein, has a momentary lapse when he says that it was inspired by his friend's 'envy' of Garrick.

That so many people made the same mistake suggests that this was not simply a matter of jokes misfiring. When Goldsmith paraded a brightly coloured new suit in Boswell's Bond Street chambers and informed the assembled company that his tailor had instructed him to pass on his address to all enquirers, he was accepted on the strength of his own words by at least one of his fellow guests as a grotesque and very ungentlemanly dandy; when on a visit to the puppet-show in Panton Street he insisted "Why, give me but a Spontoon now and I'll play as good tricks myself" yet another demonstration of egregiousness was added to the score. It was only natural for Johnson, congratulating a friend on the skill of his coachman, to add '. . . were Goldsmith here now he would tell us he could do better.'[30]

But were Reynolds, Boswell, Johnson and several other contemporary observers wrong to take Goldsmith at his word? Perhaps a solution to the problem can be found in the very ambivalence which allowed Reynolds to see in the same incident an example of envy and of an elaborate sense of humour. Reynolds had seen as convincing a demonstration of envy as Boswell had of vanity, while Johnson was probably correct in anticipating yet another situation in which Goldsmith, in his familiar role of Bully Bottom, would claim the capacity to do practically everything under the sun better than anyone else. (At the St James's coffee house one evening he mounted a chair and attempted to prove that he was just as skilled an orator as Burke.)[31] Something more than 'dead-pan' humour is at issue, for an acute observer like Reynolds would not have missed the joke simply because the joker had failed to smile at the right moment.

Goldsmith's writing, besides being full of lively and subtle comedy, is characterised by his continuing need to stand back from himself and, through the creative fantasy, to come to terms with those aberrations of his own mind and behaviour of which circumstances so often forced him to take note. By 1764 he had begun to associate with some of his most able contemporaries. Their achievements must have seemed daunting to a man who, in Reynolds' phrase, had 'come late into the great world.' That Reynolds, in fact, had a sympathetic understanding of Goldsmith's difficulty is shown in the sentences that follow this revealing statement:

> All his old habits were against him. It was too late to learn new ones, or at least for the new to sit easy on him. However, he set furiously about it. For one week he took one for a model and for another week [another] . . .

One asks at this point if Reynolds had found exactly the words he needed to convey his insight. If they are taken literally Goldsmith has to be imagined sustaining recognisable impersonations of Johnson, Burke or Beauclerk for hours at a stretch—clearly a preposterous idea. If, however, Goldsmith was 'taking for a model' not one *person* but a moral quality, like characters from the drama of the previous era which he so greatly preferred to that of his own day, then it is possible to see him combining a social rôle with the acting out of a fantasy.

Too often, observers were drawn into that fantasy. This is what did his reputation such harm. He was found to be '*envious* of Garrick', or, perhaps anticipating George Bernard Shaw again, 'envious of Shakespeare.'[32] There is also the possibility that, like a Pirandellian hero, the fantasist himself was drawn dangerously far into the fantasy. Much of the evidence suggests that Goldsmith was one of those 'natural' comedians whose 'act' is an extension of their psychic life at its deepest level.

The psyche is dangerous territory for a biographer, but the possibility of an analogy with Johnson's well-recorded physical disabilities suggests a possible approach. Johnson had suffered as a child from tubercular glands and since then had had to cope with the disability popularly known as St Vitus's Dance. It was something which nearly every memoir-writer who met him felt obliged to record, and when a writer like Mrs Thrale or Fanny Burney sets it down as an inexplicable phenomenon of nature the description of the grinding jaws and flailing hands is curiously cold-blooded. When Fanny Reynolds, too, embarks on a sketch of Johnson entering the house with Miss Williams, she attains the heights (or depths) of black comedy:

> On entering Sir Joshua's house with poor Mrs Williams, a blind lady who lived with him, he would quit her hand, or else whirl her about on the steps as he whirled and twisted about to perform his gesticulations; and as soon as he had finish'd, he would give a sudden spring, and make an extensive stride over the threshold, as if he was trying for a wager how far he could stride, Mrs Williams standing groping about outside the door, unless the servant or the mistress of the House more commonly took hold of her hand to conduct her in, leaving Dr Johnson to perform at the Parlour Door much the same exercise over again.[33]

It is this same lack of empathy revealed in the desire to record only the surface of existence which was to result in so many literal commentaries on Goldsmith's social behaviour. Yet there is clearly a link between the neurological compulsion which worked upon the muscles of Johnson's powerful but lethargic body and Goldsmith's need to act out undesirable moral qualities. In a sense, the man who could so easily be put down by an insolent girl or by a coffee-house pundit who buttonholed him to point out exactly what was wrong with his new play, was too passive. He needed some other method of ensuring that muscles which on those occasions were apparently slack, were actually in good working order; and it was when he had the attention of a roomful of people that he became the Narcissus or the Bully Bottom. Mrs Thrale was to record him in the former role:

> The Doctor was a Man eminently ugly, but wonderfully fond of his Person; they told him Kelly's Play was applauded—his was hissed—yet he did not seem to fret much—after a Pause he was heard to say—"A handsomer Fellow than Kelly however . . ."

what was the amazement of his Friends to see he was sitting over against a Glass.[34]

That a man who, as Reynolds saw, had a craving for affection should have risked alienating people in this way strengthens the impression that Goldsmith's compulsion was as pathological as Johnson's, for he must have known that, unlike Lien Chi Altangi who immediately saw through the Man in Black's affectation of surliness and parsimony to the compassion that underlay them,[35] he could not rely on the intuitive powers of a Mrs Thrale, for all her cleverness. Yet he continued to challenge his contemporaries in this way even to the extent of rounding off his evening at a tavern by setting up elaborate conditions for telling a story in the cobbler-and-bailiff tradition, demanding to know why no one laughed and leaving the room to all intents and purposes in great mortification.[36] Rather than respond to an almost manic humour of this kind the average observer preferred to trust the evidence of his eyes. But behind the angry or puzzled face with its deeply entrenched furrows, there must have been an intelligence alternately delighted and appalled by the wild logic with which it was pursuing the spirit of comedy—a logic which to a great degree it controlled but which might, unpredictably and dangerously, sweep the reasoning individual helplessly along in its train.

Whether understood or not, Goldsmith was much *talked about* in the literary and artistic circles of his time, and this is what he seems to have wanted. In Reynolds' words, 'to draw the attention of the company upon [himself he would] sing, stand upon his head, [or] dance about the room'. He gave very good value. Even people who felt that they had to brush themselves down, give themselves a shake, and return to normal by way of a disparaging comment as soon as he left the room, must have felt that they were in the presence of a strong personality, a force. Goldsmith as captured in Reynolds' word-sketch is really dynamic. In his last play he would describe how Mrs Hardcastle 'fidgets and spits about like a Catherine-wheel', and one feels that this might well have been applied on occasions to himself.

*

Boswell's recollection of a conversation with Goldsmith shortly after their first meeting in 1763 shows that there was a strong element of hero-worship in Goldsmith's attachment to Johnson:

> 'He had increased my admiration of the goodness of Johnson's heart, by incidental remarks in the course of conversation, such as, when I mentioned Mr Levet, whom he entertained under his roof: "He is poor and honest, which is recommendation enough to Johnson;" and when I wondered that he was very kind to a man of whom I had heard a very bad character; "He is now become miserable, and that insures the protection of Johnson." [37]

However sententious the expression, Goldsmith's feelings were evidently sincere; he returns to the theme on a later page when Boswell quotes his more memorable comment on Johnson's notorious prickliness: 'He has nothing of the bear but his skin'. Hero-worship can be dangerous to the recipient but, as Reynolds saw, Johnson's 'great pleasure was to talk to those who looked up to him';[38] and if he did leave the door wide open to disciples it is also true that he treated them generously once they had crossed the threshold. There might of course be an induction course: the persistent young Boswell had worse snubs to endure than jokes about Scots leaving Scotland, but it was not long before he was being persuaded to stay until two in the morning. Boswell's relationship with Johnson was cemented when, on their fourth encounter over supper at the Mitre, he introduced the subject of his religious difficulties, hinting that he was being drawn back towards orthodox Christianity: this was the moment when Johnson exclaimed, 'Give me your hand; I have taken a liking to you.'[39] The recurring theme of Christian apologetics and the outburst against Rousseau, when Boswell on his return from the continent confessed that he had sat at Rousseau's feet in Geneva, give the impression that Johnson saw the spiritual redemption of the future Laird of Auchinlech as a moral imperative.

He loved the company of young people. When two young ladies visited him to ask his advice about Methodism they were invited to dine at the Mitre, and one of them sat on his knee.[40] The social climate of the eighteenth century. however, made it inevitable that he would find himself more frequently in the company of young men. Bennet Langton, inspired by the *Rambler*, had gone to see him while still a schoolboy and when he went up to Oxford a few years later Johnson visited him there, Topham Beauclerk, an apparently unlikely friend for the bookish, unworldly, rather indecisive Langton, was introduced, and it was in Beauclerk's company that Johnson took a jaunt to Cambridge at the beginning of 1765. Sentimental Miss Reynolds thought they were like Socrates and Alcibiades. 'Sir, I love the acquaintance of young people,' he told Boswell, soon after their first meeting; 'because, in the first place, I don't like to think myself growing old. In the next place, young acquaintances must last longest, if they do last; and then, Sir, young men have more virtue than old men; they have more generous sentiments in every respect. I love the young dogs of this age, they have more wit and humour and knowledge of life than we had . . .'[41]

Goldsmith, who was thirty-four when he met Johnson, still had enough of the spirit of youth in him to fit, for a time at least, into this pattern; and there are many indications of Johnson's adopting a paternal and slightly protective attitude. The Wine Office Court episode indicates that there were times when Goldsmith thankfully accepted such a relationship, and as Johnson's interest in the staging of both Goldsmith's plays would demonstrate, it was not the last occasion on which he would help him to get his work before the public. There was an odd strain of ingenuousness in Goldsmith (perhaps another mental 'muscle' that had to be exercised) and Johnson's rock-like presence seems to have brought it into play. It was to Johnson that he confided, 'Whenever I write any thing, the publick *makes a point* to know nothing about it,' and although Boswell suggests that Johnson found this 'ludicrous', he allows us to see elsewhere that Johnson's concern for Goldsmith took very much the same form that it had done in his own case.[42] Johnson speaks of Goldsmith in 1763 as 'one of the first men we now have as an author, and he is a very worthy man too. He has been loose in his principles, but he is coming right.'[43] He may have believed—as in the case of Boswell—that he himself would play an active part in this process.

Johnson had been one of the first people to recognise the merit of the 'Chinese Letters' and other essays, and he remained a loyal advocate of Goldsmith's work, even if on occasions he felt compelled to make an invidious distinction between the merits of the writing and the writer. He defended Goldsmith against would-be detractors, speaking generously of his talent as both creative writer and compiler. Goldsmith in turn showed his respect for Johnson by attending those levées at Inner Temple Lane and later in Johnson's Court where, about noon, Bennet Langton, Topham Beauclerk, George Steevens the Shakespearean scholar, Arthur Murphy the dramatist and other friends, including on occasions 'learned ladies', might be found.[44] On the evening when he and Boswell found Johnson slumped in one of those depressions which preceded his nervous breakdown in 1766 he acted on the principle that help in times of distress was a mutual obligation. Seeing that something was wrong he tried to shake Johnson out of his mood. (Boswell, while saving yet another episode from oblivion, gives no sign of having understood its significance.)

Another evening Dr Goldsmith and I called on him, with the hope of prevailing on him to sup with us at the Mitre. We found him indisposed, and resolved not to go abroad. "Come then, (said Goldsmith), we will not go to the Mitre tonight, since we cannot have the big man with us." Johnson then called for a bottle of port, of which Goldsmith and I partook, while our friend, now a water-drinker, sat by us.

GOLDSMITH: "I think, Mr Johnson, you don't go near the theatres now. You give yourself no more concern about a new play, than if you had never had any thing to do with the stage."

JOHNSON: "Why, Sir, our tastes greatly alter. The lad does not care for the child's rattle, and the old man does not care for the young man's whore."

GOLDSMITH: "Nay, Sir; but your Muse was not a whore."

JOHNSON: "Sir, I do not think she was. But as we advance in the journey of life we drop some of the things which have pleased us; whether it be that we are fatigued and don't choose to carry so many things any farther, or that we find other things which we like better."

BOSWELL: "But, Sir, why don't you give us something in some other way?"

GOLDSMITH: "Aye, Sir, we have a claim upon you."

JOHNSON: "No, Sir, I am not obliged to do any more. No man is obliged to do as much as he can do. A man is to have part of his life to himself. If a soldier has fought a good many campaigns, he is not to be blamed, if he retires to ease and tranquility. A physician, who has practised long in a great city, may be excused, if he retires to a small town, and takes less practice. Now, Sir, the good I can do by my conversation bears the same proportion to the good I can do by my writings, that the practice of a physician, retired to a small town, does to his practice in a great city."

BOSWELL: "But I wonder, Sir, you have not more pleasure in writing than in not writing."

JOHNSON: "Sir, you *may* wonder."

He talked of making verses, and observed, "The great difficulty is, to know when you have made good ones. When composing, I have generally had them in my mind, perhaps fifty at a time, walking up and down my room; and then I have written them down, and often, from laziness, have written only half lines. I have written a hundred lines in a day. I remember, I wrote a hundred lines of 'The Vanity of Human Wishes' in a day. Doctor, (turning to Goldsmith,) I am not quite idle; I made one line t'other day; but I made no more."

GOLDSMITH: "Let us hear it; we'll put a bad one to it."

JOHNSON: "No, Sir; I have forgot it."[45]

Compliments passing between Goldsmith and Johnson on a literary score must have been welcome on both sides, for they were working within the same tradition. Both insisted that the decasyllabic couplet as brought to perfection by Alexander Pope was the ideal form for English verse—an assumption that, by the 1760s, was not unassailed—and in their different ways they were both masters of prose style. They had a common admiration of Dryden and of the dramatists of the late seventeenth century, and a distrust of innovators like Gray and Sterne.

Goldsmith and Johnson shared a cautiousness about new developments other than those in the literary field. Although Johnson showed a sounder knowledge of economics than Goldsmith and refused to assume that every change in life styles was a symptom of national decadence, there was some truth in Goldsmith's remark in the course of a debate on Luxury that they were really arguing on the same side, both believing that a grotesquely disproportionate amount of the national wealth was reaching the men and women who actually produced the goods. Johnson's Toryism was more deeply engrained than Goldsmith's, as is seen by a belief in birth and family which was more emotional than rational, and to which Goldsmith could not have subscribed. Johnson was not a snob, but it mattered to him that Langton should be able to trace his descent from Norman forbears, and that Beauclerk was a great-grandson of Charles II; and he believed that a lord should dress and behave like a lord. But they were both ardent monarchists and felt a strong sense of personal loyalty to George III. Boswell (who was not there) ascribed Goldsmith's silence to envy when in Reynolds' house one day in 1767 he sat on the fringe of the group to which Johnson recounted his conversation with the young King. It is far more likely that Goldsmith was living out a fantasy in which he, and not Johnson, had been surprised in the library of Buckingham House, and this is confirmed by his albeit rather bald confession, when 'he sprung from the sopha, advanced to Johnson, and in a kind of flutter, from imagining himself in the situation which he had just been hearing described, exclaimed, "Well, you acquitted yourself in this conversation better than I should have done; for I should have bowed and stammered through the whole of it." '[46]

For Johnson, one of Goldsmith's great virtues must have been that in his mid-thirties he was still a bachelor. Johnson liked his friends to be available and appears to have resented changes of status. When Beauclerk married the eldest daughter of the Duke of Marlborough four days after she had admitted her adultery with him in order to be released from her marriage to Lord Bolingbroke, Johnson spoke about the lady in harsh terms; if his laughter at the expense of Bennet Langton is a fair indication, there is reason to believe that his feelings for this old friend changed too after his marriage to the widow of a Scots nobleman; and his reaction to Mrs Thrale's re-marriage is notorious. He wanted his friends to be available, and however much his reason and highly developed moral sense informed him that matrimony was 'necessary and honourable' there was an element of bohemianism in his personality that was attracted by people whose domestic arrangements were as odd and possibly as uncomfortable as his own. As a young man he had walked round and round St James's Square all night with the

homeless Richard Savage.[47] He had redeemed Samuel Boyse's
clothes from the pawnbroker and loved to tell stories about this
improvident poet who, on a visit to his publisher, had unsuccessfully
tried to conceal his lack of breeches by wrapping himself in his coat.
Unlike Boyse, Oliver Goldsmith may never have had to make himself paper cuffs and frills for lack of linen, but the possibility must
at times have seemed imminent and Johnson would not have loved
him the less for it.[48]

It was a legal phrase, *cum privilegio*, that Boswell used to convey
the fact that Goldsmith was allowed to make remarks which would
not have been kindly received from other members of the circle.
Once the stage of simple hero-worship was passed Goldsmith's
closeness to Johnson and their similarity of tastes made him a shrewd
observer of the Doctor's real (as opposed to fortuitous and external)
idiosyncrasies. His insights were sometimes communicated behind
his friend's back, as was probably the case when he applied to him a
line from Colley Cibber: 'There is no arguing with Johnson; for
when his pistol misses fire, he knocks you down with the butt end
of it'.[49] But often Johnson was challenged to his face. When Goldsmith made his comment on Johnson's tendency to 'argue for
victory' he was speaking from experience, because he enjoyed
issuing the challenge, and it is by no means evident that he was
always the loser. Something of the atmosphere of their relationship
at its best can be seen from Boswell's account of an argument
between them at a dinner-party given by General Oglethorpe when
Goldsmith, absolutely convinced that he is right but knowing that
he is going to be argued down, nimbly side-steps (and one imagines,
though Boswell gives no stage directions, sets the company laughing)
while Johnson, just as agile for all his heavy weapons, makes a
split-second recovery:

JOHNSON: ". . . Sir, no nation was ever hurt by luxury; for, as I
said before, it can reach but to a very few. I admit that the great
increase of commerce and manufacturers hurts the military
spirit of a people; because it produces a competition for something else than martial honours,—a competition for riches. It
also hurts the bodies of the people; for you will observe, there is
no man who works at any particular trade, but you may know him
from his appearance to do so. One part or the other of his body

being more used than the rest, he is in some degree deformed: but, Sir, that is not luxury."

GOLDSMITH: "Come, you're just going to the same place by another road."

JOHNSON: "Nay, Sir, I say that is not *luxury*. Let us take a walk from Charing-cross to Whitechapel, through, I suppose, the greatest series of shops in the world, what is there in any of these shops, (if you except gin-shops,) that can do any human being any harm?"

GOLDSMITH: "Well, Sir, I'll accept your challenge. The very next shop to Northumberland-house is a pickle-shop."

JOHNSON: "Well, Sir: do we not know that a maid can in one afternoon make pickles sufficient to serve a whole family for a year? nay, that five pickle-shops can serve all the kingdom? Besides, Sir, there is no harm done to any body by the making of pickles, or the eating of pickles."[50]

Arthur Murphy believed that Johnson had a talent for 'incomparable buffoonery'[51] and the evidence suggests that Goldsmith was a good partner on occasions when he wished to indulge it. "Sir," Johnson commented on being informed that Goldsmith was anxious to go to the Far East, "he would bring home a grinding-barrow, which you see in every street in London, and think that he had furnished a wonderful improvement."[52] But if there was an element of rough-and-tumble the advantages were not all on Johnson's side. Two evenings after General Oglethorpe's dinner-party, they met again at the house of the exiled Corsican leader, General Gian Battista Paoli, and the subject of literary dedications was raised. Johnson was known to be always ready to prepare a baited hook for some needy friend to use, but Goldsmith felt this was beneath him and had the courage to say so:

JOHNSON: "Why, I have dedicated to the Royal Family all round; that is to say, to the last generation of the Royal Family."

GOLDSMITH: "And perhaps, Sir, not one sentence of wit in a whole dedication."

JOHNSON: "Perhaps not, Sir."[53]

Both Johnson and Goldsmith had embarked on their friendship

with certain illusions about each other. Inevitably they shed them, but the relationship seems to have remained in good working order—at least until the last difficult months of Goldsmith's life.

*

Unlike Johnson, Joshua Reynolds was a man for whom the discipline of work was essential. He found access to the best in his own personality in his studio, just as Goldsmith did when forced, rather reluctantly, to sit down and write. It may have been a common need to catch hold of life through art that cemented the friendship between these two men. Mrs Thrale found Reynolds a cold and grey person and both she and Fanny Reynolds hint that there was an absence of feeling in Goldsmith too at moments when it might reasonably have been expected; but Mrs Thrale had noticed the affection that existed between the painter and the writer and Miss Reynolds, who deeply resented her own neglect, confirms Mrs Thrale's view by her evident jealousy of her brother's friend.

Mrs Thrale was sufficiently perceptive to see that at least there was no coldness in Reynolds' painting, and she recognised that the work and the life were complementary. Reynolds himself admitted that he was a perfectly happy man simply because he loved his work and was extremely well paid for doing it. His estimated £5,000—£6,000 a year is a really prodigious figure for the times.[54] He had a daily routine which was rarely interrupted; a preoccupation which to some people would inevitably have seemed selfish rather than single-minded. Ostensibly he was far from selfish, lending large sums of money to a friend like Burke and giving it away unprompted to fellow painters in distress. Even emissaries from the slums and thieves' kitchens of London might owe him a debt of gratitude once they had drifted into his sphere of influence. When one of his servants (the black man who had modelled the figures of attendants in various paintings) had his pocket picked in the watch-house where he had taken shelter, and was later called as a witness for the prosecution, Reynolds went to considerable trouble to get the subsequent death penalty commuted to transportation, and sent the servant to the prison with gifts of food and clothing.[55] As the first president of the Royal Academy he was considerate and tactful, insisting that a fair number of his own exhibits at the annual exhibition should be hung in the undesirable corners. Poor Miss Reynolds, however, had to have paints smuggled out to her from the painting-room, and the pupils who were always on the Leicester Square premises received very little tuition, having to pick up what knowledge they could by painting draperies and backgrounds and by copying Reynolds' canvases (a practice which he himself considered to have comparatively little educational value).

The octagonal studio buried away in the depths of an outwardly unassuming London house was a spider's web into which royalty, statesmen, aristocrats, soldiers and sailors, actors, actresses and writers were only too pleased to walk. Away from the easel, Reynolds was perpetually mild, good-mannered, unruffled, a man to respect— as Johnson respected him, failing to produce a diminutive version of his name (as he was in the habit of doing for his friends), and emphasising his soundness when he spoke about him to Boswell: 'When Reynolds tells me something I consider myself as possessed of an idea the more.'

Reynolds cultivated the society of strong personalities. In later years he would rationalise this by suggesting that the study of people was essential to the cause of progress in one's art: 'In reality indeed it appears to me, that a man must begin by the study of others. Thus Bacon became a great thinker by first entering into and making himself master of the thoughts of other men.'[56] The need for vicarious excitement was probably deeper than this suggests and led to the gaming tables of St James's as well as to friendships with John Wilkes and the banker, Fordyce, and those women who modelled for him—Nelly O'Brien, Kitty Fisher and the actress Mrs Abington—who had used their beauty and charm to break free from the social strait-jacket in which circumstances had placed them. At the dinner-parties which he gave once a week there was never enough glass or cutlery; some of the guests would have been invited at the last minute; Burke might arrive with Irish relatives in tow. Differences of rank were ignored and it was taken as a house-rule that, while fending for oneself, one must adopt a platonic attitude to such distractions as food and drink and concentrate on things of mind.[57] Reynolds, directing his ear-trumpet here and there, must have taken a quiet but deep pleasure in all the bustle and wit which he, as hub and axle of the wheel, had set in motion.

Bustle, and if not wit then an original brand of humour Goldsmith could also provide and since it was combined with qualities
of intuition of the same order as Reynolds', it is hardly surprising
that the outwardly urbane painter and the writer who by the
standards of his age was constantly on the verge of one solecism or
another, should have become the intimate companions who were so
often seen about London together.

Goldsmith's temperament was the reverse of Reynolds'. He was
volatile and quick-tempered. John Eyles, the man-servant who
looked after him in the Temple during the last years of his life,
described how he had sometimes been led to exploit this facet of his
employer's personality, for angry words were usually followed by a
handsome tip.[58] The writer probably found the painter's constant
equanimity reassuring: Reynolds was undemonstrative but on the
other hand he was unlikely to perpetrate those sudden withdrawals
of affection against which a man with Goldsmith's psychological
problems had to be on guard. He also received the benefit of
Reynolds' knowledge of the world, and particularly of the 'great
world', at a time when he was beginning to acquire more social
mobility. In their opinions as in their temperaments there was
enough to supply the necessary ingredients for a life-long companionship. They were on opposite sides politically, and Goldsmith
would have disliked his friend's addiction to aesthetic theory, even
if he refrained from pointing out that Reynolds contradicted his
well-publicised preference for the sublime effect rather than the
revealing detail every time he took up his brush. For Reynolds' part
it would be possible to read a sneaking admiration into his comments
on Goldsmith's refusal to talk intelligently about his writing:

Perhaps one of the reasons why the Doctor was so very inexpert
in explaining even the principles of his own art was his ignorance
of the scholastic or technical terms by which similar things are
distinguished. He professed himself an enemy to all those
investigations which he said did not at all increase the powers of
doing, but only enabled a person to talk about it, of those researches of which you receive the full result and advantage
without study or attention equal to those who had spent their life
in the pursuit. He considered this as superfluous and needless a
science as that which was taught the *bourgeois gentilhomme*, who

was persuaded he had made a great proficiency in rhetoric when he knew the operation of the organs of speech, or, as he himself says, what he did when he said *u*. No man ever wrote so much from his feelings as Dr Goldsmith. I do not mean here the vulgar opinion of being himself possessed with the passion which he wished to excite. I mean only that he governed himself by an internal feeling of the right rather than by any written rules of art. He judged, for instance, by his ear, whether the verse was musical, without caring or perhaps knowing whether it would bear examination by the rules of the *prosodia*.[59]

Both Reynolds and Goldsmith were essentially humble men. While Goldsmith's humility was accompanied by a lack of confidence in himself which was detrimental to his art, Reynolds' is well illustrated by the manner in which as an old man he discussed with Edmund Malone his notorious lack of success in his experiments with colour (he had been lampooned for his inability to stop the carmine from fading):

I tried every effect of colour, by leaving out every colour in its turn, showed every colour that I could do without it. As I alternatively left out every colour, I tried every new colour; and often, as is well known, failed. The former practice, I am aware, may be compared by those whose first object is ridicule, to that of the poet mentioned in the Spectator, who in a poem of twenty-four books, contrived in each book to leave out a letter. But I was influenced by no such idle or foolish affectation. My fickleness in the mode of colouring arose from an eager desire to attain the highest excellence . . .[60]

A painter who could discuss failure as ingenuously as this was clearly a man after Goldsmith's own heart.

*

Within a few months of the Club's foundation Reynolds had his first opportunity to take Goldsmith's measure as a writer, though they were probably not yet friends. He was enthusiastic about the poem which appeared in December, 1764. In his view it was 'a small, well-polished gem . . . more completely finished than any of

H

his other works', and he found in it qualities of both simplicity and grandeur.[61] This enthusiasm is understandable because, of all Goldsmith's works, it is the one which most closely conforms to Reynolds' artistic theory. With its avoidance of the particular and its brilliant generalisations on the national characters of the Italians, the Swiss, the Dutch, the French and the English, the poem which had existed as a fragment since the end of Goldsmith's continental travels was to prove one of the last achievements of the slowly dying age of classicism. It is almost defiantly so, for the opening section with its romantic emphasis on loneliness and a longing for a particular place is deliberately disowned. It is to equip himself as a citizen of Europe and understand the effects on individuals of different geographical and sociological conditions that Goldsmith's *Traveller* discards the emotional luggage that threatens to chain him to one nostalgia-soaked scene.[62] His imagery is public rather than private, having been placed at the service of the reasoning mind at moments when the mind itself takes an intuitive leap in the dark.

Both the enthusiasm Goldsmith's contemporaries felt for this poem and their bewilderment that he could have written it are understandable. Johnson, of course, already knew the identity of the anonymous writer of the 'Chinese Letters' and had read at least part of *The Vicar of Wakefield* by the time Goldsmith showed him his not quite finished poem. Given that, in his opinion, the couplet was the ideal form for English verse and that neither the technical innovations nor the romantic feeling of Thomas Gray's poems could be comfortably assimilated, the welcome he gave *The Traveller* was predictable. Once published he awarded it almost the highest praise it was possible for him to give. 'Such is the poem, on which we now congratulate the public,' he wrote in the Critical Review,[63] 'as on a production to which, since the death of Pope, it will not be easy to find anything equal.'

The Traveller, which had originally been given the title *A Prospect of Society*, was sold to Newbery for twenty guineas in October or November 1764. Thomas Percy, who was back in London for the autumn, had seen the manuscript, every space filled with corrections and revisions. Johnson was also involved, especially after Newbery's compositor by inadvertently reversing the order of the galleys provided further opportunities for revision.[64] The ending, in particular, was re-worked and it was at this stage that Johnson contributed his 'dozen or sixteen lines'. (Towards the end of his life, at Boswell's request, he marked nine as being definitely his own.) Percy was busy too this autumn, preparing the *Reliques* for the press, and the sense of purposeful activity within the Johnson circle can be felt on a page of his appointments book:

Tuesday,	November 13	Dined with Mr Johnson at ye Mitre Tavern. Supped with Mr Dodsley.
Wednesday,	November 14	Called on Mr Tonson, on Mr Johnson . . .
Saturday,	November 17	Drank tea at Mrs Williams. Dr Goldsmith supped with me.
Wednesday,	November 21	Dined at Mr Thomas Davies in Russel St., with Johnson, Goldsmith, Hoole, who spent the evening with me.
Thursday,	November 22	Dined with Goldsmith and spent the evening with him and Mr Johnson, tea at Mr Allen's.
Monday,	November 26	Dined with Apperley. Met Dr Goldsmith who spent the evening with me.
Wednesday,	November 28	Went to the Museum. Spent the evening at Mr Hoole's with Johnson Goldsmith, and a Mr White.
Wednesday,	November 30	Called on Johnson and Goldsmith, Mr Rivington and Mr Newbery . . .[65]

When the poem appeared six days before Christmas, with the Bible and Sun imprint and the name Oliver Goldsmith, M.B. on the title page, it was immediately acclaimed. The anonymous critic on the *London Chronicle*, evidently a man who knew Goldsmith slightly and who felt obliged to make something of a public recantation, wrote: 'It were injustice to this ingenious gentleman not to allow him a degree of poetical merit beyond what we have seen for several years, and we must acknowledge him possessed of a strength and connexion of thought which we little expected to see'. The reviewer on the *Monthly* was forced to the conclusion that the poem whose imagery he had found 'just and magnificent' was 'a work of very considerable merit'. The review in the *Gentleman's Magazine* must have been particularly consoling to Goldsmith for, perhaps prompted by the wording of the dedicatory letter addressed to Henry, the reviewer went out of his way to compare *The Traveller* with poems which had engaged the public's attention in recent years:

> After the crude and virulent rhapsodies upon which caprice and faction have lavished an unbounded praise, that if known to any future time will disgrace the present, it is hoped this poem will come with some advantage, and that a general encouragement of real merit will show, that we have not totally lost the power to distinguish it.[66]

The dedication had given Goldsmith the opportunity to indulge in some of the fashionable 'sentiment' on which the poem itself seemed to turn its back: readers were reminded of the perpetual curate 'who, despising Fame and Fortune, has retired early to Happiness and Obscurity, with an income of forty pounds a year'. Although there is a degree of contrivance behind this picture of a bucolic philosopher, it is not hard to sympathise with Goldsmith's real motive for using his brother as a stalking-horse. For several years now his resentment against a public which seemed preoccupied with the most tiresome kind of literary, theatrical and political squabbles had been slowly mounting. 'When the mind is once infested with this disease,' Goldsmith writes, 'it can only find pleasure in what contributes to encrease the distemper. Like the tyger, that seldom desists from pursuing man after having once preyed upon human flesh, the reader, who has once gratified his appetite with calumny, makes, ever after, the most agreeable feast upon murdered reputation. Such readers generally admire some half-witted thing, who wants to be thought a bold man, having lost the character of a wise one. Him they dignify with the name of poet; his tawdry lampoons are called satires, his turbulence is said to be force, and his phrenzy fire.'[67]

There were rare moments when, freed from despondency on the one hand and the praises of his friends on the other, Goldsmith knew that he was an artist. William Cooke, a neighbour in the Temple, caught him at one of them when he was working on *The Deserted Village*. Goldsmith read ten lines of his poem, and then:

> "Come," says he, "let me tell you, this is no bad morning's work; and now, my dear boy, if you are not better engaged, I should be glad to enjoy a Shoe-maker's holiday with you."

It is the voice of a humble man wanting to share his pleasure that imagination has imposed order on experience, that something has 'come right'. Unfortunately such confidence was intermittent and punctuated by self-doubt often in an overwhelming form, and out of this doubt sprang the kind of envy which the dedication of *The Traveller* conveys, an envy which is easier to assimilate when it is remembered that at thirty-six Goldsmith was putting his name to a publication for the first time. He at once knew his own worth with all the certainty of someone who had spent mornings condensing his impressions of Europe into tautly-knit couplets, and refused to believe in it because (until these reviews began to come in) the majority of his literary-minded contemporaries in a small city where personalities and reputations were a matter of everyday conversation had refused to give his talent its due. Unlike that humour of Envy which he grotesquely parodied, this was a mean and uncomfortable emotion which plagued him until the end of his life. He made efforts to control it, and the parody of Envy may have been part of this effort. Reynolds believed that his poetic achievement was of the same order as Addison's,[68] and it is surely significant that, arguing with Johnson about the respective merits of Dryden and Pope, Goldsmith should have quoted the lines on Addison, with their analysis of literary jealousy, as proof of Pope's 'deep knowledge of the human heart'.[69] That Goldsmith's jealousy was directly related to a lack of confidence in himself is suggested by his reaction to the attack on him by the scurrilous Dr William Kenrick in the last year of his life, while the extent of his endeavour to overcome the disability is seen by his frank and open relationships, once he had bound them to himself with bonds of affection, with some of the most famous and successful figures in the cultural circles of his day.

In the spring of 1765, Goldsmith's doubts as to 'what reception a Poem may find, which has neither abuse, party, nor blank verse to support it' may have seemed justified, for *The Traveller* got off to a poor start commercially. It was March before a second edition was needed, but then the tide turned in Goldsmith's favour and a third and fourth edition came out in the course of the year. He was at last 'a notable man'.

*

In the month of publication recognition came promptly from an unexpected quarter. Robert Nugent, M.P., the son of a Colonel Michael Nugent of Carlanstown, County Westmeath and therefore a kind of neighbour, chose this moment to establish an Irish connexion. Although neither he nor Goldsmith was to leave any indication as to what they thought of one another, it is almost certain that, for Goldsmith, this was another important friendship, and it is a surprising association when Goldsmith's remarks about squireens to Bob Bryanton are recalled, for this loud-mouthed, boisterous, athletically-built gentleman of sixty-two with the florid complexion and Mr Punch profile must in youth have had more than a touch of the squireen about him. Although their relationship is almost entirely undocumented, access to Nugent's house in Essex or his lodgings on North Parade at Bath was obviously an important feature of Goldsmith's life from now on. No letters have survived apart from that epistle in verse which Goldsmith composed after a visit to Essex in 1773 and the unexpected arrival on his return to London of a haunch of venison—an appropriately hearty gift from a hearty man.[70] Nugent's entry into Goldsmith's story produces a temporary change of key and perhaps for that reason underlines some of the qualities which Goldsmith as an Irishman needed to find in his life, and which London had not provided.

For Nugent, two things had determined a future rather different from that of his typical Irish counterpart: he was extremely ambitious, and while still a boy was involved in a scandal with his cousin who claimed that he was the father of her illegitimate son. Nugent had fled to London to escape the necessity of marrying her and although he returned to Ireland for a few years (and for a brief marriage to the Earl of Fingal's daughter, who died giving birth to his son, Edmund), London and especially the London political scene had captured his imagination. Having furthered his ambitions by a timely conversion to protestantism (he would revert to his old faith only on his death-bed) he acquired an estate, a fortune and a pocket-borough at the age of thirty-four by marrying Anne Craggs, a stout, jolly widow five years older than himself. By the time he introduced himself to Goldsmith he had had a long career in the Commons as M.P. for Bristol, was a figure of some influence in the Treasury and, since 1759, Vice-Treasurer of Ireland. Within a year of Anne Cragg's death he had married yet another widow, the Countess of Berkeley, from whom he was now estranged.[71]

Nugent's greatest asset seems to have been his rather flamboyant charm. He inspired affection in both men and women, though on the one side there might be a clear recognition that politically he would support the party that had most advantages to offer and on the other that he was sexually promiscuous. To Horace Walpole he was 'an Irish stallion' who had fallen into a comfortable, easy relationship with a rich, plain woman who was prepared to use her influence with friends like Lord Chesterfield to promote his parliamentary career, and Alexander Pope to encourage him in his endeavours as a fluent but uninspired writer of verse. Benjamin Franklin, who had been questioned by a parliamentary committee on which Nugent was sitting, adopts an ambivalent tone when describing their subsequent tête-a-tête dinner, but even through the medium of his cautious irony we can see the effect that Nugent might have had on contemporaries who welcomed an occasional holiday from English reserve:

> He gave me a great deal of flummery,—saying that though I had answered some of his questions a little pertly, yet he liked me from that day, for the spirit I shewed in defence of my country; and at parting, after we had drunk a bottle and a half of claret each, he hugged and kissed me, vowing he had never in his life met with a man he was so much in love with. This I write for your amusement . . .[72]

As M.P. for Bristol his concern for trade went hand in hand with liberal tendencies, but his belief, in the early stages of the American dispute, that the colonists should be allowed to trade freely, and his support for the Jews' Naturalisation Bill, were not pursued beyond a point at which he would have come into conflict with government policy, and the acquisition of two Irish peerages within ten years (he became Lord Clare in 1766 and Baron Nugent in 1776) was an indication of this willingness to conform to the official line as much as of a royal reluctance to make a cash settlement of the money he had lent to the King's father. But there was one cause in which he was prepared to risk his political neck: this was Ireland. Nugent's seeking out a fellow Irishman who had had a literary success was in keeping with his repeated attempts (by no means popular with his Bristol constituents, who in the end rejected him) to have the Irish commercial embargo lifted.

There seems to have been no question of Nugent's becoming a patron in the traditional sense. Goldsmith remained true to his Johnsonian principles, though he was to show every sign of enjoying access to Gosfield Hall and the opportunities this offered both for botanising and for advising Nugent as to how the rather featureless terrain could be improved. Perhaps it was when the landscape theme began to pall that he was encouraged to design an ice-house. Goldsmith would have needed less curiosity and a stronger will than he in fact possessed to reject the flattering approach that was made to him this December, especially when it came from a man whose noisy humour and elaborate absurdities he could easily understand. Perhaps too he had some rapport with that incongruous vein in Nugent's personality where the Camillas and Corinnas and Clarissas of a would-be poet existed side by side with ruminations in verse on the nature of the Holy Trinity.[73]

From Nugent's point of view, as he hailed people from the window of White's in a stentorian voice or slapped them on the back, punctuating his conversation with coarse jokes and his speeches with anecdotes and homely allusions, the important thing was to be regarded as the Good Fellow, or at least the Honest Rogue, who had knocked about a bit but could do no serious wrong. And it was incumbent on a good fellow to do something for a deserving neighbour, ideally not by embarking on any personal expense but by hooking them up to one of the many national funds to which at this time a skilful politician had access. In short, Nugent's aim that December was to make Goldsmith a pensioner on the Irish Establishment. Plans were made for the poet to be interviewed by the current viceroy, The Earl of Northumberland, who was now in London and, within a few days of the publication of *The Traveller*, Goldsmith presented himself at a forbidding

Jacobean mansion at the corner of Whitehall and the Strand. The result of that interview would be more than enough to convince anyone who was still in doubt of his startling inability to look after his own interests.

*

The career of the Earl of Northumberland, like that of Robert Nugent, was one of the great success stories of the age, but in his case the tree of Fortune had needed only the gentlest of shakes. Hugh Smithson, who had started life with the comparatively simple prospects of the younger son of a Yorkshire squire, had by the time he was twenty-four inherited both a title and a fortune and married the girl who through the female line had inherited the great north-country Percy estates. An intelligent and handsome extravert without strong political ambitions, he had deployed his wealth in acquiring even grander titles than his baronetcy, beginning with the extinct earldom which he and his wife were allowed to assume together with the old family name of Percy.[74]

At a time when England was a Utopia for the wealthy and the ennobled, the Northumberlands gave every indication that they were vastly enjoying themselves. They employed the Adam brothers to alter their several houses, carried out extensive improvements on the Alnwick estate, and advertised their belief in conspicuous consumption by holding spectacular parties. The Countess was a friend of Queen Charlotte, and the King's birthday might be celebrated with a reception for 1,500 guests at Northumberland House or a firework display and fête at Sion, their second Thames-side residence. Lady Northumberland, a romantic who dabbled in verse and liked the well-corsetted ballads which Thomas Percy was soon to supply, would be piped into her ancestral hall by Scots retainers, and had to be reproved by the Queen for employing more servants than the Royal Family itself. She had a lively mind which delighted in new people and new places, and was equally at home shut up in a drawing room with a royal family determined to economise on candles or, at an election, haranguing the temporarily mesmerised Common Man from a window in Covent Garden.[75] At a time when History was being discovered as a popular entertainment and Shakespeare's plays (including, of course, *Henry IV*) were gaining ground in the theatre, she revelled in the ancient Percy connexion. The Revd. Thomas Percy was soon to be taken up by the Northumberlands not only because of his publishing success in 1765 but for his ability to trace his descent from a distant Earl. Horace Walpole may have forgiven 'Earl Smithson' and his jovial wife their flair for acquiring titles but it must have been galling for a man whose carefully disposed 'Gothic' pinnacles at Strawberry Hill were constantly being vandalised, to contemplate that the 'Duchess of Charing Cross', as he inevitably dubbed her when Smithson achieved his dukedom, had inherited not only a romantic ruin at Warkworth but an inhabitable castle which was ripe for embellishments in that new style he was doing so much to promote. It was an unfortunate irony that an explosion in the tower at Sion where Lord Northumberland kept his fireworks should have blown out four of Walpole's stained-glass windows.[76]

The Northumberlands courted popularity and although as viceroy in Ireland the Earl no doubt accepted a situation which men of the calibre of Johnson could see to be iniquitous, he and the Countess had gone to Dublin with the determination to make friends. To a great extent they succeeded, and now, on a short return visit to London, the Earl set time aside from his other affairs to see the expatriate Irish poet whom Nugent had drawn to his attention.

As Lord-Lieutenant of Middlesex he also had occasion to see John Hawkins, one of the county magistrates, and although in one sense it was unfortunate that Goldsmith should encounter a fellow Club member at Northumberland House, the meeting was to afford a unique opportunity for gauging the exact relationship of a Goldsmith story to its factual base. Hawkins in the account of the episode in his *Life of Johnson* interestingly lets fall that, although he had arrived in the busy ante-room after Goldsmith, he was given precedence, county affairs evidently being considered more important than poetry:

Having one day a call to wait on the late Duke, then Earl of Northumberland, I found Goldsmith waiting for an audience in an outer room: I asked him what had brought him there; he told me an invitation from his lordship. I made my business as short as I could, and as a reason mentioned that Dr Goldsmith was waiting without. The Earl asked me if I was acquainted with him; I told him I was, adding what I thought likely to recommend him. I retired, and staid in the outer room to take him home. Upon his coming out, I asked him the result of his conversation. His lordship, says he, told me he had read my poem, meaning *The Traveller*, and was much delighted with it; that he was going Lord Lieutenant to Ireland, and that, hearing that I was a native of that country, he should be glad to do me any kindness.—

—And what did you answer, asked I, to this gracious offer?

—Why, said he, I could say nothing but that I had a brother there, a clergyman, that stood in need of help: as for myself, I have no dependence on the promises of great men; I look to the booksellers for support; they are my best friends, and I am not inclined to forsake them for others.

As he waited for Hawkins to emerge from the Earl of Northumberland's presence, Goldsmith may have had time and inclination to reflect on the change of climate between the literary world of the 1760s and that of the Augustan golden age in the first two decades of the century. About to be 'patronised' for the first time in his life he may have recalled the dramatic changes which intelligent patronage had effected in the lives of earlier writers. His own circumstances, as he waited in the ante-room while the earl and the lawyer conferred seemed to reflect the price that poets had paid for that independence advocated by Pope. The man from Lissoy, who was rather inclined to share the inverted snobbery of the mid-century man of letters and to believe that he would be disparaged in this aristocratic setting because he wrote for money, may have recalled that scene in another ante-room where, with the plans for his Dictionary in his hand, Johnson had waited while the Earl of Chesterfield entertained Colley Cibber.

Like Johnson, Goldsmith was being turned into a courtier. However graciously condescending, however polite the manner in which the subject was broached, Lord Northumberland was asking him to beg and Goldsmith, who only two years previously had sent a lucidly reasoned memorial to Lord Bute requesting a travel grant, refused to do so. His hint that Henry should be helped (hardly necessary perhaps in view of the indication he had given of his brother's low status in the Church of Ireland in the dedication to his poem) was not taken up—perhaps because it had been made in so casual a manner as to appear a deliberate snub. Into Thomas Percy's rather anxious little rider to the incident in the Memoir, where he insists that Lord Northumberland 'often regretted that he was not then made acquainted with Dr Goldsmith's plan and desire to explore the internal regions of Asia; for if he had . . . he would have procured him a sufficient salary on the Irish establishment', it would be possible to read an admission on the earl's part that he had mishandled the affair. While Lord Halifax had stepped forward at the right moment to prevent Addison from going into the church or presented Congreve with a rich government sinceure, Northumberland had waited for a request as his steward might have waited for a tradesman to present a bill.

Hawkins' presence might have been the determining factor as far as Goldsmith was concerned. He had not only been expected to petition Lord Northumberland, but a member of the Club was there to watch the performance. It could well have been the streak of theatricality in his nature that tipped the balance in favour of silence. It was an expensive luxury. The one thing gained from his visit to Northumberland House was a story and he was still telling it (to Percy rather surprisingly) nine years later. With a wave of the story-teller's wand Hawkins has disappeared and been replaced by a 'groom of the chambers'. To this gentleman the inexperienced (but dazzled) poet—who thinks that a man of such magnificence can be no less a personage than the earl himself—makes the speech which he has so carefully rehearsed. Too late he discovers his mistake. By the time the would-be patron appears the cupboard is bare and there is simply nothing left to say to the great man.[77]

This is Goldsmith in a typically self-deflating vein, but the satire, though gentler, is as unmistakeable as Horace Walpole's sneers about the parvenu who is beginning to set himself up as a patron of the arts—' . . *price* is no article, or rather *is* a reason for my Lord Northumberland's liking anything . . .'.[78] John Hawkins was exasperated by Goldsmith's apparent naivety: 'Thus did this idiot in the affairs of the world trifle with his fortunes, and put back the hand that was held out to assist him!' But the licensed fool had kept his independence and the literary world had one more story to tell about the preposterous Dr Goldsmith.

NINE

The Good-Natured Man

GOLDSMITH'S INVISIBLE earnings from *The Traveller* were to be out of all proportion to the twenty guineas that Newbery paid him for his poem. 'By Oliver Goldsmith, M.B.' Newbery had announced and the appearance of the same name on other title pages would, in the long term, make a vast difference to the writer's income. Goldsmith had received £21 for the *History of England in a Series of Letters from a Nobleman to his Son* published six months before *The Traveller*, but a few years later he would be commissioned to write a similar work for over ten times this sum.

In the early months of 1765, however, the immediate financial prospect was not promising. The previous autumn he had received ten guineas from James Dodsley (and possibly another ten from Newbery) for an oratorio libretto called *The Captivity*. It was a competent script but it was not to be printed until 1820 and was probably never performed.[1] During this year he also seems to have acted on a hint from Thomas Percy who had now been taken up by the Earl and Countess of Northumberland. Goldsmith composed a little ballad, *Edwin and Angelina*—based on one of the ballads in Percy's collection—and had it printed privately 'for the Amusement of the Countess of Northumberland'. He had probably had time to regret the attitude he had adopted in his interview with the Earl. If there had been an implied snub on Goldsmith's part the ballad was an ample apology, and it is almost certain that there would have been some return, one hopes not in kind though the Countess was a competent writer of light verse. *Edwin and Angelina* was subsequently to be incorporated into the text of *The Vicar of Wakefield*.

Goldsmith still owed money to Newbery and work on the *Survey of Experimental Philosophy*, for which he had already been paid, had hardly begun. But success was obviously in the air for, by mid-summer, he had decided to return to Fleet Street. He installed himself in lodgings in the Inner Temple at No. 3 King's Bench

Walk in time to keep an eye on the sales of the collection of twenty-five reprinted *Essays by Mr Goldsmith* with which Newbery, in conjunction with William Griffin of Fetter Lane, set out to capitalise on the success of *The Traveller*. They were received with enthusiasm for their 'most natural humour, together with the deepest strength of judgment, and the widest range of understanding.' Nine months later the appearance of *The Vicar of Wakefield* would consolidate Goldsmith's success. The more domestic link with Newbery, through Miss Fleming, was still intact and Goldsmith returned to Canonbury House for occasional visits when London became either too airless or too distracting (or perhaps when a creditor had to be avoided).

As today, the Inns of Court of which the Inner and Middle Temple were a part were associations with the function of maintaining a professional code for barristers and of educating recruits to the legal profession. As in the universities, the residential qualification for entrants had become more important than any formal teaching they might receive. The Inns with their conveniently situated chambers attracted well-to-do bachelors from outside the legal profession as the Albany would later do: in particular they provided a fashionable address for people associated with the arts. There was no danger of Goldsmith's flirting with the prospect of a legal career; he had put that behind him with the trip to Dublin in 1752. But other literary acquaintances like his compatriots Hugh Kelly, who also lived at the Temple, and Arthur Murphy, who had chambers for a time at Gray's Inn, had legal ambitions which were later realised; and Johnson, who was still living in rooms at 1 Inner Temple Lane, appears to have known at least as much law as the average professional resident. In their different ways all these writers were continuing a tradition which had its roots in the middle ages when the inns of court combined the functions of a forum of wits and a finishing school for the upper classes.

The lawyers seem also to have clung to a tradition which in Shakespearean times had produced the kind of revels and amateur dramatics which Leslie Hotson has described in *The first Night of Twelfth Night*. By the mid-eighteenth century they had dwindled into amateur censors of the professional theatre, getting up parties to attend new plays, sometimes supporting a favourite dramatist,

sometimes if a writer had infringed their code organising themselves into a claque to ensure that the first night should also be
the last. A visiting Frenchman, the Abbe LeBlanc, had become
aware of this phenomenon in the summer of 1737 when he visited
Covent Garden theatre on the night following the introduction
of the Theatrical Licensing Act. On this occasion it was the new
restrictions rather than the play which caused the disturbance,
but the effect was the same: the actors were driven off the stage.
LeBlanc was surprised to learn that it was professional men rather
than apprentices, clerks or mechanics who had been responsible:

> ... they were men of a very grave and genteel profession; they
> were lawyers, and please you, a body of gentlemen, perhaps, less
> honoured but certainly more feared here than they are in France.
> Most of them live in colleges, where, conversing always with one
> another, they mutually preserve a spirit of independency through
> the body, and with great ease form cabals. These gentlemen, in
> the stage entertainments of London, behave much like our
> footboys in those at a fair. With us, your parti-colour'd gentry
> are the most noisy; but here, men of the law have all the sway, if
> I may be permitted to call so those pretended professors of it, who
> are rather the organs of chicanery, than the interpreters of
> justice. At Paris the cabals of the pit are only among young
> fellows, whose years may excuse their folly, or persons of the
> meanest education and stamp: here they are the fruit of delibera-
> tions in a very grave body of people who are not less formidable
> to the minister in place, than to the theatrical writers.[2]

Living in this environment Goldsmith not surprisingly began to
turn his thoughts once more in the direction of the theatre. It had
always appealed to him and he knew other writers in London who
had been paid handsomely for successfully running plays. George
Colman's first comedy, *The Jealous Wife*, was still in the repertoire;
and Arthur Murphy, a neighbour from Roscommon, had written
his first plays while still an actor at Drury Lane and had more
recently had a comedy and a farce successfully produced at Covent
Garden in the '63-'64 season.

Goldsmith's acquaintance with Arthur Murphy and his association with the *Critical Review* at a time when contributors to that
paper had gained a reputation for hostility towards the court of

King David, were determining factors in the direction his own
theatrical career would take. Murphy's relationship with Garrick
was an uneasy one and during the *Rosciad* 'debate' which had
embraced national as well as theatrical politics he had written pamphlets attacking the Churchill-Colman faction.[3] He was thus
committed to the lobby which refused to see Garrick's managership
of Drury Lane as an entirely unmixed blessing. Although Goldsmith had refused to participate in so futile a squabble, thus avoiding
the mistake he had made in his *Enquiry into the Present State of
Polite Learning*, he was associated with Murphy both in his political
opinions and in his allegiance to Johnson. The two Irishmen
frequently found themselves in each other's company at Tom's
coffee house, in Johnson's rooms and, after the following summer,
in Southwark or Streatham at the homes of the eminently civilised
brewer, Henry Thrale, to whom Murphy had introduced Johnson.
Hester Thrale, although the subtleties of Goldsmith, the 'odd
little doctor', were lost on her, greatly admired the conversational
powers and pleasing manners of Arthur Murphy. He was 'so willing
to amuse you, to divert your Company, to inform, to sooth: yet no
Buffoonery, no Coarseness, no meanness, but a Behaviour perfectly decorous; and a Conversation so happily made up of Narration
and native good Sense, of Fact & Sentiment, that it is impossible
to image a more agreeable Man.' Johnson believed that Murphy 'by
some happy Skill displays more knowledge than he really has; like
Gamesters who can play for more Money than they are worth';[4]
Mrs Thrale would not have agreed. In spite of Murphy's long-
standing devotion to an actress, she was infatuated by him. Goldsmith hardly endeared himself to her by hinting as much:

Murphy was too fond of telling Stories of Foote, and Dr Goldsmith who was no match at all for him in general Conversation
could only watch that Propensity and mark it. He stood behind
my Chair one afternoon, and as fast as Atty came out with his
stories, he kept whispering to me—Story the first, and by and by—
Story the 2nd he went on to the 4th I remember, and then I said,
how have done Doctor, or I swear I'll tell: he had done in a
Moment, for he both fear'd Mr Murphy's Powers, and envy'd
his elegance of Dress and Behaviour: What now you like Mr
Murphy says he to me, because of that Hat I suppose.[5]

5 *The Times I* by Hogarth, September 7, 1762

Bute, advocating peace with France, mounts the fire engine with which he is
trying to quench the flames of global conflict. William Pitt, on stilts, applies
bellows to the flames, while his brother-in-law, Lord Temple, provides further
discouragement for Bute from a first-floor window. A fresh supply of fuel in
the shape of the *Monitor* and the *North Briton* is being trundled towards the
conflagration. Parodying the Union Fire Office emblem, the new inn sign which
is being manoeuvred into position on the left suggests a far from united kingdom

6a Robert Chambers

6b Edmund Burke

6c Bennet Langton

6d Topham Beauclerk

7a Thomas Percy

7b Samuel Dyer

7c John Hawkins

7d Anthony Chamier

8a Mary and
Catherine Horneck
by Reynolds, 1766

8b Robert Nugent (Lord Clare) with his sister, Peggy,
his daughter and his son Lieutenant Colonel Edmund Nugent, M.P.
by Zoffany

Murphy's early career in the theatre was in some ways a curtain-raiser for Goldsmith's briefer but more significant experience as a dramatist. In Goldsmith's case there were to be the same difficulties with Garrick, and the same dissatisfaction with the prevailing dramatic taste which, for Goldsmith, would eventually lead to a success snatched from the jaws of the failure that the managers had predicted.

*

As the newspaper battle of 1761 demonstrated, the London theatre of the third quarter of the century had a prestige out of all proportion to its artistic achievement. In many ways it has an affinity to the Hollywood of the nineteen-thirties. Its leading players were highly paid and socially in demand and the smallest items of back-stage gossip would find their way into the press. It had its own talent-scouts, like Paul Hiffernan, a bothersome acquaintance of Goldsmith's; its press relations officers, like Colman and Robert Lloyd who had run the *St James's Chronicle* as a mouthpiece for Garrick; and leading ladies like Mrs Abington who could start a fashion by appearing in a new cap or throw Drury Lane into chaos by refusing to attend rehearsals. For matinée idols there were Barry and Holland and 'Gentleman' Smith: for popular comedians, Woodward and Ned Shuter—Shuter could make or break a new author: everything depended on whether he was drunk or sober on the first night. The analogy certainly holds where the status of writers is concerned. Dramatists were expected to attend the rehearsals of new plays and might be assailed with demands for instant re-writing. Mrs Bellamy (in her twenties) prided herself on having reduced the poet Edward Young (in his seventies) to a state of impotent fury by insisting in front of the assembled company that his favourite line was unspeakable; but when, at the end of a hopeless first night she found another clergyman-dramatist weeping quietly amongst the props of his turgid tragedy, she was kind and promised to use her influence to obtain him a chaplaincy.[6] The prestige of these leading players was reflected in the salary structure: at the height of his career Garrick as actor and manager was drawing approximately £1,300 per season; Powell, in the year which saw the production of Goldsmith's first play at Covent Garden, had a salary somewhere in the region of £650, while humbler members of the company would have been on scales of between 15s. and 30s. a week.*

If Hollywood aimed at providing a society with a flattering image of itself, the same is true of the London theatre of the mid-eighteenth century. When he was not watching eviscerated dramas about Greek heroes and moorish potentates the middle class Englishman of the period was revelling in drawing-room comedies whose protagonists voiced genteel sentiments or represented stereotyped and instantly recognisable villainy. The term middle class is used advisedly. The early decades of the century had witnessed the managers' long and successful wooing of those respectable city folk whom Jeremy Collier had frightened away when he represented Congreve as a threat to the moral fabric of society.

By combining some of the stock situations and types of full-blooded restoration comedy with the expression of handsome sentiments and a hero who was obligingly ready to miss his chance with the heroine in order to be decent to everyone else, Richard Steele had attempted to restore the good image of the drama in his play *The Conscious Lovers*. This had many good scenes and when the genteel folk threatened to become immobilised by their delicate consciences, a team of well-portrayed servants took over in a lively way. But the continuing popularity of this play half a century after its first performance was having a harmful effect on the theatrical repertoire since less able dramatists were still reproducing Steele's formula.

The theatre companies had little to offer more intelligent members of the public apart from heavily cut versions of the Restoration dramatists and a handful of Jacobean plays. A small but constantly widening selection of Shakespeare productions made an exception to the rule. But Shakespeare was still presented with whatever mutilations and embellishments the actor-manager thought fit. Garrick prided himself on his 'improved' version of *Hamlet*; and turned *A Midsummer Night's Dream* into a musical comedy, without the Mechanicals.

The two patent theatres of Drury Lane and Covent Garden were national institutions and could never be entirely unfashionable

*These figures, calculated from salary lists reprinted by G. W. Stone in *The English Stage*, do not include earnings from benefit nights.

while their actor managers donned court dress and circulated amongst the courtiers at St James's Palace on a royal birthday; but although the Italian opera in the Haymarket was packed with wealthy and fashionable patrons, at Drury Lane the beautiful Peggy Woffington might find herself playing to a crowded gallery and empty boxes.[7] Kitty Clive got a measure of revenge by doing an impersonation of Signora Regina Mingotti as a party-piece; but the Great still showed a preference for the society of Italian singers and opened their country houses to them when the season ended at the beginning of June.[8]

A benefit night for a popular actor or actress usually attracted coaches from the St James's end of town (and Garrick himself was known to come running if certain monogrammed equipages drew up at the stage door), but many of the patrons who bought a gold ticket had come to look round the house from a box rather than attend to the unexceptionable and mildly democratic sentiments voiced from the stage. The real audience was elsewhere, crowding into the pit to enjoy their corporate power and see the actors go through their paces, like the Abbé LeBlanc's claque of lawyers, or into the middle and upper galleries where a predominantly lower middle class audience avid for politeness and decorum acted as censors of the stage, hissing at any impropriety and making mental notes as to the way in which the Lovewells and Harriots and wicked Lady Altons comported themselves.

The theatre belonged to its public. This was strongly felt and while it was accepted as seemly and appropriate that David Garrick should wait on the King at a levée, it was also right that a humbler actor should acknowledge the power of his audience, perhaps by making a real submission to its whims. This was probably one of the reasons for the ambiguous status of the acting profession and the continuing idea that for an actor to be a 'gentleman' he must either have a cast-iron pedigree or be very successful indeed. Garrick had waited until his mother's death before seizing his chance and appearing, well-disguised as a black man, in a performance of *Oroonoko* at Ipswich; and Goldsmith was strangely horrified when Daniel Hodson's son arrived in London and announced his intention of going on the stage.[9]

London audiences were feared. They were kind to beginners, but could confront an established actor with nasty exhibitions of group hostility. One of Garrick's actors, Moody, famous for his stage Irishmen, had in the course of a riot at Drury Lane snatched a lighted torch from the hand of a demonstrator who showed every intention of setting fire to the auditorium: his action was considered to be disrespectful to the public and Garrick was forced to suspend him for a few performances until the customers deemed him to have purged his contempt. That audiences could be roused to the pitch of collective sadism is illustrated by the ugly scene at Covent Garden when the septuagenarian Macklin—something of a trouble-maker but an actor who had done a lot to promote the cause of naturalism in the theatre with his famous Shylock (he was now performing Macbeth in a kilt)—was requested to kneel and beg the audience's forgiveness for an imagined offence. He refused and was shouted off the stage.[10]

In another way these audiences were easy to please. It was too early for a concept like Coleridge's 'willing suspension of disbelief'. Only a very limited degree of illusion was demanded. In many respects a performance was riddled with conventions, from the guardsmen who mounted duty on either side of the proscenium arch to the little pages who, in plays like *All for Love* and *The Rival Queens*, would trot along behind their royal mistresses and re-arrange their trains after each dramatic sweep across the boards.[11] As tradition associated a tragic heroine with a black dress even Juliet might appear prematurely in full mourning. Scenery was stored and re-used repeatedly. Long after Garrick had brought the designer de Loutherbourg from Paris, audiences could expect to find familiar back-drops, costumes and props reappearing from one production to the next. (In contrast, to Goldsmith's disgust, the ever-popular harlequinades were lavishly mounted with transformation scenes and artificial waterfalls.) Leading performers seem to have been left to their own devices with regard to costumes. An actress with rich patrons would enjoy decking herself out in borrowed diamonds and the extravagant Mrs Bellamy, in the part of the Empress Fulvia, effectively up-staged her Roxana (Peg Woffington dressed in a straw-coloured 'good-as-new' dress that had belonged to the Princess of Wales) by sending privately to Paris for a costume of yellow satin which she wore with a purple robe.

The theatrical memoirs of the period are full of stories about people who stepped out of their rôles while still on stage. Garrick was effectively neutralised by a leading lady who saw an unusually long speech as an opportunity to re-tie her glove-knots and Mrs Bellamy was inclined to break into laughter whenever accidents befell other performers. Like her, the clever young impersonator Tate Wilkinson found the audience sympathetic when his sense of the ridiculous got the better of him; while, at a performance of Congreve's *Mourning Bride* in Edinburgh, the good lady who had stood in at short notice for her sister, Mrs Kennedy, reduced the rest of the cast to jelly by rising from the couch on which she had recently expired and stepping to the edge of the stage to rebuke the restless audience—before re-arranging herself between the mutes and covering her face with a veil.[12] Even at Drury Lane the great Mrs Cibber, playing Ophelia at her own benefit at the age of forty-seven, was to be seen dropping deep curtseys during the 'Mousetrap' scene.[13] (She was not protesting against the tradition that the Player King and Queen should perform with their backs to the Court of Denmark, but simply acknowledging the presence of friends in the audience.)

Such stories, coupled to George Colman's statement that a *coup de théatre* would set the spectators in the upper gallery rapping the panelled walls in appreciation,[14] suggest that the playgoers of this age went to the theatre to see 'Acting' as a series of brilliant theatrical moments rather than as a consistent bodying-out of a dramatic role. Watching David Garrick dressed in the uniform of one of George III's generals amongst a bevy of witches who performed a 'fantastical dance' under three enormous chandeliers, they must have remained rather more detached from the concept 'Macbeth' than a modern audience would expect to find itself.[15] By the standards of James Quin's day Garrick's performances were 'naturalistic' (it was known that he had gone to Tower Hamlets to observe the behaviour of a madman when preparing himself for Lear) but even Garrick was pleased when a performance was interrupted by one of the proscenium guards who broke down and wept; he rewarded the man with half-a-crown. With audiences willing to settle for a very slight degree of illusion it was not surprising that the emphasis should be on performance rather than on what was performed, and the result was a repertoire which groaned under the weight of 'tragedies' like Arthur Murphy's *Grecian Daughter* with its flabby blank verse and cardboard 'politeness'

(Mrs Thrale considered it the finest tragedy of her day) and comedies in which the situation of the young lovers, the intransigent father, the unwanted suitor and the malevolent older woman (she was usually titled) was constantly re-explored. On a spring evening in 1767 when the choice happened to lie between *The Jealous Wife* at Drury Lane and *The Suspicious Husband* at Covent Garden, even the most seasoned playgoer must have had to pause for a moment and perform some mental exercises.

While so many writers were filling newspaper columns with theatrical gossip, Goldsmith kept his independence as an occasional —and often severe—commentator on the state of the theatres. Although he carefully moderated his critical disdain when discussing a derivative and wordy 'tragedy' like Murphy's *Orphan of China* or as lack-lustre a farce as Townley's *High Life Below Stairs*, he spoke out against the vogue for maudlin dramas and those 'weeping comedies' which turned the stage into a platform for sententious debate.[16] He was far from convinced that acting had reached the apex of naturalism. He claimed that many of the performances he saw were closer to mimicry than to that interpretive quality which could get to the heart of a rôle and produce the living embodiment of a character. In contrast, he praised Mlle Clairon (whom he had probably seen in Paris) for appearing to be less aware of the audience than of her fellow actors and for achieving a natural co-ordination of voice and gesture: 'She sometimes begins with a mute, eloquent attitude; but never goes forward all at once with hands, eyes, head, and voice.'[17] He resented the trivialisation of the stage—the spread of dancing, harlequinades, pantomimes and those tawdry processions for which Rich at Covent Garden had been notorious. Having to decide whether an increasingly frivolous audience or the theatrical managers were to blame, he came down against the latter who 'think they deal generously with us if they give one new play during the whole season'. He thus keeps his faith in theatre-goers whom he imagines to be, like himself, tired of the insipid fare the two patent theatres are offering: 'Sorry I am to think that the stage . . . should thus be made a scene for absurdity, that men who come to be rationally amused, should, upon recollection, blush to think of the futility of their passing the evening.'[18]

*

When in the late summer and autumn of 1766 Goldsmith turned his thoughts to a dramatic venture of his own he could have looked back on the preceding theatrical season and observed that the state of the theatre was very much what it had been when he voiced these strictures in the *Weekly Magazine* six years earlier. At Covent Garden the singer John Beard had produced only three new shows in his last year as actor-manager, one a musical comedy and one a two-act farce designed to round off the long theatrical evening to which the playgoers of this time were accustomed. (Curtain-up was usually at 6.30 and as dancing as well as a farce running between thirty minutes and an hour were included in the entertainment the evening would not have ended until after 11.0.) Apart from performances of the major Shakespearean tragedies, together with *Julius Caesar, Richard III, Henry IV* and *The Merry Wives of Windsor*, the bulk of the repertoire had consisted of plays written at the beginning of the century, like Congreve's *Way of the World* and *Love for Love* and Farquhar's *Beaux' Stratagem* and *The Recruiting Officer*. Drury Lane had been enlivened by the return of Garrick to play a handful of rôles which he had perfected in his early years on the stage, but as far as the repertoire was concerned there was little to choose between his management and Beard's. At the senior theatre Shakespeare and the restoration dramatists (including Dryden and Otway) again predominated. *The Beggar's Opera* had been revived and recent plays by Colman and Murphy kept in the repertoire, together with popular and well-tried historical pieces like *Jane Shore*, an appendage to *Richard III*, and a play about Queen Elizabeth and Mary Queen of Scots, *The Rival Queens*. There was also a thin sprinkling of fashionable comedies with varying degrees of the Steele-inspired sentimentalism. It was an indication of the weak stomachs of the audience of the 1760s that the restoration plays should have been 'adapted' and that Wycherley's *The Country Wife*, now as effectively emasculated as its hero had ever claimed to be, should have made its reappearance this season reduced to a mere after-piece. There had been only four new plays at Drury Lane this season, representing a total of forty-nine performances. Two of them were after-pieces and two full-length comedies: William Kenrick's unsuccessful pastiche of Shakespeare, *Falstaff's Wedding*, and the play on which Garrick and Colman had begun to collaborate before Garrick's departure for France, *The Clandestine Marriage*.

Goldsmith may have approved of the heavy weighting in favour of dramatists like Vanbrugh and Farquhar, both of whom he admired. But the lack of support for new plays, startlingly illustrated by the withdrawal of Kenrick's play after a single performance, was daunting. In his *Good-Natured Man* he introduced two broadly-conceived 'humours' characters in the Farquhar tradition and a plot which took its momentum from coincidences and farcical misunderstandings rather than from those more or less 'pathetic' complications arising in the lives of over-scrupulous young lovers.

There was a snag. For Goldsmith the inspiration for any piece of writing which led to real imaginative involvement was the continuing problem of his own wayward life and character. The best parts of the 'Chinese Letters' had sprung from his experience of London as a stranger and expatriate, *The Vicar of Wakefield* had contained much autobiography, overt or concealed, and *The Traveller* had taken the homesickness of the wandering exile as its springboard. Now, as he turned his thoughts towards a play and, inevitably, towards some aspect of his own situation which could be explored dramatically, he fell into that sentimental trap which, as he had seen, had already claimed so many willing victims among his contemporaries. He presented a spuriously problematical situation which arose less from a real observation of life than from a desire to present society with a flattering image of its essential 'niceness'. In Goldsmith's defence it can be said that a tough and realistic presentation of his own weaknesses in the character of Honeywood appears to have been modified in the interests of producing a suitably bland and innocuous hero for the polite 'sixties.

When Goldsmith handed the contents of his writing-table drawer to Percy in the spring of 1773 there were several begging letters from writers in the collection, one in elegant verse, one trying to appear light-hearted and jocular, another announcing that its bearer was the sick author's wife.[19] Attracting greater financial rewards than other forms of creative writing, a play could be expected to produce such a crop; but the publication of a successful poem in 1764 had probably already made him a natural target for both the genuinely unfortunate and the scroungers against whom he was so dangerously short of natural defences. It was this aspect of his life and personality that Goldsmith now decided to stress, perhaps feeling that it provided the kind of dialectic hinge which contemporary taste demanded. Young Honeywood's problem is that, while remaining impervious to requests for payment from his tailor and grocer, he feels compelled to respond to nearly every other suitor. These range from the casual beggar to the quarrelling husband and wife who simultaneously demand his moral support and reassurances.

Part of Honeywood's disability can be laid safely at Goldsmith's door. But it is hard to see him as a yes-man, even though an anecdote of Mrs Thrale's shows that he had enough tact and verbal dexterity to soften an unwelcome reply:

> Mrs Montagu says She was vastly struck with him the first Time they met: it was at some great Table I forget what—but Lady Abercorn was there—a Lady of about seventy six or eight Years old—and the Company remarking how Young She looked, were led to mention her Age & apply to the Dr—I am no great Judge says Goldsmith, for I never saw an old Woman before; except I mean an Applewoman or a Beggarwoman or some such Body—*Ladies* always look *young* I think, for they are finely dress'd up—so I can't tell whether this *Lady* looks well of her Age or no——'tis a new Species to me.—[20]

Did Goldsmith come any closer to himself in his sketchy analysis of Honeywood's weakness? A minor character is allowed one damaging hit: Honeywood's fabled good nature arises, he claims, 'rather from his fears of offending the importunate, than his desire of making the deserving happy'. The progress of the play, however, fails to develop this hint: the general effect is that of the true sentimental comedy: of parading a 'fault', which is only a virtue in disguise, to show what nice people the protagonists are. True to form, Honeywood undergoes only the mildest of catharses before being rescued from his difficulties by the appropriately named Miss Richland.

The only casualty here, one feels, is Goldsmith himself. He has fallen clumsily between two stools: on the one hand he has brought into question the motives behind his own indisputable generosity: on the other—having failed to carry this theme through—he has appeared to congratulate himself in the sententious, vapid manner of his most mawkish contemporaries.

The Good-Natured Man had been completed by the early part of

1767 and now Reynolds demonstrated his friendship for Goldsmith by attempting to set things right between him and the reigning theatrical monarch, David Garrick. He contrived an encounter between them at 47 Leicester Square—with every sign of success: Garrick was interested to hear about the play, and wanted to read it.[21]

For Goldsmith it would have been immediately obvious that his future as a dramatist was assured. Reynolds was probably less sanguine. He understood the complexities of Garrick's character: the desire to please which led to sudden enthusiasms and promises which couldn't be kept, and the deeply-ingrained vanity which allowed old grudges to rankle under a vivacious and genial façade. Arthur Murphy, whose place as Drury Lane's leading dramatist had been taken over by Colman, had discovered that to be a member of Johnson's circle was by no means an automatic recommendation to Garrick. The obverse side of the actor's hunger for publicity was that he was abnormally sensitive to criticism, and he suspected that amongst Johnson's friends there was a pocket of resistance to the charm which he made elaborate efforts to project. The relationship with Johnson himself was always a love-hate affair. Johnson enjoyed putting 'Davy' down. "Punch has no feelings," he had muttered in the wings at Drury Lane at a rehearsal after Garrick had protested that the sound of Johnson's off-stage conversation was making it impossible for him to get the feel of the character he was impersonating;[22] and Garrick could always be persuaded to 'do Johnson'. This meant the re-enactment of a scene which he claimed he had observed through the bedroom keyhole when a pupil at Johnson's school. Letty Johnson urged her husband to come to bed while he sat reading aloud to her from his tragedy *Irene* absent-mindedly trying to stuff the bed-sheets into the top of his breeches.[23] There had recently been some bad feeling over Johnson's edition of Shakespeare, Garrick seeing the omission from it of any reference to himself as a calculated snub.

Garrick received Goldsmith's manuscript—and kept it. Goldsmith waited until July when the ending of the theatrical season deprived the actor-manager of further excuses for delay, and then went to see him. With the retirement of Beard and the dissolution of the partnership between Garrick and Colman this summer there had been a ministerial reshuffle in the theatrical world. Colman had persuaded Garrick's leading actor, William Powell, to leave Drury Lane and, with himself and two backers, to take up the Covent Garden patent. Garrick regarded the double defection as a personal betrayal and it would have been wise of Goldsmith not to tell him that he had already been in touch with Colman. As the interview was afterwards described as 'warm' it is likely, however, that the rival theatre did come into their conversation. By the end of the month the neglected manuscript had been redeemed and was in the hands of Colman.

Though in the event Garrick really did behave badly over the production of *The Good-Natured Man* it would not be too difficult to sympathise with him at this juncture. In spite of the streak of sentimentalism in Goldsmith's play, some of its best scenes were farcical. The current taste was for plays which created the comforting illusion that the refinements of life in St James's and Mayfair could be purchased with a shilling ticket, and Garrick was the servant of his audience, particularly of the arbiters of taste in the upper galleries who were now on guard against all signs of 'lowness'. Both Murphy, who had begun his career with some lively farces, and Colman, whose début had consisted of a satirical attack on the sentimental genre, had learned this lesson and were now providing the kind of tunes for which the pipers upstairs were prepared to pay.

It is doubtful if Colman himself was much more enthusiastic about Goldsmith's play than Garrick had been, but at this period of coolness in his relationship with Garrick he would have been open to the suggestion that he might gain prestige by being decisive while his rival dithered. Now, some powerful persuasion was effected by Edmund Burke who had joined forces with Reynolds in his support of Goldsmith.[24] Colman committed himself to taking on *The Good-Natured Man*, and it was scheduled for production shortly before Christmas.

Having missed his chance with Goldsmith's play Garrick now betrayed signs of wanting to minimise its chances of success. By the beginning of the new season he had discovered a new playwright, Hugh Kelly, who seemed perfectly designed to satisfy his patrons' craving for gentility. Kelly had endeared himself to Garrick the previous year by writing a poem, *Thespis*, which in the true *Rosciad* tradition had denigrated several members of the Drury Lane company before paying homage to their manager; and Garrick, however anxious he might be to be popular in the green room, loved praise too much to resent such invidious distinction. He met the man who had pointed out that one of his leading ladies 'waddled and bawled' and that another was 'withering swiftly on the stalk of time' and by the summer was writing in fulsome terms about the play on which Kelly had been working since Easter. 'There are thoughts in it worthy of an angel,' Kelly was informed;[25] and with Goldsmith's play taken over by Colman it was now Garrick who was inclined to act decisively. He took on *False Delicacy* and, when Colman set a date for the first night of Goldsmith's play, announced (not unpredictably) that Kelly's play would be staged the same evening.

Hugh Kelly was a young Irishman who even at this early stage in his career was seen to have played all his cards extremely well The son of a Dublin tavern-keeper, he had had little formal education and had come to London seven years earlier as a corset-maker. He confessed candidly that he was not a great success at this trade because of sweaty hands which soiled the materials on which he worked. In any case he was much more interested in the theatre. He patronised the taverns where actors congregated, was an avid reader of plays and, after working for a while as a copying clerk at fifteen shillings a week, graduated to journalism where as a free-lance 'paragraph-writer' he could earn up to two guineas.[26]

Unlike Goldsmith, Kelly had welcomed every opportunity to put himself in the way of some of the best pickings of journalism by writing political pamphlets and theatrical gossip and now, at the early age of twenty-eight, his success was marked by his editorship of the Public Ledger. This post had brought him into contact with Goldsmith at about the time when his fellow-countryman was enjoying his newly won fame as the author of *The Traveller*. Kelly was bland in conversation and appearance. Fair-haired, round-faced, carrying too much weight both for his height and age, he had a flair for good-natured chat. He had begun to drop names and, a little self-consciously, to add cautious refinements to his Irish brogue in keeping with the sword, bright waistcoats and bag-wig which he was beginning to sport. However sharp he had been at the expense of his friends the actors, socially he was amiable and pleasant, showing enough ingenuous satisfaction with himself and his achievements to win a degree of affection and esteem. When he stepped forward to congratulate Goldsmith on the success of his poem, he was identifiable as a more than usually prosperous member of the younger set of expatriate Irishmen who lived in or near the Temple.

Goldsmith had at first been amused by Kelly's blend of candour and self-importance and had a little unkindly answered his overtures in Kelly's own terms: 'I would with pleasure accept your kind invitation, but to tell you the truth, my dear boy, my *Traveller* has found me a home in so many places, that I am engaged, I believe, three days—let me see—today I dine with Edmund Burke, tomorrow with Dr Nugent and the next day with Topham Beauclerk—but I tell you what I'll do for you, I'll dine with you on Saturday.' He did, and at once saw that he could not afford to be either satirical or patronising. The young journalist had patently managed things much better than he could have done. For one thing, Kelly, who had married at the age of twenty-two, had a pleasant home life. Within a short time Goldsmith had paid the sincerest compliment to what he observed within-doors by confiding in Kelly that the wisest thing he himself could do would be to marry Kelly's sister-in-law. Kelly, either because he thought disparagingly of the prospective suitor's financial prospects or because he had seen no more than a flash of sentimental enthusiasm in the confession, persuaded him to think more deeply before he committed himself. Nothing more was heard of the proposition.[27] During the summer while he waited anxiously for some word from Garrick, Goldsmith was brought to a thoughtful pause for at least the second time by the fast-working young Kelly. He accompanied another common friend, the Irish musical-comedy writer Isaac Bickerstaffe to a reading by Kelly of the play which he had recently finished. Although Bickerstaffe, having praised Kelly to his face, confided to Goldsmith on their way downstairs that the play was rubbish,[28] Goldsmith knew enough about the theatre to realise that a serious rival had appeared on the scene.

False Delicacy lacks the high spirits which occasionally bring a scene from *The Good-Natured Man* to life, but is a far better constructed and also more 'modern' play than Goldsmith's. Kelly had a talent for smooth, realistic dialogue together with the born dramatist's knack of getting his characters efficiently on and off the stage and of bringing a scene to an effective climax; but even more important, in view of the audience for which Garrick was catering, he displayed all the hero-worship of a young man who had seen 'society' through a lighted window in one of the spacious new streets of Mayfair and gone home to dream about the elegant and— ideally—golden-tongued and courteous men and women who had floated gracefully across his line of vision. All this had gone into *False Delicacy*—a play which remained popular for years to come and which is a recognisable ancestor of Shaftesbury Avenue comedies which still flourished up to twenty years ago.

Although Garrick was a notoriously bad judge of plays, the success of *False Delicacy* showed that he had been wise to back Kelly, while the mixed reception given to *The Good-Natured Man* suggested that he had not been entirely wrong about Goldsmith. The first nights had been postponed, that of *False Delicacy* until the 23rd of January and that of *The Good-Natured Man* until the 29th, Colman having bowed to Garrick's superior advance publicity and decided to allow Kelly's play a clear run before risking a production in which even at rehearsal stage he had lost faith. Kelly won the acclaim that had been predicted. Three thousand copies of his play were sold on the day of publication and his total receipts were said to be about £700. While at Drury Lane, King and Mrs Dancer were well satisfied with Kelly's smooth lines, Powell at Covent Garden considered Honeywood an impossible rôle. By now he may have been regretting the £1,000 which he had forfeited on breaking his contract with Garrick the previous year. Powell was famous for his old man parts and was considered by some to be a finer Lear than Garrick himself: he was probably right in thinking that no-one could have done anything with the insipid, passive young Honeywood. Beard's niece, the singer Mrs Bulkley, was satisfied with the self-assured, rather managing Miss Richland, and there were good opportunities for the two comedians who were the mainstays of the Covent Garden company—the difficult, sardonic Henry Woodward and Ned Shuter, who when passably sober was the darling of the gods. For them, Goldsmith had created two 'humours' characters which left maximum scope for their own inventiveness, Shuter as Croaker—a disaster-relisher based on one of Johnson's word-portraits in the *Rambler*—and Woodward as Lofty the 'smoke-seller'.

In the event the first night was tricky. Thanks to the jeremiads of

Colman and Powell (who as two of the four patentees had most to lose if things went wrong) Goldsmith was in a demoralised state in spite of a loyal turnout of friends. Johnson had contributed a prologue which suggested an analogy between the feelings of the author and those of the candidates in the coming general election. Not unreasonably, Goldsmith begged him to replace the phrase 'our little bard' with 'our anxious bard'.[29]

The predicted anxiety had reached its peak in Act III when Honeywood, receiving a visit from Miss Richland shortly after the bailiffs had taken possession of his house, tries to pass off the unwelcome visitors as footmen. At this point the gallery-critics began to protest noisily, though the scene is arguably the best in the play. Goldsmith, with his total freedom from social prejudices, had presented his bailiffs as people with a language, opinions and a will of their own, so that there is a genuine clash of cultures between them and the, for once, nonplussed Miss Richland. They are not only in possession of Honeywood's house: they are also entirely self-possessed and on a small scale, as they attempt to engage Miss Richland in a conversation about the law and habeas corpus, Goldsmith creates the effect of a hole suddenly appearing in the social fabric—as it was later to do in the tea-party scene in Shaw's *Pygmalion*. The contrast between this and the depiction of conventional comic servants in the popular *High Life Below Stairs*, an afterpiece in which the Revd. James Townley had pampered to all the petty snobberies of his audience, reveals yet another of the chasms between Goldsmith and his contemporaries.

Ned Shuter, sensitive to his audience and no doubt with more tricks up his sleeve than had shown themselves in rehearsal, was afterwards thought to have brought the play through. Goldsmith rushed back-stage at the end to congratulate and thank him, and later in the season presented him with £10 on his benefit night.[30] The fact that the curtain had finally come down on the sound of laughter ensured that he was over the first hurdle: the play was requested for a second night, and in the course of the next three weeks there were nine subsequent performances, which denoted it a moderate success. Under the traditional system whereby, after the deduction of house expenses, the proceeds of every third performance (up to a maximum of three benefits) went to the author, Goldsmith received his reward. Though not on the same scale as Kelly's this was perfectly respectable, but it had only been achieved by deferring to the gallery pundits, for the bailiffs' scene was cut after the first performance.[31]

The Club had been determined, whatever happened, to treat Goldsmith's theatrical début as an excuse for celebration. This Friday was designated a Club night Extraordinary and after the back-stage visits had been paid the members carried their friend off to supper. He responded as was expected of him, appearing to be in particularly good form and, by special request, singing the song 'about an old woman toss'd in a blanket seventeen times as high as the moon.' No-one had observed that Goldsmith was not eating and Johnson, when the other members had departed and they were alone, was startled to find his friend in tears.[32] The outbreaks of hissing at Covent Garden, however much to be expected on a first-night, had brought reality crashing into whatever fantasies Goldsmith had still been able to harbour about the instant recognition the new dramatist would receive, and with characteristic imprudence he had created circumstances that would make his first night a war of nerves. Anticipating success, he had purchased a long lease on a set of chambers in the Temple (where he had rented rooms for the past three years). In these circumstances the hissing inspired by his bailiffs must have had the same effect as real bailiffs knocking at his new front door. In the mood of black despair induced by this experience he assured Johnson that he would never write for the theatre again.

Kelly's easy triumph was bitter to him. The booksellers were so delighted with their sale of 10,000 copies of *False Delicacy* that Kelly was fêted at a public breakfast in the Chapter coffee house and presented with a piece of plate valued at £20. Goldsmith went on record, when he heard that the play was going to be translated into French and Portuguese, as saying 'It must be done for the purpose of exhibiting it at the booths of foreign fairs, for which it is well calculated.' This was naturally repeated to Hugh Kelly. Visiting Covent Garden one morning, Goldsmith found his Drury Lane rival installed in the green room. His unconvincing speech of congratulation was met with a sharp rebuff from Kelly: 'I cannot thank you, because I cannot believe you'. One of their contemporaries, Cooke who recorded the incident, was satisfied that they never spoke to one another again.

But, if Cooke's estimate of £500 is correct, Goldsmith had done well out of his play and it must have seemed that he could afford to indulge tastes which had already been evident two years earlier when Boswell found his room in King's Bench Walk furnished in a 'quite magnificent' manner.[33] The inventory drawn up for the sale on Goldsmith's death shows that the colour scheme at the new chambers was blue. In the dining room, blue upholstered chairs round a mahogany dining table matched the heavy blue moreen curtains. Both this room and the drawing room were panelled and had Wilton carpets, and the furnishing had clearly been undertaken with an eye to entertaining. The drawing room contained a mahogany sofa, eight matching chairs and two compass-front card tables. The reflections of the large gilt-framed chimney glass which must have dominated this room would have been echoed in four oval glasses, two of them with candle sockets and lustres. Besides the two principal rooms there was a small closet bedroom containing a four-poster bed with red and white hangings, and a large mahogany framed dressing glass. At the end of Goldsmith's life these chambers housed a library of about a thousand books, in which travel, the natural sciences and modern French literature were well represented.[34]

*

At about the time of the move to Brick Court, John Newbery died. It was an event which in the long run would have serious repercussions for Goldsmith for he had come to depend both on the discipline which, in a friendly way, the publisher had imposed and on the flexibility of their business dealings. But the immediate result of his death was that he lost a retreat which had become all the more welcome now that he was a marked figure in the London literary world. The need to find a substitute for Canonbury brought him closer to Edmund Bott, a young barrister of independent means who was also known to Reynolds.[35] Of this friendship no record has survived, though it was clearly of some importance. Bott seems to have been without literary aspirations of his own (as its title suggests, his own book, *A Collection of Decisions of the Court of King's Bench Upon the Poor Laws*, first published in 1773, is an anthology of legal judgments) but he evidently put a high price on his friend's

J

achievements and, perhaps, his ability to give him the entrée to literary and theatrical circles. When Goldsmith died £2,000 in debt, Edmund Bott was the principal creditor.[36] In the summer of 1769, after Goldsmith had rejected Percy's offer of the loan of his rectory at Easton Maudit in Northamptonshire, he and Bott agreed to share the tenancy of a little villa on the edge of the Cannons estate at Edgeware. Their landlord was a shoemaker who had laid out his half-acre with fountains and flying Mercuries. Goldsmith and Bott named their four-roomed cottage 'The Shoemaker's Paradise'.[37] By the end of 1769 Bott had moved from the Inner Temple into chambers just across the landing from Goldsmith's rooms in Brick Court.[38] The Edgeware arrangement probably survived until 1771 when Goldsmith installed himself in a new country retreat. Even if his interest in the Poor Laws was professional rather than humanitarian, it is difficult not to credit the shadowy Edmund Bott with a genial image. The only other anecdote to have survived is of his driving Goldsmith up to Edgeware at the end of a mellow evening in town, when he narrowly avoided tipping his friend into a ditch.[39] But whether the friendship was strong enough to survive the strain imposed on it by Goldsmith's considerable indebtedness is a matter of conjecture.

A second death, in May 1768, could have brought no material changes to Goldsmith though one imagines it affected him deeply. The news came from Ireland that Henry, the contented perpetual curate, had died in early middle-age.

*

Although Newbery's death, for better or worse, marked a turning-point in Goldsmith's career, the immediate effects were far from unpleasant. The writer had acquired a name and he was now available to the highest bidder. When Thomas Davies, representing a consortium, offered two hundred and fifty guineas for a *Roman History* it became evident that the bids were going to be reassuringly high.[40] Shortly before this work was published in the spring of 1769, Goldsmith received the first part of an advance of eight hundred guineas from a former associate of Newbery's, William Griffin, for the *History of the Earth and Animated Nature* which was to occupy him during the last years of his life.[41]

In London the Club had been expanded. Thomas Percy, who had been in the employment of the Duke of Northumberland for the last two years, was now a member and, perhaps as a reward for his somewhat reluctant support of Goldsmith, George Colman was admitted a fortnight after the first night of *The Good-Natured Man*.[42] At the same time Johnson's interest in the law and his connection with Oxford were acknowledged in the election of the young law professor Robert Chambers. Apart from Goldsmith himself, several of the Club's members could be regarded as having expanded too over the preceding four years. Burke had distinguished himself in parliament during the short-lived Rockingham Ministry of '65 to '66 and was becoming one of the principal theoreticians of the group. The Rockingham Whigs had now entered a long period of apparent political eclipse, but thanks to Burke it would be seen in retrospect as having marked a stage in the evolution of such basic constitutional concepts as 'party' and 'opposition'. With the financial help of the Marquis of Rockingham (and possibly Reynolds) Burke this year purchased an estate at Beaconsfield and became at least a junior member of that club of landowners to which he was politically allied. He took a keen interest in estate management and lived, in Mrs Thrale's account, 'among Dirt Cobwebs, Pictures and Statues that would not have disgraced the City of Paris itself: where Misery and Magnificence reign in all their Splendour, & in perfect Amity'.[43] In spite of the King's mistrust of his bias towards the Rockingham party, Joshua Reynolds received his knighthood this year. After years of committee work and discussion in which he had played a leading part, the Royal Academy had been founded and he had been elected as first president.

Early in 1769 three of the Club members, Johnson, Percy and Goldsmith, received an invitation to spend a few days at Oxford. It came from Robert Chambers and was issued primarily to Johnson. The young Vinerian professor, daunted at the prospect of following William Blackstone, had turned to Johnson for encouragement. Johnson had responded generously by helping him to compose his lectures, and his presence was now requested at a lecture to be delivered in the Bodleian on Wednesday, February 15th. Percy was also an Oxford man, and in this company Goldsmith must have seemed a natural choice as travelling companion. Though such qualities might at times puzzle and scandalise, his freshness and spontaneity would have perfectly suited the traveller's holiday mood. He had the gift of helping one to observe the world anew and of being able to make things happen—pleasant things on the whole. Perhaps, if Johnson and Percy had been able to foresee the scrape in which the trip to Oxford was going to involve them, they would have needed every reminder they could muster that their friend really was at heart a very delightful man.

At what point in the proceedings it was decided that Goldsmith should acquire an Oxford degree is not known; neither is the extent, if any, of Goldsmith's own involvement in the affair. Johnson had been 'Doctor' Johnson since 1765 by courtesy of Trinity College Dublin, and as they travelled up to their own university in the company of a Trinity College man whom they believed to be in possession of an M.B. awarded by that university, it might have occurred to either Johnson or Percy that they should provide their friend with the right of entry to yet another club by arranging for the conversion of that degree into its Oxford equivalent—*ad eundem gradum*. It was little more than a courteous formality.

Although Goldsmith had not returned to Dublin to acquire a medical degree, as he had evidently intended to do when attempting to make contact with his family in 1755, it had been generally assumed amongst his London acquaintances that he possessed a medical qualification of some kind. There was confusion about the validating university, however. The Milners had been told that he was a Bachelor of Medicine and former Edinburgh acquaintances appear to have believed that he had taken a degree at either Padua or Louvain during his absence on the Continent. But friends without Irish links, like Johnson and Percy, seem to have been reasonably sure by the mid-sixties that Goldsmith's 'degree' had been awarded in Dublin. They would have been less prone to rely on hearsay, or on Goldsmith's word, if they had known about the humiliating failure to obtain any kind of certificate from the College of Surgeons in 1758.

It seems unlikely that Goldsmith was particularly degree-conscious at this moment in his life. It was generally accepted that he was 'Doctor Minor' to Johnson's 'Doctor Major'; his entitlement to an M.B. had passed unquestioned when his name appeared for the first time on a title-page five years earlier; and he was now far too busy as a popular historian to devote time to a medical practice which could never have been large and had by now probably withered away. It seems most probable in these circumstances that, in good faith, the two Oxford men either acted independently without informing Goldsmith of their intention or that, if their friend filed the *ad eundem* application himself, it was only as a result of their persuasion. Goldsmith's feelings must have been divided between an appalled realisation that he had been hoist with his own petard and a glow of interior satisfaction at being about to receive— at last—official recognition for being an immensely 'notable man'. He might have reminded himself that even the odious William Kenrick had become a 'Doctor', having been awarded an LL.D. by St Andrew's University for his translation of Rousseau. Goldsmith's French was just as good as Kenrick's.

Arriving at Oxford, Goldsmith, Percy and Johnson at once entered on both the social and academic life of the university, as Percy's appointment book indicates:

Tuesday	February 14	Went to Oxford with Mr Johnsonand and Dr Goldsmith. Got there in the evening.
Wednesday	February 15	Was in the Bodleian and heard Mr Chamber's Lecture. Afterwards dined in the Hall of University College and tea at Sir John Peshals.
Thursday	February 16	Was in the Bodleian, and in the Ashmole Library etc. Dined with Mr Morthwaite at Queen's. Supped with Mr Trevor.
Friday	February 17	Breakfast with Mr Huddesford. Dined at Thomas Warton's. Evening at Mr Chambers's.
Saturday	February 18	We returned to Town.

Probably on one of these occasions the question of Goldsmith's *ad eundem* was raised. Jackson's *Oxford Journal* picked up a rumour and, in spite of the fact that the University itself left no record of a meeting of Congregation on the day in question, stated that a degree had been bestowed on the poet on February 17th. On the strength of the existing evidence it is impossible either to resolve the problem of the supposed *ad eundem* degree or to say at what stage in the affair, if any, Johnson and Percy realised that Goldsmith's claim to a medical degree was false.[44] By the time he came to write his Memoir, Percy himself was in no doubt that his friend's M.B. was bogus, and there are indications that within Goldsmith's lifetime Johnson too was disillusioned. Whatever rumours the Oxford affair may have started it was clearly unfortunate in one respect, for the entry in the *Oxford Journal* had tethered firmly to Trinity College Dublin that 'degree' which could have been more safely left to wander, in its disconcerting way, round the various universities of Europe.

*

The Club pointedly ignored what was to have been the big event of the year: the 'Shakespeare Jubilee' which Garrick organised on the water-logged banks of the Avon in September. The local aldermen were delighted and—when it was learned that heavy rains and outrageously high prices had dampened the spirit of celebration —so were those who had stayed away. Boswell had scented an opportunity for masquerading and had gone to Stratford in the costume of a Corsican bandit to advertise his travel book: Garrick, equally publicity-conscious, had recited his *Ode to Shakespeare* in a damp marquee to the accompaniment of chorus and orchestra—but no word of Shakespeare's had been spoken.

The following month the Johnson circle was plunged into a crisis. Johnson's friend, Joseph Baretti, a linguist whose criticisms of the authorities in his native Italy had led to exile, was accosted by a prostitute as he walked down Panton Street one night. A man who refused such invitations ran the risk of being described as a 'French bugger', and on this occasion Baretti struck the woman who had insulted him. He was immediately set upon by her protectors. His glasses were knocked off and, virtually blind without them, he struck out wildly with the fruit-knife he kept in his pocket. One of his assailants was wounded (and later died), and Baretti blundered into a shop, announcing that he wanted to give himself up. News of these events reached Goldsmith while Baretti was still at the magistrate's house. He had never liked the stiff and brusque

Italian, but his wretched situation was an appeal he was unable to resist, and with characteristic impulsiveness he went at once to Bow Street arriving in time to accompany Baretti to the Bridewell in Tothill Fields.[45] Two weeks later he appeared in court together with Johnson, Burke, Reynolds and Garrick, ready to appear for the defence as Baretti was tried on a murder charge. Baretti was acquitted, but the members of the Club, with impressions of Newgate fresh in their minds, must have felt unpleasantly brushed by that other London of St Giles' and Saffron Hill which, since John Wilkes' return to England the previous March, had made its presence felt more and more frequently in outbursts of street violence.

TEN

Exiles

T HE SEVENTEEN-SIXTIES had seen an economic recession in which prices had risen and wages had remained unaltered in the interests of an economic theory which stressed the importance of competitiveness abroad. As a result of bad summers in the middle of the decade great hardship was caused by the increased price of wheat which between then and the mid-seventies rose by about a third. Throughout the country there were sporadic outcrops of violence, usually in the form of attacks on mills and bakeries.

While a considerable part of the community worked long hours in return for pitiful wages and little security apart from the highly inefficient safety-net of the Poor Laws, it was probably wise of the authorities to tolerate a certain amount of therapeutic boisterousness. A blind official eye was turned on the bands of apprentices who sometimes, in the evening, cordoned off a section of Fleet Street and turned it into a football field;[1] and at the dissolution of parliament the mock elections of 'Mayors of Garratt' up and down the country channelled off some of the frustrations of the politically unrepresented, who took to the streets and enacted a noisy satire on the departed members of parliament and the ruling class they represented. The chosen Mayor had to be either a clown or a ne'er-do-well, and his supporters decked themselves out in pointedly absurd imitation of people of fashion.[2]

In normal times violence for its own sake seems to have been confined to the occasional molesting of foreigners (particularly Frenchmen, who were fiercely unpopular): visitors to London drew a sharp contrast between the courteous help they received from the genteel and the gratuitous insults of the mob.[3] The Wilkes troubles, however, produced demonstrations specifically against those who by their manners and dress could be assumed to be hand-in-glove with the persecutors of the editor of the *North Briton*. The Austrian ambassador was taken out of his coach and held upside down while the figures 45 were chalked on the soles of his shoes, and people being carried to the assembly rooms in Soho Square were liable to have the windows of their sedan chairs broken—or so Mrs Cornelys implied by inserting advertisements in the newspapers which advised her patrons to travel with the blinds or shutters up.[4]

Deserted by his former allies once Burke had succeeded in buying his continued absence from England, John Wilkes had languished on the continent until 1768 when, heavily in debt and in danger of being forgotten, he returned home to try his luck as a political martyr. As there was no longer any prospect of support from Lord Rockingham he looked for it to the mercantile class which had enjoyed its first brief taste of power as a pressure-group during the short-lived Rockingham ministry three years before,[5] and was now becoming increasingly frustrated as the government pursued American policies which were detrimental to trade. For city merchants it was an entirely academic point whether or not the American colonies should be forced to contribute to the cost of their own defence; what concerned them was that exports wilted as American resentment against direct and indirect taxation grew.

It was amongst the radical elements of the London hinterland, however, that Wilkes won his first victory when in the election of March 1768 he was returned as a member of parliament for Middlesex. Three weeks later he insisted on being arrested; and although in April Lord Mansfield, perhaps anticipating the troubles to come, had found a way of dropping the outlawry charge on a legal technicality, in June Wilkes was sentenced to twenty-two months in the King's Bench Prison on the charges relating to the *North Briton* and the obscene *Essay on Woman*. When troops opened fire on a crowd that had gathered outside the prison in St George's Fields several people, including passers-by, were killed, and public opinion was aroused by the fact that the incident was officially condoned.[6]

As a symbol of Liberty, John Wilkes could draw support from many currents of mid-eighteenth century feeling. Journalists had kept alive sentiments that probably had their origin in the political strife of the early years of the previous century, and drew contrasting pictures of the clubs of St James's where scented and empty-headed placemen courted the rich and powerful, and the coffee-houses of Cornhill where thrift, sobriety, good business sense and a love of worthy causes were the order of the day.[7] This had been John Newbery's territory and even the children's books which he was producing at the end of his career convey the same sense of middle class assertiveness. Recalling a theme from Johnson's *Rambler*, *Little Goody Two Shoes*, one of the publications that was to ensure him lasting fame, drew attention to the disadvantages of a man of moderate means when involved in a civil case against a wealthy landowner. At the end of the tale the virtuous and hard-working Margery, by becoming 'Lady Jones', acquires a title that seems better designed to give her prominence in the City of London than for a life at court.[8]

The same mood, in a much sharper form, is felt in the 'Definitions' section of Hugh Kelly's journal the *Babler*:

A Tradesman: A superior sort of Coach-horse, created entirely for the convenience of the great, without either passions, resentment, understanding, or inclination.

Debt: A word under which persons of fashion have a right to rob the honest and industrious, without the fear of suffering from the laws of the kingdom, or the reproach of their acquaintance.

A Free-Born Englishman: One who is continually bragging of liberty, and independence, when he has neither will nor property of his own, and laughs at the wretchedness of other countries, while he himself is indulged with no other privilege than the right of nominating the person by whom he chooses to be enslaved.

But Kelly, no advocate of Wilkes, was now writing for the government. Similarly, Goldsmith, though he shared the anti-establishment attitudes of Wilkes' followers, had already revealed his dislike of both the demagogue in Wilkes and the mercantile interests on which his power was based.[9] Goldsmith made no direct comment on the recent troubles but Johnson was forthright in his support of the House of Commons' action in declaring Wilkes' election illegal. 'That a man was in jail for sedition and impiety', he wrote in *The False Alarm*, 'would, I believe, have been within memory a sufficient reason why he should not come out of jail a legislator'.

Much of Wilkes' support came from those skilled workers who were now having to spend a higher proportion of their incomes on such a basic commodity as bread. The silk-weavers of Spitalfields were particularly restless: their standard of living had dropped sharply when the clandestine importation of silk had been resumed after the Peace of Paris. In 1765 the weavers had seized 'a large book of French patterns containing several thousands of samples from 5s to £5 per yard; which book had been secretly handed about among the mercers by French agents'.[10] At the same time the hand-weavers were under threat from the new engine-looms. Although within the various trades friendly societies provided mutual help, while the apprenticeship system restricted the number of recruits and so stabilised wages, there was a general feeling that they were losing ground. Spitalfields, where there was much un-employment, had a foretaste of Luddism in 1768 when engine-looms were smashed by armed gangs. In a letter to the Duke of Bedford, the leader of one of the most powerful factions of the period, a weaver pointed out that, if they changed places, the Duke would have to accustom himself to living upon 10d a day.[11] Agitation amongst the weavers, touched off by Wilkes, inevitably spread to other dissatisfied groups. There were strikes of sailors and coal-heavers, in the latter case accompanied by violent picketing.

The House of Commons was ultimately divided over the issue of whether or not the Middlesex electors had the right to be repre-sented by Wilkes. The government attempted to squash him by declaring his election invalid, and thereupon followed the farce of three subsequent re-elections and, at the fourth, the admission of the runner-up, Colonel Luttrell, to the seat. The question at stake was the extent to which force was being brought to bear on the Commons. When the parliamentary session of 1768 opened with crowds of disaffected and striking workmen standing in Palace Yard it seemed clear that the Wilkites were attempting to intimidate M.P.'s. To this it was possible to answer that under the old New-castle system of jobs and government rewards the Commons had long been responsive to other more attractive forms of outside pressure which were just as real a threat to the constitution.

Wilkes' supporters in the City were well organised. Running battles in the street between sailors and Irish chairmen were an accident of the new situation but when, in March 1769, a group of merchants and tradesmen on their way to present a loyal address to the King was attacked by a mob which succeeded in fighting its way into the yard of St James's Palace, it would have been evident that there had been some effective organisation behind the incident. The Wilkites themselves appear to have been a little alarmed by the forces they were unleashing and at the first Brentford election 40,000 handbills advocating orderly behaviour were distributed with the help of the weavers. One of the men who attracted attention in these years was the unclubbable lawyer, John Hawkins, who earned himself a knighthood by successfully confronting rioters at Brentford and Moorfields.

Although fourteen days of rioting after Wilkes' imprisonment must have created the impression that the country was on the verge of a proletarian revolution, a large sale of commemorative china indicates where Wilkes' most effective support lay.[12] With the beginning of the new decade the middle class factor was seen to be increasingly important. A Society for the Defence of the Bill of Rights was formed with branches in the principal towns. Petitions and remonstrances to the King were drawn up. The Address of Remonstrance which the Lord Mayor and Aldermen of the City of London presented to the King at St James's Palace on March 7th, 1770 contained allusions to 'the Misdeeds of Your Majesty's Ministers' and, even more pointedly, to the obduracy of the Stuarts in the previous century. The King's carefully worded reply adopted a 'more in sorrow than in anger' stance but the effect was spoiled when, as the petitioners were withdrawing, he was observed to turn to his courtiers and laugh.[13] 'These fellows,' Samuel Foote had commented on the Wilkites, adopting a more serious view of the situation than George III, 'will take a place for the King in the Dover coach and put his mother in the basket.'[14]

Within the fold of the City which had chosen him as its figurehead Wilkes prospered. He became an alderman and subsequently Lord Mayor. In 1775 he reappeared again in the Commons. His fame was widespread. Mrs Thrale was told that a merchant arriving at a port in China was greeted with 'Ah Master John! your mandarine want to bamboo Wilkie, but Wilkie bamboo mandarine!' Without the panoply of martyrdom he was revealed as something less than a hero, too taken up with his own financial problems to show any concern for his printer, Bingley, who became a real martyr by going to prison for three years rather than give evidence against Wilkes before Lord Mansfield.[15] He was a poor speaker and was in turn abandoned by his more serious-minded supporters. The Revd. Thomas Campbell on his visit to London in 1775 saw him at the Guildhall where he was speaking on behalf of the American colonists:

> He labours under baldness, increpitude, and want of teeth: from the hedge of the teeth being removed, his tongue is for ever trespassing upon his lips, whereof the undermost, together with the chin, projects very far. He went to the front of the Hustings, where he was clapped as a player more than once before he spoke, tho' I was removed from him but the breadth of the green table, I could not make out all he said . . .[16]

The principal outcome of the Wilkes troubles, apart from the devotion of time and energy to the issue in the Commons which might have been more profitably devoted to the American problem, was the Spitalfields Act which established machinery for the periodic review of weavers' wages. Another sign of a changed social climate is that readers of daily newspapers were now far more likely to find indignant paragraphs about semi-starvation amongst the poor.

One of the victims of the agitation had been Hugh Kelly whose comedy *A Word to the Wise* was refused a hearing by a hostile audience in 1770. However immediately profitable the exercise might be, it was a bad time to write government propaganda. Kelly's career as a dramatist was not over but from now on his plays had to be attributed to other writers before they could be safely staged.[17]

*

Goldsmith was not taken in by the 'Liberty' theme promoted by Wilkes' wealthy supporters in the City. His experience of life in counties Westmeath and Roscommon ensured that he would never forget the realities that underlay the claptrap. Dealing with 'Quadrupeds of the Cow Kind' in his *History of the Earth and Animated Nature* he wrote:

> There are many of our peasantry that have no other possession

but a cow; and even of the advantages resulting from this most useful creature, the poor are but the nominal possessors. Its flesh they cannot pretend to taste, since then their whole riches are at once destroyed; its calf they are obliged to fatten for sale, since veal is a delicacy they could not make any pretensions to; its very milk is wrought into butter and cheese for the tables of their masters; while they have no share even in their own possession, but the choice of their market. I cannot bear to hear the rich crying out for Liberty, while they thus starve their fellow-creatures; and feed them up with an imaginary good, while they monopolize the real benefits of nature.

But in spite of his strong views he was thoroughly a-political. There is nothing in his writing to suggest that he, any more than his contemporaries, could envisage the rooting out of such evils by legislation, and an economist who took the trouble to analyse his recurring 'Luxury' theme would probably have little difficulty in making him seem ridiculous. He had been infected by something that was very much in the air. Public figures like General Oglethorpe and private men like Thomas Turner, the Sussex grocer, expressed their fears about the rising standard of middle class living. Turner was convinced that 'the exorbitant practice of tea drinking' had 'corrupted the morals of people of almost every rank'. Only a hedonist, a cynic, or men of the intellectual stature of Samuel Johnson and Adam Smith were prepared to oppose this view. The superficial changes were so striking, and the evidence for the capital investment[18] which was preparing the way for the industrial revolution so hard to come by, that people generally accepted that Britain was becoming dangerously soft and wasting money on inessentials. To this Goldsmith added his theory (which he later anchored to his reading in the later history of the Roman empire) that a small country was gravely imperilling itself through the dispersal of population and diffusion of talent that was demanded by imperial expansion. In the short term Goldsmith was wrong, both politically and economically. In the long term it remains an open question whether or not he had been acute enough to perceive signs of incipient growths that would indeed prove malignant within the social system. Johnson's views were robustly laissez-faire:

A man gives half a guinea for a dish of green peas. How much gardening does this occasion? How many labourers must the competition to have such things early in the market keep in employment? You will hear it said, very gravely, "Why was not the half guinea, thus spent in luxury, given to the poor? To how many might it have afforded a good meal." Alas! has it not gone to the *industrious* poor, whom it is better to support than the *idle* poor?[19]

Though he could never have argued so effectively, Goldsmith was more subtle in his realisation that, as certain sections of the community increased the distance between themselves and the mass of the people by means of increasingly opulent display, unhealthy strains were created within the state. He saw that in certain situations the appearance could be far more important than the reality.

Other observers than Goldsmith had commented on the changing style of life amongst the upper classes and the prosperous section of the middle classes who were beginning to adopt refinements which a generation earlier would have been considered well beyond their reach. Colman and Bonnell Thornton had described in the 'fifties how French cuisine had triumphed in the houses of the rich (the traditional roast beef having been banished first to the sideboard, where it could be half hidden behind the guests' hats and thence to the servants' hall). More seriously they had pointed out that as they became more conscious of 'refinement' the middle classes were beginning to foster snobbish attitudes in their children. The disparaging view of Trade which was rife in Jane Austen's time could hardly have been felt a hundred years earlier when the younger sons of noblemen were being apprenticed in the City. Before Goldsmith drew his disparaging contrast between the decorative lady of his times and the enterprising mistress of a sixteenth century household,[20] Colman and Thornton had commented on the declining patronage of Kidder's Pastry School in Holborn, which was now attended by young women destined for domestic service rather than by future housewives. On the other hand a distinctly lower middle class fear of being overtaken by 'upstarts' can be sensed in the verses written in 1772 by Charles Jenner, who describes the assemblies that are beginning to be held in such unexpected places as Rotherhithe and Wapping:

> Where ev'ry month the powderd white-glov'd sparks,
> Spruce haberdashers, pert attorneys clerks,
> With deep-enamour'd prentices, prefer
> Their suit to many a sighing milliner:
> In scraps of plays their passions they impart,
> With all the awkward bows they learn from *Hart*.
> 'Tis here they learn their genius to improve,
> And throw by *Wingate* for the *Art of Love*;
> They frame th'acrostic deep, and rebus terse,
> And fill the day-book with enamour'd verse;
> Ev'n learned *Fenning* on his vacant leaves,
> The ill-according epigram receives,
> And *Cocker's* margin hobling sonnets grace
> *To Delia, measuring out a yard of lace.**

If there was any snobbery in Goldsmith's nature it was inverted snobbery: when, like his contemporaries, he criticised the spread of Luxury he was inclined to look far higher up the social scale and criticise people whose lives bore ample witness to 'Convenience, plenty, elegance, and arts' The bar-sinister of puritanism is evident on at least one side of his nature and although in religious matters his stance was one of broad church Anglicanism, he had a sneaking admiration for George Whitefield, a persuasive preacher with a large lower middle class following at the Methodist tabernacle in Moorfields.[21]

With a deep need for an intellectual framework for his life, Goldsmith remained as consistent in the attitude he had adopted on the Luxury issue as he did in his toryism and anti-colonialism. Escaping the absurdities of people who condemned tea-drinking or who had been alarmed by the sight of boatmen in silk stockings, he expressed views in *The Deserted Village* which had first been voiced in his little magazine the *Bee* eleven years earlier and repeated in *The Vicar of Wakefield*: that while people went hungry and poorly clothed they were gratuitously insulted by the flamboyant display of wealth. General Oglethorpe, who had spent a lifetime promoting social improvement on either side of the Atlantic, was willing to back his judgment that Goldsmith had a genuine concern for the

*Jenner is referring to popular handbooks on book-keeping, arithmetic and grammar.

unfortunate by sending him money to distribute as he saw fit.[22] Perhaps such a testimonial is necessary, for it is obvious that by this time Goldsmith was becoming increasingly identified with a way of life which he had so frequently condemned. The inventory for the Brick Court apartment hardly suggests frugality: nor do Mr Filby's accounts. Between October '69 and June '73 he spent over £220 at the tailor's alone. The bulk of this sum went on suits, breeches and waistcoats for himself but included a suit of livery and a crimson collar for his occasional servant, John Eyles, and £35 for clothes which his nephew had been invited to order at his expense. In the last year of his life, shortly before attending a dinner-party given by the Duke and Duchess of Northumberland at Sion House, he is found spending four guineas on a single 'rich straw silk tamboured waistcoat'. To use the kind of argument that he might have employed against Johnson, it would have taken the man who wove this silk on a Spitalfields loom at least six weeks to earn the money that Goldsmith had spent on the one item.

His style of living was still modest in comparison to that of Burke (even more deeply in debt than himself) or of Reynolds or of Topham Beauclerk who was creating a library at the back of his house in Great Russell Street which, in Walpole's phrase, 'stretched halfway to Highgate' and threatened to rival the British Museum as an attraction. Nevertheless, the extravagant purchase of an embroidered waistcoat is clearly the act of a man who, in Reynolds' account, had 'arrived late in the world' and was anxiouse to demonstrate that he had left a provincial upbringing well behind him. At Pallas and Ballymahon he had known what it was for a family to have middle class status without the adequate means to support it, and in the streets of Dublin he had worn the red cap which proclaimed him a second class member of Trinity College. Once Ireland was behind him he had been kindled to the point of fierce competition by the sight of the thriving English as opposed to the wilting Irish middle class. It was the classic recipe for the making of a snob. Miraculously he escaped this fate but although in private he was content with a bowl of bread and milk for his supper or the simple provisions that a farmhouse could provide, when he visited the luxurious houses to which he had access in this last period of his life he felt compelled to emulate what he saw there. He was also intensely inquisitive. At the Thrales' Streatham villa, left alone with Johnson in a room which contained an intriguing locked chest, he wanted his friend to try his own keys on it; and on another occasion Mrs Thrale was irritated to learn that, in her absence, he had wandered into her boudoir, prying into boxes and examining the contents of her stationery rack.[25]

Perhaps behind this curiosity there was also an impish desire to mock. During a stay at Bath with Lord Clare he acted out a curious charade with the Duke and Duchess of Northumberland who had lodgings in the next house. This involved walking into their dining room at breakfast time one day and throwing himself on to a couch as if he and not they were in the right place.[26] It was a situation which he had found ready-made for him in *The Absent Man*, a farce by his friend Isaac Bickerstaffe. On being 'disillusioned' he maintained his act so effectively that the Northumberlands, kindly inviting him to return to dinner, seem to have had the impression that they had helped him out of a genuine embarrassment.

*

The tailor's bills to which James Prior had access provide an opening onto the darker, compulsive side of Goldsmith's split personality. But it is only fair to remember that schizophrenic symptoms are to be encountered not only in his mind but throughout the society in which he lived. While Arthur Murphy was congratulating his contemporaries on their taste for romantic novels on the grounds that they could 'lead us through a Train of pleasing and unexpected Events, to a Knowledge of the Passions, a Taste for Virtue, and the refined Enjoyments of an enlightened Understanding',[27] he was actively encouraging a retreat from the realities of hunger, of the sale of children, and of the prostitutes packed into the newly completed terraces to the north and south of Oxford Street before the sale of leases to more respectable tenants.[28] The Taste for Virtue was often a matter of form alone: spending an evening in fashionable company at Bath, Thomas Campbell found both matrons and girls 'kicking with laughter' when a girl of aristocratic Irish descent gravely sang a ballad which was packed with sexual innuendo.[29]

The yearning for sentiment which Sterne had playfully exploited in his last book has to be offset by a penal code which, in terms of stolen property, fixed the value of a man's life at a surprisingly low rate of exchange. Goldsmith had made an eloquent attack on this particular obscenity. At Green Arbour Court he had lived only a few yards away from St Sepulchre's Church where once or twice a month the execution carts on their way from Newgate to Tyburn would stop for the gruesome ritual of the tolling bell and the prayers for the dying. Boswell, who had once prepared himself for an interview with Rousseau by gulping down the 'romantic prospect' of a Swiss valley,[31] was an afficionado of executions: in October 1769, having witnessed the hanging of six men at Tyburn he contributed a paragraph on the subject to the *London Chronicle*, congratulating himself on his ingenious solution to the problem of getting as near as possible to the gallows: he had sat on a hearse waiting to carry away one of the bodies.[32]

*

Luxury was at its most seductive in the late 'sixties and early 'seventies when Goldsmith was to be found in blue velvet or peach-coloured satin at public assemblies and masquerades, at the picture gallery in Spring Gardens or (between the months of May and August) at Vauxhall or one of its many imitators. Vauxhall itself had kept its popularity and, even when allowances have been made for cool summers and for the industrial pollution only a little way downstream, it must have been a delightful place. Basically a grove with illuminated walks, the trees themselves acting as standards for hundreds of oil lamps, the focal point was a rotunda approached under a portico which was decorated with murals. By this time, Hogarth's 'Henry VIII and Anne Boleyn' had been replaced by Hayman's depiction of 'the last conquests of the English in the four quarters of the world', Canada being represented by a panel in which a general, whose countenance revealed 'a tender and noble compassion', distributed food to the inhabitants of fallen Quebec.[33] Under the trees which surrounded the rotunda were supper-boxes in the form of Chinese kiosques where private parties ate rather expensively. In the 'fifties an evening at Vauxhall for four people had cost about thirteen shillings.[34] This would have included rather dubious wine. M. Grosley was convinced that

good Burgundy and Bordeaux were being adulterated with fermented
fruit and turnip juice to make the 'port' which was everywhere on
sale in London.

Gardens, lamplight, supper, and a high standard of musical
entertainment were the ingredients for Vauxhall's imitators,
Ranelagh upstream at Chelsea where there was a far more impressive rotunda, and the exclusive Marylebone Gardens, approached either from Marylebone High Street or by a footpath
across the allotments to the north-west of Cavendish Square.[35]
Incidental attractions varied from place to place, like the artificial
ruin and the cascade at Vauxhall and, at Marylebone, the fireworks,
cheese and almond cakes made by the proprietor's daughter and, in
1774, William Kenrick lecturing on Shakespeare. The most
serious competition seems to have been musical. The rival extablish-
ments had their own orchestras (indoor at Ranelagh, outdoor under
covered stands at Vauxhall and at Marylebone, where Pergolesi was
musical director at this time) and, under contract for the season,
singers who could draw large audiences.

The high priestess of Luxury at this time was Mrs Cornelys, a
blonde Austrian woman who had made her first appearance in
London twenty years back as a singer at the Opera in the Haymarket.
After wandering around Europe, including Holland where she had
acquired her Dutch name, she had returned in the late 'fifties with
the intention of setting herself up as official hostess to London
society. The house in Soho Square which she took over from
the Earl of Carlisle had ceased to be in the first rank of fashion
as a private residence but it promised to give her the space she
needed for assemblies. Settling here she had begun to demonstrate the skills of an impresario and soon established enough
confidence to be given access to the £2,000 needed for her scheme
of extending and renovating the house.[36] By the end of the decade,
when Goldsmith and Reynolds were among her patrons she
was employing J. C. Bach and C. F. Abel as musical directors
and for a time her oratorios were so successful that the Italian
Opera felt sufficiently threatened to invoke the theatrical licensing
act against her. She had other resources, the chief of which was
the masquerade which evoked memories of her youthful days
in Venice and which now gave London its chance to indulge
a taste for display instant history and occasional transvestism.

A combination of theatrical sense and organisational qualities which General Burgoyne might have envied emerges from Mrs Cornelys' elaborate advertisements:

Ante-Masquerade Intelligence.—For the information of such of our readers as intend to be at the Masquerade at Soho tomorrow night, we are happy to lay before them the following particulars of the manner in which that elegant Entertainment is to be conducted. The doors will be opened at eleven o'clock precisely. The Company are first to assemble in the Tea-rooms. As soon as these are sufficiently full, the doors leading to the Great Gallery will be opened, and the Masks will enter through an elegant green walk with flowers and shrubs planted on each side. In the Gallery, which will be curiously illuminated, a Band of Music is to be placed for *Contre Dances*. The Bridge-room will be opened at the same time, and the circular space under pavilion [sic] is to be appropriated [sic] for dancing Cotillons [sic]. The Pavilion will be ceiled with looking-glasses, which must produce a most charming reflection. The rest of that elegant apartment is laid out in a delightful Garden, perfumed with the odoriferous scent of the choicest flowers which the season can afford, and bordered with a Thicket of the most curious Shrubs, which will at once inspire the mind with the most rural ideas, and after the fatigue of the Dance, will afford a most desirable refreshment by the coolness of the shade. At one o'clock a Band of Music will announce the opening of the Supper Rooms by a march, and proceed at the head of the company up the great front stairs to the door of the Star-room, at the entrance of which the most rural and delightful prospect will open upon the eye. In the middle of the great Supper-room will appear an elegant Walk, bordered with two regular green Hedges; on each side of this beautiful walk is raised a curious Platform, where Supper will be laid out on large round tables, each of which is enriched with trees, under whose embowering shade the Masks will sup, as if they were *en pleine Campagne*, with the pleasure of seeing the rustic Swains and their Lasses mix in the gay Dance on the green turf beneath them. Those who may not find room at these tables, may pass by the Great Back-stairs into the Stage-room, which is laid out in a Shrubbery with extraordinary taste; in this and the Bridge-room, tables will be also laid for Supper, and the Masks, as they return into the Gallery, will be agreeably surprized by the opening of the Chinese-room, which will be so decorated, as to afford the most enchanting *Coup d'oeil*. Upon the whole, there is every reason to believe that this will prove one of the most pleasing Entertainments that has been given to the Town for many years, and that the night will be spent with true Arcadian felicity in this *Paradis Terrestre*.[37]

London had discovered the joys of dressing up. Royal princes, aristocrats and members of the government put themselves on display with the assistance, on a typical evening, of four thousand wax candles and a hundred musicians. Men dressed as women, women as men. Dancing bears, Irish haymakers, friars and abbesses with fleets of novices in tow walked about the rooms attempting to maintain the characters they had chosen. Sometimes one of Mrs Cornelys' patrons went too far. A young lord was frowned upon for appearing as Adam in flesh-coloured silk and 'a garland of flowers and fruits', and the ladies were not amused when the occupant of Wilkes' seat in the Commons, the sinister Colonel Luttrell, stalked through the rooms in a shroud with his coffin on his back. One of them decided to put him in his place: 'Your character of tonight will no doubt reconcile you to every freeholder of Middlesex; for you are certainly now the representative of what they all most heartily wish you the reality.'[38]

Garrick refused to compete with the would-be actors and actresses who appeared at Carlisle House in recognisable dramatic rôles. He wore a simple domino, and so escaped the strain of having to remain in character throughout the masquerade.[39] Reynolds, too, preferred this easy solution to the problems posed by fancy dress. But Goldsmith clearly enjoyed the opportunity to give vent to the theatrical vein in his personality. He liked to appear in 'old English' costumes. But for the man whose volatile sympathies were easily brought into play by the sight of suffering there were uncomfortable moments when, in the early hours of the morning, he walked out into Soho Square and looked into the faces of the wretched men and women who had waited in the hope of inspiring pity in the masqueraders. Visiting Brick Court one afternoon, Reynolds found his friend kicking the previous night's costume about the room in disgust.[40]

As Mrs Cornelys' advertisements suggest, visual tastes in the 'sixties and 'seventies were more subtle than they had been in the middle of the century. Mrs Primrose's dress of crimson paduasoy would no longer have been acceptable in any but the most rustic society. This was the period which Gainsborough commemorated. Blendings and contrasts of colour became less obvious and clothes had more natural lines. Both gold lace and the crinoline had disappeared. The French style in tall, plumed head-dresses had been adopted by the women and, now that Canada was a British territory, fur trimmings were in plentiful supply. The architectural settings for such fine clothes were being shaped under the predominating influence of John and Robert Adam and James Wyatt. The new sophistication of dress was matched by interiors which, from their overall dimensions to the loving detail of hearth-furnishings and fingerplates, showed a coming together of opulence, archaeological study, and a taste for the new and the elegant while, outside, the so-called 'Chinese' style of gardening which Sir William Temple had first talked about at the turn of the century was producing the great gardens which are to be seen in their maturity today.

The national imagination however, was not entirely given over to the arts of display. This of course was the age in which, in some sections of the community, a combination of religious revivalism, the desire for improved standards in public as well as private life, and the fashionable cult of the Man of Feeling were producing small but significant social changes. Jonas Hanway was collecting statistics which could be used to effect improvements in the lives of parish children and apprentices. General Oglethorpe was campaigning for the more rational and humane treatment of debtors; groups of men and women all over the country were coming together to promote the founding of a charity school or an infirmary, and members of parliament were lobbied for support when local improvements could only be effected by means of new legislation. Even though Goldsmith's practical share in this groping towards social justice was by now limited to spontaneous hand-outs of money, he was publicly committed to the causes of humanitarianism and moderat on, receiving a letter and possibly a visit from Tom Paine, who wanted his support in obtaining better conditions of service for excise officers, and encouraging his apothecary, William Hawes, in founding what was to become the Royal Humane

Society.[41] But however much the public acclaimed him as a man of conscience, he himself knew that he had been seduced by that very Luxury which he had so forcefully condemned; and when not engaged in bouts of frenetic socialising, he was too much given to morose fits of introspection to escape the feeling that he had betrayed his own better instincts. Out of this dichotomy of idealism and private indulgence a new poem was to spring.

*

If Johnson, Percy and Goldsmith travelled to Oxford by the more attractive Thames valley route in February 1769 they would have found on the last stage of their journey, four miles out of Dorchester, that the high road lay between recently constructed cottages evenly spaced on either side like a modern council estate. This was the new village of Nuneham Courtenay, and a road-book of the period would have informed them that between the road and the river Thames to the west lay the new mansion and pleasure grounds which had been created for Lord Harcourt between 1760 and 1761. The chronically short-sighted Johnson was indifferent to houses, landscapes and improvements: his companions were enthusiasts. Like Goldsmith himself at Gosfield, Percy had access to an estate which was being remodelled: his interest in Alnwick would later lead to the angry exchange between himself and Johnson which Boswell was to record.

To achieve his Arcadian landscape, Lord Harcourt had destroyed a Gothic church and an entire village with its parsonage, ale-house, cottages and long-established gardens on a bluff overlooking the Thames; its duck-pond had been expanded into a lake, and a Grecian temple did service as a parish church, although in their new cottages on either side of the main road the villagers were now a mile and a half away.[42]

Seven years earlier Goldsmith had written a hostile essay about such clearances. The *Revolution in Low Life*, which has been described as 'a *Deserted Village* in prose', deplores 'enclosures destined for the purposes of amusement or luxury', and mentions a specific instance of the destruction of a village 'distant about fifty miles from town, consisting of near an hundred houses': disguised as a 'correspondent' Goldsmith informs the editor of *Lloyd's*

Evening Post that he had actually stayed there in the summer of 1761.[43] There is no need, of course, to accept this letter as being strictly autobiographical: Goldsmith, as an anonymous journalist 'whose life had been spent in cities', was clearly inventing some of his circumstantial facts to make the article more lively. He could no doubt have read about the demolitions at Nuneham Courtenay in the year when Lord Harcourt was in the public eye as a functionary at the coronation, or he might have heard accounts from Percy of the improvements at Easton Neston, ten miles away from Percy's rectory at Easton Maudit in Northamptonshire, where another village had disappeared in the interests of landscaping.[44] But whatever his source of information, Goldsmith strongly condemned the insensitivity to the feelings and needs of simple people which was displayed on these occasions by the improvers.

For the purposes of his essay the villagers are not simply tidied away into 'improved dwellings' along the main road but are entirely dispossessed:

> I was grieved to see a generous, virtuous race of men, who should be considered as the strength and the ornament of their country, torn from their little habitations, and driven out to meet poverty and hardship among strangers. No longer to earn and enjoy the fruits of their labour, they were now going to toil as hirelings under some rigid Master, to flatter the opulent for a precarious meal, and to leave their children the inheritance of want and slavery.

Was the distortion deliberate or did it arise from an inadequate knowledge of the facts?—The strong tone of *The Revolution in Low Life* suggests that Goldsmith is confusing examples of local distress in England with a more widespread and searing process in Ireland. Burke, in the journal he had conducted as an undergraduate at Trinity College, Dublin, had in the course of an analysis of the Irish agrarian problem described the process of rack-renting which culminated in the emigration of the cottiers to America or England:

> ... The poorer kind of Farmers ... hold larger Quantities of Land, but at such a Rent as both hurts them and the Landlord. Gentlemen perceiving that in England Farmers pay heavy Rent, and yet live comfortably, without considering the Disproportion

of Markets and every Thing else, raise their Rent high, and extort it heavily. Thus none will hold from them but those desperate Creatures who ruin the Land (in vain) to make their Rent: they fly; the Landlord seizes, and to avoid the like Mischance, takes all into his own hands; which being unable to manage, he turns to grazing; thus one part of the Nation is starved, and the other deserted . . .[45]

The element of confusion in Goldsmith's essay was to be carried over into the poem and, after its publication in May, 1770, to give rise to a protracted debate in the newspapers: *The Deserted Village* was greatly admired but few people were prepared to accept that English village-folk were being forced to emigrate to Georgia. A temporary solution to this difficulty was found when Goldsmith's Irish friends and relations, with some justice, laid claim to 'sweet Auburn' as the village of Lissoy where he had spent his youth. The slow-flowing and sedgy River Inny was a likely haunt of the 'hollow sounding bittern', the sounds of the village at evening did rise up the knoll where Goldsmith had liked to sit close by his parents' house. Although the portraits of the schoolmaster, the parson and the pathetic old woman who gathers water-cress from the stream are generalised portraits in the eighteenth century manner, even they were identified.[46] In the eagerness to locate George Conway's ale-house, the mill and the 'hawthorn bush with seats beneath the shade', the introductory letter which Goldsmith addressed to Reynolds was conveniently overlooked. Here he had claimed: 'I have taken all possible pains, in my country excursions, for these four or five years past, to be certain of what I alledge, and . . . all my views and enquiries have led me to believe those miseries real, which I here attempt to display.'[47] It might be inferred from this reiterated belief that there were deserted villages within easy reach of London that Goldsmith would have been the last person to welcome any attempt to prove that he had written a poem of nostalgic regret for the Ireland of his youth.

It is difficult to escape the mood of lost innocence and spiritual exile that pervades *The Deserted Village*: when the poem communicates this message arguments on behalf of either Nuneham Courtenay or of Lissoy fade into comparative insignificance. But behind a dispute which at first seems to be a biographical rather than an aesthetic concern, it may be possible to detect reasons for the enduring appeal of the work.

The breakdown in logic lies somewhere between the pathetic ruins of the opening description and the landscaped garden which Goldsmith envisages when he warms to his social theme—and which he and Percy may have explored if, on their way to Oxford, they exercised their rights as travelling gentlefolk to 'inspect the improvements'. At the beginning of the poem he imagines that, in a ghostly way, he has returned to a ruined, deserted Auburn to stroll 'Amidst thy tangling walks, and ruined grounds'. Images from the Lissoy of his youth seem to be recalled:

> Sunk are thy bowers in shapeless ruin all,
> And the long grass o'ertops the mouldering wall[48]

This was a familiar part of the Irish landscape: by the end of the next century, the Goldsmith homes at Pallas, Lissoy and Bally-mahon would themselves have been reduced to just such a condition. But later in the poem Auburn is seen not as a mature ruin but as an ornamental park—'a garden, and a grave'—from which humbler gardens and dwellings have been cleared:

> . . . The man of wealth and pride,
> Takes up a space that many poor supplied;
> Space for his lake, his park's extended bounds,
> Space for his horses, equipage, and hounds;
> The robe that wraps his limbs in silken sloth,
> Has robbed the neighbouring fields of half their growth;
> His seat, where solitary sports are seen,
> Indignant spurns the cottage from the green;
> Around the world each needful product flies,
> For all the luxuries the world supplies.
> While thus the land adorned for pleasure all
> In barren splendour feebly waits the fall.[49]

Behind the logical flaw in *The Deserted Village* arises the fundamental biographical problem of Goldsmith's failure to return to Ireland. As his letter to Contarine from Leyden indicates, he had originally planned to return to Trinity College to complete his medical studies, and in 1755/6 only a breakdown in communications had hindered his return home. Since the early 'sixties when he had proved that he could secure an income for himself with his pen, there had been nothing to stop him from visiting his family. The journey would have taken just over a week,[50] but neither time nor expense are factors which Goldsmith might have been expected to take into account. By the end of the decade however, the wish to see Lissoy again had faded. In terms of psychic energy much of that original desire had been diverted into the opening lines of *The Traveller* and the recollections of Lissoy life in *The Vicar of Wakefield*. By the time he came to write *The Deserted Village* he had probably admitted to himself that he would never return. Henry had died and, with one important exception, there was no-one left who might have been expected to exert a pull strong enough to get him back across the Irish Channel. The exception, of course, was Anne Goldsmith. She was now in her early seventies, infirm and blind,[51] and more than ever an object of pity since the death of her eldest son.

Pity may have made up the bulk of Goldsmith's feeling for his mother at this time. A decade earlier he had been unforgiving towards the woman who in her wilful, managing way had pushed him forward as a precocious child and, later, withdrawn her affection when he began to show every sign of having turned into an unsatisfactory, feckless young man. The sourly ironical references in the letter sent to Bryanton from Edinburgh suggest that the family quarrel at which Catherine Hodson hinted had included a humiliating attack by Anne Goldsmith on her son.[52] In the absence of further evidence it is impossible to say whether the breakdown in their relationship was complete, or whether bitterness had been followed in time by remorse. Significantly, the only person Goldsmith encounters as he wanders in memory about ruined Auburn is the feeble old woman, a widow, who with difficulty stoops to pull watercress from the brook. It is very unlikely that Mrs Goldsmith had been reduced like this 'sad historian of the pensive plain' to living off the land, gathering her own firewood and residing in a hovel, but it is far less unlikely that Goldsmith was trying to salve an open wound in the pathos of these lines.[53] If he had once cheered himself up by striking attitudes about being both unsuccessful and thirty in a rhetorical letter to Henry, one should not be surprised to find him attempting to neutralise a more profound pain through the medium of poetry. Less creditably it may have been a way of quietening a conscience that was reminding him of his duty to visit his mother: under the poetic symbolism of the 'widowed solitary thing' she could be more conveniently consigned to the care of art and posterity. And this may have been a kinder fate than a reunion with a son who had outgrown any love he had once felt for her.

Apart from the problem of his relationship with his mother, Goldsmith probably knew that the gap between his London life and the intellectual narrowness of Lissoy was too great to allow for a home-coming that would be happy on either side. The unexpected arrival of his brother Charles in 1757 and Maurice's letters hinting that Oliver should help to set him up in London had warned him what to expect.[54] Neither of the brothers had attained the standard of literacy they would need to find places as clerks. So long as he remained out of Ireland Goldsmith could consign his family to the edge of his vision where the image was blurred with nostalgia. When someone who *could* be helped emerged out of the haze he would devote all his energy to assisting him: in 1770 his nephew, William Hodson, would be dissuaded from going on the stage and sent to a great surgeon, Dr Hunter, to complete his medical studies.

It is impossible to tell whether distance and nostalgia had introduced an element of fantasy into his feelings for his elder brother; but Henry's simple nobility of character had been an *idée fixe* for many years, and he seems a better subject than his father for the portrait of the Village Preacher of the poem. Goldsmith's mixed feelings about the kindly but improvident Charles Goldsmith had settled down in *The Vicar of Wakefield* into a picture of a man whose virtues were both enhanced and off-set by his endearing and sometimes comic unworldliness. Henry is recalled in the preface to *The Deserted Village* when Goldsmith, in order to free himself from the imputation that he is dedicating it to Reynolds simply because he is a powerful figure in the artistic world, hints that his feelings for this friend are similar to those that his brother once inspired. At the heart of so elegiac a poem it seems appropriate that there should be an elegy to this dead brother:

> But in his duty prompt at every call,
> He watched and wept, he prayed and felt, for all.
> And, as a bird each fond endearment tries,
> To tempt its new fledged offspring to the skies;
> He tried each art, reproved each dull delay,
> Allured to brighter worlds, and led the way.[55]

Henry Goldsmith had shown both his affection for Oliver and his understanding of him when he extricated him from the Wilder *débacle* and took him back to complete his degree course at Trinity College. The idea of returning home as a successful writer to a welcome from such a man must have been attractive. With Henry's death all prospects of a pleasant homecoming outside pure fantasy had come to an end; and if at this period in his life Goldsmith felt the need to envisage Lissoy as a deserted village, the possibility must be considered that it was because it had been deserted, for ever, by himself.

*

It is interesting to notice how closely the 'tyrant' who is behind all the unhappiness of the poem can be identified with Goldsmith's own life at this period. Ostensibly he is a landowner who has either foreclosed his leases or actually razed the village to the ground; but within the symbolism of this work the tyrant is also Luxury, laissez-faire economics and conspicuous consumption. When one looks at the imaginative embodiment of the symbol one finds oneself thrust into the very heart of Goldsmith's Brick Court existence. The masquerade itself becomes an important element in the symbolism as a hectic antithesis to the innocent village sports recalled from the old days:

> But the long pomp, the midnight masquerade,
> With all the freaks of wanton wealth arrayed,
> In these, ere trifflers half their wish obtain,
> The toiling pleasure sickens into pain;
> And, even while fashion's brightest arts decoy,
> The heart distrusting asks, if this be joy.[56]

Reaching the city, the uprooted villagers are confronted by a scene which one might be excused for associating with Mrs Cornelys' assembly rooms in Soho Square on an evening when the 4000 candles were alight:

> If to the city sped—What waits him there?
> To see profusion that he must not share;
> To see ten thousand baneful arts combined

To pamper luxury, and thin mankind;
To see those joys the sons of pleasure know,
Extorted from his fellow-creature's woe.
Here, while the courtier glitters in brocade,
There the pale artist plies the sickly trade;
Here, while the proud their long drawn pomps display,
There the black gibbet glooms beside the way.
The dome where pleasure holds her midnight reign,
Here richly deckt admits the gorgeous train,
Tumultuous grandeur crowds the blazing square,
The rattling chariots clash, the torches glare;
Sure scenes like these no troubles ere annoy!
Sure these denote one universal joy!
Are these thy serious thoughts—Ah, turn thine eyes
Where the poor houseless shivering female lies.
She once, perhaps, in village plenty blest,
Has wept at tales of innocence distrest;
Her modest looks the cottage might adorn,
Sweet as the primrose peeps beneath the thorn;
Now lost to all; her friends, her virtues fled,
Near her betrayer's door she lays her head,
And pinch'd with cold, and shrinking from the shower,
With heavy heart deplores that luckless hour,
When idly first, ambitious of the town,
She left her wheel and robes of country brown.[57]

It would be nearly half a century before another poet, publicly castigating himself as

                                        a youth
Who ne in virtue's ways did take delight;
But spent his days in riot most uncouth,
And vex'd with mirth the drowsy ear of Night,[58]

was eagerly read, lionised and pursued by fashionable ladies. Such a situation would have been very hard to envisage in the year 1770. Without risk of offending his audience, Goldsmith had presented himself in *The Traveller* as a homesick exile; but if now, in his new poem, he had openly announced that he had betrayed all his finer instincts he might well have been either ridiculed or consigned to oblivion. The Man of Taste of this period would have found a Byronic parading of weakness and failure offensive if not anti-social. (It was in the following year that the authorities intervened to prevent Jean-Jacques Rousseau from giving public readings of his *Confessions* in the drawing rooms of Paris.) Just as Sterne's sense of alienation had been carefully disguised by the rich characterization and the humour of *Tristram Shandy*, Goldsmith was conveying his helpless awareness of having taken a wrong turning through a poem which, in its apparent detachment and its uniformity of tone, kept well within the framework of objective, socially-oriented eighteenth century verse.

It seems likely that at least one of Goldsmith's friends would have recognised the personal implications of his poem. Sir Joshua Reynolds was his constant companion at Vauxhall and at the Carlisle House assemblies, and on canvas he had already portrayed Goldsmith as a man who was introspective and even morbidly sensitive. By the time he reached the comparison between Luxury and an overdressed woman decked out

> In all the glaring impotence of dress[59]

he must have been startled to find his friend treading such dangerous ground. Goldsmith's clothes were one of the long-standing jokes of London. Yet it is difficult to escape the conclusion that, in a poem which he appears to have held up in the press for six months for the sake of further revisions, Goldsmith knew perfectly well that he was presenting Reynolds, in the absence of Henry, with a personal confession.

One of the recurring images of *The Deserted Village* is pain, both of mind and body. It is sometimes associated with over-indulgence and guilt, and the consistent inner logic of the poem leads to the image of Luxury poisoning the body-politic and causing it to swell dropsically into

> A bloated mass of rank unwieldy woe[60]

It is significant that one of the ideas of the *revenant* in its opening section is that, if all had been well, he could have returned to Lissoy to die; and that the Village Preacher is imagined, in particular, as bringing comfort not simply to a countryman who is

taking leave of the idyllic, pastoral life portrayed in the opening
lines, but to a man who is with

> . . . sorrow, guilt, and pain, by turns dismayed.[61]

To these problems, that of continuing exile has to be added, for
Goldsmith is identified with the uprooted villagers as much as with
the masqueraders who parade under the chandeliers while a
wretched woman sits outside in the cold. But perhaps he is now
thinking less in terms of homesickness, for which there was an
obvious cure, than of the state of being exiled from his own better
nature. This is suggested by the re-introduction of imagery which,
under the influence of William Chambers' highly-coloured account
of the gardens he had seen in China, he had used in one of the
'Chinese Letters'. The garden that Goldsmith had imagined in that
essay was arranged to demonstrate a contrast between the initial
difficulties and rich rewards of virtue and the seductiveness and
diminishing returns of vice. The visitor to the garden was confronted by two gates: the gate of Virtue was appropriately gloomy
and uninviting: the opposite gate, labelled *Facilis Descensus*, a piece
of 'light, elegant and inviting' architecture attractively overgrown
with climbing plants and ornamented with statues of nymphs: but
the stranger who entered this gate would soon discover his mistake:

> Immediately upon his entering the gate of vice, the trees and
> flowers were disposed in such a manner as to make the most
> pleasing impression; but as he walked farther on he insensibly
> found the garden assume the air of a wilderness, the landskips
> began to darken, the paths grew more intricate, he appeared to
> go downwards, frightful rocks seemed to hang over his head,
> gloomy caverns, unexpected precipices, awful ruins, heaps of
> unburied bones, and terrifying sounds, caused by unseen waters,
> began to take place of what at first appeared so lovely . . .[62]

It was this piece of rather over-wrought prose which was to provide
a basis for the picture of the villagers in exile, and whereas the lines
in the poem may leave something to be desired as an account of
Georgia they have power when approached as a landscape of the
mind, or as a symbolic representation of the half-squalid, half-
opulent London of the 'sixties in which Goldsmith himself had lost
his way:

K

Through torrid tracts with fainting steps they go,
Where wild Altama murmurs to their woe.
Far different there from all that charm'd before,
The various terrors of that horrid shore.
Those blazing suns that dart a downward ray,
And fiercely shed intolerable day;
Those matted woods where birds forget to sing,
But silent bats in drowsy clusters cling,
Those poisonous fields with rank luxuriance crowned
Where the dark scorpion gathers death around . . .[63]

On the publication of *The Deserted Village* there was disagreement amongst the critics over the interpretation of the 'farewell to poetry' with which it ends. Some thought that Goldsmith was saying that the age was inimical to poetry; others that he had decided to write no more poems of his own. At a Royal Academy dinner a year or two later when asked by Lord Lisburne why he was writing histories instead of poetry, he replied 'My Lord, by courting the muses I shall starve, but by my other labours I eat, drink, have good clothes, and enjoy the luxuries of life.'[64]

There was some exaggeration here: William Griffin had given Goldsmith a hundred guineas for his poem.[65] But there would be no more poetry in this vein, though he would write a series of fine verse portraits of his friends before he died. In May 1770 there was more than one apparently good reason for taking leave of poetry. In the first place, its writing absorbed a great deal of his time and energy, and it was becoming more and more necessary for him to make money fast. With an eye on the large advances he could now command he had already postponed work on his study of natural history in order to embark on the *History of England* commissioned by Thomas Davies.[66] At a deeper level he may have felt that he could go no further, either in exposing his own nature or in adapting the essentially objective medium of Augustan verse to explorations of his psyche. Within the scheme of the poem it was appropriate that the man who had come adrift from his ideals should symbolically bid farewell to what was best in himself.

But having reached this point via the nightmare imagery of a spiritual wilderness, he found himself incapable of bringing *The Deserted Village* to the temperate conclusion that the good manners of his age demanded. It may have been this, rather than any other difficulty, which caused the delay of six months after Griffin had announced the imminent appearance of the new poem at the end of 1769.[67] Once more it was Johnson who came to his rescue to provide two concluding couplets. It would be dangerous to assume that Johnson failed to see the hidden significance of *The Deserted Village*; but he chose to ignore it and the lines he wrote, however impressive in themselves, have the effect of an anti-climax. Perhaps this was necessary. Ironically it was these couplets, based on the minor theme, that touched off the debate. By postulating quite un-Johnsonially that Britain's ills could be attributed to mercantile expansion, they left the impression that the poem sprang from a dubious political theory, rather than from the remorse of a complicated and perhaps deeply unhappy man.

ELEVEN

Nobody With Me At Sea But Myself

GOLDSMITH'S APARTMENT in Brick Court had two front doors: the innermost panelled and the outer, lying flush against it, a solid barricade of oak reinforced by iron bars. Traditionally this was the ultimate line of defence: by closing both doors on himself the tenant would have been 'sporting his oak' and giving a clear indication that he was not to be disturbed.

It has to be assumed that Goldsmith rarely used his outer door. His expensive furniture was intended to indicate that he was taking his rightful place in the social life of the capital, and there are enough stories from this period involving a casual caller to suggest that he was all too accessible.[1] In the evening the mahogany card-tables were in use, while the long dining table in the outer room awaited the extravagant meals which would be sent round from Middle Temple Hall or a nearby tavern. He wanted to impress his guests. Hence his nickname for the parties he gave: his 'little Cornelys'.[2] But socialising wasn't restricted to the evening. The man who took Johnson as his model must have his levée as well, even if he lacked Johnson's guaranteed income or his ability to write at considerable speed when it was absolutely necessary to do so.[3] Before he had time to consider the drawbacks of the new environment he was creating for himself, he must have been swamped with callers ranging from old friends to idly curious tavern acquaintances. It is not surprising that he needed to escape at times to suburban retreats, or that Sir William Blackstone, in the chambers below, should have departed not very long after his arrival.

Goldsmith needed casual acquaintances and thrived in their company. But the right setting for these encounters would have been the tavern, from which he could withdraw whenever he wanted to and where the reckoning was shared. He already belonged to an informal club which met at the Grecian Tavern[4] and whose members included William Cooke, Isaac Bickerstaffe and William Frederick Glover. Cooke was a young lawyer from Cork whom Goldsmith had helped when he came to London after the death of his first wife. Bickerstaffe came from a family which was part of the Dublin establishment. Glover, a popular, handsome, lazy man in his early thirties who, without much success, had tried his hand at writing and acting before leaving England for a brief but promising career as a surgeon in Dublin, had recently returned with a large family to eke out a Micawber-like existence in London. Goldsmith, playing his flute, singing a song or two and losing money at whist with unvarying good grace, must have sometimes recalled George Conway's inn at Ballymahon when he was with these friends. Here he could probably indulge his taste for rôle-playing and get a sympathetic reception for his jokes even when the warning signal was a frown rather than smile.

In the tavern he was a free agent, but installed in Brick Court Goldsmith must have begun to discover all the disadvantages of being the Irishman who had taken London by storm. Irish families on tour with letters of introduction would present themselves at the door on no. 2 staircase expecting to make the acquaintance first of Dr Goldsmith and then of Dr Johnson. Goldsmith had no defence: yet another supper party would be arranged. Surprisingly, Johnson could make a delightful impression on such occasions, perhaps because Goldsmith had warned the travellers of the danger they would find themselves in if they moved away from Irish topics and entered areas where gaps in either information or understanding might be discerned.[5] Sometimes the callers were émigrés rather than tourists—like the young man who after persuading Goldsmith to procure him a job as a teacher, turned out to be a thief. Another young Irishman was installed at 47 Leicester Square, again without much success since although he could draw well he lacked the experience with oil-paint which alone could have made him a useful member of Reynolds' team.[6]

The writer whose standard of living seemed to proclaim ready access to money was an obvious target for the professional hangers-on like Paul Hiffernan and John Carteret Pilkington. Hiffernan was an able but perverse man in his early fifties. Short and thickset with an aquiline nose, ruddy complexion and keen black eyes, in his youth he had trained for the priesthood in France; he had also acquired a medical degree and practised for a time as a doctor back at home in Dublin, but he now made a precarious living by acting as a theatrical agent and writer of paragraphs for the newspapers. These might be commissioned either for political purposes, or merely for self-advertisement, and Hiffernan was not above exploiting the opportunities for discreet blackmail which his access to the newspaper columns gave him. To some extent he redeemed his unpleasant image and earned himself a much needed place at friends' dining-tables by being well informed and an amusing conversationalist, though he spoiled everything when he was drunk by becoming coarse and abusive and, sometimes, by falling asleep after dinner.[7] Goldsmith felt obliged to remonstrate with this pensioner of his after an unfortunate episode in Bickerstaffe's rooms. The host had given his friends supper as a prelude to the reading of his new play. But he read badly, stumbling and hesitating in an unpleasantly thick voice. Hiffernan had managed to stay awake until the end of Act One when, rather grudgingly, he joined in the general commendations but by the middle of Act Two he was asleep. Goldsmith, raising his voice above the sound of Hiffernan's snoring, came to the defence of the humiliated playwright: 'Never mind the brute, Bick; go on—so he would have served Homer if he was here, and reading his own works'. He spoke to Hiffernan the next day. Hiffernan was unabashed: 'It's my usual way—I never can resist sleeping at a pantomime.'[8]

Pilkington was the complete drifter. His mother was an Irish poetess who had been a favourite of the ageing Swift before she disentangled herself from a boorish husband and came to London to make a reputation as a wit and to be 'protected' by a series of noblemen. John Carteret had made half-hearted attempts to exploit his mother's reputation by tacking some correspondence between her and one of her lovers on to an insipid memoir of his own. Thus armed he had set out to extract subscriptions from anyone who was willing to respond to his easy charm. He had a fair degree of success in this venture though he shared with Goldsmith the dubious distinction of having fallen foul of Ralph Griffiths (Letitia Pilkington's publisher). Acting on his usual form, Griffiths spread vicious rumours about the relationship between the memoir-writing mother and son.

It is Pilkington who features in the most famous of the 'gullibility' stories to be pinned to Goldsmith. He arrives at Brick Court with the news that, on behalf of a duchess with a taste for unusual pets, he has secured a pair of white mice 'now in the River, on board the Earl of Chatham Indiaman, just arrived'. The only thing that prevents him from delivering them in person is the lack of a suitably splendid cage. Will Goldsmith oblige with a loan? Goldsmith's pockets are fortunately empty—of all but his gold watch. To Pilkington this suggests an obvious solution, and the poet looks on helplessly as it is carried off to the pawnbroker, to be redeemed several months later by Goldsmith himself. In the victim's account, there is a sequel to this episode: '. . . after staying away two years, he came one evening into my chambers half drunk, as I was taking a glass of wine with Topham Beauclerk and General Oglethorpe; and, sitting himself down, with the most intolerable assurance enquired after my health and literary pursuits, as if we were upon the most friendly footing. I was at first . . . so much ashamed of ever having known such a fellow, that I stifled my resentment, and drew him into a conversation on such topics as I knew he could talk upon, and in which, to do him justice, he acquitted himself very reputably; when all of a sudden, as if recollecting something, he pulled two papers out of his pocket, which he presented to me with great ceremony, saying, 'Here, my dear friend, is a quarter of a pound of tea and a half pound of sugar I have brought you, for though it is not in my power at present to pay you the two guineas you so generously lent me, you nor any man else shall ever have it to say that I want gratitude.' This was too much . . . I could no longer keep in my feelings, but desired him to turn out of my chambers directly, which he very cooly did, taking up his tea and sugar, and I never saw him afterwards.'[9]

The retrieved tea and sugar brand the White Mice story with the mark of the sophisticated humourist and brings into question its relationship to the moral fable which had appeared amongst the 'Chinese Letters' about a prince who neglected his bride in order to pursue a mouse with green eyes.[10] By telling William Cooke and others that he had been grossly imposed upon by Pilkington Goldsmith was inviting his friends to regard him as a credulous, as well as a good-natured man. Although his motives for allowing himself to be cheated were probably different from George Primrose's in *The Vicar of Wakefield*, there is a similarity of attitude. After describing how a rogue has promised him a job as secretary to 'an embassy . . . from the synod of Pennsylvania to the Chickasaw

Indians' George comments, 'I knew in my own heart that the fellow lied, and yet his promise gave me pleasure, there was something so magnificent in the sound.'[11] There is probably more at stake, both here and in Goldsmith's account of his dealings with Pilkington, than the born raconteur's willingness to sacrifice himself to his own story. If, as the personal theme of *The Deserted Village* suggests, he was living with the knowledge that he had betrayed his own principles, there may have been comfort in the thought that, as a man who was guileless to the point of idiocy, he himself was entirely exploitable. At Brick Court he had created a situation in which his part-time servant could have robbed him with impunity if he had had the mind to do so. Large sums of money were kept in a drawer to which he had free access for household expenses.[12]

Goldsmith's need to trust people at least one remove from himself—a drinking companion, a notorious lounger, a woman in the street with a sad story—should perhaps also be treated with caution. Fundamentally there is less altruism here than the spirit of the compulsive gambler. But there were other occasions when he applied experience and mature judgment to the task of helping people in difficulties. In particular this is true of his relationships with young men who were attempting to launch themselves in London as he had done only fifteen years before. At about the time of the publication of *The Deserted Village* two emissaries from Lissoy had arrived at Brick Court: his thirty-four-year-old brother, Maurice, and Daniel and Catherine Hodson's eldest son, William. He at once took to his nephew and set about assisting him in the very spheres where he himself had encountered disappointment and humiliating failures. William was to remain under his wing in London for about a year during which time Goldsmith had hopes of securing him an appointment as a surgeon with the East India Company.[13] Maurice, on the other hand, returned to Ireland after only a short stay: William could be helped; Maurice with his poor command of literary skills could not. As Katharine Balderston has suggested, there was probably only one way in which Maurice's interests could have been promoted and this was to introduce him to Lord Clare.[14] Goldsmith's uncharacteristic cautiousness in concealing this friendship from his family could have sprung from a variety of motives: an unwillingness to place himself under a real obligation to the Irish peer; a reluctance to bring a thoroughly provincial younger brother to the attention of his London friends; perhaps also a recognition that Maurice's lack of direction at this comparatively late age was a sign of a dangerous tendency to think in terms of what could be done for him rather than what he could do.

There were other Irishmen who would leave records of the simple friendliness and consideration that Goldsmith had shown them as unknown young men newly arrived in London. John Day, with a distinguished legal career behind him by the time James Prior asked him for his impressions of Goldsmith, indicated a friendship between the writer and the young Henry Grattan who arrived from Trinity College Dublin to share Day's chambers in the Middle Temple in 1767. Suffering from a double bereavement and intent on studying the oratory which would later help him to become one of the great Irish political and social reformers of the later years of the century, Grattan was at this time a rather withdrawn and melancholy boy; but an account of Goldsmith from another stranger who found himself alone in London suggests, as might have been expected of the man who detected the note of distress in a street-singer's voice as he played whist with Sir William Chambers,[15] that he was responsive to his companions' moods and could meet them at least half way. It was during a break from his work on the *History of Animated Nature* while he was strolling in the Temple gardens that he came across the eighteen-year-old M'Veagh M'Donnell studying his volume of Boileau. M'Donnell's brother had died on their arrival in London en route to Ireland from France where, as Roman Catholics, they had both been educated. There was 'a great deal of conversation' in the garden and later, taking up an invitation to visit Goldsmith in his rooms, M'Donnell received not only good advice but also a job on the translation of Buffon's *Histoire Naturelle* which was the basis of Goldsmith's own work. 'In London, nothing is to be got for nothing,' Goldsmith warned him. M'Donnell, who was to become a well-known London doctor, recalled Goldsmith's kindness in a conversation with James Prior shortly before his own death:

It has been said he was irritable. Such may have been the case at times; nay I believe it was so; for what with the continual pursuit of authors, printers, and booksellers, and occasional

K*

pecuniary embarrassments, few could have avoided exhibiting similar marks of impatience. But it was never so towards me. I saw him only in his bland and kind moods, with a flow, perhaps an overflow, of the milk of human kindness for all who were in any manner dependent upon him. I looked upon him with awe and veneration, and he upon me as a kind parent upon a child.

His manner and address exhibited such frankness and cordiality, particularly to those with whom he possessed any degree of intimacy. His good nature was equally apparent. You could not dislike the man, although several of his follies and foibles you might be tempted to condemn. He was generous and inconsiderate; money with him had little value.

I was abroad at the time of his death, and wept bitterly when the intelligence first reached me. A blank came over my heart as if I had lost one of my nearest relatives, and was followed for some days by a feeling of despondency.—Poor Goldsmith was himself subject to frequent fits of depression as I heard from those around him.[16]

Some time between August 1770 and April 1771 a tragedy involving another young stranger to London had come to the notice of Goldsmith and the members of the Club. His attention would have been easily engaged by the story of the Bristol boy, Thomas Chatterton, who had taken a fatal dose of arsenic in a garret room not far from Green Arbour Court. Certainly the question of the 'Rowley' poems was to concern him intermittently for the last three years of his life, at one time imposing a strain on his friendship with Thomas Percy. Percy was understandably annoyed when Goldsmith refused to accept expert evidence that the poems were forgeries, clinging quixotically to his belief in the mediaeval poet and the chest in the tower of St Mary Redcliffe at Bristol where the 'manuscripts' were said to have been found.[17]

*

'The Club commenced again on last Monday,' Johnson wrote to Bennet Langton on October 24th 1770. 'Dr Goldsmith has been at Paris with the Hornecks not very delightfully to either side . . .'[18] Johnson had met the beautiful Mrs Horneck, wife of Captain Kane Horneck, at a dinner party given by Reynolds eight years before.

She came from Devonshire and was now introducing her two daughters to the world. They were both considered to be as beautiful as herself. Even Horace Walpole was impressed by the elder of the two, Catherine, whom he encountered at a reception shortly after her marriage. '... I was in love till one o'clock, and then came home to bed,' he wrote. Goldsmith accompanied the three women to France when the younger sister, Mary, was sixteen. He had probably agreed to the journey in order to please Reynolds, but however willingly the travellers had fallen in with each other's plans as they set out from London there are hints in the second of two letters written to Reynolds from France that they eventually succumbed to the occupational disease of travelling companions and got in one another's way.

Reynolds may have believed that Goldsmith, with his fluent French, would smooth the Hornecks' path for them: a complicating factor, however, was that by the time they reached Paris they were seeing a great deal of Reynolds' lawyer, the wealthy Joseph Hickey, who had gone there to bring his daughters home from a convent and who very much prided himself on *his* French.[19] Goldsmith was not an obvious choice as an escort for a genteel lady with two beautiful daughters. In many ways he was still a bit rough as Henry Thrale had discovered when, in the course of a sumptuous dinner party at Streatham, Goldsmith had enquired how much he earned in a year.[20] He was never at his best, anyway, in the company of women, his jocularity mounting as rapidly as his jokes failed.[21] Goldsmith had embarked with his charges at Dover armed with remarks about sea-sickness and determined to keep everyone's spirits up but, perhaps before they had arrived at the Hotel d'Angleterre in Calais, Mrs Horneck had begun to have doubts about the whole undertaking. Goldsmith's own excitement at being back in France after a world war and an absence of fourteen years, can be felt in the first of his letters. So can his determination that the Hornecks are going to enjoy themselves come what may:

My dear Friend,
    We had a very quick passage from Dover to Calais which we performed in three hours and twenty minutes, all of us extremely sea-sick, which must necessarily have happened as my machine to prevent sea-sickness was not completed. We were glad to leave

Dover, because we hated to be imposed upon, so were in high spirits at coming to Calais where we were told that a little money would go a great way. Upon landing two little trunks, which was all we carried with us, we were surprised to see fourteen or fifteen fellows all running down to the ship to lay their hands upon them, four got under each trunk, the rest surrounded and held the hasps, and in this manner our little baggage was conducted with a kind of funeral solemnity till it was safely lodged at the custom house. We were well enough pleased with the peoples civility till they came to be paid; every creature that had the happiness of but touching our trunks with their finger expected six-pence, and they had so pretty civil a manner of demanding it that there was no refusing them. When we had done with the porters, we had next, to speak with the custom house officers, who had their pretty civil way too. We were directed to the Hotel d'Angleterre where a valet de place came to offer his service and spoke to me ten minutes before I once found out that he was speaking English. We had no occasion for his service so we gave him a little money because he spoke English and because he wanted it. I can't help mentioning another circumstance, [?Mary] bought a new ribbon for my wig at Canterbury, and the barber at Calais broke it in order to gain six-pence by buying me a new one.[22]

Only a few days later the atmosphere had changed. Perhaps to spare Reynolds' feelings, perhaps (as he suggests) because he intended to show the letter to his companions, Goldsmith only hints at the causes of friction, but from the letter sent from the Hotel Dannemark, rue Jacob, Fauxbourg St Germain, one senses that the Hornecks were homesick and found Goldsmith ill-bred, and that Mrs Horneck, in particular, was scandalised by his attitude to money. 'I have been thinking of the plot of a comedy,' he observes to Reynolds, 'which shall be entitled a journey to Paris, in which a family shall be introduced with a full intention of going to France to save money . . .'[23] Striving rather desperately to amuse them he took them to Versailles where, as they stood beside an ornamental pool, he claimed that one could easily leap onto the island in the centre. He proceeded to demonstrate—and fell in. The tone of his subsequent relations with the Horneck sisters had been set.[24]

In the letter to Reynolds Goldsmith announced the intention of parting company with the Hornecks as soon as they got back to Dover. He wanted to explore Kent, he said. When the time came he abandoned this idea and they presumably travelled back to London together: but the feeling behind the plan to take leave of his travelling companions at the earliest possible moment adds to the impression that the holiday had not been a success.

All the same, they had spent a month together and there must have been enough shared incidents by the end of it to make a reunion welcome to both sides once the frictions of living too close to one another had been forgotten. A new setting for this friendship was provided when Catherine ('Little Comedy', as Goldsmith had nicknamed her)[25] married Henry Bunbury, a gifted caricaturist and the younger brother of a Suffolk baronet whose home, Barton Hall near Bury St Edmund's, now became accessible to all of them. It was here that Goldsmith had his last holiday in the severe winter of '73–'74. Any restraining influence that Mrs Horneck had exercised was lessened by Catherine's marriage and at Barton Goldsmith was in demand as a willing object of practical jokes. 'Accidents' happened to his wig and, very mysteriously, the efforts of Henry Bunbury's valet to repair the damage only added to the comic effect; his black silk coat acquired inexplicable embellishments of white paint; and during a boating party, in an attempt to prove that it was quite possible to retrieve a guinea from the shallow bottom, he fell into the pond.[26]

The public which wept over the tribulations of Parson Primrose and the dispossessed villagers of Auburn might have been surprised to learn what the famous Oliver Goldsmith was suffering at the hands of Devonshire and Suffolk gentlefolk. Possibly Goldsmith himself was a little surprised when he stood back from the situation. At the beginning of his acquaintance with the Hornecks he had attempted to administer a reproof when, a mere two or three hours before the event, he had received a summons to attend a supper party in London at the house of one of their friends. He had refused the invitation and sent back a message in doggerel that hinted that this was 'not how things were done'.[27] The lines were clumsy enough, and the Hornecks may very well have been as insensitive as Goldsmith's pork-butcher friend on another occasion, to the point that their delightfully odd little Doctor was making. By

Barton days he had clearly given up the struggle and, perhaps needing the family atmosphere created by the Hornecks as much as the merry sisters needed him, he settled down into the rôle in which he found himself cast.

At least one of Goldsmith's biographers[28] has suggested that his need of the Hornecks could be narrowed into a specific attachment to the younger sister, Mary, whose nickname 'the Jessamy bride' had been incorporated into his facetious verses.

But although some of his contemporaries found Goldsmith attractive when the dark, sensitive eyes kindled and brought animation to the plain, pock-marked face,[29] he was not a natural object for a young girl's calf-love, even before he had revealed his zest for falling into the water. A few years later, Mrs Thrale noticed that Mary, as strikingly beautiful as Catherine, had overtaken her sister in intelligence and powers of conversation, so even at this time there might have been an intellectual meeting place between her and Goldsmith.[30] But there is nothing to suggest that Mary Horneck could have appreciated her friend's manic sense of humour. Ironically, two of the stories which were to have such a damaging effect on his reputation have Mary as their source: the visit to the puppet-show and the 'There are times and places where I am also the object of admiration' incident at Calais. It was Catherine not Mary who invited Goldsmith in anapaestic couplets to join them at Barton and who received his reply in the same form, and it is easier to imagine a relationship between Goldsmith, the willing butt, and the safely married 'Little Comedy' than between him and the beautiful, clever—and perhaps humourless—younger sister.

From Goldsmith's side, of course, the relationship might be seen in a more serious light and, in the absence of any other known romantic attachment it is tempting to do so. Mary, when he first met her, was little more than a child but here was a man who loved the company of children, and as she developed into the beautiful Miss Horneck she could have become for Goldsmith an important exception in his predominantly uneasy relationships with women.

Reynolds noticed that his friend was not at his best in female society: 'When in company with ladies he was always endeavouring after humour, and as continually failed; but his ill success was equally diverting to the company as if he had succeeded. If they laughed, he was happy and did not seem to care whether it was with him or at him'.[31] The 'did not seem to care' is revealing. A critic who, on the strength of Goldsmith's literary output up to the year 1771, came to the conclusion that he was a misogonyst would seem to have a good deal of justification for such a finding. Whether in the journalism or in his novel, Goldsmith's women tend to be un-reliable, manipulative and overbearing. This is unlikely to have escaped intelligent women like Miss Reynolds and Mrs Thrale and, in addition to his lack of decorum, there may have been something in his attitude towards them that inspired dislike. At Edinburgh, contemplating his lack of success at the Assembly in spite of his 'rich Sky-blew sattin' and white gloves, he had adopted a broadly satirical stance before confessing to Bob Bryanton: 'But how ill my Bob does it become me to ridicule woman with whom I have scarce any correspondence . . . An ugly and a poor man is society only for himself . . .'[32] Since that time, at one level of experience as Reynolds noted, he had kept women at arm's length under a barrage of hit-or-miss jokes, while at the deeper level he had revealed a pathological mistrust. In consequence he became awkward in female company, and was self-conscious enough to build upon his awkwardness, so that for an Irish visitor to London the memory of dancing a minuet with him was one of universal mirth.[33] There were obviously important exceptions including the Catherine of his boyhood (who had jeopardised his Trinity College prospects by seducing Henry's pupil); and Jane Contarine (who had failed to answer his letters). There was also a succession of women, from casual beggers in the street to Mrs Butler of Green Arbour Court or the Misses Gun near the Temple, who took in sewing, to whom he could relate simply because, as objects of condescension or charity, they were already safely at one remove. He still visited Mrs Butler, taking her money, old clothes and food, and the Gun sisters worshipped him.

Mary Horneck could have been another such exception. In one way, her youth would have been in her favour. But if Goldsmith *had* fallen in love in early middle age it is extremely unlikely that he believed for a moment that there could be any response. He saw his own circumstances too clearly. In May 1761 one of the last 'Chinese Letters' had been headed 'Whether love be a natural or a fictitious passion'. For the most part the debate evades the issue, though it seems to lead to the same conclusion as the comments on marriage scattered about Goldsmith's journalism: that a prolonged relationship is in a sense artificial, but something to be striven for with all the powers of will and intelligence by civilised people in a civilised community. A little rag-bag of odds and ends, the essay was probably written at pressure while the printer waited; but of course it was at such moments that the writer took himself by surprise and sometimes got through to the best in his own nature. The sentence that follows is surely a clear indication that the man who submitted to having his wig and his new suit spoiled was more aware of the fundamental issues at stake than might have been supposed: 'Tho' [love] cannot plant morals in the human breast, it cultivates them when there: pity, generosity, and honour receive a brighter polish from its assistance; and a single amour is sufficient entirely to brush off the clown . . .'[34] Perhaps the pet-name 'Jessamy Bride', whether bestowed by Goldsmith or not, sets the tone of his relationship with Mary Horneck. She was seen as the child-bride of a *Jemmy Jessamy*, a Jack-a-Dandy who in his bright foppish clothes was something between a changeling and a household pet.

Goldsmith was under no illusions about the Hornecks' ability to see beneath the clown's mask. Even when he was the victim, he probably found their high spirits attractive, but he knew that they were just as incapable of understanding his curious style as so many of his other London acquaintances. In his answer to Catherine's clumsy verses he made a last-minute revision. She had made free with his bad luck at cards and his weakness for flashy clothes. He in reply imagines the sisters in the dock of the Old Bailey to answer a charge which he has brought against them. The attention of the court is drawn to himself:

But pray who have they pilfered? A Doctor I hear.
Yon handsome fac'd well looking man that stands near . . .

On re-reading the couplet Goldsmith correctly surmised that Catherine and Mary were incapable of responding to even the very obvious irony of 'handsome fac'd' and before the letter was posted the words were scratched out and replaced by the unequivocal 'solemn fac'd odd looking man'. If Goldsmith had indeed fallen in love with one of the Horneck sisters, he knew perfectly well that he could expect neither understanding nor a response to his tender feeling.

*

9a Hugh Kelly

9c George Colman
by Gainsborough

9b Arthur Murphy by Dance

10a James Boswell by Willison

10b Mrs Thrale by an
unknown Italian artist,
circa 1784

10c Horace Walpole
by T. Lawrence

11 Oliver Goldsmith by Henry Bunbury

12 David Garrick between the Comic and the Tragic Muse, by Reynolds (Mrs Abington as the Comic Muse)

The emotional life of a man who could only gain access to the deeper side of his nature through his art was predictably unsatisfactory. The letter which he wrote to a friend, John Bindley, in July 1766 contains a possible danger signal:

> ... I am heartily sorry for your brother's illness, for with great truth I may say that I never knew any one so short a time whose mind I fancy'd more like my own, that is in other words that I loved better ...

Even by the standard of the age this was an effusive way of speaking about someone he had met only once before—and nothing else is heard of his friendship with either of the brothers.[35] But if there is a hint here of the egoist's unattainable dream of finding a soul-mate who is really himself in disguise there are plenty of indications elsewhere of the inevitable isolation that awaited the man who had embarked on such a quest.

There were compensations: in the first place, acquaintances who remained part of the back-drop of his life simply because they were kept at arm's length, as drinking-companions perhaps or dependents (for while Johnson's pensioners invaded his life and his home, driving him out eventually to the Thrales', Goldsmith's remained on the fringe, as casual scroungers or recipients of visits and gifts). The friendship of a man like Nugent was probably important because whatever lurked at the core of his personality was well hedged round with noise and bluff Irish jokes. Offering security of a very different kind there was Johnson like a lighthouse emitting signals from the solid outcrop of reason, which was both a haven and a peril.

Johnson represented intellect and this was an essential *point d'appui*, for Goldsmith clung tenaciously to intellectual consistency. Here was order, control, sanity as opposed to the chaos in which the darker, compulsive side of his nature constantly threatened to plunge him. But Johnson was also the father-figure who on many occasions seems to have awoken a deeper emotional need in Goldsmith. To reveal that need was probably a mistake, for Johnson could not answer him on this level. He could resolve his friend's finanical crises with the help of Newbery, but he could not respond to the other, silent appeal that was being made by such tokens as an uncorked bottle of madeira. When Goldsmith burst into tears after the first night of *The Good-Natured Man* Johnson was all too probably disconcerted. Later he was shocked to hear other friends being informed about the incident which he felt to be in some way shameful.[36] And one might conjecture from his concluding couplets to *The Deserted Village* that he was also inclined to close his mind against the buried confessional theme of that poem.

Although at moments of crisis Goldsmith turned instinctively to Johnson, it was in the company of the outwardly bland Joshua Reynolds (who by this time had probably rejected finally the possibility of marriage with Angelica Kaufmann)[37] that Goldsmith came closest to expressing affection. Mrs Thrale was sharp enough in her observation to be credited on this point; and Reynolds himself seems to bear it out: 'The author was intimately acquainted with Dr Goldsmith. They unbosomed their minds freely to each other, not only in regard to the character of their friends, but what contributed to make men's company desired or avoided . . .'[38] Perhaps the limitations of even this relationship can be seen in the gap between promise and realisation that seems to reveal itself in Reynolds' measured phrases.

Laughing as he lost money at whist, frowning dreadfully as he indulged his taste for droll stories, Goldsmith seems to have lived out his public existence in the spirit of the masquerade. Perhaps it was inevitable that a writer who hid behind masks of good nature or simple buffoonery should have been deeply attached to the theme of disguise and mistaken identity. In *The Vicar of Wakefield*, one of these disguised characters, Sir William Thornhill, is closely identified with Goldsmith himself. Like the hero of *The Good-Natured Man*, Sir William has used reckless philanthropy as a substitute for giving at a deeper level. As Sir William, disguised as Burchell, tells his own story, Goldsmith seems to come close to an important realisation about his own condition; but he stops short at the very moment when—like Sir William who nearly gives his disguise away in his absent-minded use of the personal pronoun—he seems to be on the verge of the truth:

He now therefore found that such friends as benefits had gathered round him, were little estimable: he now found that a man's own heart must be ever given to gain that of another. I now found, that—that—I forget what I was going to observe: in short, sir, he resolved to respect himself, and laid down a plan of restoring his falling fortune . . .[39]

Other compensations than literature and friendship were readily available to unattached males in the London of the mid-eighteenth century. The Temple was only superficially a monastic establishment: a blind eye was turned on the comings and goings of prostitutes; and for men who were too fastidious to enjoy the kind of adventures in which Boswell indulged in the dark courts and alleyways off the Strand, other possibilities presented themselves in the theatrical green-rooms, from which Johnson had exiled himself because as he told Garrick 'the silk stockings and white bosoms of your actresses excite my amorous propensities'.[40] Arthur Murphy had set up an actress in her own apartment, and George Colman had married another with whom he had lived for several years.

In Goldsmith's case the lack of any clear evidence of promiscuity is not conclusive: even Boswell's escapades seem to have been a well preserved secret until the publication of the Malahide papers. But in view of Goldsmith's flair for attracting anecdotes to himself it is a little curious that none that survived, with the exceptions of the Wine Office Court *fracas* and a story of his leaping into a post-chaise at Hyde Park corner to accompany a lady to Bath,[41] presents him in anything approaching a sexual context. In contrast, everyone knew that Charles Churchill had woken up early one morning in a bed of asparagus at Battersea to find a prostitute asleep at his side. He was so relieved that she hadn't stolen his watch that he had her admitted to the Magdalen, a home for 'fallen women' in St George's Fields.[42] The only suggestion of a hidden side to Goldsmith's life comes from the mock epitaphs which were composed by fellow members of the Club which met at the St James's coffee house in the last year or two of his life. Garrick's extempore epitaph on Goldsmith was the famous couplet

> Here lies Nolly Goldsmith, for shortness call'd Noll
> Who wrote like an angel, but talk'd like poor Poll.

But after Goldsmith's effective analysis of his own character he produced, under the heading *Jupiter and Mercury : A Fable*, a more elaborate portrait which took the writer's dual personality as its theme and contained enough innuendo to suggest that he was a philanderer:

Here, Hermes, says Jove, who with nectar was mellow,
Go fetch me some clay—I will make an odd fellow.
Right and wrong shall be jumbled, much gold and some
                                                    dross;
Without cause be he pleas'd, without cause be he cross:
Be sure as I work to throw in contradictions;
A great lover of truth, yet a mind turn'd to fictions.
Now mix these ingredients, which warm'd in the baking,
Turn to learning and gaming, religion and raking;
With the love of a wench, let his writings be chaste,
Tip his tongue with strange matter, his pen with fine taste.
That the rake and the poet o'er all may prevail,
Set fire to his head, and set fire to his tail.
For the joy of each sex on the world I'll bestow it,
This scholar, rake, christian, dupe, gamester, and poet.
Tho' a mixture so odd, he shall merit great fame,
And among brother mortals be Goldsmith his name.
When on earth this strange meteor no more shall appear,
You, Hermes, shall fetch him, to make us sport here.[43]

There is one other commentator who might be regarded as having
thrown light, however obliquely, on this subject. Horace Walpole,
who tried to keep as great a distance as possible between himself
and the Johnson-Goldsmith circle, informed a friend at the time of
the poet's death that he had died 'of a purple fever'.[44] One medical
authority appears to have used this hint as a basis for his theory that
Goldsmith's final illness was complicated by venereal disease.[45] It
is very slender evidence, and again the source is potentially un-
reliable: Walpole was a gossip, albeit an astute one and, after the
references to his friends and possibly himself in *She Stoops to
Conquer*, he would have been unable to resist such an item however
dubious its provenance. Whether the recurring idea of pain and the
nightmare imagery in *The Deserted Village*:

> Those poisonous fields with rank luxuriance crowned
> Where the dark scorpion gathers death around[46]

could refer to a sexual jungle of which he was aware, or into which
he had strayed, must remain an open question. His journalism of
the early 'sixties shows that at that time Goldsmith was something

of a puritan, but certainly neither a humourless nor a squeamish one: there is no mincing of words in the 'Chinese Letters' when he condemns the current vogue for titillation.[47] As for close relationships, he was under no illusions about the demands they imposed. Beneath the ambiguities of *The Vicar of Wakefield* and the farcical situation of *She Stoops to Conquer* he acknowledges the difficulties and seems to bestow a tacit approval on the badly matched couples who have weathered the storm together and settled down into a way of life which is both tolerant and civilised.

*

If Katharine Balderston's conjecture is right and Reynolds forwarded his friend's mail from the porter's lodge at the Temple, then it was probably while he was in Paris that Goldsmith received the news of his mother's death.[48] In this case it is almost certain that he kept his silence and that not even Reynolds was informed of his bereavement. A lingering sense of duty ensured that he would observe the forms and, on his return to London, he went into mourning; but by putting on grey instead of one of the black suits which he clearly enjoyed wearing he probably hoped to escape questions. Unluckily, Fanny noticed that his appearance was unusually drab. On enquiry she was informed that Goldsmith was indeed in mourning, 'for a distant relative'. When she learned the truth, her love of him was not increased by what must have appeared a heartless and cold remark. The death of the woman who had once fought a battle on his behalf and insisted on the 'liberal education' that was to be the basis of his future career had apparently caused little more than a ripple across the surface of his life. But there was another play to be written and his final portrait of himself could only have sprung from an attempt to come to terms with a relationship which had evidently gone very wrong indeed.

*

If Maurice Goldsmith read to his blind mother the letter he received a few months before her death Mrs Goldsmith would have had the satisfaction of knowing that Oliver was receiving high honours in London. In it he had written, obviously with an eye on a larger audience than Maurice alone, 'The King has been lately pleasd to make me Professor of ancient history in a Royal Academy of Painting which he has just establishd, but there is no sallary anex'd and I took it rather as a compliment to the institution than any benefit to myself. Honours to one in my situation are something like ruffles to a man that wants a shirt . . .'.[49] This, of course, like Johnson's chair of Ancient Literature, was a Reynolds appointment Goldsmith omitted to say that one of its perks was a seat at the Royal Academy dinners, the first of which was held on the eve of the summer exhibition on April 23rd, 1771. Another guest on that occasion was Horace Walpole and for him it was to be an evening he would probably have preferred to forget. Goldsmith was on the point of departure for Bristol and the conversation turned to Thomas Chatterton and the manuscripts which he was supposed to have discovered in the church of St Mary Redcliffe. The object of Goldsmith's journey was to locate and try to buy them. Walpole, a celebrated amateur antiquarian, had received a letter from Chatterton two years earlier but after an initially enthusiastic response to the fragment of 'mediaeval' poetry the boy had sent him, he had grown more cautious and, discovering that he was a lawyer's clerk, advised him to forget about literature until he had made his fortune.[50] It was unlucky for Walpole that a year and a half later Chatterton should have poisoned himself, perhaps as E. H. W. Meyerstein suggested, during an intense bout of pain induced by long-neglected gonorrhoea. As far as Walpole knew, Chatterton had simply returned to his office stool. Goldsmith was better informed. He knew that the young poet was dead and announced the fact at the dinner.[51]

Whether or not he considered Walpole to be responsible for this death, as many people were to do, Goldsmith seems to have identified himself to some extent with the boy from the provinces, and he knew about Walpole's involvement. The journal to which Chatterton had contributed in the last months of his life was the *Town and Country Magazine*, edited by William Hamilton, a son of Smollett's former business associate. It was most probably from this source that Goldsmith had received his information and learned that Chatterton had been known in London as 'the Young Villain'. He was now in correspondence with Lord Hardwick and was firm in his belief that the 'Rowley' manuscripts really existed.[52]

Perhaps a pre-Romantic yearning, buried so deeply within his own poetry, gave a fascination both to 'Gothic' fragments and to the tragic young man who had claimed to discover them. Although it was most probably Thomas Percy who put the issue before the Club, Goldsmith's enthusiastic embracing of the cause must have done much to keep it alive. Club members were still talking about Chatterton and Rowley two years later.[53]

It was Goldsmith's second visit to the west country in two months. In the second week of March he had travelled to Bath in the company of Lord Clare's son, Edmund Nugent.[54] With them travelled Lord Clare's sister, Peggy, only a few years older than her nephew, for whose upbringing she had been partly responsible. Nugent, an M.P. and Lietuenant-Colonel in the First Foot Guards, had joined his father at Bath in January in search of a cure. He was now going back there as a dying man and Lord Clare had invited Goldsmith to join the family group at their lodgings at 11 North Parade. Edmund Nugent died in Bath six weeks later, the day after Goldsmith's departure from London for Bristol. There was a tragic irony in the fact that, having been pilloried for his failure to recognise the 'Robert Nugent' who claimed to be his illegitimate son, Clare should now have lost his legitimate male heir.[55] He was irreconcilably estranged from his third wife and by now the title he had worked so hard to procure must have begun to have a hollow ring. This invitation to join the family at a sad time indicates both a bond between the elderly worldling and the improvident writer, and a combination of generosity and tact in the latter which too many of his contemporaries had failed to notice.

TWELVE

Hodge

'SINCE I had the pleasure of seeing you last,' Goldsmith wrote to Bennet Langton on September 7th, 1771, 'I have been almost wholly in the country at a farmer's house quite alone trying to write a Comedy. It is now finished but when or how it will be acted, or whether it will be acted at all are questions I cannot resolve. I am therefore so much employd upon that that I am under a necessity of putting off my intended visit to Lincolnshire for this season. Reynolds is just returned from Paris and finds himself now in the case of a truant that must make up for his idle time by diligence. We have therefore agreed to postpone the affair till next summer when we hope to have the honour of waiting upon her Ladyship and you and staying double the time of our intended visit. We often meet, and never without remembering you. I see Mr Beauclerc very often both in town and country. He is now going directly forward to become a second Boyle. Deep in Chymistry and Physics. Johnson has been down upon a visit to a country parson Doctor Taylor's and is returned to his old haunts at Mrs Thrale's. Burke is a farmer en attendant a better place, but visiting about too. Every soul is visiting about and merry but myself. And that is hard too as I have been trying these three months to do something to make people laugh. There have I been strolling about the hedges studying jests with a most tragical countenance. The natural History is about half finished and I will shortly finish the rest. God knows Im tired of this kind of finishing, which is but bungling work, and that not so much my fault as the fault of my scurvy circumstances. They begin to talk in town of the opposition's gaining ground, the cry of Liberty is still as loud as ever. I have published or Davi[e]s has published for me an Abridgement of the History of England for which I have been a good deal abused in the newspapers for betraying the liberties of the people. God knows I had no thoughts for or against liberty in my head. My whole aim being to make up a book of a decent size that as Squire Richard says

296

would do no harm to nobody. However they set me down as an
arrant Tory and consequently no honest man. When you come to
look at any part of it you'l say that I am a soure Whig. God bless
you, and with my most respectful compliments to her Ladyship I
remain dear Sir

Your most affectionate

Temple Brick Court   humble Servant,

Sepr. 7th 1771   Oliver Goldsmith'[1]

The arrangement with Edmund Bott had come to an end, and
Goldsmith had found accommodation at Hyde in a farmhouse a little
to the west of the Edgeware Road at the sixth milestone from Hyde
-Park. It was far enough from that dubious mixed belt of tea gardens
villas, brick-kilns, middens and nurseries to be 'real country', and it
was still a charming place when Prior visited it early in the nineteenth century: 'The house is of the superior order of farm houses,
and stands upon a gentle eminence in what is called Hyde Lane,
leading to Kenton, about three hundred yards from the village of
Hyde on the Edgeware Road, and commands a view of an undulating
country directly opposite, diversified with wood, in the direction of
Hendon.'[*2] At harvest time there was an influx of Irish farm-
workers to the area and as he walked about the fields and lanes Goldsmith must often have been within sound of the familiar brogue.[3]

Away from Brick Court he could live simply. He had rented a
single room at the front of the house on the first floor and his meals
were sent up to him, though when London friends were invited out
for the afternoon or evening a parlour downstairs was put at his
disposal. He had come to work. When Boswell made an unexpected
call, in his absence, he found notes for the *History of Animated
Nature* scribbled round the walls of the room.[4] But Goldsmith could
never be the complete hermit for long. His landlord's son, then
about sixteen, later recalled being taken in a carriage to Hendon
with other young people to see a company of strolling players, and
an impromptu dance was held in the parlour one day when London
visitors were temporarily marooned by heavy rain. The great
virtue of the Hyde lodgings was that casual or begging or idly

*Like Reynolds' house in Leicester Square, 'Hyde House' survived until the
1930s when it was demolished to make way for a housing estate. The site is
marked by the junction of Derwent Avenue with Kingsbury Road.

curious visitors would for the most part have been deterred by the six mile journey. Amongst the people who *did* come were Sir Joshua Reynolds and Sir William Chambers.[5] Goldsmith was given both the time he needed for the completion of his Natural History and the freedom from distraction for a new creative work. The play to which he had referred in his letter to Langton and which on the eve of its performance would be called *She Stoops to Conquer* had a rural setting. But this may have less to do with the farmhouse at Hyde than with another friend, Isaac Bickerstaffe, who visited him this summer.[6]

Bickerstaffe was one of the most talented men working for the London theatre at this time. He had made his name in the early sixties with a comedy interspersed with songs called *Love in a Village*. Set to music drawn from a variety of sources, it was the great commercial success of the decade and had been revived every season at Covent Garden since its first performance in 1762. When, Bickerstaffe left Covent Garden for Drury Lane at the end of Beard's managership Garrick seized the opportunity to lay claim to the work, with the result that for a season two rival productions could be seen. The success of *Love in a Village* had been repeated by such words as *The Maid of the Mill* and the musical after-piece *Thomas and Sally*, with the music by Thomas Arne. Although Bickerstaff's lyrics appealed to the taste of the age, he was no poet; but as a dramatist he was more than competent and a farce like *The Absent-Minded Man* reveals a talent quite capable of cutting itself free from the prevailing sentimentalism of the 'sixties. *Love in a Village*, which was virtually a straight three-act comedy with songs inserted at appropriate moments to melodies borrowed from Handel, Boyce, Arne, Galluppi and several other composers, was based on an idea which Bickerstaffe had taken from Marivaux's *Le Jeu de L'Amour et du Hasard*.

In Marivaux's play the two parties to an 'arranged' engagement decide independently to change places with their servants in order to buy time in which to observe the intended partner. Bickerstaffe had used half this plot. His Rosetta and Young Meadows, who have both run away from home to avoid the alliance which their fathers have arranged for them in childhood, meet at the country house of the Woodcocks and fall in love with each other disguised respectively as lady's maid and gardener. To this plot Bickerstaffe added the complications of a second love affair between Lucinda Woodcock and Eustace who, having been brought into the house when the family is supposed to be attending the village sports, has to be passed off as a music master when Lucinda's suspicious Aunt Deborah unexpectedly returns. Rosetta's problems are easily solved when Meadows Senior makes his appearance in the last act and is reunited with a friend of his youth, Hawthorn, a neighbour who prides himself on his simple country ways and who has discovered Rosetta's identity. Although the other love problem seems intractable in the face of Aunt Deborah's hostility, yet another happy coincidence is discovered in the fact that old Meadows knows Eustace's father and can speak persuasively enough on his behalf to convince Justice Woodcock that he has found the right man for his daughter.

In terms of plot, the relationship between Bickerstaffe's Lucinda and Eustace, Rosetta and Meadows and Goldsmith's Constance Neville and Hastings, Kate Hardcastle and Marlow, will seem sufficiently obvious. But the similarity between *She Stoops to Conquer* and *Love in a Village* does not end there. In Bickerstaffe's play one of the most effective characters is Hodge, a servant of Justice Woodcock's who does duty sometimes as a groom and sometimes as a rustic Figaro, carrying messages and, in his idiosyncratic manner and at his own pace, helping Lucinda when the complications of her love affair threaten to become overwhelming. Hodge is both satyr and peasant, in hot pursuit of the disguised Rosetta but boorish with the servant-girl who is pregnant by him, astutely weighing up new arrivals to the village inn, surrendering information cryptically and with reluctance and goading his employer's sister when it is clear that she is to be on the losing side. With his stable metaphors, his oaths and his tendency to describe intransigent ladies as 'cross-grain'd toads', Hodge is an excellent comic invention. He is also, of course, the literary progenitor of Tony Lumpkin.

For other features of the plot of the new comedy, Goldsmith was indebted to an earlier 'Bickerstaff', for Richard Steele had used this as his pseudonym in the Spectator, and it was probably here that he found the stories of the traveller who mistook a palace for an inn, and of the lady who, after announcing her intention to live no longer with her incompatible relations was driven round in a circle

and brought back to the same house.[7] It is likely that by this time
Goldsmith was already working on a new edition of the *Spectator*
at the invitation of a Dublin publisher.[8]

The contemporary attitude to literary 'borrowing' is curious. It
would probably be an over-simplification to draw a line between the
borrowing of incidents from essays written half a century earlier
(or from a foreign play) and the lifting of a plot and at least one
character from a comedy that was still part of the Covent Garden
repertoire, and to suggest that the first would have been considered ethical and the second not. As far as the author (as opposed
to publisher) was concerned there was no concept of literary owner-
ship at this time: a bizarre example was provided in the '72–'73
season when Colman turned a play of William Mason's into a
musical comedy without bothering to inform him. Mason only
became aware of what was happening when his publisher discovered
that an unexpected run on the book could be entirely accounted for
by the need for rehearsal copies.[9] The fact that Bickerstaffe himself
was now borrowing money from his friends in spite of having plays
in the repertoire at both the leading theatres, is a sufficient reminder
that, apart from the retaining fee which he received when he was
working for Garrick, his payment for each new production was
limited to the receipts of three benefit nights after the house
expenses had been deducted. The borrowing of plots and characters
was widely practised. If there were any 'unwritten laws' they were
not universally accepted. That accusations of plagiarism were a
highly selective weapon is suggested by the detailed analysis of
Arthur Murphy's indebtedness to French and Latin sources that
appeared in the pro-Garrick *St James's Chronicle* at the very time
when the paper was stimultaing interest in Goldsmith's new play.[10]
Not all sections of the literary world would have shared Mason's
indignation about the *Elfrida* affair. As William Kenrick had put it,
'The republic of letters is ever in a state of civil warfare; in which
every man, being an enemy to his neighbour, takes the spoil of his
goods for lawful plunder.'[11]

Contemporary critics might seem to have been condoning the
practice by their failure to draw attention to Goldsmith's indebtedness to Bickerstaffe, though there were other possible reasons for
this silence. The friendship that existed between the two writers
is a complicating factor. As Bickerstaffe visited Goldsmith while he

was working on his play, there is a strong possibility that he himself had suggested the reworking of the *Love in a Village* plot. Failing that, Goldsmith would have anticipated with a certain uneasiness an evening in the future when the curtain went up before his unsuspecting friend. He could not have foreseen that by that time Bickerstaffe would no longer be in London but hiding under an assumed name in France.

Whatever the circumstances of its composition may reveal about his motives for writing a play, a comparison between *She Stoops to Conquer* and *Love in a Village* displays yet again Goldsmith's flair for embellishing whatever he borrowed. On one level he was the least inventive of writers, and yet he gave a distinctive patina to whatever he touched. Paradoxically, as far as the double plot of the lovers is concerned, it seems fairer to think of Bickerstaffe in terms of re-worked Marivaux than of Goldsmith in terms of re-worked Bickerstaffe. *She Stoops to Conquer* is one of the great theatrical survivors (as at least two commercially successful London productions in the last thirty years indicates): no sterile plagiarism could possess this enduring vitality. Although Goldsmith was drawing upon a contemporary source, he could fairly be put in the category of those dramatists like Giraudoux and Jean Anouilh who have adapted the themes and dramatis personae of existing plays for their own purposes. In an age of 'improvements' he was improving what came immediately to hand.

One of his changes was to simplify the Marivaux story even further, so that mistaken identity applied only to the 'Rosetta' character, Kate Hardcastle. Another was to combine the personages of the rugged countryman, Hawthorn, and the village squire into that of Mr Hardcastle. Bickerstaffe's Deborah now became Dorothy and Hardcastle's wife rather than sister. All these changes are in the interests of clarity and leave more space for the development of comic personalities and the creation of memorable *coups de théatre*. The hint for Hardcastle's servant problem had been given by Justice Woodcock, but Hardcastle after a single scene in which he tries to turn his farm-workers into footmen is more memorable than his counterpart in Bickerstaffe's play. Kate Hardcastle is a resourceful, witty young woman with a will of her own, Marlow a man with a problem which immediately engages an audience's attention, whereas Rosetta and Meadows remain a fairly conven-

tional couple well within the range of an actor and actress who would
have been chosen for their voices rather than powers of impersonation. In both these instances Goldsmith's hero and heroine owe
more to his observations of life than to their purely literary source.

It may have been the country setting of *Love in a Village* that
prompted a fresh bucolic breeze to blow through *She Stoops to
Conquer*. In spite of talk of improvements out of doors the Hard-
castles seem far removed from the world of Marlow and Hastings:
their servants panic as the gentlemen from London ride up to the
front door and Hardcastle's only response to his wife's craving for
'fashion' is to offer her his old wig as a *tête*. Like the Three Pigeons,
all this was to some extent Lissoy-inspired. But there were other
things in Goldsmith's head, including perhaps rumours about the
state of affairs at Bennet Langton's home in Lincolnshire.

The tall, stooping, scholarly Langton was one of those men who
for no apparently good reason inspired laughter, and his eccentric
family was very much part of the joke. Since they were hospitable
people there were plenty of visitors to bring back strange stories to
London, some of which, beginning with Bennet's father and uncle,
Mrs Thrale recorded in her diary:

'. . . with all this I have heard that he was positive enough,
though supreamly wrongheaded; he had dug a Ditch, and the
Damms being too low at one End, the Water run over; You
should raise the Earth higher there Sir, said one of his Neighbours
to keep the Water *in*, No Sir says Mr Langton I will dig the
Ditch deeper *just in that Place*, which will answer the End better
& no body could convince him. His Batchelor Bro^r lived better
on two hundred than he did on two Thousand a Year—his
Friends twitted him sometimes—Ay replies Mr Langton 'tis easy to
be an Economist with a Little. His eldest Daughter was a strange
Being I believe, wore her Aprons unmade as I have been told,
and said in Conversation—to a Gentleman—that She would be a
W[hore] but for three Reasons—one that it would endanger her
Salvation, one that it would endanger her health, & the other I
have forgot, but it was not that She should disgrace her Family;
for says Johnson who told it to me—No hang her She was *above
that*. The Wife of this Heroines Brother or Father was a *London
Lady*, always teizing her husband to go to Town, and never

regulating her Family for twenty Years, never buying a Cow, never putting up a Fowl to feed,—never repairing their Furniture or house in Lincolnshire where they always lived because they were to go to London next Year forsooth and see the Players, who made all the Subject of her Conversation, settling the Merits of Mrs Cibber & Mrs Pritchard in the midst of a Family ruined by Mismanagement, and running to speedy Decay; and in a Neighborhood of Country Gentlewomen who had never seen nor were likely to see them.'[12]

Goldsmith is almost certain to have had access to such stories about a fellow Club-member, even if he had not already been to Lincolnshire himself, and there were enough hints here to provide inspiration for both Mr and Mrs Hardcastle if not the resourceful and articulate Kate.

The actress Mrs Abington may also have made a contribution towards the creation of his heroine. She was a friend of Reynolds and the Club had a collective devotion to her, going as a group to her benefit nights.[13] There was talk at the time, rather unusual in the circumstances as she was at Drury Lane and not Covent Garden, that Goldsmith had written the part of Kate Hardcastle for her.[14] She did not in fact play Kate, but as her dramatic strengths lay in both her sophistication and her skill in impersonating chambermaids[15] it seems perfectly credible that Goldsmith should have had the mannerisms and attitudes of the actress before him as he created this character. Marlow, the young Englishman who is overbearing in the bar parlour and tongue-tied in the presence of ladies could have come from one of several pen-portraits in the journalism, especially the French journalism, of the period. Perhaps he is also Goldsmith's revenge on some of those stolid men he had encountered in tavern and coffee house, who seem to have been so impervious to his oblique and subtle humour.

But at the heart of *She Stoops to Conquer* there remains a debt to Bickerstaffe which cannot be overlooked: this is in the form of the one character who in the original text is always heralded by his first name alone. Both in general outline and in verbal mannerisms Tony Lumpkin comes straight out of *Love in a Village*: Goldsmith's innovation was to bring a minor character forward and make him the mischievous instigator of the play's action. In order to do this, he had to upgrade him socially and bring him to the heart of the family circle so that Hodge the groom is turned into Tony Lumpkin Esquire, the egregious result of Mrs Hardcastle's first marriage. Whether or not Goldsmith was fully conscious of the effect he was producing, it was this transformation of Bickerstaffe's satyr/peasant which would produce a dramatic impact still capable of holding an audience's attention today, for Hodge/Lumpkin now becomes a throw-back, graceless, illiterate, unwilling or unable to adopt the tone and even the grammar of his own class, the complete anti-thesis of Lord Chesterfield's perfect gentleman as he lies, steals, cracks Constance Nevill's skull, torments his mother and glories in his ascendency over barmaids and the patrons of the village inn. The Hodge who, in *Love in a Village*, had provided a respite from the problems of politer lovers has been elevated in Goldsmith's play into a half-comic, half-malevolent Lord of Misrule.

Perhaps acting on a hint provided by the Bickerstaffe episode in which Hodge crosses Aunt Deborah and gets his ears boxed for having attempted to help Lucinda and Eustace, Goldsmith sets at the heart of *She Stoops to Conquer* one of the most grotesque relationships in the theatrical repertoire, that of Tony Lumpkin and Dorothy Hardcastle. The joke centres on the mother's inability to accept that her son, however unsatisfactorily, has already realised his graceless potential. The concealment of the fact that Tony is of age is insignificant in comparison to the self-deception which allows her to see her son as the 'naughty boy' who will come right in a year or two (ideally by marrying Constance Nevill). Far more absurdly she insists that he is a delicate youth who needs her continuing maternal care. At moments when, even to her besotted eyes, Tony seems to be something less than the ideal young man and when it is all too clear that he is beyond control, she breaks down into less and less articulate fury and, on two occasions, is on the verge of physical violence as she pursues him off the stage. By removing Hodge's 'Margery' from the action and relegating his own Bett Bouncer to the wings (like Hodge's other attachment Bett Blossom) Goldsmith is able to focus attention entirely on the grotesque mother/son relationship, and also perhaps to ensure a more sympathetic reaction to Tony than it is possible to have towards the Hodge who refuses to accept that he is 'obligated in conscience' to his girl.

She Stoops to Conquer is the reverse of a 'literary' play. Quite apart from inconsistencies of plot which reveal themselves in reading, the action moves too swiftly to allow literary qualities to emerge in any one big scene. Many of the most effective touches can only be fully realised in the theatre. Tony Lumpkin is heard whooping and roaring off-stage while Mrs Hardcastle justifies having kept him at home on account of his health; Hardcastle's patience slowly crumples as Marlow and Hastings, mistaking him for a meddlesome innkeeper, deliberately keep up their smart 'London' conversation against him; the illiterate Tony tries desperately to decipher Hastings' letter and, when Miss Nevill pretends to read it aloud inventing a suitably neutral theme for Mrs Hardcastle's ears, becomes so excited at references to stables and horse-dealing that he forgets the need for caution. But although Goldsmith's play belongs squarely within the walls of the theatre it is easily spoiled by the kind of production which treats eighteenth century comedy as an opportunity for a romp. The freshness of its language alone should warn a producer of the psychic energy which has gone into the creation of Goldsmith's updated 'Vice', into the contortions of Marlow when confronted by Kate Hardcastle and into a mother/son relationship which has the makings of *Oedipus Rex* re-written by Aristophanes.

Although Goldsmith's debt to Bickerstaffe was considerable, there is no inconsistency between the exceptionally high level of literary plagiarism in *She Stoops to Conquer* and the fact that when the last debt has been ferretted out one is still left with a strong sense of creativeness and originality. Confronted with a blank sheet of paper Goldsmith was as helpless as any child who asks 'But what shall I write *about*?' On the other hand he possessed the kind of egotism, the need to project and come to terms with his emotional problems, that could seize hold of the material that came to hand and irradiate it with creative energy, and although the area of interest may seem disappointingly narrow the soil was deep and fertile.

As Goldsmith loved music and was a keen theatre-goer it seems reasonably safe to conjecture that on more than one occasion between 1762 and the summer of 1771 he had sat in the pit at Covent Garden and watched a performance of *Love in a Village*. His theatrical criticism shows that he took plays seriously, demanding a

L

higher degree of illusion than would have contented the average playgoer; and this suggests that he felt an emotional need to project himself into the action. For a man who was fascinated by disguise the element of concealment and mistaken identity in Bickerstaffe's musical comedy must have been attractive. But it was clearly the character of Hodge, vicious and comic, ignorant and cunning, amorous and brutal, which fully engaged his attention. And part of Hodge's appeal must have been his confrontation in the course of his duties as go-between with a narrow, bad-tempered and domineering woman.

During this decade when his writings were winning for him the reputation of an always rational observer of the social scene, of a man whose lucid style combined common sense with intuition and humour with feeling, it must have been deeply refreshing for Goldsmith to relapse into the temporary anonymity of a playgoer and, through this short but vital dramatic rôle, to enjoy vicariously the pleasures of a thoroughly disreputable existence. The need to put Hodge at the centre of his own play, even at the risk of producing an anomalous and *déclassé* character, suggests that there had been an imaginative spilling-over from an area of his personality where the identification with a Vice/satyr figure was not only possible but psychologically necessary. The difference between appearance and reality was a theme which for a long time had hovered uncertainly on the borders of the terrain over which he had imaginative control. There had been an attempt to take it up in the previous play but, after hints that Honeywood's seeming altruism sprang from a less worthy impulse, he had failed to develop the theme. By the time of his withdrawal to Hyde in the summer after the publication of *The Deserted Village* there was a much more pressing need to come to grips with it, and this need would give his play its dynamic. Whether it is Marlow veering from insolent self-assurance to stammering inadequacy, or the heir to £1,500 a year with the manners and tastes of a peasant, or the mother who clings stubbornly and against all the evidence to the belief that her ugly duckling is about to turn into a swan, the consequences of illusion are to be encountered at every turn.

It has already been suggested that behind Deborah Primrose and Dorothy Hardcastle it is possible to detect the shadowy figure of Anne Goldsmith. The fictitious characters resemble one another particularly in their attitudes towards their sons. Moses, the precocious twelve-year-old in *The Vicar of Wakefield*, is brought forward with maternal pride to be shown off to visitors, but when he returns home with his gross of green spectacles he is made to feel very small indeed. For Dorothy Hardcastle, Tony Lumpkin is alternately the 'dear, sweet, pretty, provoking, undutiful boy' who 'would charm the bird from the tree' and a 'blockhead', a 'monster' and 'great ill-fashioned oaf'. *She Stoops to Conquer* is a farce, but no admirer of Georges Feydeau will doubt that, although the appropriate feelings have been deliberately syphoned off, the issues at stake are potentially as serious as in the most complex drama. At the heart of this mother/son relationship, grounds for resentment—possibly even estrangement and hatred—can be detected. Although spoken in a moment of fury, that last phrase of Mrs Hardcastle's with its emphasis on physical shortcomings, has the impact of a bitter truth. Transferred from farce to a real-life situation like the family inquest described by Catherine Hodson in her letter to Percy it would be capable of leaving scars even on sons as apparently brazen as Tony Lumpkin.

The honours between mother and son are even in Goldsmith's play. Dorothy Hardcastle is a grotesque or, to use her own terminology, a 'Gothic' character, but her curious passion for Tony has an inner consistency. In the broad comedy of the last act after she has emerged from the horse-pond 'draggled up to the waist like a mermaid', she is allowed a redeeming act which in a 'tragedy' by Arthur Murphy or one of his contemporaries would have had all the force of a climactic moment: overcoming her terror of the 'highwayman' (Mr Hardcastle) who is holding Tony in conversation in the dark garden, she comes forward, throws herself on her knees and begs her astonished husband to 'take my money, my life, but spare that young gentleman, spare my child . . .'[16] Tony is equally consistent. As unmoved by such maternal heroism as he is ungrateful for the waistcoats she embroidered for him, he coolly observes at the end of the scene, 'Ecod, mother, all the parish says you have spoil'd me, and so you may take the fruits on't.'[17]

At one level, if it is correct to see a reconstruction of the relationship between Goldsmith and his mother at the heart of *She Stoops to Conquer*, the question of good taste can hardly be avoided. Even when allowances have been made for the more robust attitudes that lay so close to the 'polite' surface of life in the eighteenth century, it is not easy to assimilate the fact that this theme was being explored within a year of Anne Goldsmith's death.

Mrs Hardcastle's principal complaint whenever she showers abuse on her son's head is that he is 'unfeeling'. There was to be a curious echo to this in remarks made in private about Goldsmith after his death, in one case by a close friend. If Tony Lumpkin is Goldsmith's culminating self-portrait, it is clearly a portrayal of the *id* rather than the *ego-ideal*, and for the detached and reasoning mind to gain access to the spontaneous, buried, dynamic side of the personality was an achievement far beyond the boundaries within which Good Taste was still a meaningful concept. It is, of course, Goldsmith himself who raises the question of his lack of feeling for a mother who, if she is accurately reflected in Mrs Hardcastle, was as likely to engage in acts of domestic heroism on his behalf as to inflict psychological wounds. In his mother's account Tony Lumpkin was a monster. Was Goldsmith, in pre-Freudian times, examining his inability to respond in an adequate human way to the fact that his own mother had died? The complete inability to feel is of course a pathological symptom. That Goldsmith himself might have been a psychopath seems to be ruled out, however, by his very awareness that Tony as well as Dorothy Hardcastle has behaved badly. But the possibility remains that it was the very energy that he had failed to expend in mourning his mother that was channelled through the deliberate detachment of farce into a depiction of an incapacitating neurosis.

*

Garrick's *Jupiter and Hermes* was still in the future but, in 1771, the year in which Goldsmith began to write his play, a satirical poem addressed to him had appeared in the *Morning Chronicle*, preceded by an epigraph taken from *The Traveller*:

> Say, should the philosophic mind disdain
> That good, which makes each humbler bosome vain?
> Let school-taught pride dissemble all it can,
> These little things are great to little man . . .

At least one person in London had picked up the hints scattered through *The Deserted Village*, and he was now making explicit Goldsmith's own hidden message: turned against their author, the lines from *The Traveller* drew attention to the fact that this 'little man', far from cultivating a philosophic detachment, was irresistibly drawn to such 'little things' as fine clothes and furniture and masquerades at the Pantheon or Carlisle House:

> How widely different, Goldsmith, are the ways
> Of doctors now, and those of ancient days!
> Theirs taught the truth in academic shades,
> Ours haunt lewd hops, and midnight masquerades!
> So chang'd the times! say philosophic sage,
> Whose genius suits so well this tasteful age,
> Is the Pantheon, late a sink obscene,
> Became the fountain of chaste Hippocrene?
> Or do thy moral numbers quaintly flow
> Inspir'd by th'Aganippe of Soho?
> Do wisdom's sons gorge cates and vermicelli
> Like beastly Bickerstaff or bothering Kelly?
> Or art thou tir'd of th'undeserv'd applause
> Bestow'd on bards affecting virtue's cause?
> Wouldst thou, like Sterne, resolv'd at length to thrive,
> Turn pimp and die cock-bawd at sixty-five,
> Is this the good that makes the humble vain,
> The good philosophy should not disdain
> If so, let pride dissemble all it can,
> A modern sage is still much less than man.[18]

Reading these lines in a daily newspaper, Goldsmith must have had the nightmare feeling of being found naked in the street. He had no defence. His attacker was criticising him on the very same grounds as the concealed confession in his recent poem. With his tendency to exaggerate setbacks Goldsmith may have thought that there was nothing more to lose as far as his social reputation was concerned, and this too would have determined the width of the gap between the personae he had adopted in *The Good-Natured Man* and in *She Stoops to Conquer*.

The writer of the lines in the *Morning Chronicle* was William Kenrick to whom, a few years earlier, Ralph Griffiths had assigned the altogether congenial task of damning Goldsmith's first publication. He was the son of a Watford corset-maker. Himself apprenticed to a scale-maker, it was probably as a youth that he surrendered to one of the two great passions of his life, the study of physics.[19] If Goldsmith sometimes appears to have been the clown of the London literary world, Kenrick was certainly the Caliban. Like Goldsmith, he loved to find himself the centre of attention, taking on all comers. His positions were usually just as indefensible: the difference being that while Goldsmith adopted them in the spirit of comedy, Kenrick enjoyed the fight on account of its opportunities for malevolence and for the mud that was frequently churned up. Any literary figure who enjoyed fame or passing attention was challenged.

Kenrick's reviewing for the *Monthly*, on which he was an important figure in the early 'sixties, was predominantly hostile, but it had enough literary flair to be credible and the width of his interests as well as his knowledge of French literature had made him a useful member of the Griffiths' team, until Griffiths himself became an object for attack.[20] Kenrick's talent showed itself in his dramatic writing. In 1760 he had written a clever pastiche of Shakespeare (his second passion). His play was a kind of *Henry IV, part 3* called *Falstaff's Wedding* and it contained Eastcheap scenes with some good jokes on such familiar themes as Bardolph's nose in a clever imitation of Shakespeare's prose style. Even though the play failed to live up to its opening scenes and Falstaff himself dwindled rather unconvincingly into a double agent between the new King and the Scrope/Cambridge faction, it deserved more than its solitary performance six years after publication on the benefit night of Love, the leading Falstaff of the day. Another play, *The Duellist*, which was at least as good as many comedies already in the repertoire, had a similar fate: it fell foul of an audience-versus-manager quarrel at Covent Garden and had to be withdrawn after a single night. It was not altogether surprising that more than a fair share of Kenrick's otherwise indiscriminate hostility should be directed against dramatists and the two principal theatrical managers.

A Caliban could be humoured, even treated like a pet, and this seems to have been true of Kenrick. He was feared, propitiated and at the same time indulged as something of a joke: he accepted all these rôles with gusto. He would spread scandal, apologise profusely, and the next moment repeat his stories. His ideal opponent had been Christopher Smart who in his Newbery days had seemed to enjoy his running battle against Kenrick. Kenrick's main contribution to the campaign had been a scatological poem in absurd imitation of Milton to which was appended both a 'translation' in heroic couplets and a prose transcript with key.[21] Johnson had simply ignored his critic when the *Shakespeare* came under attack, but Goldsmith had felt obliged to comment. Kenrick had described himself in his review as a man who had 'laboured long in the literary vineyard'. 'Yes,' Goldsmith was reported to have said, 'like a mole'.[22] He himself was as vulnerable to Kenrick's brand of cheerful scurrility as he had once been to the bullying of a sadistic tutor. The streak of egotism in his personality made him particularly sensitive to criticism and Kenrick, with all the instincts of a bully, was shrewd enough both to recognise this and to know where to apply the goad. It has been suggested that when about this time Goldsmith's publisher, Griffin, asked him to collaborate with Bickerstaffe and Kenrick on a new magazine, the *Gentleman's Journal*, Goldsmith agreed simply in order to propitiate Kenrick.[23] But although it was not unusual for Kenrick's victims to have dealings with him at one of the apologetic stages of their relationship, as was demonstrated by both Colman and Garrick, Goldsmith's motive is just as likely to have been the financial one of having to meet his obligations to Griffin for advances already received. The *Journal* survived only a few months and died, in Goldsmith's account, 'of too many Doctors'.[24] William Cooke believed that each of the parties had embarked on the project in the belief that the others were going to do the work.

Kenrick's satirical lines on Goldsmith were true enough to be hurtful, but were at least polite, even mild by his usual standards. His accusation against Garrick the following summer was damaging, venomous and almost certainly untrue. It was triggered off by a scandal involving the same Lieutenant Bickerstaffe to whom Goldsmith was by now deeply indebted. Bickerstaffe was generally known to be a homosexual who had left the army in mysterious circumstances and who still indulged his weakness for guardsmen. He appears to have fallen into the hands of a blackmailer[25] and in the spring of 1772, when he could no longer meet the demands that were being made on him, he faced exposure for offences which, on the statute books, still carried a capital penalty. In May he slipped out of the country, probably never to return although he lived on into the early years of the nineteenth century as an exile in France and Italy.[26]

Since prising him away from Covent Garden in 1767 Garrick had been inclined to make a fuss of the writer who could be relied upon to produce entertaining after-pieces whenever box-office receipts threatened to decline. Short notes to Bickerstaffe on theatrical matters were phrased in affectionate terms and, on receiving a dozen or so elegant couplets requesting the loan of £10, he would respond promptly. There was no evidence that the relationship had gone further and the tone of the letter in French which Bickerstaffe sent from exile in St Malo and which Garrick preserved with the endorsement 'from that poor devil Bickerstaffe' indicates that there had been nothing between them other than a friendly working partnership.[27] Kenrick, however, had seen his opportunity and, shortly after Bickerstaffe's flight, a scurrilous poem, *Love in the Suds, a Town Eclogue, Being the Lamentation of Roscius for the loss of his Nyky*, was in circulation creating the impression that Garrick and Bickerstaffe had had a homosexual love affair. Although Garrick was demonstrably one of the most happily married men in London he had laid himself open to attack through a predilection in his own plays for farcical situations involving effeminate men. Now he was to be kept on the rack for several months, unwilling to give wider publicity to Kenrick's libel by taking him to court and unable to pin him down to a firm retraction. Throughout the summer the actor-manager who had for so long been able to control important sections of the press found that he himself had become good copy in a thoroughly hateful way. Kenrick returned intermittently to the attack, sometimes with black humour, for when Garrick wrote anonymously to the *Morning Chronicle* signing his letter 'Candour', Kenrick also wrote: 'Dear Madam,' he began.[28] When at last he was forced to withdraw he shrugged off the affair as a joke: 'I only did it to plague the fellow,' he confessed to his publisher.[29]

It was remarked at the time that Johnson alone was surprised to discover the reason behind Bickerstaffe's disappearance,[30] and it can be assumed that, whether or not the subject was ever raised between them, Goldsmith was aware of his friend's sexual tastes. One would have expected him to be highly vulnerable to attack himself in the summer of '72. He clearly enjoyed the male-oriented nature of the social life of his times, seems to have found more sustenance in the company of men like Reynolds and Johnson than with the Hornecks and, like Johnson himself, enjoyed the company of young men, particularly those rather serious youths who, temperamentally, seemed to be his exact opposites. This year, for example, besides setting M'Veagh M'Donnell to work on the translation of Buffon, he had become friendly with Joseph Cradock, the thirty-year-old owner of an estate near Leicester, and through an intermediary had been persuaded to write a prologue to *Zobéide* the play Cradock had written in the rather unlikely dramatic form of Miltonic blank verse.

Kenrick would have liked to inflict on Goldsmith the same kind of blow he had aimed at Garrick, and within a year of publishing *Love in the Suds* he would indeed be turning his attention once more towards the successful author of *She Stoops to Conquer*. But when that time came he could extract nothing more scandalous from his supposed love life than the name Mary Horneck. Goldsmith, like other members of the Club, had appeared in *Love in the Suds* where Bickerstaffe was imagined in the dock at the Old Bailey, like Baretti before him, with the Johnson set ready to give evidence for the defence. But the accusation of homosexuality was levelled exclusively at Garrick. Strangely enough one of the results of the *Love in the Suds* affair is that although Garrick, almost certainly without intending to, has raised the possibility of bi-sexuality in *Jupiter and Hermes*, the odious Kenrick, equally unintentionally, has scotched it by showing that the very weapon that would have been most destructive of all in the aftermath of the Bickerstaffe affair was simply not available for use.

*

Goldsmith had problems of his own in 1772 apart from the fate of his friend and literary godfather. His play underwent frequent revisions, a fact which makes Bickerstaffe's appearance at Hyde all the more interesting. Some time in the course of the '71–'72 season it was given to George Colman, but as late as the winter of '72–'73 he was begging the manager to come to a decision. There is a hint of desperation behind the depressed, even abject tone of his letter:

L*

Dear Sir

I entreat you'l relieve me from that state of suspense in which I have been kept for a long time. Whatever objections you have made or shall make to my play I will endeavour to remove and not argue about them. To bring in any new judges either of its merits or faults I can never submit to. Upon a former occasion when my other play was before Mr Garrick he offered to bring me before Mr Whitehead's tribunal but I refused the proposal with indignation: I hope I shall not experience as hard treatment from you as from him. I have as you know a large sum of money to make up shortly; by accepting my play I can readily satisfy my Creditor that way, at any rate I must look about to some certainty to be prepared. For God sake take the play and let us make the best of it, and let me have the same measure at least which you have given as bad plays as mine.

I am your friend
and servant
Oliver Goldsmith[31]

Goldsmith's difficulty in getting his play performed would become one of the set-pieces of theatrical history, and after the successful first night Colman was mocked for his blindness to it theatrical virtues. But no satisfactory explanation exists for a delay which seems all the more extraordinary in view of the fame that Goldsmith now enjoyed and of their belonging to a club which still limited itself to only twelve members. Colman must have had strong reasons to risk offending not Goldsmith alone but the other members who in some ways appear to have assumed a collective responsibility for one another. Were his fears limited to the belief that an audience still in love with its ultra-polite image of itself would find the play too broad and farcical? He was clearly very uneasy and even this pathetic appeal failed to push him towards a decision. In February 1773 when it was already becoming late in the season to introduce a new play, Goldsmith acted on impulse, reclaimed the manuscript on which Colman had been pencilling his objections, and took it to Garrick. It was Johnson who convinced him that this was a false move,[32] and within twenty-four hours he was writing to Garrick begging him to return the play and forget the incident. Events had moved swiftly. Colman had relented under

Johnson's persuasion, and although he still made it clear that he had little faith in the play he was prepared to put it on. That the go-between had had to mollify Goldsmith's feelings as well as apply some pressure on the manager is suggested by the phrasing of Goldsmith's letter to Garrick:

> ...I therefore request you will send my play by my servant back, for having been assured of having it acted at the other house, tho' I confess yours in every respect more to my wish, yet it would be folly in me to forego an advantage which lies in my power of appealing from Mr Colman's opinion to the judgement of the town...[33]

An attempt was being made to cheer him up and remind him of a court of appeal behind George Colman.

The efforts made on his behalf by fellow Club-members in the early months of 1773 are perhaps an even more valuable testimonial to Goldsmith's character than the epitaph which, little more than three years later, Johnson was to compose for the tablet to his memory in Westminster Abbey. It is fairly obvious that they were concerned about him. His financial situation was worsening, as it was for many people either in or around the Club at this time. The new decade had seen the culmination of a period of intense speculation in East India stock and the Burkes had been implicated in the crash that followed.[34] In the summer of '72 there was a fresh disaster in the failure of Fordyce's bank, and the financial difficulties of Henry Thrale in the same year are probably symptomatic of a generally uncertain economic climate.[35] In this year too, one of the Club members, Samuel Dyer, lost the fortune which he had inherited a little time before, and when he died in September there were rumours of suicide. Goldsmith had received a large advance in 1769 for the *History of the Earth and Animated Nature*—a work which was still largely monopolising his energies. In 1770 he had been commissioned to write biographical prefaces to works by Parnell and Bolingbroke which Thomas Davies was publishing; and in the summer of 1771 he would have received £500 for the *History of England* which Davies had commissioned two years earlier. [36] Probably in 1773, there were two more commissions, for an abridged *History of England* and, from Griffin, who gave him an advance of £250, for a *Grecian History*.[37] But Goldsmith had failed to offset the effects of John Newbery's death by devising means of spreading over a period of years the advances which at first sight would have presented the dangerous illusion of wealth. A temporary solution had been to borrow between £200 and £300 as an advance against a work, unspecified, which he would produce for John Newbery's nephew and successor.[38] Now, Francis Newbery was requiring Goldsmith to honour his obligation and, probably in 1772, he made a half-hearted attempt to write a novel—which was rejected on the grounds that it was simply a re-working of *The Good-Natured Man* in narrative form.[39]

Relief had come from an unexpected source in February '72. The Dowager Princess of Wales had died and Goldsmith received a request from Mrs Cornelys, through her agent, the journalist and former printer William Woodfall, to write the text for a 'threnodia' which could be performed in her honour at Carlisle House to the adapted music of Handel and Purcell. Once again Mrs Cornelys was demonstrating her skill as an impresario, in her sense of occasion as well as her choice of poet. Goldsmith insisted on remaining anonymous and described his text as a compilation rather than a poem, but his lines have a clear resonance and dignity. This time the principal quarry was his own verse, and on the evening of February 20th his Auburn villagers made a brief reappearance, now in the Great Room of Carlisle House rather than the inhospitable square outside, as the pensioners whom the Princess had supported at Kew.[40]

Whatever Mrs Cornelys paid for the Threnodia, the circumstances of Goldsmith's invitation to write it are in complete contrast to the treatment he was about to receive from Colman. To William Woodfall and his employer, Dr Goldsmith was a man to defer to in every possible way. Woodfall seemed to go through every contortion of embarrassment as he pointed out that, because of the difficulty of transporting musical instruments to Brick Court, Goldsmith would have to go to the composer, Matthias Vento, for the fitting of libretto to music, rather than the composer to him.[41] His obsequious letter provides a brief glimpse of the writer as he appeared to those beyond his immediate circle and makes his treatment at Covent Garden all the more surprising.

The death of Samuel Dyer had taken place on September 15th. By the end of the same month members of the Club would have heard that now Goldsmith was seriously ill at his chambers in the Temple.[42] It was probably an attack of the dysuria, a bladder complaint symptomatic of some more radical disorder, which eighteen months later would be a contributory factor to his death. For those members who were inclined to see a link between Dyer's financial troubles and his subsequent death, Goldsmith's illness must have been a sharp reminder that something must be done to help him. The immediate need was recovery and convalescence, and this autumn, while the manuscript of his play stagnated with Colman, Goldsmith accepted invitations to stay at Gosfield with Lord Clare, with Joseph Cradock at Gumley (where he offered to design another ice-house) and probably with the Langtons.[43]

Once Colman had been persuaded against his judgment to stage Goldsmith's still unnamed play, the Club seems to have turned its attention to Garrick who five years previously, when *The Good-Natured Man* was produced, had made a deliberate attempt to steal Covent Garden's thunder. Either on his own initiative or at the prompting of his friend, Goldsmith had inserted a compliment to Garrick in his February letter: it was only expediency he had implied, which compelled him to accept Colman's last-minute offer; he would, of course, have preferred his play to be staged at Drury Lane. Goldsmith's supporters seem to have expected Garrick, on this occasion, to behave more reasonably. Only this assumption can explain the current belief that when at last the play was staged, Mrs Abington, Garrick's leading lady, would create the part of Kate Hardcastle. The loan of an actor or actress to the rival theatre was very rare and Garrick's co-operation would naturally be required. In the event the question did not arise as Mrs Abington was said to have 'greatly mortified' Goldsmith by rejecting the part.

At Covent Garden all the appearances suggested that, there too, Goldsmith and his play were being massively snubbed. 'Gentleman' Smith refused the part of Marlow, which was then allotted to Lee Lewes, a young harlequin who had never been trusted with a speaking part of any significance before Shuter prompted him to put himself forward for this rôle.[44] A little known actor called Quick was given Tony Lumpkin after the fifty-six-year-old Woodward—probably to the relief of Jane Green who was to play Mrs Hardcastle—refused the part.[45] This extraordinary suggestion that Woodward should play Lumpkin can be partly accounted for by

Colman's lack of interest in the play, which was demonstrated again by his refusal to spend money on new scenery and costumes.[46] (Goldsmith's gratitude to Quick for accepting and making a success of Tony Lumpkin showed itself in the trouble he took over the adaptation of Sedley's *Grumbler* for Quick's benefit a few weeks later.)[47] The new comedy was rushed into rehearsal for performance in the middle of March. Only in this way could a run of nine nights be fitted in and this, of course, was needed if Goldsmith was to get his full financial reward.

After the first night on Monday March 15th the story of Covent Garden's lack of faith in *She Stoops to Conquer* would be as great a nine days' wonder as the *Rosciad* 'debate' a decade earlier. Colman had to retire to Bath to escape the lampoons and wrote to Goldsmith begging him to do or say something that would bring the ridicule to an end.[48] But in view of the fact that, on paper at least, the new play bore such a remarkable resemblance to the musical comedy which appeared at Covent Garden ten times this season, his nervousness is understandable. It might be possible to detect it in the fact that with the exception of the indispensable Ned Shuter, who was Justice Woodcock in *Love in a Village* and Hardcastle in *She Stoops to Conquer*, no members of the company who appeared in Bickerstaffe's play were given parts in Goldsmith's: Colman may have been attempting to minimise the chances of an audience's noticing and disapproving of the resemblance.

The air of impending doom at Covent Garden in the first fortnight of March must have been sensed by Goldsmith's friends. The attendance of Johnson, the two Reynoldses, brother and sister, and the Hornecks at rehearsals may have been part of an attempt to restore morale, but not a particularly happy one as Shuter disliked rehearsing in public.[49] Richard Cumberland's account of the first night supports the view that the Club was determined to rescue Goldsmith from his financial embarrassment by doing everything possible to ensure the play's success. Although a rival dramatist's story has to be treated with caution and although, in the event, the first-night audience needed little prompting, it is probably true that Club-members and other friends of Goldsmith had arranged to sit in various parts of the house and to laugh at pre-selected moments in the action.[50] But however calculating their behaviour may seem by modern standards of theatrical decorum they were mere amateurs in comparison to King David who had now over thirty years' experience of public relations to his credit. With so much depending on a first night towards which the Covent Garden management was drifting with every sign of apathy, it can hardly be a coincidence that, at this point, a long-standing embargo should have been lifted and Garrick invited to join the Club. Goldsmith himself seconded the proposal to admit him.[51]

Garrick had maintained a dignified silence over what must have been an increasingly hurtful slight since his friends Johnson and Reynolds had drawn up their scheme for an informal Academy nine years earlier, and the connection between the production of *The Good-Natured Man* and the admission to it of his former associate George Colman could not have escaped him. At this point he seems to have been determined to prove his clubbability and to embrace Goldsmith's cause. It was probably made easier by the different impression he had received of his former detractor when they had been brought together in the discussions over the organisation of Baretti's defence in 1769.[52] When he at last took his place at the table in Gerrard Street on the evening of March 12th,[53] three days before the opening of the new play, he had probably already composed the prologue which Woodward was to deliver; and it is reasonable to guess that this was envisaged as the opening shot in a campaign which would be launched in the press to stimulate interest in the new comedy after the first night.

Although he had expressed himself fulsomely on the subject to Hugh Kelly, Garrick's support for his and Cumberland's senti-mental comedy had been expedient rather than sincere. Even in a prologue to one of Kelly's plays he had been unable to resist the observation that the stage was being turned into a pulpit.[54] Knowing that Goldsmith's play was more farcical and that much of the strength of the Covent Garden company lay in its comedians, Shuter and Woodward, he saw that the most effective way to promote *She Stoops to Conquer* was to grasp the nettle and appear to declare war on the sentimental *genre*. Woodward, dressed in black and with a handkerchief to his eye, was to recite a prologue[55] which took up the theme of an essay which Goldsmith had contributed to the *Westminster Magazine* in January: that the Comic Muse was wasting away under the influence of that 'mulish production' the 'Weeping Sentimental Comedy'.[56] With plays by Kelly and Cumberland still an important part of the Drury Lane repertoire, Garrick must have satisfied himself that any debate on this theme would be good for their plays as well as Goldsmith's; but in the aftermath of a stormy first night which he had attended at the Little Theatre in the Haymarket the previous month, he sensed a change in the public's mood. This new entertainment of Samuel Foote's had demonstrated the absurdities of sentimental comedy through the simple device of relegating his company to the status of puppets who gave a wooden enactment of a story based on Richardson's novel, *Pamela*.[57] Two of the immediately identifiable targets of Foote's satire were Richard Cumberland and Goldsmith's new friend, Joseph Cradock. There had been clamorous protests but with some modifications Foote's play survived its first night and had settled into its successful career. It was by taking up Foote's theme that Garrick now made himself acceptable to his new supper companions in Gerrard Street.

When the curtain went up at Covent Garden at 6 p.m. on the evening of Monday, March 15th Goldsmith was not in the theatre. Circumstances had combined to make the dramatist feel more than usually irrelevant on his own first night. After months of uncertainty the fate of his play was now in the hands of Colman and his company and of the theatrical column-writers and the friends who had loyally turned out in its support. Whereas at cards he could lose his guineas with a cheerful air, the stakes this evening were so high that he probably doubted his ability to convey the degree of sangfroid that was expected of him. However closely his imagination had ultimately been engaged he had almost certainly begun to write this play with the sole intention of making money. If it succeeded he could hope to collect at least £400 from the box-office manager in a fortnight's time.[58] If it failed, as Colman was evidently expecting it to do, he would get nothing and his creditors would be alerted to the fact that they had backed a bad risk. At the dinner in the Shakespeare Tavern where his friends had asembled to drink success to his play, he had occupied an unusually silent place at the top of the table by Johnson's side,[59] and before the time came for them to adjourn to the theatre he slipped away.

Psychologically, it would have been the moment to believe that Bickerstaffe rather than himself should be responding to the toast, for Goldsmith was the last person to have known how much of his own style and personality he had injected into the original material. He had reached the stage of neither wanting to see the play nor talk about it. 'Did it make you laugh?' he later asked the young James Northcote who seemed to be hesitating on the brink of a critical analysis.[60] That was all he wanted to know. In this frame of mind he went off for a walk and in the course of the evening a shocked acquaintance came across him in the Mall.[61] Wasn't it necessary for an author to be present on his own first night? Wouldn't he have to be consulted if last minute cuts were made? The chance meeting shook him out of his mood. He turned his steps towards the theatre and arrived at the beginning of the fifth act when Mrs Green and Quick were on the stage, with Colman watching from the wings. Colman had already been proved wrong. The audience's warm response had launched *She Stoops to Conquer* on its long theatrical career. But the first sound Goldsmith heard as he went to stand by Colman's side confirmed all his fears: someone in the audience hissed, drawing attention to the improbability of Mrs Hardcastle's mistaking her own garden for Crackskull Common. Goldsmith blurted out his anxieties to Colman, and Colman showed less tact than honesty to his own mood in his reply: 'Psha! Doctor, don't be fearful of squibs, when we have been sitting almost these two hours upon a barrel of gunpowder.'[62]

Although it had appeared too late in the season to have the long run it deserved before the summer recess, the pleasure the play had given its first audience and the outbreak of comment in the news-papers during the next few days ensured its survival. In subsequent months it became the kind of play that Colman could promise to put on when an audience objected to the billing of some less fortunate work, and on a November evening the following season, when Mrs Catley the singer was indisposed, it was staged at the last moment instead of *Love in a Village*.

If members of that first audience had recognised Goldsmith's debt to Bickerstaffe, none of the reviewers made the point. This could have been for a variety of reasons. It was still the time of rigid classification in dramatic theory and the gap between a three-act comedy with music and a five-act comedy without may have been considered too great to bridge. It might equally have been that Bickerstaffe's was a name which, in polite circumstances and literature, was no longer mentioned. Theatre audiences certainly felt so. They continued to enjoy *Love in a Village*, *The Maid of the Mill* and *Thomas and Sally*, but they did not wish to be reminded that someone called Isaac Bickerstaffe had written them. This had been demonstrated at Drury Lane the previous month on the first night of a comedy with music by Dibdin: a rumour circulated that the text was by Bickerstaffe and the performance was not allowed to proceed until Dibdin had been persuaded to go on stage and claim the entire authorship of the work himself.[63]

Whether Bickerstaffe was aware of Goldsmith's debt to him in the summer of 1771 may never be known. For obvious reasons no significance could be attached to his failure to attend his friend's first night. But certain possibilities are raised by the fact that within five weeks of its first performance in London the *Morning Chronicle* of April 24th should be claiming that Goldsmith's play was also a subject of conversation in Paris.[64] It would have been at least appropriate if Bickerstaffe, with his vested interest in *She Stoops to Conquer*, had found a means of supporting himself in exile by capitalising on Goldsmith's success.

∗

William Woodfall, for all his grotesque flattery the previous year, followed the prevailing trend of *Monthly Review* policy towards Goldsmith when composing his anonymous notice on the publication of the play. Admittedly, the dramatist had made his characters on stage 'talk very funnily', but Woodfall believed that 'the Reader must peruse the present Comedy without pleasure, while the representation of it may make him laugh'.[65] The house of Newbery, however, having accepted *She Stoops to Conquer* as a settlement of Goldsmith's obligations, had got a bargain: 4,000 copies were sold within three days.[66] In subsequent comment, the *St James's Chronicle*, with its strong Garrick connection, played the leading part, and the worst possible motives were attributed to Colman. Goldsmith, in the course of the dedication (appropriately enough to Johnson) contented himself with a single reference to the feelings that Colman demonstrated during rehearsals, but other commentators extracted as much fun as possible from the manager's loss of face. One of them was John Wilkes:

TO DR GOLDSMITH

Has then (the question pray excuse,
For Doctor you're a droll man),
The dose that saved the Comic Muse,
Almost destroyed poor Colman?

How drugs, alike in strength and name,
In operation vary!
When what exalts the Doctor's fame
Undoes th'Apothecary![67]

*

Wilkes' squib, of course, simply exploited a conceit which Garrick had built into his witty prologue. In view of the title which was now inseparable from Goldsmith's name it was an idea which came immediately to hand and made an irresistible point: Comedy was dying of a surfeit of fine sentiments, and here was Oliver Goldsmith, M.B. to prescribe a remedy. But Garrick's conceit was perhaps less innocent than it appeared. The *ad eundem* escapade at Oxford had produced a flood of illumination on an area better suited to the darkness and confusion which had prevailed up to this point. Goldsmith's degree was now firmly tethered to Trinity College Dublin, and even if none of the many Trinity College men in London had taken the trouble to check his credentials, the sudden withdrawing from the universities of Louvain and Padua of the honour of having conferred medical status on him must have looked suspicious. Garrick had evidently picked up a rumour that Goldsmith was sailing under false colours and, once he had embarked on his medical theme, he was unable to resist an allusion to it.

By pointing to a way in which *She Stoops to Conquer* might be turned into a *cause célèbre*, Garrick would have felt that he had treated Goldsmith generously, and at the end of his prologue he reserved a compensating *bonne bouche* of mischief for his own pleasure. The sick-patient conceit was good fun and would get the comedy off to a rousing start, but the sting was in the tail:

> . . . One hope remains—hearing the maid was ill,
> A *doctor* comes this night to shew his skill.
> To cheer her heart, and give your muscles motion,
> He in *five draughts* prepar'd presents a potion:
> A kind of magic charm—for be assur'd,
> If you will *swallow it*, the maid is cur'd:
> But desp'rate the Doctor, and her case is,
> If you reject the dose, and make wry faces!
> This truth he boasts, will boast it while he lives,
> No *pois'nous drugs* are mix'd in what he gives;
> Should he succeed, you'll give him his degree;
> If not, within he will receive no fee!
> The college *you*, must his pretensions back,
> Pronounce him *regular*, or dub him *quack*.[68]

The hint was so delicate that only those whose suspicions were already aroused would respond. But of course Garrick had gone straight to Goldsmith's weakest spot: the college which he claimed to have validated his medical degree had no record of the event.

Garrick clearly had no desire to ruin Goldsmith's reputation (even if Londoners of the time would have seen the matter in so serious a light). He simply found the situation comic and in a humorous way was settling an old score. Goldsmith, however, seems to have been alarmed. He was caught neatly in a trap. He needed Garrick's support, and could hardly refuse the prologue especially if it had been bespoken by Johnson or some other of Garrick's friends in the Club. The dangerous lines had to stand unless he was to incriminate himself by objecting to them. But he quite lost his taste for being called 'Doctor'. Obviously puzzled by his wish to revert to a simple 'Mr', Cooke suggests, not too convincingly, that it may have been inspired by an ambition to cultivate the image of the man of fashion. But whatever Goldsmith's motive for trying to shed it, the title was fixed in everyone's mind and he was simply not allowed to retract:

> This period, too, is farther remarkable for our Author dismissing the title of *Doctor* from his address, and calling himself Mr Goldsmith. Whether he had only then decided never to practise the profession he was bred to, or that he thought *Mr.* a more familiar manner of launching himself into the fashionable world,

which he was then vain enough to affect to be fond of, it is now hard to decide; this, however, was the fact, that the world would not let *him lose his degree*, but called him *Doctor* to the end of his life.[69]

The effect of Garrick's declaration of disbelief (as it would immediately have seemed to Goldsmith) was to create a curious rapport between the two men. As the hidden message in *The Deserted Village* indicates, Goldsmith had a need at this stage in his life to share his sense of personal failure. Johnson would in some ways have been a good confessor (the young Boswell had found him so) but the signs are that he failed to meet Goldsmith on this level. Now, Garrick in an amused and not unfriendly way was nudging Goldsmith and calling him a fraud. The hole that he had pricked through the mask was too small for any risk of public exposure and it may even have offered a kind of relief. He was an odd successor to Henry, but this was what in a way he now became and there are two striking examples of the intimacy which in the last year of Goldsmith's life existed between them. Goldsmith had borrowed money from Garrick on the strength of an offer to alter *The Good-Natured Man*, in any way Garrick wished, for a revival at Drury Lane,[70] and one of his letters on the subject of this loan ends almost as surprisingly for Garrick, one imagines, as his prologue had ended for Goldsmith, with an allusion to Garrick's lack of inches, a topic which all his contemporaries from Samuel Foote to Mrs Bellamy had used whenever they wanted to deflate him. ('Will your figures be as large as life, Mr Foote?' someone had asked when the manager of the Little Theatre was preparing to stage *Piety in Pattens*. 'Oh, no, my lady,' he replied, 'not much larger than Garrick'.)[71]

My Dear Friend,

I thank you! I wish I could do something to serve you. I shall have a comedy for you in a season or two at farthest that I believe will be worth your acceptance, for I fancy I will make it a fine thing. You shall have the refusal. I wish you would not take up Newbery's note, but let Waller teize him, without however coming to extremities, let him haggle after him and he will get it. He owes it and will pay it. Im sorry you are ill. I will draw upon you one month after date for sixty pound, and your acceptance

will be ready money part of which I want to go down to Barton
with. May God preserve my honest little man for he has my heart.

ever

Oliver Goldsmith[72]

That extraordinary flourish sets the tone for the entertainment
which the actor and playwright had contrived between them this
same December. The Beauclerks had given a party at their new
house overlooking the Thames in Adelphi Terrace. Their neighbours, the Garricks, had been invited together with Goldsmith and,
perhaps with the intention of convincing him that Goldsmith was
not such a bad fellow, Horace Walpole. Walpole had probably been
right in the spring to discover references to his friend Miss Rachel
Lloyd (and possibly to himself) in Goldsmith's new play.[73] In the
printed text Goldsmith had changed the original 'Rachel' to
'Biddy' when Marlow claimed membership of an exclusive dining
club, The Female Coterie, to which both Walpole and Miss Lloyd
belonged:

> At the Ladies Club in town, I'm called their agreeable Rattle.
> Rattle, child, is not my real name, but one I'm known by . . .
> There's Mrs Mantrap, Lady Betty Blackleg, the Countess of
> Sligo, Mrs Langhorns, old Miss Biddy Buckskin, and your
> humble servant, keep up the spirit of the place . . .[74]

Walpole had not been amused, and was to be even less so by the
'entertainment' which Goldsmith and Garrick were to provide.
Perhaps Goldsmith's hand can be detected in the simultaneous
announcement that something amusing was to happen and that the
guests would have to wait several hours to discover what it was as
Garrick was performing at Drury Lane that evening: in the same
fashion the 'Cobbler' story that Reynolds recalled had staggered
forward with grim determination towards its long-delayed anti-
climax. The stiff-necked, self-consciously witty Horace Walpole
was incapable of responding to such humour.

'I dined and passed Saturday at Beauclerk's,' he writes to the
Countess of Upper Ossory, 'with the Edgecumbes, the Garricks,
and Doctor Goldsmith, and was most thoroughly tired, as I
knew I should be, I who hate the playing off a butt. Goldsmith is
a fool, the more wearing for having some sense. It was the night

of a new comedy, called *The School for Wives*, which was exceedingly applauded, and which Charles Fox says is execrable. Garrick has at least the chief hand in it. I never saw anybody in a greater fidget, nor more vain when he returned, for he went to the playhouse at half an hour after five, and we sat waiting for him till ten, when he was to act a speech in *CATO* with Goldsmith, that is, the latter sat on t'other's lap, covered with a cloak, and while Goldsmith spoke, Garrick's arms that embraced him made foolish actions. How could one laugh when one had expected this for four hours?'[75]

Other people did laugh, and for a little girl, one of Reynolds' nieces, who witnessed a repeat performance at Leicester Square in which, reversing their rôles, Garrick recited one of his most famous pieces, Hamlet's speech to his father's ghost, and Goldsmith 'put out his hands on each side of the cloth . . . tapping his heart and putting his hand to Garrick's head and nose, all at the wrong time', it was a matter of laughing till one shrieked and remembering the party into one's old age.[76]

THIRTEEN

Between The Comic And The Tragic Muse

THE SUCCESSFUL production of his new play and the attendant publicity had made Goldsmith vulnerable to attack from one obvious quarter. Perhaps resenting the atmosphere of congratulation (and quite possibly self congratulation) which now surrounded him, William Kenrick reacted as Theaker Wilder had once done and looked for the readiest means to send him publicly reeling. As he had severed his relationship with Griffiths, the channel that suggested itself was a newspaper, the *London Packet*, and to its editor, the same William Woodfall who had acted as Mrs Cornelys' agent the previous year, he submitted a typically scurrilous piece attacking both play and playwright.[1]

Even if Goldsmith was sufficiently sure of himself to know that Kenrick's opinion of his writing was worthless, this article would have caught him on the raw coming from a man who had at least had a chance to familiarise himself with the furnishings of the Brick Court chambers and who knew that he was a friend of the Hornecks.

TO DR GOLDSMITH
Vous vous noyez par vanité

Sir,

   The happy knack which you have learnt of puffing your own compositions provokes me to come forth. You have not been the editor of newspapers and magazines, not to discover the trick of literary *humbug*. But the gauze is so thin, that the very foolish part of the world see through it, and discover the Doctor's monkey face and cloven foot. Your poetic vanity, is as unpardonable as your personal; would man believe it, and will woman bear it, to be told, that for hours, the *great* Goldsmith will stand surveying his grotesque orang-outang figure in a pier glass. Was but the lovely H——k as much enamoured, you would not sigh, my gentle swain, in vain. But your vanity is preposterous. How will this same bard of Bedlam ring the changes in praise of Goldy! But what has he to be either proud or vain of? The Traveller is a flimsy poem, built upon false principles; principles diametrically opposite to liberty. What is the Good Natured Man, but a poor, water-gruel, dramatic dose? What is the Deserted Village, but a pretty poem, of easy numbers, without fancy, dignity, genius or fire? And pray what may be the last *speaking pantomime* so praised by the Doctor himself, but an incoherent piece of stuff, the figure of a woman, with a fish's tail, without plot, incident or intrigue. We are made to laugh at stale, dull jokes, wherein every scene is unnatural, and inconsistent with the rules, the laws of nature, and of the drama; viz. Two gentlemen come to a man of fortune's house, eat, drink, sleep, &c. and take it for an inn. The one is intended as a lover to the daughter; he talks with her for some hours, and when he sees her again in a different dress he treats her as a bar-girl, and swears she squinted. He abuses the master of the house, and threatens to kick him out of his own doors. The Squire whom we are told is to be a fool, proves the most sensible being of the piece; and he makes out a whole act, by bidding his mother lie close behind a bush, persuading her that his father, her own husband, is a highwayman, and that he is coming to cut their throats; and to give his cousin an opportunity to go off, he drives his mother over hedges, ditches, and through ponds. There is not, sweet sucking Johnson, a natural stroke in the whole play, but the young fellow's giving the stolen jewels to the mother supposing her to be the landlady. That Mr. Colman did no justice to this piece, I honestly allow; that he told all his friends it would be damned, I positively aver: and from such ungenerous insinuations, without a dramatic merit, it rose to public notice, and it is now the *ton* to go to see it; though I never saw a person that either liked it or approved it, any more than the absurd plot of the *Homes'* tragedy of *Alonzo*. Mr. Goldsmith, correct your arrogance! Reduce your vanity; and endeavour to believe, as a man, you are of the plainest sort; and as an author, but a mortal piece of mediocrity.

> Brise le miroir infidèle,
> Qui vous cache la vérité.

> "Tom Tickle."[2]

It was a cunningly contrived lampoon with all the ingredients to make Goldsmith wince, from its obtuse disregard of his individual vein of humour to its far more astute recognition of a writer's lack of confidence in himself. But the surest stroke of all turned out to be the mention of Mary Horneck. One side of Goldsmith's personality aspired towards the freedom, security and refinements of bourgeois living. Now Kenrick had created a situation in which the standards of the bourgeoisie would be invoked to embroil him in a skirmish far more humiliating than the episode a quarter of a century ago at Trinity College. On Friday March 26th, two days after the appearance of the article, Goldsmith dined with the Hornecks in Westminster and found the family going through all the motions of high indignation at the 'compromising' of Mary in a newspaper. Mary's brother, Captain Charles Horneck was present and it was brought home to Goldsmith that action must be taken. The two men set out by coach for Paternoster Row that afternoon.[3]

Evans, the publisher of the *London Packet* was apparently alone in his shop when they arrived and Goldsmith delivered a speech which, (if he had been trying since dinner-time to feel his way into his companion's mood) may indeed have been as stagey as Prior's record of it suggests. 'I have called in consequence of a scurrilous attack in your paper upon me (my name is Goldsmith) and an unwarrantable liberty taken with the name of a young lady. As for myself I care little, but her name must not be sported with.' Perhaps as he heard his own words he lost his temper. As Evans stooped to reach for his file, no doubt having bought time by claiming ignorance, Goldsmith struck him across the back with his cane. Evans retaliated, and in the scuffle a lamp was broken, showering them with oil and cutting Goldsmith's face. At this point Kenrick coolly appeared from the inner room in time to help bundle the bruised and bleeding writer back into the coach.[4]

Goldsmith's day was not yet over. He had hardly set foot in his chambers before Garrick and Topham Beauclerk appeared to accompany him to Gerrard Street.[5] Behind his façade of languor and disenchantment Beauclerk was sufficiently fascinated by the child of the provincial Irish parsonage to make frequent calls at Brick Court. He may have found Goldsmith genuinely refreshing, but it is more probable in the light of what happened now that, like the folk at Barton, he looked for entertainment on a more superficial level.

That Goldsmith's clothes should have become daubed with blood and oil was a joke very much in the Barton tradition and Goldsmith, despite his bruises, was probably prepared to play up to it for a time at least. Perhaps encouraged by their host to overlook the more serious implications of this scrape, the visitors saw the opportunity of exploiting another excellent Goldsmith story. Keeping up the exhilarating post-battle spirit, they persuaded Goldsmith to demonstrate his unconcern by accompanying them *as he was* to Gerrard Street.

The Club had expected nothing more dramatic this evening than a reading of the Rowley poems by a new member, Lord Charlemont.[6] The arrival of the incongruous trio from Brick Court—two suave and self-possessed gentlemen and a poet who looked as if he had just emerged from a Butcher Boy brawl on the banks of the Liffey— was both startling and irresistibly comic. However doubtful Beauclerk's own motives may have been, Goldsmith was too well- liked for any immediate response other than concern; but already he had had time for reflection and must have picked up certain tremours in the air not completely compatible with universal sympathy. He realised too late that by appearing in his torn clothes with a swollen, blood-stained face he had committed a solecism: the only thing to do was to withdraw with as much dignity as could be salvaged from such a wretched situation. But as he took his leave his own sense of the comedy which Beauclerk and Garrick had inveigled him into providing got the better of him—as Thomas Percy recorded without apparently detecting the irony in his friend's parting remark:

> The poor Doctor had every attention paid him which his painful situation required, but it was impossible for the most serious not to relax from his gravity at the oddity of the scene and the comic circumstances of the narrative. Long however from civility and tenderness, they repressed the inclination to smile, till our unfortunate Bard, who remarked the constrained silence which pervaded the Company, and who was suffering great pains in body and mind, desired leave to retire, "as he found he only made them melancholy".

It was a bold but—as Percy's failure to see the joke would prove— not a wise stroke: a little too late in one sense, but certainly before he was down the stairs, he would have heard the great burst of laughter which his observation had released.[7]

Kenrick had done his job well. The scene in Evans' shop gave him ample material for another squib in which he gleefully drew attention to the parallel between Goldsmith and Johnson, who had once knocked his publisher, Osborne, to the ground. 'He has sucked the nipple of nurse Johnson's bubby so long,' Kenrick proclaimed, recalling a salient aspect of Goldsmith's literary and social careers, 'that the manners, not the wit, of the former are become his own'. 'Adieu dear Goldee,' he concluded; 'don't spare pomatum; reduce the swelling of your face, and your vanity, and it will be the most beautiful alteration in your grotesque character and figure'.[8]

Goldsmith was still reluctant to let Kenrick have the last word and, failing to act on his own dictum that 'a Grub-street writer never thinks his pamphlet succeeds until it is answered', he sent a short, dignified letter to the *Daily Advertiser*. In it he set out the case for higher ethical standards in journalism. He lamented its 'inroads upon private life', its turning 'from combating the strong, to overwhelming the feeble', and pointed to his own unblemished record in writing for the press.* 'Every man,' he concluded, 'should singly consider himself as a guardian of the liberty of the press, and as far as his influence can extend, should endeavour to prevent its licentiousness becoming at last the grave of its freedom'.[9] It was such a good letter that many people assumed that Johnson had written it, but when Boswell put this to Johnson he replied 'Sir, Dr Goldsmith would no more have asked me to write such a thing as that for him, than he would have asked me to feed him with a spoon, or to do any thing else that denoted his imbecility'. But he added sternly that if Goldsmith had consulted his friends 'he would not have been allowed to publish it'.[10]

*

'This is a new plume to him,' was Johnson's bitterly ironical comment to Boswell on Goldsmith's part in the Evans affray, and it

---

*This is largely true, though the satirical portrait of his former *Monthly Review* associate Theophilus Cibber, after Cibber had been drowned at sea, might be considered an exception. It is possible to see in this ironical biography a pointer to Goldsmith's later identification with the Hodge/Lumpkin figure.

is only one of many hints that something had gone wrong with their friendship. On Goldsmith's side there was evidently still a certain reverence for Johnson's moral strengths: it can be detected in the kind of remarks which in his serious vein he felt compelled to utter in Johnson's presence. Three weeks after the scuffle in Paternoster Row, when he and Johnson were together at General Paoli's lodgings, they argued about the advisability of Martinelli, a fellow guest, continuing his *History of England* up to the present age. Johnson took the side of prudence and expediency, saying that the Italian would run into prejudice and make dangerous enemies if he did. Goldsmith took the unwordly, idealistic view.

GOLDSMITH: There are people who tell a hundred political lies every day, and are not hurt by it. Surely, then, one may tell truth with safety.

JOHNSON: Why, Sir, in the first place, he who tells a hundred lies has disarmed the force of his lies. But besides; a man had rather have a hundred lies told of him, than one truth which he does not wish should be told.

GOLDSMITH: For my part, I'd tell truth, and shame the devil.

JOHNSON: Yes, Sir; but the devil will be angry. I wish to shame the devil as much as you do, but I should choose to be out of the reach of his claws.

GOLDSMITH: His claws can do you no harm, when you have the shield of truth.[11]

At one level such a stand from Oliver Goldsmith had its obviously absurd side—but absurd rather than hypocritical. The man who had idealised his brother was still capable of being drawn out of his depth by his dazzled recognition that Johnson was a living monument to certain Christian virtues. Johnson himself, on this and every other occasion but one, repressed the devastating reply with which by this time he could have crushed him. The exception was his comment on Goldsmith's style of story-telling, where it is possible to detect a shade of grimness beneath the humour. Goldsmith had confessed to sometimes embroidering or otherwise improving an anecdote: but 'he said he only indulged himself in white lies, light as feathers, which he threw up in the air, and on whomever they fell nobody was hurt'. 'I wish,' Johnson replied, 'you would take the trouble of moulting your feathers'.[12] It was little more than a warning growl. His moral judgments of course, could be far more clear-cut and severe than that. His answer to Boswell's claim that, although divorced, Lady Diana Beauclerk had really been the less guilty party in her previous marriage, was 'My dear Sir, never accustom your mind to mingle virtue and vice. The woman's a whore, and there's an end on't.' So often tolerant and compassionate in practice, Johnson would have been uncompromisingly severe about any hints of disingenuousness, muddle or dishonesty in Goldsmith's dealings with him.

Goldsmith was arguably the most honest of men. He kept his distance from the lucrative party-hack journalism of his age; he blurted out statements which his contemporaries would have suppressed as naked and naive; he acknowledged the envious streak in his nature by grotesquely parodying it. In his writing, through the images of disguise and the masquerade, and in his life, through the alternating suits of black and gaudy colours, he had advertised the dual nature of his personality. He had also, of course, involved Johnson, Percy and Chambers in an act of deception which could have had embarrassing repercussions for all three.

At the time of the Bickerstaffe scandal Johnson had adopted the stance of a man who preferred to ignore his friends' moral shortcomings; but it is very unlikely, even if he kept his silence, that he could have failed to pick up the warning signals in the aftermath of the *ad eundem* affair and, even without the reminder built into Garrick's prologue, the episode would have rankled with the man who valued very highly indeed his right of entry to the senior common rooms of Oxford. The issue was extremely delicate —too delicate in fact to be given a public airing beyond coffee-house gossip and innuendo, however firm a line Johnson might have adopted privately.

In this last phase of his life it was quite evident that, by Johnson's standards, Goldsmith had not 'come right' as his friend had once confidently predicted; and it is now that Johnson's voice is heard at its sternest. 'He knows nothing,' he told Boswell on Good Friday, 1773; 'he has made up his mind about nothing'; and a few days later he returned to this theme in the presence of Reynolds: 'It is amazing how little Goldsmith knows.' (If there were good reasons for regarding Goldsmith as a moral delinquent it was much safer to transfer any condemnation to the intellectual plane.) But a few days later when he made a similar remark to Reynolds the criticism was softened by warm praise of Goldsmith as a writer: 'Whether, indeed, we take him as a poet, — as a comick writer — or as an historian, he stands in the first class.'[13]

Johnson himself had been an influence on Goldsmith's literary career in other than practical ways. In the subtle generalisations and closely-knit style of *The Traveller* there is a conscious intention to emulate the brilliant, taut rhetoric of *The Vanity of Human Wishes*, although there was to be a departure from that classical standard in the second major poem where the nostalgia which had been rejected in the earlier work was now deliberately exploited. *The Deserted Village* with its emphasis on mood, on the poet's relation to the places described and on landscapes of the mind anticipates the development of poetry beyond the age of Johnson, while at their most original the essays offer a foretaste of Charles Lamb. It is significant too that his novel should have won the admiration of Goethe while Fanny Burney was evidently puzzled by its effect of blurred focus and swift modulations from major to minor keys. But unlike the writers of the last years of the century, Goldsmith was moving away from the standards of the classical era instinctively and unconsciously. When he *thought* about literature he adopted Johnson's criteria wholesale and, although there were moments when his appreciative faculties were demonstrably more acute than those of Johnson himself, he was content for the most part to remain in Johnson's shadow, regrettably taking on his friend's prejudices with regard to such eminent contemporaries as Gray and Sterne. If Johnson was a haven of security in the intellectual and moral sphere, so were the preconceptions of the classical literary theory to which Goldsmith consciously adhered even while instinctively groping forward to greater freedom in the expression of idiosyncracy and shades of feeling.

One of the most puzzling features of Goldsmith's literary career is his changing attitude towards the novel and his failure to build on the success of either *The Vicar of Wakefield* or the fictional element in the 'Chinese Letters'. In one of his essays in the *Bee* in 1759, Goldsmith had included Smollett amongst the men who were entitled to take a place in the stage-coach of fame. 'A well-written

romance is no such easy task as is generally imagined,' the in-
quisitorial coachman tells the novelist.[15] This was before Goldsmith
met Johnson. At the end of his career, in the essay about sentimental comedy which had preceded the production of *She Stoops
to Conquer*, he writes with the utmost disparagement about the art:

> But there is one Argument in favour of Sentimental Comedy
> which will keep it on the Stage in spite of all that can be said
> against it. It is, of all others, the most easily written. Those
> abilities that can hammer out a Novel, are fully sufficient for the
> production of a Sentimental Comedy.[16]

Goldsmith was indirectly reminding his public that people like
Hugh Kelly and Mrs Griffiths, besides writing plays, had also made
their contributions to a market now flooded with popular romances.
Charles Jenner had also recorded the phenomenon:

> Thrice happy authors, who with little skill
> In two short weeks can two short volumes fill!
> Who take some Miss, of Christian-name inviting,
> And plunge her deep in love, and letter-writing;
> Perplex her well with jealous parents' cares,
> Expose her virtue to a lover's snares;
> Give her false friends and perjur'd swains by dozens,
> With all the episodes of aunts and cousins;
> Make parents thwart her, and her lover scorn her,
> And some mishap spring up at ev'ry corner;
> Make her lament her fate, with *ahs* and *ohs*,
> And tell some dear Miss Willis all her woes,
> Whilst now with love and now with grief she rages;
> Till, having brought her through two hundred pages,
> Finding, at length, her father's heart obdurate,
> Will make her take the 'Squire, and leave the Curate;
> She scales the garden wall, or fords a river,
> Elopes, gets married, and her friends forgive her . . .

With hindsight it is clear that the achievements of Goldsmith
himself and Fanny Burney, like Jane Austen at the beginning of
the next century, dwarf the popular fiction of their day; but to the
practitioners on the ground this would have been far less obvious.
It was unfortunate that the man who had so much influence over

Goldsmith both as critic and friend should have belittled the art of Fielding and, by association, of Smollett. (The only novelist to whom Johnson gave unqualified praise was Richardson.) Newbery's delay until 1766 in publishing Goldsmith's novel does not seem to have been offset by any promptings from Johnson that might have persuaded Goldsmith to write another, and by the time *The Vicar of Wakefield* appeared its author had committed himself to the long labours of compiling.

Over this aspect of Goldsmith's career Johnson was both complacent and patronising. When he claimed that his friend was a better historian than Hume and Robertson he was paying a compliment to his graceful narrative style rather than making a serious assessment of his completely unoriginal work. When the *History of the Earth and Animated Nature* began to dominate his working life, Johnson simply found that he had a wealth of material for Goldsmith jokes. 'He is now writing a Natural History,' he announced, 'and will make it as entertaining as a Persian tale'. In his turn, emerging from the long hours he had spent grappling with Buffon or Lucretius, Goldsmith could be relied on to scatter nuggets of science or pseudo-science into the conversation, sometimes with a positively Johnsonian turn of phrase as when he talked about the 'nidification of birds'. 'There is a general abhorrence in animals at the signs of massacre,' he informed Johnson and Henry Thrale on a different occasion. 'If you put a tub of blood into a stable, the horses are like to go mad'. The possibilities for entertainment at Goldsmith's expense were legion, and Thrale promptly offered his own stable for an experiment; but Johnson, to his credit, stepped in to save his friend:

Nay, Sir, I would not have him prove it. If he is content to take his information from others, he may get through his book with little trouble, and without much endangering his reputation. But if he makes experiments for so comprehensive a book as his, there would be no end to them; his erroneous assertions would then fall upon himself; and he might be blamed for not having made experiments as to every particular.[17]

It would, of course, be unfair to attribute too much blame to Johnson for failing to react more strongly to this waste of Goldsmith's talent. He had brought it on himself through his improvi-

M

dence, and he was still a comparatively young man: Johnson could not have foreseen that he had only a few more months to live. It would also be wrong to exaggerate the shortcomings of *The History of the Earth and Animated Nature*. This was a lucid and immensely readable work which kept its popularity: only by the 1840s had its built-in obsolescence begun to show itself. But Johnson had obliquely stated the vital, lamentable and necessary fact: that Goldsmith, who had been no more than an enthusiastic amateur when his eyes had been opened to the lucrative possibilities of popular science, had spent the better part of five years re-arranging other people's findings.

Johnson would have had to be a saint to resist the temptation to exploit his reputation for intellectual rigour and pugnacity. His greatest quality was probably humour rather than sanctity and he enjoyed the licence which his fabled bear-like qualities gave him for the exercise of a ruthless wit. Often he went too far and was penitent: but members of his circle, Boswell amongst them, were all too willing to create the conversational moments when Johnson could be proved to be in good form, cutting through muddle with the laser beam of a brilliant discursive mind. In their different ways many of his contemporaries revealed their fear of the humiliation Johnson was capable of inflicting on them. Some, like Horace Walpole or the aristocratic friend of Reynolds who confessed that he would 'rather dine at the same table with two tygers' than with such 'formidable' people as Johnson and Goldsmith,[18] stayed out of reach. Others practised brinkmanship. Arthur Murphy was adept at this art: when arguing with Johnson he rarely offered an idea as his own, but would place it in a conversational no-man's-land where Johnson could do with it what he would.[19] There were also the sycophants and, in Joseph Cradock's opinion Tom Davies, the gentleman-bookseller of Russell Street was one of them, dancing attendance on Johnson during a dinner at the Mitre or the Globe, ostentatiously smoothing the paths and getting snubbed for his pains.[20]

Goldsmith was no more prepared to accept the rôle of courtier with Johnson than with the Duke of Northumberland. His own distinctive brand of humour, his need to be noticed and his courage had won him the status of licensed fool or even, as he himself probably saw it, of Jack the Giant Killer. Although he revered Johnson as a writer he was not prepared to defer to his moods or even his opinions, though on many issues they were in basic agreement with one another. A message incidentally communicated by Boswell's *Life of Johnson* is that Goldsmith's willingness to begin conversations or introduce new topics made him one of Johnson's most valuable friends. Johnson himself was constitutionally reluctant to take the initiative and it was sometimes after he had been stimulated into activity by Goldsmith's tenacity in argument and, on occasions, by the subtlety of his thinking, that he produced memorable sayings for Boswell to record. And in the heat of argument Goldsmith sometimes revealed, without perhaps realising it, that he had left behind those mid-century positions to which consciously he still clung.[21]

It was a good partnership. Unfortunately, too many of their contemporaries underestimated Goldsmith's contribution. Goldsmith smarted under sneering references to 'Doctor Minimus' and was provoked into a sharp reply when the Swiss secretary to the Royal Academy, Michael Moser, stopped him in full flow with 'Stay, stay, Doctor Shonson is going to say something'. 'Are you sure that *you* can comprehend what he says?' Goldsmith asked him.[22] And on another occasion, 'This is a fellow to make one commit suicide,' he commented to Johnson when an Eton schoolmaster pointed out that an invitation addressed to Johnson had not included Goldsmith.[23] But Johnson himself was complacent about the effect on his friend of such invidious distinctions. As his actions in various crises had proved he had Goldsmith's best interests at heart, but with the scent of battle in his nostrils he tended to forget that Goldsmith deserved some reward for the very special kind of social service he was providing. He knew his worth. 'A very great man,' was the phrase he used in a letter to Bennet Langton three months after Goldsmith's death.[24] But no-one would have been more amazed than Goldsmith himself by such a tribute: too often in their encounters with one another it must have seemed that he was if anything undervalued by Johnson. On occasions when Johnson seemed depressed or unwilling to be brought into the conversation, it was often Goldsmith who took upon himself the delicate task of shaking him out of his mood, but too often his only reward, when the change in gear had been effected, was the brusque aside: 'No more fooleries!'[25]

This was the least attractive aspect of Johnson's personality.

Perhaps conscious of his own massive infirmities, he underestimated the needs of other people as social animals. The danger was inherent in the freedom with which he would talk (even when they were not present) of 'Goldy' or 'Atty' or 'Mund'.[26] Sometimes he underestimated his own strength or was carried away in the heat of conversation to say things he afterwards regretted. There are several signs in Boswell's account of the spring of 1773 that Johnson was in an overbearing mood (perhaps a prelude to his illness during the summer).

Goldsmith was Johnson's opposite in this respect. On his best form, he had social tact of so high an order that he was prepared to offer himself as sacrificial victim whenever the wheels threatened to grind to a halt. He knew when the moment had come to take a conversational risk, to create a diversion by drawing attention to his new bloom-coloured suit or even, perhaps, to fall into the lake. He must also have known when it was appropriate to adopt a completely different stance: when Johnson and Burke were in full flood the members of the Club would not have tolerated a man who simply wanted to chatter. Even if there is an element of truth in Johnson's claim that he was badly informed, when Goldsmith condemned Johnson for monopolising the conversation he was not simply registering a peevish resentment at being unable to keep up. In accusing Boswell of 'making a monarchy of what should be a republick',[27] he was implicitly condemning all those people who, when they deferred to Johnson or treated him as a one-man entertainment, were encouraging him in all his less admirable tendencies.

*

Boswell's detailed account of a series of dinner parties in April and May 1773 suggests that members of Johnson's circle took it for granted that he and Goldsmith were complementary to one another. On Tuesday April 13th the two friends had their debate about Luxury at General Oglethorpe's. Two days later they were together again at General Paoli's, the following Wednesday at the Thrales', on Thursday 29th at Oglethorpe's again and on Friday, 7th May at a dinner given in the City by two sociable publishers, the Dilly brothers. Boswell's faithful record of these occasions shows that both men were on their mettle. Besides the Luxury issue and their argument about Martinelli's *History of England* they found themselves at issue on such questions as whether suicide was an act of courage or cowardice (Goldsmith taking the latter view), on the difference between flattering and respecting a monarch, on the stylistic problems of writing fables, on freedom of conscience and the moral implications of martyrdom. But for Goldsmith, already a sick man, the strain of these public contests, coming after the anxiety over his play, was considerable. 'We should change companions oftener,' he told Johnson, 'we exhaust one another, and shall soon be both of us worn out.' Mrs Thrale added the rather complacent rider, 'It had been better for *him* perhaps'. But it was true. Goldsmith played these contests on his nerves while Johnson with his more robust intellectual resources sailed on imperturbably. Even an apparent handicap like his deafness became an advantage when he was in a mood for talking other people down.

Goldsmith made light of his own poor health. He had appeared to make a good recovery from the illness which had laid him up in the summer of '72, and in the last year of his life, in spite of increasing worry and a poor appetite, he often gave the impression of enhanced mental vigour. On a stroll through London, as they passed within sight of the rotting heads on Temple Bar he had quoted back at Johnson the verse from Ovid which Johnson had recited in Westminster Abbey a little while before,

Forsitan et nostrum nomen miscebitur *istis**28

suggesting that with their political views (and Johnson's affection for the Stuarts) they were as likely to achieve fame here as on the walls of the Abbey.

In their discussion of suicide it is Goldsmith's intuitive grasp of the suicide's mentality that makes Johnson's robust logic seem shallow in comparison; and undoubtedly it was Goldsmith who was right, in the face of Johnson's incredulous laughter, in insisting that in a fable little fish must talk like little fish.29

But they were too much in each other's company. By May 7th when they met at the Dilly brothers' house in the Poultry Goldsmith was exhausted and Johnson himself was probably sickening for the illness which he later recorded amongst his Prayers and

*Perhaps one day our name will be mingled with theirs.

Meditations for the year. Besides Boswell and Bennet Langton, Edward and Charles Dilly's guests included three clergymen, one of them a dissenter. After some discussion of Captain Cook's recent voyage to the South Seas the conversation turned in the direction of religious toleration. It was the dissenting Dr Mayo who raised the question of martyrdom and Goldsmith who developed the theme by enquiring if this were not really a form of 'voluntary suicide'. For once his and Johnson's rôles were reversed: it was Goldsmith who appealed to reason and Johnson who adopted the idealistic viewpoint. They were on dangerous ground as soon as Goldsmith quoted a specific instance of martyrdom, 'Our first reformers who were burnt for not believing bread and wine to be Christ', for Johnson hated discussing the more intimate aspects of his faith in public and the effect of Goldsmith's remark was to underline the difference between his broad-church protestantism and Johnson's anglo-catholicism. Boswell's designation of Johnson's 'Sir, they were not burnt for not believing bread and wine to be Christ, but for insulting those who did believe it' as an *interruption*, is a danger signal.

After Boswell had stepped in with a remark which effectively neutralised Goldsmith's unfortunate intervention, he, Johnson, Dr Mayo and the other clergymen continued to pursue the topic of religious toleration. Goldsmith himself was silent and it would seem from what happened later—although Boswell puts a different interpretation on it—that he was brooding under a sense of injury. In the heat of the argument he had made a false move and Johnson's pointed interjection must have seemed like a snub. Perhaps angry with himself as much as with Johnson and very probably suffering discomfort from his bladder complaint, he took his hat in readiness for departure. But the discussion continued, and he was unable to pull himself away. It was clear by now that Johnson's temper had also risen: he was stern with Dr Mayo when Mayo showed signs of repeating himself. Unluckily Goldsmith was sitting at the other end of the table and it was probably a genuine accident that his friend simply overrode him as he tried to re-enter the conversation. Goldsmith's temper snapped. He threw his hat onto the floor, muttering 'Take it' but, whether it was intended as a declaration of war or as an ironical submission, Johnson ignored the gesture as he had ignored the remark and continued talking. Though hostile to Goldsmith,

Boswell's terse account of what happened next preserves all the embarrassment of the scene:

> When Toplady was going to speak, Johnson uttered some sound, which led Goldsmith to think that he was beginning again, and taking the words from Toplady. Upon which, he seized this opportunity of venting his own envy and spleen, under the pretext of supporting another person: "Sir, (said he to Johnson,) the gentleman has heard you patiently for an hour: pray allow us now to hear him."

> JOHNSON: (sternly) "Sir, I was not interrupting the gentleman. I was only giving him a signal of my attention. Sir, you are impertinent." Goldsmith made no reply, but continued in the company for some time.

As it was Friday (the day on which the Club met at this period) the two men were due to encounter one another again in the evening, and during the interim there was time for both to regret their quarrel. When Johnson arrived in Gerrard Street Goldsmith was unaccustomedly silent. Again, unluckily, a distance separated them but Johnson, perhaps beginning to feel some remorse, was intent on putting things right. It was not the ideal way, but circumstances dictated it, and the apology, like the reprimand, was public:

> Johnson . . . said aside to some of us, "I'll make Goldsmith forgive me;" and then called to him in a loud voice, "Dr Goldsmith, —something passed today where you and I dined; I ask your pardon." Goldsmith answered placidly, "It must be much from you, Sir, that I take ill." And so at once the difference was over, and they were on as easy terms as ever, and Goldsmith rattled away as usual.[30]

In spite of the satisfactory note on which the affair seemed to have ended, Johnson's apology had not been enough to undo the damage. Boswell must have realised as much when he called at Brick Court three days later to say goodbye before returning to Scotland. Goldsmith had managed to produce a gracious reply to Johnson's apology, but he was still full of resentment: 'The jealousy and envy which, though possessed of many most amiable qualities, he frankly avowed, broke out violently at this interview.'[31] Boswell was able to tell him that Johnson had at last promised to visit Scotland: in the late summer they were to make a walking tour of the Highlands and Hebrides. The force of Goldsmith's bitterness can still be felt in his reaction to the news: 'He now seemed very angry that Johnson was going to be a traveller; said "he would be a dead weight for me to carry, and that I should never be able to lug him along . . ." ' Transferring his attack to a more rational level as Boswell began to praise Johnson, he enquired sharply, 'Is he like Burke, who winds into a subject like a serpent?' It was the same mood that Henry Thrale was to encounter when, discussing Johnson's depressed state after an illness (perhaps the fever which overtook him not long after the evening in the Poultry) Goldsmith commented a shade too complacently that Johnson 'would never more be the man he was'.[32] Johnson for his part was bewildered by the resentment he had aroused. Even when allowances have been made for the exaggerations of a man in the grip of depression his remark to Mrs Thrale on July 18th was too strong not to suggest that, in his belief, something had gone seriously wrong with the friendship:

'And who will be my biographer (said he), do you think?' Goldsmith, no doubt, replied I, and he will do it best among us. 'The dog would write it best to be sure, replied he; but his particular malice towards me, and general disregard for truth, would make the book useless to all, and injurious to my character.'[33]

One of the unluckiest features of the quarrel had been its timing. Johnson's illness this summer would have kept him at Streatham, so that after the unfortunate climax to a period in which the friends had certainly seen too much of each other there was by contrast a gap in which, on Goldsmith's side, resentment could continue to fester. On August 6th Johnson left London for Scotland and did not come back until November 26th. Nor is it likely that he saw very much of Goldsmith on his return for during December and the early months of 1774 he had persistent bronchial trouble and was at the same time working hard on his *Journey to the Western Islands of Scotland*. The last occasion on which they can be placed together in the same room with reasonable certainty is the dinner-party which Goldsmith gave in Brick Court shortly before Johnson's departure for Scotland.[34] On this occasion it is Johnson's practical nature that makes itself felt though, at the time, Goldsmith is unlikely to have seen it in that light. Although he was now extremely worried about his financial position, he had put on the usual extravagant display for guests who included Reynolds, Dr Kippis and several literary men apart from Johnson. The first course was a dinner in itself, and when the second appeared Johnson, as principal guest, refused it and caught Reynolds' eye. Within a few moments it had been rejected by everyone at the table. Johnson's initiative could only have been intended as a kindness, for whether a nearby tavern or the Middle Temple kitchens had been responsible for the catering, Goldsmith would presumably not have had to pay for a course that was returned untouched. That it was an altogether tactful gesture remains in doubt. Goldsmith was observed to be 'mortified' as the covered dishes were borne away.[35]

*

The person who was least interested of all in the expensive meal he had ordered for his guests was the man who sat at the head of the mahogany dining-table. For some time it had been noticed that while his companions were doing justice to veal and ham and beef-steak pie in the taverns of Fleet Street, Goldsmith would be eating poached eggs and spinach.[36] Joseph Cradock, returning to London with his wife after an absence of some months was shocked by the change in his appearance. Goldsmith was fond of the young couple and accepted an invitation to dine with them at their lodgings in Norfolk Street. But he ate nothing apart from some biscuits which he took with a little wine. During dinner he sat at table or walked about the room and 'amused himself with pen and ink.'

Apart from the recurring dysuria he was preoccupied with his money difficulties and the closely related problem of the direction he should now follow in his career as a writer. If Reynolds was right in his estimate of Goldsmith's debts, the receipts from the three benefit nights at Covent Garden in March had provided little more than temporary relief. The nature of these debts is not known. As his principal creditor was his neighbour Edmund Bott, they may have accumulated over several years. 'Coins of all sizes,' as he had observed thirteen years earlier, had a 'surprizing facility of slipping from him';[37] and he had not lost his taste for gambling. The card games which were such a fatal snare to him were even built into the social life of the times, as he had recognised when purchasing two fine baize-covered tables for his rooms. Joseph Cradock understood what a snare this represented to a man of his temperament: 'The greatest fault of Dr Goldsmith was, that if he had £30 in his pocket he would go into certain companies in the country, and in hopes of doubling the sum, would generally return to town without any part of it'. Too many of Goldsmith's friends seem to have lacked Cradock's perspicuity. Like the great ladies who cultivated Mrs Abington's acquaintance and got her into debt simply by assuming that she could afford the same stakes as themselves,[38] people like the Hornecks and the Nugents and Sir William and Lady Chambers, living on an entirely different scale from Goldsmith, would have failed to realise that when he lost three or four pounds at a game of whist (which he played very badly)[39] he was bravely smiling in the face of a considerable setback.

It was far easier for Goldsmith to give than to receive and he was evidently too proud to disillusion these friends. But the correspondence with Garrick and the obligations to Edmund Bott indicate that he was now in a situation where access to some financial source other than the booksellers had become essential. The acceleration of this problem had begun with the death of John Newbery six years previously. His income from that quarter had been small in comparison to receipts from Griffin and Davies, but Newbery had understood Goldsmith's problem and formulated a way of dealing with it, whereas the large advances which had come into his hands when the Newbery connexion was broken had encouraged him to be reckless and created an illusory sense of freedom. Now Goldsmith's relationship with the publishers was deteriorating. Griffin, who five years earlier had taken a great risk in putting the first £500 instalment of an £800 advance into Goldsmith's hands, had been forced to sell his interest in the *History of the Earth and Animated Nature* to another publisher, John Nourse;[40] and Goldsmith, who was having his usual difficulties in bringing his work to a conclusion, had still not produced the book. It was advertised for the first time in February, 1774, but would not be published until June, two months after his death. The work which had launched Goldsmith on his career as a popular science writer, the *Survey of*

Experimental Philosophy undertaken for Newbery, appears to have
been abandoned after the publication of Volume I, though Newbery's
nephew would issue a companion volume in 1776.[41] Such experiences
may have had the effect of warning other publishers off, and
although, as Thomas Davies realised, in an emergency Goldsmith
could dream up half-a-dozen projects, they would have been more
reluctant now to surrender large advances to a writer who had
acquired a reputation for being dilatory. Davies who, in his agree-
ments cautiously stipulated payment on receipt of the manuscript,
was probably thinking of his own dealings with Goldsmith (in
which Johnson would have been the likely intermediary) when he
described the bad reputation which he had by this time acquired in
the book world:

> After much and disagreeable altercation, one bookseller desired
> to refer the matter in dispute to the doctor's learned friend, a
> man of integrity, and one who would favour no cause but that of
> justice and truth; Goldsmith consented, and was enraged to find
> that one author should have so little feeling for another, as to
> determine a dispute to his disadvantage, in favour of a paltry
> tradesman.[42]

In his eagerness to help find a solution to Goldsmith's difficulties
in the winter of 1773–1774, Joseph Cradock had been unrealistic in
suggesting that a new edition of *The Traveller* and the even more
recent *Deserted Village* should be published by subscription. Goldsmith's hopes were invested instead in an idea for a *Universal
Dictionary of the Arts and Sciences*, to which Reynolds, Johnson,
Burke, Garrick and Charles Burney had agreed to contribute under
his own general editorship. No one was better equipped than
Goldsmith for the task of co-ordinating the work of some of the
leading figures of his age who were also, of course, his friends. He
had made a good job of the prospectus, he felt, and was elated, when
Cradock called on him one morning, at the prospect of the advance
that must surely now be forthcoming:

> I one morning called upon him ... and found him infinitely
> better than I expected, and in a kind of exulting style he ex-
> claimed, "Here are some of the best of my prose writings; I

have been hard at work ever since midnight, and I desire you to examine them." "These," said I, "are excellent indeed."[43]

His hopes were soon to be dashed. No consortium presented itself to purchase the scheme, and Davies who might have been expected to be interested even though his own financial position was precarious, ascribes the blame equally to the size of the project and the booksellers' diminishing faith in Goldsmith himself:

> The booksellers, notwithstanding they had a high opinion of his abilities, yet were startled at the bulk, importance, and expense of so great an undertaking, the weight of which was to depend upon the industry of a man with whose indolence of temper and method of procrastination they had long been acquainted: the coldness with which they met his proposals was lamented by the doctor to the hour of his death, which seems to have been accelerated by a neglect of his health, occasioned by continual vexation of mind, arising from his involved circumstances. Death, I really believe, was welcome to a man of his great sensibility.

The five years between the inception and first signs of a publication date for the *History of the Earth and Animated Nature*, the failure of *The Gentleman's Journal*, the squabbles at which Northcote and Davies hint, had all contributed to the creation of an atmosphere prejudicial to Goldsmith's career as a compiler. For the writer who was experiencing a recrudescence of intellectual vigour as his health deteriorated, the sound of this door closing must have been ominous.

However inaccurate it might be to describe someone of Goldsmith's temperament as 'facing his problems', as the severe winter of '74 gave way to a wet spring[44] he was showing every sign of resilience and courage. The frequency with which the idea of suicide had occurred in his conversations with Johnson the previous spring suggests that an obvious solution to his difficulties had at least crossed his mind. But suicide he had argued, was a form of cowardice. In December he had planned his ventriloquist entertainment with Garrick, rallied himself to write a verse letter to Catherine Bunbury and after Christmas gone down to Barton for another bout of teasing and practical jokes. He embarked on a second project to change his fortunes: a novel. It amounted to a few chapters at the time of his death.[45] But characteristically the principal achievement of this last period was a handful of verses, privately circulated, which were a by-product of his social life rather than a money-making proposition.

He was a member of a club that had sprung out of an attempt by Burke to perpetuate a successful dinner party at 47 Leicester Square; it met occasionally at the St James's coffee house. It was probably David Garrick who had the idea of a competition in epitaph-writing. He had no doubt come armed with his 'Poor Poll' couplet,[46] and Goldsmith himself, of course, was the most popular subject in the versifying that ensued. As always he had been the focal point of the reunion, doing his turn as Bully Bottom and offering to challenge the entire company at their particular skills— no mean undertaking as (in addition to Garrick) Johnson, Burke and Percy were present besides Richard Cumberland, Joseph Hickey, Burke's cousin and brother, Caleb Whitefoord (who ran a newspaper spot for 'crossed-readings which Goldsmith found very amusing) and Dr Thomas Barnard, Dean of Derry, who at the time of the Black Dog Riot had stood with Goldsmith before the disciplinary committee at Trinity College.[47] Goldsmith was unprepared for Garrick's firework. In Garrick's own account 'upon the company's laughing very heartily, [he] grew very thoughtful, and either would not, or could not, write anything at that time'.[48] Other members of the party were already joining in the fun, amongst them Caleb Whitefoord who produced some vaguely offensive lines on 'Oliver Pug', which made free with Goldsmith's 'vanity' just as Garrick had done with his idiosyncratic style in conversation.[49]

Between Whitefoord's vulgarity and Garrick's wit, Goldsmith had much to think about. Both had reiterated that Johnsonian theme which was now a cliché: the gulf between the writer and the man; both had chosen to ignore that talent for *camaraderie* into which he had diverted so much of his energy. It was very much a time for retaliation and, as William Cooke put it, for realising that 'a little sprinkling of fear was not altogether an unnecessary ingredient in the friendships of the world'. Cooke was not a member of the Johnson/Reynolds circle and may have been exaggerating when he claimed that after Goldsmith's own verse-portraits had begun to circulate 'he was treated with more civility and seeming affection; his peculiarities were found to possess some degree of humour, and his taste was consulted in all discussions on literary subjects'; but the psychology fits the situation: for years Goldsmith's unflagging good nature had simply been taken for granted.

The little portraits in anapaestic couplets which Goldsmith now began to hand about with invocations to secrecy—a game which Burke flatly refused to play, guessing rightly that he had shown them to other people than himself[50]—contained insights as sharp as most of the portraits of Goldsmith had been obtuse. The sketches of Garrick and Burke were particularly fine. The seven couplets on Burke contained all the ingredients of his subsequent career in their central paradox of a talent that was both fostered and confined by the needs of party politics, while the portrait of Garrick went straight to the heart of the occupational hazards of the actor's vocation with a deft analysis of his driving need to manipulate audiences both inside and outside the theatre.[51] The tone was right: avoiding both flattery and malice, the portraits combined an admiration of his friends' achievements with a candid inspection of their shortcomings. In both penetration and generosity they surpass all contemporary views of himself with the single exception of Reynolds' fine essay. Yet the humdrum movement of the anapaestic lines seemed designed to blunt the cutting edge of his observation: the connoisseur of disguises was offering psychological insights of the calibre of Pope's in the metre of a nursery rhyme. There is no portrait of Johnson, nor apparently was there intended to be, though in Cradock's account he was present at the St James's Coffee House and in very good form on the day when the epitaph contest was proposed.

The lines on Reynolds are affectionate but incomplete: it is interesting to note that the qualities Goldsmith most admired in him are his evenness of temper and his unvarying good manners. Only one dispute between these two friends has been recorded. Three years earlier Dr James Beattie, the author of the meretricious *Essay on Truth* much admired by George III, had come to London with a letter of introduction from Boswell to Johnson. Goldsmith resented the acclaim with which Beattie's work had been received and was disingenuous enough to say so—and earn himself a Johnsonian sarcasm.[52] But when he visited Reynolds at his studio and found his friend at work on a canvas in which the figures of Hume and Voltaire, apparently representing atheism and falsehood, lay at Beattie's feet, he returned to the attack: 'It very ill becomes a man of your eminence and character, Sir Joshua, to condescend to be a mean flatterer, or to wish to degrade so high a genius as Voltaire before so mean a writer as Dr Beattie; for Dr Beattie and his book together will, in the space of ten years, not be known ever to have been in existence, but your allegorical picture, and the fame of Voltaire will live for ever to your disgrace as a flatterer.'[53] It was the voice of authority, and one imagines that Reynolds at least would not have been taken by surprise by that 'other' Goldsmith who, as it seemed to some of the members of the St James's club, revealed himself for the first time in *Retaliation*.

*

After his holiday at Barton Hall in January Goldsmith retreated to Hyde for a final onslaught on the *History of the Earth and Animated Nature*, probably revising and rearranging his verse portraits as a relaxation from the daunting task of getting the future contents of eight octavo volumes ready for the press. A Middlesex farmhouse was a less attractive proposition in a damp January and February than it had been in the summer months, but he deliberately kept himself at a distance from London, even to the extent of writing to Percy when he found a gap in his text and asking him to go to Brick Court to look up a reference for him.[54] He was presumably well advanced in his work when he came down to attend the meeting of the Club at the beginning of March at which he made an unsuccessful attempt to secure Gibbon's election.[55] On March 10th he was again at the Turk's Head, dining alone with Thomas Percy.[56] He was far from well. His dysuria was worse and accompanied now by a general feeling of malaise. At Brick Court on the afternoon of March 25th he was forced to take to his bed by a rapid pulse and violent headache. He prescribed two ounces of ipecacuanha wine for himself, but as the symptoms had not abated by the late evening he sent for his apothecary, William Hawes.[57]

*

Hawes was a gifted man who was later to acquire a medical degree in the course of a distinguished career. But for seventeen years his patient had lived out the pretence (or the fantasy) of being a qualified doctor, and it soon became evident to the mere apothecary that he had been summoned not so much to give advice as to listen to Goldsmith's own diagnosis of his ailment and to dispense the necessary drugs. Goldsmith appears to have been suffering from cystitis induced by a stone in the bladder and it was probably an infection of the kidneys arising from this complaint that caused his death.[58] The emphasis on fluids in accounts of his diet in his last years suggests that here he had found some relief from the dysuria, but the course of treatment he was now proposing for himself could hardly be expected to improve his condition. Hawes noticed that, despite the headache and a pulse rate of ninety, Goldsmith was not otherwise in a state of fever and ascribed his distress to a 'nervous affection'. Goldsmith agreed—perhaps with good cause—but although he tried to soften the effect of his directive by observing, a little patronisingly perhaps, "I like your mode of reasoning well," he insisted that the correct treatment would be a dose of Dr James's Fever Powders, which had seemed to pull him through his illness in the summer of '72. Hawes was in an embarrassing position. He would have liked to prescribe opiates rather than this mixture of antimony oxide and phosphate of lime which would act primarily as a cathartic, but Goldsmith, who not only laid claim to an academic knowledge of medicine but had given Hawes friendly encouragement in the founding of his charity for resuscitating apparently drowned or asphyxiated people was quite implacable in his determination to dose himself. For a while the two men humoured one another, though it became increasingly clear to Hawes both that Goldsmith's mind was made up and that there were some surprising gaps in his medical knowledge. Seeing that the problem was becoming one of protocol Hawes suggested that a qualified physician should be brought in. He mentioned Dr Fordyce, an old friend of Goldsmith's who since March 4th had been a member of the Club. But Goldsmith, perhaps feeling by this time that the situation threatened to develop into an exam like the awkward affair at the College of Surgeons, was not interested in this proposal and said that Fordyce would be in Gerrard Street, adding wistfully 'where I too should have been'.[59]

After half an hour Hawes departed having left some leeches to be applied to the forehead for the relief of the headache. He had by now decided that with or without the patient's consent Dr Fordyce must be consulted. But Goldsmith, still with his mind on Newbery's Good Samaritan, only awaited the apothecary's departure to despatch a messenger to the shop, where Hawes' assistant handed Fever Powders over the counter.[60]

Fordyce arrived in time to witness their first effects, which were as Hawes had predicted: violent purging and vomiting. These symptoms were to continue for eighteen hours. The next time Hawes saw him, the patient was exhausted and almost incapable of speech, though he managed to murmur that 'he wished he had taken Hawes' friendly advice' the previous night. This capitulation was only temporary. Goldsmith was a gambler who had had long years' experience of throwing good money after bad. In the afternoon he summoned the woman who looked after his clothes and laundry (she was the wife of the Middle Temple Porter, John Ginger, whose surname he had borrowed for *She Stoops to Conquer*) and asked her to sit with him.[61] Meanwhile the servant, John Eyles, went in search of more Fever Powders, this time from the Newbery warehouse, for Goldsmith had rallied sufficiently to convince himself that the previous evening's powders could not have been genuine. 'I am very poorly,' he replied to Mary Ginger's enquiry, but managed to add that if he had been given the right powders he would have been well by now. That evening, a nurse recommended by Mary was installed in the chambers.

Fordyce now regarded Goldsmith's condition as 'very grave' and suggested to Hawes that another physician, Turton, of whom Goldsmith had a high opinion, should be brought into consultation. But behind their backs Dr Goldsmith himself was still courageously standing by the regimen he had originally planned. He managed to eat a little chicken soup, and ordered his nurse to prepare a second dose, this time of the 'genuine' Powders.[62] These produced a repetition of the previous night's symptoms though in a milder form. At 8.00 on Sunday morning Hawes found him 'absolutely sunk with weakness', and now even Goldsmith's pathetic faith in his own medical skills seems to have wavered. He consented to see Turton and asked Hawes to order John Eyles to fetch him immediately.

During the day, there was a final burst of spirit from the man who had always lost at cards so sportingly. Having got Eyles to mix him a

final dose of Dr James's Fever Powders he ordered him to find
Hawes' bill and pay him off. It was quite obvious, Goldsmith now
insisted, that he was responsible for the unexpected course his
illness had taken. Unfortunately the bill (perhaps like many others)
could not be found. When the nurse reappeared for her night-duty
at six o'clock she was sent to fetch Maxwell, the apothecary opposite
St Dunstan's Church, whereupon there was a repetition on a
smaller scale of the original debate with Hawes. It was now Maxwell's turn to be alarmed by the doses Goldsmith wanted to prescribe for himself, though he acceded at last to the request for
'bark'. But after this last fling of the dice the patient admitted
defeat: he took a small piece of the nutmeg that Maxwell had sent
and 'after this he followed the advice of his Physicians'.[63]

The reformation had come too late, although it would be several
days before Goldsmith's friends were alerted to the fact that he was
dying. On Monday, Percy visited Brick Court and recorded no more
in his diary than that Goldsmith was 'ill of a fever'.[64] Throughout
Easter week in spite of the fact that he was sleeping badly, his
reason was clear and at times some of the old cheerfulness came to
the surface. Fordyce and Turton consulted twice daily, but there
was no rallying and Turton, like Hawes, came to the conclusion
that Goldsmith was in spiritual as well as physical distress. 'Is your
mind at ease?' he enquired. 'No,' the dying man replied, 'it is not'.
These were his last recorded words.

On the Saturday following Good Friday, readers of the *Public
Advertiser* would have found a sentence sandwiched between
accounts of a grounded ship and of a squire's son safely returned to
a rotten borough: 'We are extremely sorry to acquaint our Readers,
that the celebrated Dr Goldsmith now lies dangerously ill, and that
his Physicians have not the smallest Hopes of his Recovery.'[65] On
Easter Sunday, on the eve of his departure for the country, Thomas
Percy visited him for the last time, recording on this occasion that
he was 'dangerously ill'. The sick man lingered on into the early
hours of Monday morning. At 4 a.m. Maxwell the apothecary was
summoned and found him in violent convulsions. Three quarters of
an hour later Oliver Goldsmith was dead, at the age of forty-five
years and five months.

FOURTEEN

Aftermath

FOR YEARS Goldsmith had expended energy in maintaining a public image. Sickness had no part in this. It was an embarrassment, perhaps just as much so to his friends who would have found the gap between their exuberant Lord of Misrule and the exhausted and silent invalid too great to bridge. Horace Walpole may have been right when he claimed that they 'neglected him at last,;[1] but whether or not this was 'shameful' as he suggested, perhaps they themselves were in a better position than Walpole to judge. The last ten days of Goldsmith's life present a picture of isolation, but it may have been appropriate that, taking to his bed for the last time, he should have turned not to the men who were expecting him that evening in Gerrard Street but to someone on the fringe of his life, the laundress who responded to the request to come and sit with him.

The friends who had accepted Goldsmith's energetic self-parody and pursuit of the present moment as part of the background to their own existence were shaken to find that the dynamo had stopped. Burke wept when the news was brought to him. Reynolds was unable to find comfort even in his studio: 'Sir Joshua was much affected by the death of Goldsmith . . . He did not touch the pencil for that day, a circumstance most extraordinary for him . . .'[2] But within hours of Reynolds' entry into the Brick Court chambers where there were now affairs to be put in order, the spirit of comedy began to reassert itself.

The immediate reaction had been to plan a funeral in the Abbey to be financed out of public subscription.[3] The question of pallbearers and principal mourners was still being discussed when Reynolds brought this activity to a halt by announcing the full extent of the debts which until now had been a matter of conjecture. The effect of this revelation can be felt in a letter sent nine years later to Robert Chambers, now far away in Calcutta: 'Goldsmith died partly of a fever,' Johnson wrote, 'and partly out of anxiety, being immoderately and disgracefully in debt'.[4] Reynolds' estimate of £2,000 was a very large figure and whether it was because other friends adopted Johnson's severe attitude or because the funds from any subscription, public or private, might be more effectively deployed in reimbursing Edmund Bott, the plans for an Abbey funeral were abandoned. At 5 p.m. on Saturday, April 9th, a small group of men including William Hawes witnessed the burial in the graveyard on the north side of the Temple Church. Reynolds was represented by a clergyman nephew but no close friends were present. Hugh Kelly and one or two Temple residents mustered at the last moment were at the graveside.[5] Kelly, who had been mentioned rather ungraciously in the still unpublished *Retaliation* verses, was observed to shed tears. There had been one other gesture of sentiment. The Horneck sisters, recollecting themselves in the middle of a far more serious family crisis than the factitious episode in which they had involved Goldsmith the previous spring, sent a request for a lock of hair, and the coffin was reopened to oblige them.[6]*

The flurry of newspaper tributes and comment which the news of his death had unleashed made up for the apparent neglect shown at the funeral. There was a rush to advertise the posthumous works and to announce new editions of *The Vicar of Wakefield*, *The Traveller* and *The Citizen of the World*.[7] Even greater prominence was given to a dispute between William Hawes and Francis Newbery, the young man who had once listened to readings of *The Traveller* at Canonbury. Goldsmith's faith in Dr James's Fever Powders had got them both into trouble. Hawes was anxious to safeguard his medical reputation and Newbery the valuable patent which he had inherited from his father.[8]

---

*The absence on this occasion of Goldsmith's close friends seems extraordinary by twentieth century standards. The following account of a royal funeral, from Newbery's *Christian's Magazine* in 1766 may help to throw light on this apparent neglect:

> 'This evening the remains of his late royal highness prince Frederic William were interred. The pall was supported by the Lords Edgecumbe, Scarsdale, Boston and Beaulieu. The chief mourner, his grace the duke of Kingston, in a long black cloak ... The assistants to the chief mourner were the earls of Peterborough, Litchfield, Coventry, Ashburnham' etc. etc.

Again one notices the absence of the very people one might have expected to take part in the ceremony—in this case members of the royal family.

More comedy was provided by the launching of Johnson's epitaph two years later. 'But this is in Latin,' Goldsmith had exclaimed rather grudgingly when, competing with Johnson in the writing of an epitaph, he had been upstaged by the rapid composition of some elegiac hexameters.[9] Now, as Johnson presented the dignified tribute intended for Westminster Abbey, the friends silently echoed Goldsmith's words. But no-one had the courage to approach the author, and several notable men including Burke, Reynolds and Gibbon were reduced to adding their names to a round robin. Perhaps Johnson himself was amused: he received the petition with good grace but his unrecorded answer was probably the same as his dry comment to Goldsmith on that other occasion: 'Tis in Latin, to be sure'. He refused to give way. Although he had paid an eloquent tribute to Goldsmith as a master of English prose, he was not going to disgrace the walls of the Abbey with an epitaph in such a medium.[10]

*

If the epitaph created a problem, the biography produced endless muddle. Members of the Johnson circle were intensely aware of the need to leave records of themselves and of one another, and the year before Goldsmith's death Thomas Percy had assumed the role of official biographer by inviting Goldsmith to his rooms in Northumberland House and making notes on his early life and career.[11] When Maurice Goldsmith visited London shortly after his brother's death Percy asked him for help in gathering more material, and the immediate response was Catherine Hodson's letter. Far from relishing the possibilities which her communication revealed, Percy seems to have been all too anxious now to find an excuse for abandoning the project. This arrived in the form of the proposal that Johnson should produce a collected edition of Goldsmith's works, and perhaps with a sigh of relief Percy surrendered his own notes and other items of Goldsmith material in his possession.[12] Johnson, however, produced nothing, the immediate reason being that Thomas Carnan, Francis Newbery's partner, refused him permission to publish *She Stoops to Conquer* which was protected by copyright until 1788. It is less clear why Goldsmith's poems were not included in the *Works of the English Poets* planned by a consortium of thirty-five publishers who in 1777, commissioned Johnson to write a series of biographical prefaces.[13]

After Johnson's death in 1785 the biographical material returned to Percy, augmented by the few scraps that Johnson had gathered. Before it arrived Percy, now Bishop of Dromore in Ireland, had been discussing with Dublin publishers a scheme for a subscription edition of the *Works* with a biographical sketch which would correct the 'Innumerable Errors of Former Biographers'.[14] His intention was to help Maurice Goldsmith, but, with the pathetically thin sheaf of Goldsmith papers again in his possession, for a second time his enthusiasm waned. It would never return, for when in the seventeen-nineties, the idea of a *Collected Works* was again discussed and he was asked to contribute a Memoir, he delegated the responsibility to the Revd. Thomas Campbell. After Campbell had produced a piece of writing which he regarded as unsatisfactory, Percy made deletions, added comments of his own, and brought in yet another surrogate to tidy up this sketch of a man he had known intimately a quarter of a century before. One of Percy's most decisive actions was to put his pen through the letters M.B. which Campbell had inscribed on the title page of his manuscript.[15]

This thin, depersonalised account of Goldsmith, enlivened only by the first-hand anecdotes submitted by such Edinburgh acquaintances as Thomas Ellis and William Farr,[16] was a poor offering from a man who had once sat with his subject for an entire morning in a sparsely furnished room in Green Arbour Court, who had been present on the evening when Goldsmith and Johnson had met each other for the first time and experienced the pleasures of Gerrard Street when his friend was at the top of his form. But Johnson's failure to include Goldsmith amongst the other poets about whom he was writing in his last years seems even more regrettable. In his epitaph (which also omitted any reference to a medical degree) he had used glowing terms to acknowledge the achievements of the dead writer. Feeling guilty perhaps about his omission from the *Poets*, he paid another resounding tribute to literary talent when the time came to write about Parnell: 'The life of Parnell is a task which I should very willingly decline, since it has been lately written by Goldsmith, a man of such variety of powers, and such felicity of performance, that he always seemed to do best that which he was doing; a man who had the art of being minute without tediousness, and general without confusion; whose language was copious without exuberance, exact without constraint, and easy without weakness. What such an author has told, who would tell again? . . .' But he had still said nothing about his friend's remarkable personality and it is difficult to escape the impression that Goldsmith had fallen into disgrace with both his former travelling companions. Luckily some brief memoirs from writers who felt capable of describing the quixotic side of Goldsmith's nature while still preserving an over-all respect for him as a man were already in existence. Shortly after his death an anonymous *Life* had been brought out by the printer J. Swan, and Burke's decision to include an abbreviated version of this little pamphlet in his *Annual Register* for 1774[17] ensured its survival;* and a few years later the publisher T. Evans wrote a biographical preface for the 1780 edition of the *Poetical and Dramatic Works.*[18] Privately, of course, Reynolds had already produced his subtle and illuminating sketch. But remarks scattered through the pages of Boswell and Mrs Thrale show that Johnson's insights may have penetrated even deeper.

*

On April 27th 1773 Horace Walpole was pursuing his intermittent task of denigrating the Johnson set when he wrote: 'I have no thirst to know the rest of my contemporaries, from the absurd bombast of Dr Johnson down to the silly Dr Goldsmith, though the latter changeling has had bright gleams of parts, and the former had sense, till he changed it for words, and sold it for a pension'.[19] If it were not for the hint, conveyed in an apparently random word of abuse, *changeling*, it would be possible to dismiss this as an indication of one of Walpole's own blind spots. But the connotations of that resonant word reveal that Walpole's idea of Goldsmith's personality had a certain resemblance to Johnson's.

Johnson was a man of strong feelings. He wept at the sight of a child's grave, mourned a dead friend when one of the omelettes he had enjoyed was placed on the table and, within days of Goldsmith's death, was writing about 'poor dear Dr Goldsmith'. Yet he adopted

*Burke's attribution of the piece to 'G' led to the likely assumption that the writer, who had evidently come within close range of his subject, was William Frederick Glover.

a sceptical view of people's ability to go beyond the sphere of their own interests. 'Prithee, my dear, have done with canting,' he begged Hester Thrale when she spoke too effusively about a cousin she had never seen who had been killed in America; 'how would the world be worse for it, I may ask, if all your relations were at once spitted like larks, and roasted for Presto's supper?'.[20] He may simply have been hitting the same note when, on being informed by her that somebody had said 'Goldsmith likes Mr and Mrs Thrale vastly—he never abuses them', he shook her off again brusquely with 'No, but he would be glad to hear they were parted tomorrow Morning, never to meet more'. The fact, however, that he should have made a remark of the same order to another friend suggests that he was thinking specifically of a fundamental coldness in Goldsmith himself rather than in the human condition. 'Poor Dr Goldsmith!' Fanny Reynolds exclaimed one day. 'I am exceedingly sorry for him; he was every man's friend!'. 'No, Madam,' Johnson replied, 'he was no man's friend!'[21]

Although James Northcote, who recorded the remark, felt compelled to explain away its apparent harshness it seems almost certain that, here, Johnson the honest hater of woolliness and cant was making a dispassionate observation of the same failing that Walpole had hit upon in his choice of the word *changeling*: that Goldsmith beneath his kindness, his reckless charity and his desire to make people laugh at any price, suffered from a congenital and unnatural inability to feel. He himself had provided the clue to the absence of any strong personal ties in his life in Sir William Thornhill's realisation that no effort of good will can make up for the want of natural feeling: '. . . he now found that a man's heart must be ever given to gain that of another . . .'.

If this was Goldsmith's condition it was a crippling disability. Yet it would be a mistake to exaggerate its effects. If there was the possibility of compulsion and fantasy taking control of such a personality by filling the potential void created by an emotional impotence, it is also clear that Goldsmith had diagnosed his condition and, although there were times in his life when the destructive forces threatened to take over, he was capable of sustaining for long periods a successful fight against them. This was not simply a matter of giving away his blankets or rushing out to console a street singer. The intellect was deeply engaged in the contest, for whether it is in an argument with Johnson or a lucidly reasoned essay in the *Public Ledger*, he can be seen erecting mental barricades between himself and Coromandel. The signs of strain in the Reynolds portrait suggest that all this was achieved only by means of constant vigilance. Goldsmith's own surprising—and misleading —synonym for vigilance was 'dissipation', for it was the unreal world that had to be 'dissipated' in order to ensure continued access to the real.[22] Both daydreams and black depressions were kept at bay by means of surrendering himself to the present moment, whether it was by taking on Johnson at the Club, falling into the pond at Barton Hall or sifting through volumes of Buffon and Linnaeus at a farmhouse in Hendon. And in the meantime he had found a compensation for his disability. In that world of symbols below the level of consciousness which he was able to enter through his creative writing he found access to feelings which in actuality could be no more than simulated. Perhaps this is the reason why the writing of fiction or poetry quickly exhausted him.

Like the pock-marked little boy dancing relentlessly until the mocking fiddler was forced to admit defeat, Goldsmith as a man displayed the courage which has its roots in a chronic disability. Swaggering about the room in a ridiculous suit he created a happening, took people out of themselves. Ostensibly, he wanted to make the melancholy-eyed English laugh, but behind that there was another motive. 'The English in general,' he wrote in one of the 'Chinese Letters', 'seem fonder of gaining the esteem than the love of those they converse with . . .'[23] Though at the heart of his being there was an inability to respond other than by constantly renewed efforts of the will, he had set out to engage feelings which he himself found completely elusive. 'He had a very strong desire . . . to be liked . . .'.[24]

To be alone at the end of his life was a necessity, for once that constant, exhausting vigilance was relaxed there was no longer any safeguard against the compulsive side of his personality. The Oliver Goldsmith who accepted Hawes' arguments and then went on dosing himself with patent medicine is recognisably the man who had once run away to Cork, dreamed of becoming a nabob, and taken pleasure in being called 'Doctor'. He had nothing to do with the Goldsmith who had scored points off Johnson and who knew in his bones that he had done a good day's work after knocking a dozen lines of *The Deserted Village* into shape. In a sense, the man who at the end rejected reason and gambled his life away was the real Goldsmith. The other, the journalist who had given graceful expression to the liberal ideals of his age, the good-natured man whom children never forgot, was his own hard-won creation. He himself knew that the created image was fragile. Perhaps that was the message of the man in black, that *alter ego* of both the writings and the life: a reminder of tragic possibilities beneath the bustling activity and the jokes and the gaudy clothes. Amongst the card-tables, blue moreen chairs, lustres and mirrors that were dispersed when the chambers at 2 Brick Court were dismantled in 1774 was an incongruous item: a solitary picture. It was called '*The Tragic Muse.*'

Appendix

The departure from Arthur Friedman's dating of *The Vicar of Wakefield* perhaps demands more detailed treatment than has been given in Chapter VII. Asking the question whether or not Goldsmith had a completed book for Johnson to carry to Newbery in the late summer or early autumn of 1762, Professor Friedman comes to the conclusion that he had. Here of course he follows the most reliable version of the Bottle of Madeira story, Boswell's in the *Life of Johnson*:

> I received one morning a message from poor Goldsmith that he was in great distress, and, as it was not in his power to come to me, begging that I would come to him as soon as possible. I sent him a guinea, and promised to come to him directly. I accordingly went as soon as I was drest, and found that his landlady had arrested him for his rent, at which he was in a violent passion. I perceived that he had already changed my guinea, and had got a bottle of Madeira and a glass before him. I put the cork into the bottle, desired he would be calm, and began to talk to him of the means by which he might be extricated. He then told me that he had a novel ready for the press, which he produced to me. I looked into it, and saw its merit; told the landlady I should soon return, and having gone to a bookseller, sold it for sixty pounds. I brought Goldsmith the money, and he discharged his rent, not without rating his landlady in a high tone for having used him so ill.[1]

As Professor Friedman points out, the reference in Chapter 19 to a pro-government weekly, the *Auditor*, issued for the first time on July 15th '62 under the editorship of Goldsmith's friend Arthur Murphy, does not invalidate the novel's completion some time before October 28th (the date of Newbery's agreement with Benjamin Collins). It does imply, of course, that he was being very topical indeed and writing fast. But there are stronger grounds than this for believing that Goldsmith was still at work on his novel after 1763.

In June '64 John Newbery published the *History of England in a series of Letters from a Nobleman to his Son*, a compilation in which Goldsmith was naturally called upon to discuss two aspects of history which are dealt with in the novel, i.e. Saxon England and the Civil War of the preceding century. Two features of Goldsmith's working life have to be taken into account at this point. Although his first book and his creative works, the novel, the poems and the plays were undertaken independently, his compilations were always embarked upon *after* payment had been agreed with a publisher and usually after receipt of an advance. As for research, he was not a natural scholar with the leisure to read for the sake of reading, but a busy writer who would get up a subject for work on hand, like the *History of England* or, in the last years of his life, the *History of the Earth and Animated Nature*. Newbery's accounts for 1763 reveal that Goldsmith received two advances in that year on the *History of England*.[2] 1763, therefore, would seem to be a more likely date than 1762 for the start of this project. This would indicate that chapters 19 and 21 of *The Vicar of Wakefield*, with their references to the Civil War, and chapter 27 in which Dr Primrose alludes to Saxon attitudes to punishment in the course of his condemnation of the contemporary penal code, were written during or after 1763 (and therefore after an agreement was made with Newbery during a financial emergency in the late summer or early autumn of 1762).

Goldsmith was as reluctant to become involved in the newspaper battle which the Wilkes troubles touched off in 1762 as he had been to contribute to the trivial *Rosciad* debate the previous year. Yet, as Professor Friedman points out, Wilkes himself probably makes an appearance in Chapter 19 as the Mr Wilkinson who in the interests of Liberty would like to deny his opponents the right to speak their mind.[3] What had caused Goldsmith to break his silence?

The Wilkes press campaign against the ministry of the Earl of Bute seems to have impinged on Goldsmith's sphere of interest at two points. Besides being a monarchist in principle, he seems to have felt a measure of personal loyalty to George III, and the right time for a supporter of the King to overcome his reluctance to engage in polemics would have been in or after April 1763 when, with the resignation of Bute, Wilkes' campaign was proved to have been completely successful. At such a time supporters of the Ministry and of the Peace of Paris would have regarded the North Briton and its editor as grave threats to the constitution.

Goldsmith had a more personal reason for attacking the Wilkes and Liberty faction. In 1762 William Hogarth published a cartoon, 'The Times', in which Bute, as peace-maker, was portrayed in the act of manning a fire engine while his political opponents fed the blaze with copies of the *North Briton*. Retribution came in September in the form of the *North Briton* number 17 in which Hogarth—until now a friend of Wilkes—was savagely attacked both through his work and his private life. This was only the first shot in a long campaign to discredit Hogarth. He was assailed with cartoons, and in 1763 Wilkes' colleague, Charles Churchill, published his *Epistle to Hogarth*, a poem which opened the floodgates of the press against the unfortunate painter. Little is known about Goldsmith's friendship with Hogarth but it would have been in keeping for the man who habitually rushed to the aid of people in distress to break his silence some time between September '62 and the summer of '63 and show which side of the controversy he was on. But again it would be remarkable if Goldsmith had reacted sufficiently promptly to the attack on Hogarth in September '62 to have his Wilkinson chapter ready for Newbery to read before mid October.

The strongest evidence, however, for the sale of an incomplete manuscript comes not from the political events of these years but from a change of mood in the course of the novel which suggests a major break in its composition. Chapter 17 marks both a change of direction in the story, with the Vicar about to set off in search of Olivia, and a sudden change of tone in the writing which goes beyond the simple key-change dictated by the sad turn of events. Up to this point the book has been full of humour, sometimes directed against Primrose himself (as in the episode when Jenkinson, the confidence trickster, flatters him grossly as the author of the Whiston tracts and then cheats him out of his horse).[4] Much of it springs from his habit of seeing, and yet not quite seeing, how disgracefully his wife and daughters are behaving. With the conclusion of this chapter humour vanishes almost completely from the novel. With the exception of the last, when something of the old style returns as the Vicar tries to put his family into the right frame of mind for the wedding ceremony by reading them 'two homilies and a thesis of my own composing',[5] there are virtually no examples of the quiet, subliminal humour that one finds in the early chapters. In its place there are frequent sermons, for Primrose is made morally alert if not fluent by adversity. In these remaining fifteen chapters the opportunities for an ecclesiastical use of *thee* or *thou* are multiplied. Nothing illustrates the change of atmosphere so forcefully as the fact that on these occasions Primrose now speaks with absolute authority. In the earlier chapters, too, he had had occasion to dwell on moral issues, but these were always balanced by some absurdity or other to create an effect similar to Fielding's portrayal in *Joseph Andrews* of Parson Adams, the good man at large in a naughty world. Describing the evening spent at the cottage by the Squire and his two women friends, Primrose is delightfully unaware of his guests' true feelings:

> The two ladies . . . began a very discreet and serious dialogue upon virtue: in this my wife, the chaplain, and I, soon joined; and the 'Squire himself was at last brought to confess a sense of sorrow for his former excesses. We talked of the pleasures of temperance, and of the sun-shine in the mind unpolluted with guilt. I was so well pleased, that my little ones were kept up beyond the usual time to be edified by so much good conversation. Mr Thornhill even went beyond me, and demanded if I had any objection to giving prayers. I joyfully embraced the proposal, and in this manner the night was passed in a most comfortable way, till at last the company began to think of returning.[6]

But the pranks played on the captive Vicar in Chapter 27 are quickly brushed aside to allow him to get down to the task of saving souls:[3]

> But there was one whose trick gave more universal pleasure than all the rest; for observing the manner in which I had disposed my books on the table before me, he very dextrously displaced one of them, and put an obscene jest-book of his own in the place. However I took no notice of all that this mischievous groupe of little beings could do; but went on, perfectly sensible that what was ridiculous in my attempt, would excite to mirth only the first or second time, while what was serious would be permanent. My design succeeded, and in less than six days some were penitent, and all attentive.[7]

In the earlier part of the book the humour arose from the fact that Dr Primrose was only intermittently 'sensible' of the attempts made to undermine his authority; but now the reader is asked to feel a measure of indignation on his behalf.

I have suggested that Goldsmith ran into serious difficulties in his attempt to expand the *History of Miss Stanton* into a novel and that it was his recognition, rather late in the day, of the impossibility of allowing Primrose to fight a duel in the Stanton manner which caused a break in the book's progress in the course of Chapter 17. Could the very impossibility of staging the duel (originally intended to provide the climax of the novel) have given rise to the anti-duelling lobby which first makes itself felt at the end of this chapter? When Dr Primrose hears that Livy has eloped with Squire Thornhill his reaction is violent and he has to be restrained by Moses and Deborah (the latter acting perhaps a little out of character):

> I had by this time reached down my pistols, when my poor wife, whose passions were not so strong as mine, caught me in her arms. "My dearest, dearest husband," cried she, "the bible is the only weapon that is fit for your old hands now. Open that, my love, and read our anguish into patience, for she has vilely deceived us."—"Indeed, Sir," resumed my son, after a pause, "your rage is too violent and unbecoming. You should be my mother's comforter, and you encrease her pain. It ill suited you and your reverend character thus to curse your greatest enemy: you should not have curst him, villain as he is."—"I did not curse him, child, did I?" —"Indeed, Sir, you did; you curst him twice." — "Then may heaven forgive me and him if I did ..."[8]

From this moment duelling is frowned upon. In the course of George's narrative in Chapter 20 Sir William Thornhill strongly condemns the practice; and in the dénouement he lectures George again, this time for having challenged his nephew, 'an offence ... for which the law is now preparing its justest punishments'. Duelling, of course, was a common practice in Goldsmith's time, but it should be noticed in passing that it was more than usually a topic of conversation in November 1763 when a stomach wound received by Wilkes in a duel with the Princess Dowager's Treasurer prevented him from appearing in court to answer a charge of obscene libel.

The Bottle of Madeira story was clearly well known in its time, at least within and around the Johnson set, and once it had been incorporated in the *Life of Johnson* (1791) it was inevitable that Boswell's should become the definitive version. Publishing his *Life of Johnson* four years before Boswell, Sir John Hawkins stated that Goldsmith was working on his novel when he lived at Canonbury House, i.e. after December '62. (The year in which Hawkins might have been expected to have first-hand knowledge of Goldsmith's whereabouts and activities was 1764 since, from February onwards until Hawkins' quarrel with Burke, they were meeting regularly at that time as fellow members of the Club.) William Cooke, however, publishing his memoir of Goldsmith in the European Magazine for 1793—after the appearance of Boswell's *Life*—states that Goldsmith's novel was *finished* in Wine Office Court.[9] (Cooke himself, befriended by Goldsmith as a newcomer to London in the mid-sixties, appears to have been in Cork when Goldsmith was living at that address.

Boswell's massive authority depends more than anything else on his ability to convince one that whatever he witnessed or heard he recalled *in toto*. But he, of course, was as incapable as William Cooke of giving a first-hand account of the circumstances in which Goldsmith's manuscript was completed and sold, since he did not meet Johnson until at least eight months after the 'Bottle of Madeira' incident. Far from describing something that had happened the day before, he was obtaining his 'exact narrative' from Johnson some time after the event—and the reference to 'poor Goldsmith' suggests that he had waited until after Goldsmith's death, i.e. until twelve years had elapsed. By this time Johnson may already have given a more accurately remembered account of the incident to another friend.

In one particular Mrs Thrale's version is misleading if not dishonest. She included the story in her *Anecdotes of the Late Samuel Johnson* (1786) perhaps in order to reinforce her claim to an intimate knowledge of the great man, but as she herself did not meet him until nearly three years after the Wine Office Court affray, she is obviously wrong when she says that Johnson was in her house when he received Goldsmith's call for help. At one point, however, her version of the story has more credibility than Boswell's. Goldsmith, she writes, was 'fretting over a novel which *when done* was to be his whole fortune; *but he could not get it done for distraction.*[10] If an earlier and more accurate account has filtered down through this sentence, then the depression of the early part of 1762 (*'fretting over a novel'*) may be accounted for, and the artistic crisis ceases to be a conjecture based on an analysis of the novel itself. The qualification 'which when done was to be his whole fortune' seems to belong very much to Goldsmith's mental world.

In Boswell's version Johnson may well be telescoping certain facts. The manuscript was sold for £60, as he says, but to three publishers, not one, and the immediate crisis would probably have been resolved with an advance of only £20 (the figure given by Cooke).[11] Was his memory also taking a short-cut when he told Boswell that Goldsmith's novel was 'ready for the press'? If he had remembered this correctly, the question immediately presents itself: Why in that case had it not *gone* to the press? The virtue of Mrs Thrale's account of the incident is that the fairy-tale element which makes Boswell's unsatisfactory has been removed. It is simply too good to be true that the bailiffs should have arrived at the very moment when Goldsmith was tidying up the spelling and punctuation of a completed manuscript. There is more desperation than celebration in the Bottle of Madeira.

Finally the Percy *Memoir* deserves more credence than it has been given in this particular. As Katharine Balderston has shown,[12] Percy's informant here was Dr William Farr and one might be inclined to accept him as a reliable witness even if Goldsmith's personality had not already emerged so strongly from this episode in which he discusses the novel with his friend (see page 181 above). The point to notice here, of course, is that—besides undermining his own literary reputation so recklessly—Goldsmith was letting fall that he had been working on *The Vicar of Wakefield* two years before its publication date, i.e. in 1764.

APPENDIX

1 Boswell: *Johnson* I. 257.
2 Prior I. 479, 498.
3 *Works* IV. 103.
4 *Works* IV. 73.
5 *Works* IV. 182.
6 *Works* IV. 55–56.

7 *Works* IV. 148.
8 *Works* IV. 91–92.
9 *European Magazine* xxiv, p. 92.
10 Piozzi: *Anecdotes*, p. 99.
11 European Magazine xxiv, p. 92.
12 K. C. Balderston: *History and Sources of the Percy Memoir*, p. 57.

Notes

(References to Goldsmith's writings are to Arthur Friedman's *Collected Works of Oliver Goldsmith*, five volumes, Oxford 1966, e.g. '*Works* IV.88'. Wherever possible I have referred to Professor Friedman by name to acknowledge specific obligations to his prefaces and notes, e.g. 'Friedman, *Works* III. 188 n.2'.

References to Dr K. C. Balderston's preface and notes in *The Collected Letters of Oliver Goldsmith*, Cambridge 1928, are recorded in the same way.

References to Boswell's *Life of Johnson* are to G. B. Hill's edition, revised L. F. Powell, 1934-50, e.g. Boswell, *Johnson* II. 185).

Chapter 1 : THE PORTRAIT—AUGUST 21, 1766

1 Reynolds: Sitters' book, 1766.
2 Northcote.
3 Leslie.
4 *Survey of London*: St Anne's, Soho.
5 Leslie.
6 *Survey of London*, op.cit.
7 Paulson.
8 Malcolm.
9 Hazlitt, p. 40.
10 *Boswell on the Grand Tour*.
11 Paulson.
12 Edmund Burke : *Correspondence*.
13 Pares.
14 *Annual Register*, 1765.
15 Baker.
16 Leslie.
17 Hazlitt, p. 118.
18 Leslie.
19 J. T. Smith, p. 9.
20 *Connoisseur*, May 30, 1754.
21 Samuel Foote: *Taste*.
22 Ashton and Mackintosh.
23 Wyndham.
24 Oman.
25 Genest.
26 *Lloyd's Evening Post*, 24-27 January, 1766, quoted by Mossner.
27 Mossner.
28 R. H. Murray.

29 Boswell: *Johnson*, I. 317.
30 Charles Churchill: *The Ghost*.
31 Sherbo.
32 Welsh.
33 T. S. Ashton.
34 Grosley.
35 Chamberlain.
36 Malcolm.
37 Ibid, p. 392.
38 Chamberlain.
39 Malcolm, p. 357.
40 Quoted in *Mrs Cornely's Entertainments*, p. 6.
41 Jenner, *Time Was*.
42 *Connoisseur*, September 17, 1754.
43 Jenner, p. 27.
44 *Works* III. 47 (Weekly Magazine, 5th January, 1760).
45 Batey.
46 Glover, p. 15.
47 Colman: *Random Records*.
48 Friedman, *Works* II. xiv.
49 Pope: *Epistle to Dr Arbuthnot*, 1735.
50 Boswell: *Johnson*, I. 246.
51 Piozzi: *Anecdotes*, p. 112.
52 Ibid.
53 Northcote, I. 294.
54 Ibid, I. 326.
55 *Boswell's London Journal*.
56 *Boswell on the Grand Tour*, p. 82.
57 Boswell: *Johnson*.
58 Piozzi: *Anecdotes*, p. 128.
59 Pottle.
60 A. Sherbo (ed.) : *Mrs Piozzi's Anecdotes*, 1974.
61 Boswell : *Johnson*, I. 421.
62 Ibid, I. 411–415.
63 *Boswell on the Grand Tour*, p. 312.
64 Piozzi: *Autobiography*.
65 Hodgart.
66 Boswell: *Johnson*, II. 5.
67 Ibid, II. 235.
68 Thraliana, p. 80.
69 Reynolds, p. 42.
70 Forster.

Chapter 2 : THE DANCING BOY

1 Quoted by Patrick Murray, p. 185.
2 Prior, I. 7.

3 BM Add. Ms. 42517.
4 Prior, I. 8.
5 Goldsmith was probably mistaken when, writing to his brother in 1759, he claimed that Henry was 'seven or eight years older' than himself. The records of Trinity College Dublin, indicate that Henry was born in 1724 since, when he entered the College as a particularly able student in 1741, his age was given as seventeen. This was the age at which his father had begun his undergraduate career. Oliver was sixteen-and-a-half when he went to T.C.D. in 1745.
6 Letter from Robert Jones Lloyd of Elphin quoted in Mangin's *Essay on Light Reading* (1808). It is interesting to find that, although Thomas Percy accepted Goldsmith's word that he was born at Pallas and put this into his 1801 *Memoir*, in 1785 he believed that the birthplace was Elphin. In a letter to Malone, quoted by Katharine Balderston (*The History and Sources of Percy's Memoir*) he accuses Johnson of carelessness over the epitaph. Percy's syntax is curious but he evidently means to convey the fact that Elphin is the authentic birthplace: '[Johnson] gave a wrong place for that of his birth—*Elphin*, which is accordingly so sculptured in Westminster Abbey.' The Abbey inscription states, of course, that Goldsmith was born at Pallas. Amongst Percy's notes there is a letter to him from the Bishop of Elphin, written in 1798, stating that 'Both Oliver and his brother Henry were born at a House called Smith-Hill . . .'.
7 Prior, I. 16.
8 K. C. Balderston (ed.) *Letters* p. 29.
9 Prior, I. 94.
10 Quoted by Patrick Murray, p. 186.
11 *Letters* p. 163 (Mrs Hodson's Narrative).
12 *Works* II. 113–114.
13 Burgess Mss, County Library, Athlone.
14 Lecky.
15 Ibid.
16 Weld, p. 337 ff.
17 Burdy.
18 Burke: *Reformer* no. 7, 10. 3. 47/48., quoted by Samuels.
19 Quoted by Lecky.
20 Burdy.
21 Maxwell.
22 Gaussen.
23 Robert Bell, quoted in *Goldsmith's Poems* (ed. Newell), 1811.
24 *Letters* p. 165.
25 *Works* II. 458–465.
26 *Percy Memoir*.
27 *Letters*, p. 165.
28 G. S. MacGeough-Bond (*Family Patchwork*, 1928) states that Catherine's daughter, Anne, died in 1778 aged 35.
29 Prior, I. 49.
30 *Letters* p. 162.

Catherine Hodson states that Henry was nineteen when he married, i.e. in 1743 the year in which he won his scholarship at Trinity. She was probably telescoping events, however, when she implies that he left college at this point: '. . . he marrying a Lady he liked left the College and retired to the Country . . .'. Prior follows Catherine here: 'Finding residence in college no longer eligible, the advantages of his scholarship were sacrificed: he retired, as appears from the college books, to the country . . .'. The T.C.D. records do not, however, indicate such an absence. Henry took the Easter examinations in 1744 and won another premium, although in July he was cautioned for 'neglect of morning lectures and Greek lectures'. His B.A. was conferred at the summer commencements held in July 9th, 1745, a month after Oliver matriculated. It might be inferred from these facts that Henry's marriage had been as 'private' as Catherine's and that after it he continued to reside in college on a normal undergraduate basis.

31 Cox.
32 *Letters* p. 46.
33 Prior, I. 51.
34 Cox. (Goldsmith wrote about Carolan in the British Magazine, *Works* III. 118).
35 Kirkpatrick.

Chapter 3 : FICTION

1 Campbell: *Philosophical Survey.*
2 Kirkpatrick.
3 Ibid.
4 Burdy.
5 Barrington.
6 Walsh.
7 Kirkpatrick.
8 Prior, I. 89.
9 Ibid, I. 75.
10 B.M. Add. Ms. 42516.
11 Kirkpatrick.
12 *Letters*, p. 169.
13 Kirkpatrick.
14 Samuels.
15 Ibid, p. 204.
16 Ibid, p. 251.
17 Prior, I. 94.
18 Victor.
19 Oman.
20 The Champion, 1741, quoted in Oman.
21 Burke: *Reformer*, February, '47/'48.
22 Victor.
23 *Letters* p. 170.
24 Though obscured by the eccentric style, this seems to be implied by Mrs Hodson: '. . . the Bishop asked his age which he told was twenty and

his Lordship said he must wait till he was of a proper age for it was thought
his Lordship designd his uncles living for another as he was that time an
an old man . . .'

25 *Works* II. 115.
26 Cox.
27 Cradock; Davies.
28 Forster.
29 Prior; *Letters* p. 14.
30 *Letters* p. 10.
31 Prior.
32 *Letters* p. 12.
33 *Letters* p. 29.
34 *Letters* p. 171.
35 Northcote, I. 211.
36 *Works* II. 115.
37 Prior, I. 5.
38 *Letters* p. 177.

Chapter 4 : THE PHILOSOPHER WHO CARRIES ALL HIS GOODS
ABOUT HIM

1 *Letters* p. 3.
2 *Letters* p. 28.
3 *Letters* p. 6.
4 Forster p. 34.
5 *Letters* p. 6.
6 Arnot.
7 Graham.
8 *Letters* p. 25.
9 Bellamy.
10 Graham.
11 Forster p. 34.
12 *Letters* p. 13.
13 Boswell: *Johnson*, II. 436.
14 Graham.
15 Cox.
16 *Letters* p. 17.
17 *Letters* p. 11.
18 *Letters* p. 7.
19 *Letters* p. 16.
20 Cox.
21 *Letters* p. 5.
22 *Letters* p. 9.
23 Campbell: B.M. Add. Ms. 42517.
24 *Letters* pp. 20–21.
25 *Works* IV. 260.
26 *Letters* p. 24.
27 *Letters* p. 22.

28 Thomas Nugent.
29 *Works* I. 309.
30 *Works* II. 235.
31 *Works* II. 104.
32 *Works* IV. 261.
33 *Percy Memoir*, p. 33.
34 Ibid, pp. 34–36.
35 *Works* I. 284.
36 Prior, I. 425.
37 *Works* IV. 120.
38 Smollett: *Travels*, I. 85.
39 Glover, p. 6.
40 *Works* IV. 118.
41 Campbell: B.M. Add. Ms. 42517.
42 *Works* IV. 248.
43 *Letters* p. 26.
44 *Percy Memoir*, p. 36.

Chapter V : Empiric

 1 Turberville.
 2 Ibid.
 3 Public Advertiser, 19th August, 1756.
 4 *Percy Memoir*.
 5 Ibid.
 6 Prior, I. 215.
 7 *Percy Memoir*.
 8 Katharine Balderston identifies William Farr in the *History and Sources of the Percy Memoir*, p. 56.
 9 Prior, II. 104.
10 *Percy Memoir* p. 45.
11 *European Magazine*, volume liii. 373.
12 Cooke: *European Magazine* xxiv. 92.
13 *Works* IV. 107.
14 Forster.
15 George; Malcolm.
16 Knapp.
17 Cleland's *Memoirs of a Woman of Pleasure* was issued under the imprint 'G. Fenton'. On examination, Ralph Griffiths claimed that his brother, Fenton Griffiths, had approached him with Cleland's manuscript and asked him to advise whether or not it should be published. Fenton Griffiths is not otherwise known as a publisher (see L. M. Knapp, *The Library* XX, 1940, page 207 n. 2). A letter from him dated 1785 is preserved amongst Ralph Griffiths' correspondence in the Bodleian. (Ms. Add. C 89, f. 132). He was then living in Tavistock and was writing to tell his brother that he had recently married a widow, the daughter of a clergyman. Although the main point of the letter is to assure his brother of the lady's impeccable social

connections, he remembers to add: '. . . but what is still of greater consequence, she is of unspotted reputation and morals, religious, tho' not
gloomy, on the contrary chearfull, and of the most pleasing and gentle
manners . . .'. The brothers '*Fanny Hill* days were clearly well behind them.

18 Gentleman's Magazine lix (1789), p. 180, quoted by L. M. Knapp.
19 Burdy, p. 104.
20 *Percy Memoir*, p. 60.
21 Nangle.
22 Friedman, *Works* I. 5 n.2.
23 *Works* I. 11.
24 *Works* I. 82.
25 *Works* I. 77.
26 *Works* I. 18.
27 *Works* I. 35.
28 *Works* I. 91.
29 *Works* I. 27.
30 *Works* I. 116.
31 Percy. B.M. Add Ms. 42516.
   Percy deleted the word 'thraldom' from the original note and substituted
   'situation'.
32 Boswell: *Johnson*; I. 105.
33 *Percy Memoir*, p. 45.
34 Balderston: *Letters* pp. xxx-xxxiii.
35 *Letters* p. 50.
36 *Works* V. 37.
37 Friedman, *Works* V. 38 n.1.
38 *The Battle of the Reviews.*
39 If B. C. Nangle is correct in his identification of the 'S.T.L.' (sometimes
   'T.L.' or 'L.') of Griffiths' annotated copy of the *Monthly Review*, then one
   of the members of the reviewing team was a baronet, Sir Tanfield Leman.
   Born in 1714, he had inherited the title (but no money) from a cousin. He
   was a physician but it was probably a need of money, as Nangle supposes,
   that led him to write for the *Monthly*, where his particular interest seems
   to have been books about spas and health resorts. He contributed articles
   from August '53 until his death in 1762. Several of them were published
   during Goldsmith's time on the Review.
40 Balderston, *Letters* p. 51 (note).
41 *Letters* p. 26.
42 *Letters* p. 31.
43 John Evans—who suggests that Milner may have died between Goldsmith's
   two bouts of school-teaching.
44 *Letters* p. 50.
45 *Letters* p. 40.
   As Katharine Balderston point out, the allusions in the letter to Bryanton
   indicate that Goldsmith's thoughts had already turned in the direction of
   China.
46 *Letters* p. 35.

P

47 *Letters* p. 40.
48 Prior, I. 282.
49 I am indebted to Mr E. H. Cornelius, Librarian of the Royal College of Surgeons, for this interpretation of the significance of Goldsmith's rejection by the College.
50 *Letters* p. 56.
51 *Works* I. 118–135.
52 Boswell: *Johnson*, II. 40.
53 Samuel Foote: *The Author*, 1757.
54 Welsh. Elizabeth Kent indicates that Collins eventually acquired complete control, leaving Griffiths as editor. By the 1780s Griffiths had succeeded in buying back the Review from Collins.)
55 *Works* I. 146–162.
56 Straus.
57 *Letters* p. 66.
58 *Works* I. 318.
59 *Works* I. 305.
60 *Works* I. 319.
61 Straus.
62 *Works* I. 328.

Chapter 6 : An Amphibious Creature

1 Irving.
2 *Percy Memoir*, p. 61.
3 George.
4 *Works* I. 430.
5 *Works* II. 278.
6 Davies.
7 *Works* I. 385.
8 *Works* III. 58.
9 Prior, I. 328.
10 *Works* II. 132.
  T. Evans recounts a similar incident in Goldsmith's life in the preface to *Goldsmith's Poetical and Dramatic Works* (1780), p. xv. In this account it is Hamilton who pays off the creditor.
11 Gaussen.
12 Jones.
13 *Works* I. 449.
14 *Connoisseur*, 6th June, 1754.
15 Cooke: *European Magazine* xxiv, p. 260.
16 *Connoisseur*, 28th March, 1754.
17 *Works* III. 15.
18 *History of the Robin Hood Society*.
19 *Connoisseur*, 18th July, 1754.
20 Campbell: *English Diary*, 21st March, 1775.
21 *Works* I. 14.

22 *Works* I. 415.
23 *Works* III. 19.
24 Thomas Turner, p. 14.
25 *Works* II. 52.
26 Melville, p. 176.
27 Ibid.
28 Johnsno's *Idler*, no. 19, 19th August, 1758.
29 Welsh.
30 *Reading Mercury*, March 28, 1748.
31 1,612,800 doses had been sold by 1764. Bruce Dickins: *Life & Letters*, vol. ii, no. 8 (1929).
32 *The Midwife* (Newbery).
33 *The Lilliputian Mazgaine* (Newbery).
34 Welsh; Straus.
35 Devlin.
36 *Works* I. 444.
37 *Works* II. 20.
38 Colman: *Terrae Filius*.
39 *Connoisseur*, 24th April, 1755.
40 Ibid, 6th November, 1755.
41 *The World*.
42 *Works* II. 64.
43 *Works* II. 144.
44 Prior.
45 *Works* II. 25.
46 *Works* II. 27.
47 *Works* II. 62.
48 *Works* I. 370.
49 *Works* II. 367.
50 *Works* II. 187–190.
51 *Works* III. 1.
52 Goldsmith's debt to Marivaux was first pointed out by A. Lytton Sells.
53 *Works* III. 136.
54 *Works* II. 307.
55 *Works* II. 288.
56 *Works* II. 372.
57 *Works* II. 344.
58 *Works* II. 473.
59 Davies.
60 Goldsmith alludes to 'the ingenious Mr Hogarth' in *Polite Learning*, published April 4th, 1759. Hogarth died in October 1764.
61 Hogarth.
62 Percy *Memoranda* B.M. Add. Ms. 32, 336.
63 *Percy Memoir*, p. 62.
64 Piozzi: *Anecdotes*, p. 157.
65 Boswell's *London Journal*, quoted by Hodgart.
66 Piozzi: *Anecdotes*, p. 128.

67 Piozzi: *Autobiography*, p. 23.
68 *Works* II. 445.
69 Piozzi: *Anecdotes*, p. 147.
70 *Works* II. 221.
71 Goldsmith's evangelical strain can be felt in *A Sublime Passage in a French Sermon* (III. 49) and *Some Remarks on the modern manner of Preaching* (III. 150).
72 Northcote, II. 161.
73 *Works* II. 278.
74 Piozzi: *Anecdotes*, p. 94.
75 Ibid, p. 89.
76 Boswell: *Johnson* I. 358.
77 Ibid, I. 363.
87 Piozzi: *Anecdotes*, p. 157.

Chapter 7 : GOOSE-PIE AND GOOSEBERRIES

1   *The Critical Review*, March 1761.
2   *Works* II. 436.
3   *Works* III. 33.
4   *Works* II. 421.
5   Prior, I. 383.
6   Hogarth published his cartoon, *The Times I*, in the summer of 1762. Bute was portrayed attempting to extinguish the flames of war with a fire engine while Pitt applied a bellows to the blaze and the Duke of Newcastle hurried forward with a wheelbarrow containing a fresh supply of combustibles— copies of the *Monitor* and the *North Briton*. (See Hogarth: *Anecdotes of Himself*.) Wilkes and Churchill retaliated by pillorying Hogarth in the North Briton, no. 17).
7   *Works* II. 213.
8   *Works* IV. 98.
9   *Works* III. 197.
10 *Works* II. 246.
11 *Works* III. 128.
12 *Works* III. 132.
13 *Works* II. 229.
14 *Works* II. 296.
15 *Works* II. 475.
16 Piozzi: *Anecdotes*, p. 99.
17 *Letters* p. 60.
18 *Works* IV. 18.
19 *Works* IV. 22.
20 *Works* III. 183.
21 *Works* III. 189.
22 *Works* III. 193.
23 Goldsmith had revealed his interest in anatomy by enrolling himself in Munro's class at Edinburgh in two consecutive years. His love of botanising is revealed in his letter to John Bindley on July 12th, 1766:

'. . . I entirely agree with the gentleman that his fields are very green, but when he asserts they are as green as grass there I humbly think he wants precision. There are several kinds of grasses Mr Chairman, Linnaeus gives us a catalogue of twenty-five kinds, and all these kinds are green, but then Sir on the other hand there are several kinds of herbs that are not green at least in the flower. There is the crowfoot for instance there are several kinds of crowfoots, one of them is called geranium Roberti and this has a yellow blossom, and great quantities of this grows in the fields in question so that it gives them a yellowish greenish sort of a look so that they are not quite as green as grass . . .'
(Balderston: *New Goldsmith Letters*. Dr Balderston has a note on Geranium robertianum, a plant unknown to botanists.)

24 Friedman, *Works* V. 341 n.; Prior I. 415.
25 Land Tax books at the Guildhall Library. In 1760, Prudence Carnan was assessed at £3.12.0 (with personal estate at 10 shillings). At Green Arbour Court, Daniel Butler had been assessed in the same year at £1.16s.).
26 Balderston: op. cit.
27 B.M. Add. Ms. 42517. Percy scored out the entry in Campbell's manuscript notes. An attempt to read behind the circling pen reveals:
'. . . but not satisfied with his fees as a physician, he removed from his [room?] in the Temple to lodgings in Wine Office Court, Fleet Street. His landlady was, it seems, a [   ] or milliner, whose daughter, a smart girl, had made some impression on Goldsmith's [   ] heart, at least she honestly thought she had made a conquest of the Irish doctor. But whether this sage matron d[eemed]? him (destitute as he was of business in his profession and obliged to scribble for support) [unworthy?] of her daughter's pains [   ] but certain it is that she pressed him so sorely for the rent, which he was unable to pay, that he had no alternative but matrimony or a jail. What encouragement the virgin [milliner?] gave or whether our distressed poet would have preferred the soft chains of Hymen to the vile durance of a prison must for ever now be secret. [End of the erased passage.] The fact is, as Mrs Piozzi relates it, he was rescued from both by the friendly interposition of Dr Johnson.'
28 Boswell: *Johnson*, I. 416.
29 *The Card* by the Revd. John Kidgell, 1755. (Welsh).
30 Friedman, *Works* IV. 4–7.
31 London Evening Post, 20–23 August, 1748.
32 Glover, p. 12.
33 The informant is identified by Katharine Balderston: *History and Sources of the Percy Memoir*, p. 57.
34 J. Taylor.
35 Cooke: *Memoirs of Foote*.
36 Boswell: *Johnson* III. 141.
37 Critical Review, June, '73 (quoted by Friedman: *Works* IV. 10).
38 *Works* IV. 9–11.
39 *Monthly Review*, May '66 (*Works* IV. 9).

Chapter 8 : COMEDY OF HUMOURS

1 Prior, I. 459–60; 461–2.
2 Welsh.
3 Percy: *Letters* vol. I. 38.
4 *Works* V. 229–276.
5 Friedman, *Works* V. 290 n.i.
6 Andrews: *The Eighteenth Century*.
7 George.
8 It is unlikely to have been more than this. Goldsmith's grudging reference to the commercial rewards of painting in the preface to *The Traveller* (December '64) suggests that they were not yet the firm friends they would later become.
9 *Percy Memoir*, p. 72.
10 Boswell: *Johnson* I. 165.
11 Ibid, I. 246.
12 Reynolds.
13 Malone.
14 Northcote.
15 Reynolds' Sitters' Books seem to have been used occasionally to remind him of social engagements. The Memoranda for 1766 indicate that he had regular appointments for dinner (i.e. 4 p.m.) at the Crown and Anchor and on Thursdays at the Star and Garter.
16 *Boswell in Search of a Wife*, p. 318.
17 Hawkins.
18 A formal note from Johnson to Goldsmith dated the 23rd of April 1773 indicates that Goldsmith was chairman on the evening when Boswell's membership was proposed. (Johnson: *Letters*). Percy's Memoranda record that on 26th March 1773 Lord Charlemont gave a reading of the 'Bristol Poetry' (i.e. Chatterton).
19 Malone, p. 81 ff.
20 *Survey of London: St Anne's Soho* ('The Royal Academy').
21 Ibid.
22 Hawkins, quoted in G. B. Hill's edition of Boswell's *Johnson*.
23 Boswell: *Johnson*, V. 108.
24 Mme d'Arblay: *Diary* i.65.
25 Boswell: *Johnson*, I. 480.
26 Ibid, I. 480.
27 Frances Reynolds (G. B. N. Hill).
28 Reynolds, pp. 46–48.
29 Northcote, I. 250.
30 Prior, II. 128.
31 Cooke: *European Magazine* xxiv, p. 261.
32 Walpole: Letter to Mason, 8th October, 1776.
33 Frances Reynolds (G. B. N. Hill, p. 273).
34 *Thraliana*, p. 83.
35 *Works* II. 109.

36 Hawkins.
37 Boswell: *Johnson*, I. 417.
38 Malone, p. 30.
39 Boswell: *Johnson* I. 405.
40 Ibid, II. 120.
41 Ibid, I. 445.
42 Ibid, III. 252.
43 Ibid, I. 408.
44 Ibid, II. 118.
45 Ibid, II. 14–15.
46 Ibid, II. 42.
47 Ibid, I. 164.
48 J. L. Clifford.
49 Boswell: *Johnson*, II. 100.
50 Ibid, II. 218–219.
51 Piozzi: *Anecdotes*, p. 129.
52 Boswell: *Johnson*, IV. 22.
53 Ibid, II. 225.
54 Joseph Farington (Malone).
55 Northcote.
56 Malone, p. 30.
57 John Courteney (quoted by Northcote); Malone.
58 Glover.
59 Reynolds.
60 Malone, p. 55.
61 Reynolds, p. 53.
62 *Works* IV. 251–2.
63 *Critical Review*, December ,'64, quoted by Friedman, *Works* IV, 236.
64 *Works* IV 238–239.
65 Percy: *Memoranda*.
66 Quoted by Friedman, *Works* IV. 237.
67 *Works* IV. 247.
68 Northcote.
69 Boswell: *Johnson*, II. p. 85.
70 *Works* IV. 313.
71 Claud Nugent.
72 Ibid, p. 76.
73 Ibid.
74 Gaussen.
75 Ibid.
76 Ibid.
77 *Percy Memoir*, p. 66.
78 Walpole: Letter of October 28, 1752 to Sir Horace Mann.

Chapter 9 : THE GOOD-NATURED MAN

1 Friedman, *Works* IV. 209.

2 LeBlanc, II. Letter 82.
3 Page.
4 *Thraliana*, p. 168.
5 Ibid, p. 153.
6 Bellamy.
7 Wilkinson.
8 *The World*, Vol. 3 (1754).
9 *Letters* p. 100.
10 Malcolm.
11 Grosley.
12 Bellamy.
13 Stone.
14 *Connoisseur*, 21st November, 1754.
15 Burnim.
16 *Works* III. 210.
17 *Works* I. 389.
18 *Works* III. 54.
19 B.M. Add. Ms. 42515.
20 *Thraliana* p. 83.
21 Leslie.
22 *Thraliana*, p. 177.
23 Clifford.
24 Bryant.
25 *European Magazine*, xxiv, p. 422.
26 Ibid, p. 338.
27 Ibid, p. 339.
28 Ibid.
29 Taylor, p. 107 ff.
30 Cooke: *European Magazine* xxiv, p. 95.
31 Northcote, I. 168.
32 *Thraliana*, p. 83.
33 *Boswell on the Grand Tour*, p. 312.
34 An inventory of the contents of the Brick Court chambers is reproduced by Prior (II.579 ff.).
35 Reynolds: Sitters' Books. On April 18th 1766 Reynolds notes an appointment with 'Mr Bott, no. 19 Paper Building'.
36 Hazlitt.
37 Cooke: *European Magazine* xxiv, p. 94.
38 Prior states that Bott's chambers 'adjoined' Goldsmith's. According to the Inner Temple records, Bott sold his chambers there on November 10th 1769. This was presumably the date of his move to Brick Court in the Middle Temple.
39 Prior, II. 191.
40 Ibid, II. 203.
41 Ibid, II. 198–200.
42 *Percy Memoir*, p. 72.
43 *Thraliana*, p. 475.

44 There were two methods whereby Goldsmith, if he had been in possession of a Dublin M.B. could have converted it into the Oxford equivalent. He could have read aloud before Congregation a testimonial from his own university; or, by becoming temporarily a member of an Oxford college, he could have had his application, supported by evidence of the degree, forwarded to the Vice-Chancellor by the college. In either case the co-operation of T.C.D. would have been required. Whichever method was employed, Goldsmith's Oxford friends would have expected him to produce the necessary evidence of his Dublin M.B. and, in time, their suspicions would no doubt have been aroused by his failure to do so..

45 Thomas Davies, quoted by Forster, p. 330.

Chapter 10 : EXILES

1 George.
2 Malcolm.
3 Grosley.
4 *Mrs Cornely's Entertainments.*
5 Sutherland.
6 Postgate.
7 Malcolm; *Connoisseur.*
8 Godwin believed that Goldsmith was the author of *Goody Two Shoes* (1766). There are certainly echoes of his style and social themes here, as in other of Newbery's children's books. But the case for Newbery himself as author is stronger as the story contains a real-life incident which had been used as the starting point for an article in *The Midwife* (1750–53).
9 As Friedman suggests, Wilkes himself is probably behind the 'Mr Wilkinson' episode in *The Vicar of Wakefield*. Goldsmith's hostility towards certain features of mercantilism can be felt in *The Citizen of the World* (*Works* II. 72 and 454).
10 Noorthouk.
11 George.
12 J. T. Smith.
13 *Lloyd's Evening Post*, 5–7 March, 1770.
14 *Thraliana*, p. 151.
15 Watson.
16 Campbell: *English Diary*, 5th April, 1775.
17 *European Magazine*, xxv.
18 T. S. Ashton.
19 Boswell: *Johnson*, III. 56.
20 *Works* III. 147.
21 *Works* III. 154.
22 Prior, II. 422.
23 Ibid, II. 231–4. William Hodson came to London in 1770. See p. [269].
24 23rd May, '73—Percy: *Memoranda.*
25 *Thraliana*, p. 81.
26 *Percy Memoir*, p. 68.

27 Murphy: *Gray's Inn Journal*, no. 21.
28 Malcolm.
29 Campbell: *English Diary*, 30th April 1775.
30 *Works* IV. 149.
31 *Boswell on the Grand Tour*, p. 215.
32 *Boswell in Search of a Wife*, p. 342.
33 Grosley.
34 *Connoisseur*, 15th May, 1755.
35 J. T. Smith.
36 *Mrs Cornely's Entertainments*.
37 Ibid, p. 13.
38 Ibid, p. 10.
39 Northcote.
40 Prior, II. 353.
41 Hawes.
42 Batey.
43 *Works* III. 195.
44 Batey.
45 Burke: *Reformer*, 10.3.48 (quoted by Samuels).
46 Friedman, *Works* IV. 275.
47 *Works* IV. 285.
48 *Works* IV. 289.
49 *Works* IV. 298.
50 Oman. It took Garrick a week to travel from Dublin to London in May, 1746.
51 *Letters* p. 62.
52 *Letters* p. 14.
53 *Works* IV. 292.
54 Balderston, *Letters* p. xx.
55 *Works* IV. 293.
56 *Works* IV. 297.
57 *Works* IV. 299.
58 Byron: *Childe Harold's Pilgrimage*, canto I.
59 *Works* IV. 298.
60 *Works* IV. 302.
61 *Works* IV. 294.
62 *Works* II. 136.
63 *Works* IV. 300.
64 T. Evans.
65 Cooke: *European Magazine* xxiv, p. 171.
66 Prior, II. 322.
67 Friedman, *Works* IV. 278.

Chapter 11 : Nobody With Me At Sea But Myself

1 Reynolds, Boswell, William Cooke and Richard Pilkington are some of the visitors who arrived unannounced.
2 Prior, II. 511.

3   Cooke: *European Magazine* xxiv, p. 259.
4   Prior, II. 357.
5   Prior, II. 192.
6   Northcote.
7   Cooke: *European Magazine* xxv.
8   Ibid.
9   Cooke: *European Magazine* xxiv, pp. 259–60.
10 *Works* II. 203.
11 *Works* IV. 115.
12 Prior.
13 *Letters* p. 101.
14 Balderston, *Letters* p. xxi.
15 Prior, II. 420.
16 Prior, II. 346.
17 Cradock; Percy's letter to Lord Dacre (B.M. Add. Ms. 32, 329, f. 72).
18 Johnson: Letter to Bennet Langton, 24.10.70 (Chapman).
19 Hickey.
20 *Thraliana*, p. 83.
21 Reynolds, p. 48.
22 *Letters* p. 91.
23 *Letters* p. 95.
24 Prior, II. 288.
25 *Works* IV. 385.
26 Prior, II. 379.
27 *Works* IV. 384.
28 Irving.
29 Glover, p. 15.
30 *Thraliana*, I. 331.
31 Reynolds, p. 49.
32 *Letters* p. 13.
33 Prior, II. 193.
34 *Works* II. 450.
35 Balderston: *New Goldsmith Letters.*
36 *Thraliana*, p. 83.
37 Leslie.
38 Reynolds, p. 42.
39 *Works* IV. 30.
40 Boswell: *Johnson* I. 201.
41 Laetitia Hawkins.
    At first sight this story of a publisher who follows Goldsmith to spy on him
seems apocryphal. But the *Bath Chronicle* for Thursday March 14th 1771
indicates that Goldsmith had recently arrived in Bath in company with
Colonel *and Miss Nugent*. Peggy Nugent (1724–94) was the Colonel's aunt.
The story may throw light on the financial difficulties of Goldsmith's last
years when he was socially in demand. As Cooke suggested, it was his association with people of wealth that led him to live beyond his means. In Miss
Hawkins' story Goldsmith has gone to Thomas Cadell for an advance on his

History of England. (This was published in August 1771). She claims that he was given the £500 he demanded and that Cadell, out of curiosity over his need for such a large sum, followed him to Hyde Park Corner and saw him climbing into a post-chaise in company with a 'lady of easy virtue'. £500 was, in fact, the payment that Goldsmith was to have received on the publication of his *History*, and Cadell, with Thomas Davies and Andrew Millar, was one of the publishers. Whether or not Miss Nugent was a 'lady of easy virtue' must remain an open question, as must the fate of the £500 (if indeed Goldsmith left Cadell's premises with this large sum of money). Was he in the grip of another fantasy in which the gaming tables of Bath played a prominent rôle?

42 Cooke: *Life of Foote*.
43 Quoted by T. Evans, xxv.
44 Walpole, Letter to Mason, 7th April, 1774.
45 Sir Raymond Crawfurd. In order to sustain a theory which is extrapolated from very meagre evidence, Crawfurd gives Prior as his authority for the statement that 'Goldsmith had permanently damaged his health by his dissipated life when a student at Edinburgh'. This interpretation of Prior seems unwarranted.

    I have not been able to discover the contemporary significance of 'purple fever'. Crawfurd seems to have inferred that a purple rash was present at the time of death, but this is not exclusively associated with venereal disease.

46 *Works* IV. 300.
47 *Works* II. 221.
48 Balderston, *Letters* p. 96 n.
49 *Letters* p. 84.
50 Meyerstein.
51 Cunningham: Walpole's *Letters* vii. 339.
52 B.M. Add. Ms. 35,350 f. 41.
53 Percy's *Memoranda* reveal that the Club were discussing Chatterton at their Friday meetings in March and April 1773:
Friday March 26: . . . Lord Charlemont read the Bristol poetry . . .
Friday, April 16: . . . Mr Garrick produced Chatterton's letters . . .
Saturday, April 17 . . . Went with Dr Goldsmith and Mr Jones to inquire after the house where Chatterton died . . .
54 See note 41 above.
55 Claud Nugent.

Chapter 12 : HODGE

1 *Letters* p. 102.
2 Prior, II. 332.
3 T. S. Ashton.
4 Boswell: *Johnson*, II. 182.
5 Prior, II. 334.
6 *Letters* p. 111.
7 Ingalls.

8 Balderston, *Letters* p. 115 n.
9 Page.
10 St James's Chronicle, 3–6 April 1773.
11 Kenrick: *A Lecture on the Perpetual Motion.*
12 *Thraliana*, pp. 104–105.
13 Northcote, I. 127.
14 Ibid.
15 Davies.
16 *Works* V. 207.
17 *Works* V. 208.
18 Kenrick reprinted these lines as a footnote to *Love in the Suds.*
19 In the preface to *The Perpetual Motion* Kenrick wrote that he had 'Occasion-ally misemployed' himself in 'tagging rhimes, translating novels and scribb-ling comedies' solely in order to raise money to promote his scientific researches.
20 Kenrick referred to Griffiths in his *Review of Dr Johnson's New edition of Shakespeare* (1765) and at the same time hinted at his intention of founding a Review of his own:
 'I must own indeed that the *Monthly Review,* from its regularity in coming to town for so many years, full or empty, hath obtained the reputation of being one of the most respectable stage-coaches on the high road of Par-nassus; but Mr G———h, (that is, Mr Gee-ho, the driver) will give me leave to tell him, that, if he continues to detain his passengers such a con-founded while at Turnham Green, clogging his wheels so cursedly with the coom [sic] of dullness, to make them run smooth, some other Jehu, on the same road, will infallibly set up a post-coach with steel springs, that will beat him hollow.' Griffiths had recently bought a large villa at Turnham Green. Kenrick's own review, the *London Review of English and Foreign Literature,* on which he was assisted by his son, William Shakespeare Kenrick, was not established until 1775.
21 Kenrick: *The Old Woman's Dunciad.*
22 Kenrick: *Review of Johnson's Shakespeare,* p. 67 n.
23 D.N.B.: *Kenrick.*
24 Cooke: *European Magazine* xxiv, p. 171.
25 Garrick: *Letters* p. 688.
26 Oman.
27 Garrick Correspondence, Dyce Collection, Victoria and Albert Museum Library.
28 *Morning Chronicle,* July 2, 1772, quoted by G. B. N. Hill.
29 Oman, p. 324.
30 Piozzi: *Anecdotes,* p. 117.
31 *Letters* p. 116. (Prior's conjectured dating is January 1773).
32 Cumberland.
33 *Letters* p. 117.
34 Hickey, vol. 1.
35 Watson; Piozzi: *Autobiography,* p. 257.
36 In the agreement of 13th June, '69 (B.M. Add. Ms. 42515 f. 57) Goldsmith

promises to 'write and compile' a History of England within two years. Significantly, payment is to be on delivery of the Ms. The History was published in August '71.

37 Prior, II. 432.

38 Ibid, II. 417.

39 Ibid.
Whether completed or not, this Ms. disappeared. Robert Southey was the first to notice, in *Omniana*, that an anonymous novel, *The History of Francis Wills* translated into French, had been attributed by its Dutch publishers to 'l'auteur du Ministre de Wakefield'; this novel takes up some of Goldsmith's themes (in particular his attack on the penal code in chapter 27 of *The Vicar of Wakefield*), but it is a wretched performance with no sign of the irrepressible charm which Goldsmith's writings manifested even when produced at pressure and with the sole intention of making money. For arguments against Goldsmith's authorship of this work, see C. B. Suits, *Who Wrote The History of Francis Wills?*, *Philological Quarterly*, xliii, 2 April 1964.

40 *Works* IV. 337.

41 Balderston, *Letters* pp. xxxiii–xxxvii.

42 Gaussen indicates that Percy called on Goldsmith on September 21st and found him very ill in bed. He called again on October 4th.

43 Prior, II. 354.

44 Cooke: *European Magazine* xxiv p. 173.

45 Prior, II. 388.

46 Friedman, *Works* V. 89 n. 5.

47 Prior, II. 425.

48 B.M. Add. Ms. 42515.

49 Northcote, I. 286.

50 Cumberland.

51 Barton.

52 Oman.

53 *Percy Memoir*, p. 72.

54 Nicoll: *History of the English Drama* (1750–1800).

55 *Works* V. 102.

56 *Works* III. 213.

57 Conflicting contemporary accounts of *Piety in Pattens* suggest (1) that Foote's actors became puppet-masters, and (2) that they themselves imitated the wooden gestures of puppets. The following extracts from the *General Evening Post* for March 6–9 1773 indicate that the second view is correct:
'On Saturday noon Mr Foote's theatre was opened . . . for the rehearsal of his attempt to revive the Primitive Puppet Show. A very genteel and numerous audience were present . . . The sentimental Comedy of the *Handsome Housemaid* or *Piety in Pattens* (in which two new songs are introduced, and sung by a *Jewell* of a puppet) was performed in a manner more regular and perfect than before . . .
'Punch is introduced, and a dialogue ensues between him and Mr

Foote ... The performer who filled the character of Punch is a Mr Hutton
who never appeared on the stage before, and whose principal fault seemed
to be the want of action ...'
    Evidently both Jewell and Hutton had metamorphosed themselves into
puppets.
58 Cooke gives a round figure of £500 for the total receipts from *The Good-
Natured Man*, but this included the sale of the publishing rights. Consulting
the Covent Garden Ledger, Dr Balderston found that Goldsmith's actual
profit from the three benefit performances of *She Stoops to Conquer* was
£502.18s.6d.
59 Cumberland.
60 Northcote.
61 Cooke: *European Magazine* xxiv, p. 173.
62 Ibid.
63 Oman.
64 Friedman, *Works* V. 92.
65 *The Monthly Review*, April 1773, quoted by Friedman, *Works* V. 95.
66 Friedman, *Works* V. 93.
67 Quoted by Prior, II. 404.
68 *Works* V. 103.
69 Cooke, *European Magazine* xxiv, p. 173.
70 *Letters* p. 126.
71 Barton, p. 237.
72 *Letters* p. 127.
73 Walpole: Letter to the Countess of Upper Ossory, 27th March, 1773.
74 *Works* V. 172.
75 Walpole: Letter to the Countess of Upper Ossory, 14th December, 1773.
76 Quoted by F. W. Hilles: Reynolds' *Portraits*, p. 25.

Chapter 13 : BETWEEN THE COMIC AND THE TRAGIC MUSE

1 D.N.B.: *William Woodfall.*
2 *Percy Memoir*, p. 103.
3 Cradock, I. 233.
The Hornecks' attitude is conveyed by the fact that when Cradock himself
visited the publisher, Evans, he argued that the lampoon 'had cut off
Dr Goldsmith from the society of one of the most friendly houses that he
had ever frequented'.
4 T. Evans, xx.
5 B.M. Add. Ms. 42516 f. 68.
6 B.M. Add. Ms. 32336.
7 B.M. Add. Ms. 42516.
8 Ibid.
9 T. Evans, xxii.
10 Boswell: *Johnson*, II. 210.
11 Ibid, II, 222.
12 G. B. N. Hill, II. 223.
13 Boswell: *Johnson*, II. 236.

14 Goldsmith's sensitive response to literature is illustrated by an anecdote in Northcote's *Life of Reynolds*:
'One day Dr Johnson and Dr Goldsmith meeting at Sir Joshua's table, the conversation turned on the merits of that well known tragedy, Otway's *Venice Preserved*, which Goldsmith highly extolled, asserting, that of all tragedies it was the one nearest in excellence to Shakespeare; when Johnson, in his peremptory manner, contradicted him, and pronounced that there were not forty good lines to be found in the whole play: adding, "Pooh! what stuff are these lines: 'What feminine tales hast thou been listening to, of unaired shirts, catarrhs, and tooth-ache got by thin soled shoes?'" "True," replied Goldsmith, "to be sure that is very like Shakespeare."'

15 *Works* I. 449.
16 *Works* III. 213.
17 Boswell: *Johnson*, II. 232.
18 Northcote, I. 329.
19 Taylor.
20 Cradock.
21 Boswell's first duty was naturally to Johnson and Goldsmith's remarks are only recorded when they throw light on the main issue. Even so, there are indications of this kind, other than the remark which showed that he had a keen ear for Shakespearean verse (see note 14 above). It might be possible to read into his admiration for Burke's ability to 'wind into a subject (Johnson II. 260) an awareness of the limitations of Johnson's Augustan prose style, while in his argument with Johnson about compatibility and friendship (Johnson II. 181) the point of departure is his refusal to follow Johnson in a belief in the absolute power of reason.
22 Prior, II. 459.
23 *Thraliana*, p. 80.
24 Johnson: *Letters* 5th July, 1774.
25 Cradock, I. 302–305.
26 Goldsmith, Arthur Murphy and Edmund Burke.
27 Boswell: *Johnson*, II. 257.
28 *Thraliana*, p. 82.
29 Boswell: *Johnson*, II. 231.
30 Ibid, II. 256.
31 Ibid, II. 260.
32 *Thraliana*, p. 84.
33 Piozzi: *Anecdotes*, p. 70.
34 Dr Kippis, who told this story, said that this was 'the last, or nearly the last' of Goldsmith's dinner parties. Goldsmith was being lionised from March 15th onwards and, as Boswell indicates, receiving many invitations to dinner. It is therefore unlikely that he himself gave up entertaining until the summer. Johnson intended to leave London on August 6th.
35 Prior, II. 511.
36 Cradock.
37 *Works* III. 183.
38 Taylor.

39 John Evans.
40 Prior, II. 218.
41 Friedman, *Works* V. 341 n.1.
42 Davies, II. 150.
43 Cradock, I. 235.
44 Baker.
45 Mary Horneck informed James Northcote that Goldsmith 'read to her several chapters of a novel in manuscript which he had in contemplation; but which he did not live to finish, now irrecoverably lost.' (Hazlitt, p. 169 ff).
46 See page [291].
47 Samuels.
48 Quoted by Friedman, *Works* IV. 343.
49 B.M. Add. Ms. 36596 f. 74.
50 Cooke, *European Magazine* xxiv, p. 174.
51 *Works* IV. 353; 357.
52 *Thraliana*, p. 82.
53 Northcote, I. 299.
54 Cradock, IV. 285.
55 Garrick: *Letters* p. 923.
56 Percy: *Memoranda*.
57 Hawes.
58 I am indebted to Mr James Kemble, Ch.M., F.R.C.S., for the opinion that Goldsmith suffered from a stone in the bladder. He writes: 'This would cause cystitis followed by an ascending infection to the kidneys resulting in pyelo-nephritis and pyo-nephrosis, with final failure of kidney function and uraemic convulsions. The trouble thus beginning with a stone in the bladder, ended with death in uraemic toxaemia.' In this diagnosis it is possible to find reasons both for Goldsmith's diet in his last years, with an emphasis on liquids (which would have eased his symptoms) and for the occasions on record when he absented himself abruptly from social gatherings. As Mr Kemble has shown in his study of Judge Jeffreys (*Idols and Invalids*, 1933), in a man of very different temperament the same complaint produced far worse results than Goldsmith's display of bad temper at the Dilly brothers' house in May 1773.
59 Hawes.
60 *Public Advertiser*, 29th April, 1774.
61 Ibid.
62 Ibid.
63 Ibid.
64 Quoted by Gaussen, p. 169.
65 *Public Advertiser*, 2nd April, 1774.

Chapter 14 : AFTERMATH

1 Letter to Mason, 7th April 1774.
2 Northcote, I. 324.
3 *Percy Memoir*, p. 115.

4 Johnson: *Letters* (19th April, 1783).

5 Cooke: *European Magazine* xxiv, p. 258.

6 Hazlitt, p. 169.
   The Hornecks were preoccupied with their brother's affairs. Captain Charles Horneck had been staying with a brother-officer, Mr Scawen, at the beginning of the month when his wife eloped with their host. The story immediately circulated that Scawen had been put up to this by the regiment who had even gone so far as to raise a subscription for him with the intention of rescuing Horneck from his *mésalliance* with a nymphomaniac. Reynolds and Burke came to the family's support, Burke having to break the news to Charles that his wife and best friend had absconded.
   During the divorce proceedings Mrs Charles Horneck made an unconvincing attempt to discredit her chambermaid's evidence by saying that on an evening when the bedroom door was found to be locked Mr Goldsmith, as well as Mr Scawen, was inside the room with her on her husband's invitation. (Forster).

7 *Public Advertiser*, April 19th, 22nd, 26th and 27th, 1774.

8 Hawes: *Public Advertiser*, April 29th, May 4th and 7th, 1774.

9 Frances Reynolds (G. B. N. Hill, p. 294).

10 Boswell: *Johnson*, III. 85.

11 Balderston: *History and Sources of the Percy Memoir*.

12 B.M. Add. Ms. 42515 and 42516.

13 *The Traveller* was also a Newbery publication, but as it had been published in 1764 it was only protected until 1778. The *Works of the English Poets* was published in 1779. *The Deserted Village*, published by William Griffin, was protected until 1784, but Griffin made no objection in 1780 when Carnan, Newbery, Lowdnes, Kearsley and Evans included the poem in their *Poetical and Dramatic Works of Dr Goldsmith*.

14 Balderston: op. cit.

15 B.M. Add. Ms. 42517.

16 Balderston,: op. cit.

17 *Annual Register*, 1774 ('Characters', pp. 29–34).

18 See note 13 above. (This was not the Evans of Paternoster Row whom Goldsmith had attacked.)

19 Letter to the Revd. William Cole, 27th April, 1773.

20 Piozzi: *Anecdotes*, p. 81.

21 Northcote, I. 328.

22 *Works* II. 189.

23 *Works* II. 30.

24 Reynolds, p. 42.

Bibliography

MANUSCRIPT SOURCES

British Museum

Add. Ms. 42,515 : Correspondence from Goldsmith's desk, March–April 1773.
" " 42,516 : Notes made by Thomas Percy in preparation for his Memoir.
" " 42,517 : Campbell's *Life*, with erasures etc. by Percy.
" " 32,336 : Memoranda of Bishop Percy, 1753–1811.
" " 35,350
   f. 41 : Letter from Lord Hardwick to Goldsmith on the subject of the Chatterton poems and Goldsmith's projected visit to Bristol in 1771.
" " 32,239
   f. 72 : Letter from Percy to Lord Dacre about the 'Rowley' Manuscripts.

Royal Academy Library
Sir Joshua Reynolds' Sitters' Books (1764–1774)
The Bodleian
Ms. Add. C.89 : Ralph Griffiths' Correspondence.
Victoria and Albert Museum
Forster/Dyce Collection of Garrick's letters.

Early Biographies and Biographical Sketches of Goldsmith

(William Glover ?) : *Life*, printed for J. Swan, London 1774 (referred to in the Notes as 'Glover').
'G' : in the Annual Register for 1774, under 'Characters', pp. 29–34 (a shortened version of the 'J. Swan' sketch).
T. Evans. Preface to the *Poetical and Dramatic Works*, published by Carnan, Newbery, Lowndes, Kearsley and Evans, London 1780.
(William Cooke). Dr Goldsmith. European Magazine xxiv, August–October 1793.
Thomas Percy : *Memoir* in Volume I of the *Miscellaneous Works*, Cadell and Davies, London 1801.
John Evans. Preface to *The Poetical Works of Oliver Goldsmith*. (London 1804).*
James Prior : *Life*, two volumes, London 1837.

*Evans draws heavily on William Cooke.

Other Printed Sources

Anon. The Battle of the Reviews. (London 1760).

Anon. (T. MacKinlay?). Mrs Cornely's [sic] Entertainments. (Blackburn/ Bradford (?) 1840).

Anon. Histoire de Francis Wills. (Amsterdam/Rotterdam 1773).

Anon. History of the Robin Hood Society (1764).

Anon. Low Life. (1764).

A. A. Andrews. The Eighteenth Century. (London 1856).

A. A. Andrews. History of British Journalism. (London 1859).

Hugo Arnot. History of Edinburgh. (London 1779).

Geoffrey Ashton & Iain Mackintosh. Catalogue to The Georgian Playhouse (Arts Council exhibition, 1975).

John Ashton. Chap Books of the Eighteenth Century. (Reprinted, Seven Dials Press, 1969).

T. S. Ashton. An Economic History of England in the Eighteenth Century. (Methuen 1955).

T. H. Baker. Records of the Seasons. (London 1911).

K. C. Balderston. A Census of the Manuscripts of Oliver Goldsmith. (New York 1926).

— History and Sources of Percy's Memoir. (Cambridge 1926).

— New Goldsmith Letters. (*Yale University Library Gazette*, 39, 1964).

Margaret Barton. David Garrick. (Faber 1948).

Jonah Barrington. Personal Sketches of his own Times. (London 1827–32).

G. F. Barwick. Some Magazines of the Eighteenth Century. (*Bibliographical Society Transactions*, vol. x, 1910).

Mavis Batey. Oliver Goldsmith: an Indictment of Landscape Gardening, *Furor Hortensis*, ed. P. Willis, (Elysium Press Edinburgh 1974).

H. J. Bell. *The Deserted Village* and Goldsmith's Social Doctrines. (P.M.L.A. 59).

George Anne Bellamy. Apology. (2nd edition, London 1785).

Isaac Bickerstaffe. Love in a Village, *The British Theatre*, ed. Inchbald. (London 1824).

J. B. LeBlanc. Letters on the English and French Nations. (London 1747).

Boswell, James: Life of Samuel Johnson, (ed.) G. B. Hill, revised Powell (1934–50).

Boswell's London Journal.

Boswell on the Grand Tour, (ed.) F. Brady and F. A. Pottle. (Heinemann 1955).

Boswell in Search of a Wife, (ed.) F. Brady and F. A. Pottle. (Heinemann '57).

Edmund Bott. A Collection of Decisions of the Court of King's Bench upon the Poor Laws. (London 1773).

Robert E. Brittain. Christopher Smart in the Magazines. (The Library XXI).

D. C. Bryant. Burke and his Literary Friends. (St Louis 1939).

Samuel Burdy. Life of Philip Skelton. 1792. (Oxford 1914).

Edmund Burke. Correspondence, (ed.) Thomas W. Copeland. (Cambridge 1958).

Frances Burney. Early Diary, 1768–78, (ed.) A. R. Ellis. (London 1889).

K. G. Burnim. Eighteenth Century Theatrical Illustrations. (*Theatre Notebook* 14,1960).

G. H. Bushnell & E. R. M. Dix. Dictionary of Printers and Booksellers. (London 1932).

Thomas Campbell. A Philosophical Survey of the South of Ireland. (London 1777).

—Diary of a Visit to England in 1775, (ed.) S. Raymond. (Sydney 1854).

A. H. Cash. Lawrence Sterne. (London, 1975).

H. Chamberlain. A Complete History and Survey of London. (London 1770).

Sir William Chambers. A Dissertation on Oriental Gardening. (London 1772).

Charles Churchill. Poetical Works. (London 1804).

Sir Ernest Clarke. Medical Education and Qualifications of Oliver Goldsmith. (*Proceedings of the Royal Society of Medicine*, Vol. 7.ii., 1913).

Sir George Clark. History of the Royal College of Physicians. (Oxford 1964).

J. L. Clifford. Young Samuel Johnson. (Heinemann 1955).

A. S. Collins. Authorship in the Days of Johnson. (Holden, London 1927).

George Colman. Terrae Filius. (London 1763).

— & Bonnell Thornton. The Connoisseur. (*Harrison's British Classics*, London 1786).

George Colman the Younger. Random Records. (London 1830).

William Cooke. Hugh Kelly, *The European Magazine* xxiv & xxv (London 1793/4).

— Paul Hiffernan, *The European Magazine* xxv (London 1794).

— Memoirs of Samuel Foote. (London 1805).

M. F. Cox. The Country and Kindred of Oliver Goldsmith. (*Journal of the National Literary Society of Ireland*, I, 1900).

Joseph Cradock. Literary and Miscellaneous Memoirs. (London 1828).

R. S. Crane. New Essays of Oliver Goldsmith. (Chicago 1927).

Sir Raymond Crawfurd. Oliver Goldsmith and Medicine. (*Proceedings of the Royal Society of Medicine*, London 1914).

Alexander Cruden. The Adventures of Alexander the Corrector. (London 1754).

Richard Cumberland. Memoirs. (London 1806).

Thomas Davies. Life of Garrick. (London 1780).

Christopher Devlin. Poor Kit Smart. (Hart-Davis, London, 1961).

J. C. Dibdin. Annals of the Edinburgh Stage. (Edinburgh 1888).

L. Dickins & M. Stanton. An Eighteenth Century Correspondence. (London 1910).

(ed. G. Eland) The Shardeloes Papers of the Seventeenth & Eighteenth Centuries. (Oxford 1947).

John Forster. Life of Goldsmith. 5th edition. (London 1877).

John Galt. The Lives of the Players. (London 1831).

David Garrick. Letters, (ed.) D. M. Little & G. M. Kahrl. (Oxford, 1963).

A. C. C. Gaussen. Percy, Prelate and Poet. (London 1908).

John Genest. Some Account of the English Stage. (Bath 1832).

Dorothy George. London Life in the Eighteenth Century. (Kegan Paul 1925).

Oliver Goldsmith. Collected Works, (ed.) Arthur Friedman (Oxford 1966).

— Letters, (ed.) Katharine C. Balderston. (Cambridge 1928).

— A History of England in a Series of Letters from a Nobleman to his Son. (London 1764).

— A History of the Earth and Animated Nature. (London 1774).

— Plutarch's Lives abridged from the Original Greek. (London 1762).

H. G. Graham. Social Life in Scotland in the Eighteenth Century. (London 1906).

A. Graves & W. V. Cronin. A History of the Works of Sir Joshua Reynolds. (London 1899).

James Greig. The Diaries of a Duchess. (Hodder & Stoughton 1926).

Joseph Haslewood. The Secret History of the Green Rooms. (London 1793).

William Hawes. An Account of the late Dr Goldsmith's Illness. (London 1774).

Sir John Hawkins. Life of Samuel Johnson. (London 1787).

Laetitia Hawkins. (ed.) F. H. Skrine: Gossip about Johnson et Alia. (London 1926).

William Hazlitt. Conversations of James Northcote. (London 1830).

William Hickey. Memoirs. (ed.) A. Spencer. (London 1913).

G. B. N. Hill. Johnsonian Miscellanies. (Constable, 1966).

M. J. C. Hodgart. Samuel Johnson. (Batsford 1962).

Anecdotes of William Hogarth by himself. (London 1833).

Ludvig Holberg. A Journey to the World Underground. (Salisbury 1742).

G. V. A. Ingalls. Some Sources of *She Stoops to Conquer*. (*P.M.L.A.* 44,1929).

Washington Irving. Tales of a Traveller. (London 1834).

— Oliver Goldsmith. (London 1849).

Charles Jenner. London Eclogues. (London 1772).

Samuel Johnson. Letters, (ed.) R. W. Chapman, (Ocxford 1952).

C. E. Jones. Smollett Studies. (New York) 1970.

Hugh Kelly. The Babler. (London 1767).

— Memoirs of a Magdalen. (London 1767).

William Kenrick. Falstaff's Wedding. (London 1751).

— The Old Woman's Dunciad. (London 1751).

— Pasquinade. (London 1753).

— A Review of Dr Johnson's new edition of Shakespeare. (London 1765).

— A Lecture on the Perpetual Motion. (London 1771)

— Love in the Suds. (London 1772).

E. Kent. Goldsmith and his Booksellers. (Ithaca, N.Y., 1933).

T. P. C. Kirkpatrick. Goldsmith in Trinity College and his Connection with Medicine. (*Irish Journal of Medical Science*, 1929).

L. M. Knapp. Ralph Griffiths, Author and Publisher. (The Library 20, 1940).

— Tobias Smollett. (Princeton 1949).

Charles Knight. Shadows of the Old Booksellers. (London 1865).

W. E. H. Lecky. A History of Ireland in the Eighteenth Century. (London 1892).

R. Leslie & T. Taylor. Life and Times of Sir Joshua Reynolds. (London 1865).

A. O. Lovejoy. The Chinese Origins of a Romanticism. (*Journal of English and Germanic Philology*, 1933).

E. L. McAdam (ed.) Johnson's Diaries, Prayers and Annals. (Yale 1958).

J. P. Malcolm. Manners and Customs of London. (London 1810).

Edmond Malone. Some Account of the life of Sir Joshua Reynolds, 5th ed. (London 1819).

Edward Mangin. Essay on Light Reading. (London 1808).

Dorothy Marshall. English People in the Eighteenth Century (Longmans 1956).

C. E. Maxwell. Country and Town in Ireland under the Georges. (Dundalk 1949).

Robert D. Mayo. The English Novel in the Magazines. (Evanton 1962).

Lewis Melville. Tobias Smollett. (London 1926).

E. H. W. Meyerstein. Life of Thomas Chatterton. (London 1930).

Miss Milner. Anecdotes of Goldsmith, *The European Magazine*, cxi. (London 1808).

J. F. Molloy. The Romance of the Irish Stage. (London 1897).

The Monthly Review. (London 1749–1845). For Ralph Griffiths' annotations, Bodleian, Per. 3977 d.190.

Edward Moore (ed.) The World. (London 1754–1757).

E. C. Mossner. Life of David Hume. (Nelson 1954).

F. A. Mumby. The Romance of Bookselling. (London 1910).

Arthur Murphy. Gray's Inn Journal, Collected Edition (London 1766).

Patrick Murray. The Riddle of Goldsmith's Ancestry. (*Studies*, Summer 1974).

Robert H. Murray. Edmund Burke. (Oxford 1931).

Sir Lewis Namier. England in the Age of the American Revolution. (Macmillan 1930).

B. C. Nangle. The Monthly Review. (Oxford 1934).

John Newbery (publisher). The Little Pretty Pocket Book. (London 1744).

— The Circle of the Sciences. (London 1745).

— The Midwife. (London 1751–1753).

— The Lilliputian Magazine. (London 1752).

— The Twelfth Day Gift. (London 1767).

John Nichols. The Works of William Hogarth. (London 1835).

John Nichols. Literary Anecdotes. (London 1812).

Allardyce Nicoll. History of English Drama, 1700–1750. (Cambridge 1925).

— History of English Drama, 1750–1800. (Cambridge 1927).

George Nobbe. The North Briton. (New York 1939).

James Northcote. Life of Sir Joshua Reynolds. (London 1819).

J. Noorthouk. History of London. (London 1773).

Claud Nugent. Memoirs of Robert, Earl Nugent. (London 1898).

Thomas Nugent. The Grand Tour, 2nd edition (London 1756).

Carola Oman; David Garrick. (Hodder and Stoughton 1958).

E. R. Page. George Colman. (New York 1935).

R. Pares. George III and the Politicians. (Oxford 1953).

R. Paulson. William Hogarth. (Yale 1971).

Thomas Percy. Letters, (ed.) Nichol Smith *&* C. Brooks. (Yale 1944).

H. L. Piozzi. Autobiography, Letters and Literary Remains, (ed.) A. Hayward. (London 1861).

— Anecdotes of the late Samuel Johnson. (Oxford 1974).

—Thraliana, (ed.) K. C. Balderston. (Oxford 1942).

Raymond Postgate. That Devil Wilkes. (London 1930).

F. A. Pottle. James Boswell, the Earlier Years. (Heinemann 1966).

Peter Quennell (ed.) John Cleland's *Memoirs of a Woman of Pleasure*. (Putnam, New York).

Sir Joshua Reynolds. Portraits, (ed.) F. W. Hilles. (Heinemann 1952).

James Ralph. The Case Against Authors. (London 1758).

William Rider. Lives and Writings of Living Authors. (London 1762).

S. Roscoe. John Newbery and his Successors. (Five Owls Press 1973).

A. P. Samuels. The Early Life of Edmund Burke. (Cambridge 1923).

Robert Seitz. The Irish Background to Goldsmith's Thought. (P.M.L.A. 52).

A. Lytton Sells. Les Sources Françaises de Goldsmith. (Paris 1924).

A. Sherbo (ed.). Johnson on Shakespeare. (Yale 1968).

Christopher Smart. Poems. (London 1791).

J. T. Smith. A Book for a Rainy Day. (London 1845).

Tobias Smollett. The Adventures of Peregrine Pickle. (London 1751).

— Travels through France and Italy. (London 1766).

G. W. Stone. The London Stage, 1660–1800. (Illinois 1969).

Ralph Straus. Robert Dodsley. (London 1910).

C. B. Suits. Who wrote *The History of Francis Wills?* (Philological Quarterly 43, 1964).

Survey of London, (general editor), F. H. W. Sheppard.

L. S. Sutherland. Edmund Burke and the First Rockingham Ministry, *Essays in Eighteenth Century History*, (ed.) R. Mitchinson, 1966.

George Taylor. Theories of Acting in the Age of Garrick.

John Taylor. Records of my Life. (London 1832).

Ralph Thomas. Deathless Lady. (The Colophon, Autumn 1935).

M. F. Thwaite. The Little Pretty Pocket Book. (London 1966).

(ed.) A. S. Turberville. Johnson's England. (Oxford 1933).

Thomas Turner. Diary, (ed.) F. M. Turner. (Bodley Head 1925).

B. Victor. History of the Theatres of London and Dublin. (London 1761).

John Wain. Samuel Johnson. (Macmillan 1974).

T. G. Wainewright. Essays and Criticisms, (ed.) W. C. Hazlitt. (London 1880).

J. E. Walsh. Ireland Sixty Years Ago. (Dublin 1847).

Horace Walpole. Letters, (ed.) Paget Toynbee. (London 1905).

J. Steven Watson. The Reign of George III, *Oxford History of England*. (Oxford 1960).

Isaac Weld. Statistical Survey of the County of Roscommon. (Dublin 1832).

Charles Welsh. A Bookseller of the Last Century. (London 1885).

H. B. Wheatley. Johnson's Shakespeare. (The Atheneum, September 11, 1909).

Tate Wilkinson. Memoirs. (London 1709).

Basil Willey. The Eighteenth Century Background. (Chatto & Windus 1940).

H. S. Wyndham. Annals of Covent Garden Theatre. (Chatto & Windus 1906).

Index

Abington, *Mrs* Frances, 225, 303, 317, 346

Adventures of a Strolling Player, 147

America, 6, 7, 8, 9, 64, 104, 159, 215, 249, 253

Annual Register, 8, 359

Argens, Marquis d', 110, 138, 146

Asia, 161, 174, 220

Ballymahon, 54, 62–3, 257, 267

Baretti, Joseph, 26, 155, 246–7, 319

Barnard, *Dr* Thomas, 349

Barry, Spranger, 11–12, 58, 225

Bath, 163, 175, 295

Beard, John, 10, 231, 234, 298

Beattie, *Dr* James, 75, 350–1

Beauclerk, *Lady* Diana, 334

Beauclerk, Topham, 190, 191, 192, 200, 201, 203, 257, 279, 296, 326, 330–1

Bee, The, 130, 136, 142, 173, 256, 335,

Bell, Robert, 46–7

Bellamy, *Mrs* George Ann, 4, 58–9, 73, 120, 225, 228–9, 325

Berkenhout, John, 108

Bickerstaffe, Isaac, 237, 258, 276–7, 278, 298–301, 303–4, 305–6, 311–12, 320–2, 334

Bindley, John, 289

Blackstone, *Sir* William, 243, 276

Boswell, James, 6, 13, 24–31, 32, 75, 146, 152, 158, 190, 192, 193, 195, 198–9, 204, 207, 211, 241, 246, 259, 264, 291, 297, 332, 334, 337, 338, 339, 340–4, 350, 359, 363, 368–9

Bott, Edmund, 241–2, 297, 345, 346, 356

Boyse, Samuel, 204

Brick Court, 241, 257, 276–7

Bristol, 282, 294–5

British Magazine, The, 132, 149, 164

Brookes, *Dr* R., 175

Bryanton, Robert, 62, 63, 72, 74, 80, 110–11, 268, 287

Bulkley, *Mrs* Mary, 238

Bunbury, Catherine (formerly Horn-neck), 283, 285–6, 288, 348

Burke, Edmund, 4, 5, 7, 8, 13, 20–1, 44, 52, 56, 59–60, 99, 104–5, 116, 190, 191, 192, 193, 206, 207, 235, 243, 247, 249, 257, 265, 296, 340, 344, 349, 350, 355–357, 259

Burney, Fanny, 197, 335

Busy Body, The, 130

Bute, Marquis of, 3, 5, 6, 160–2, 174, 175, 179, 364–5

Butler, *Mrs*, 123, 147, 150, 287

Butler, Daniel, 123, 147

Byrne, Thomas, 48

Campbell, *Revd* Thomas, 253, 258, 358

Captivity, The, 221

Carnan, Anna Maria (Nancy), 134, 136

Carnan, Prudence, 176

Carnan, Thomas, 182, 357

Chambers, Robert, 191, 192, 243, 355

Chambers, *Sir* William, 139, 273, 281, 298, 334, 346

Chamier, Anthony, 21, 189, 192, 193

Charlemont, 1st Earl of, 331

Chatterton, Thomas, 282, 294–5

Chesterfield, 4th Earl of, 23, 45, 116, 129, 183, 215

China, 138–41

'Chinese Letters', 19, 20, 84, 124, 136, 138–49, 150, 153, 158, 161, 162, 164, 165, 166, 167, 168, 177, 180, 200, 232, 273, 279, 287, 293, 335, 361

Christian's Magazine, 182, 356

Churchill, Charles, 13, 157–9, 162, 224, 291, 365

Cibber, *Mrs* Susannah Maria (formerly Arne), 102, 229

Cibber, Theophilus, 102, 332

Citizen of the World, The, 20, 38, 39, 48, 58, 69, 124, 177, 356

City Night-Piece, A, 122

Clairon Mademoiselle, 130, 230

Clare, *Viscount*, 214–6, 258, 280, 289, 295, 317, 346

Cleland, John, 101

Clive, Kitty, 130, 227

'Club, The', 4, 20–1, 54, 188–93, 240, 243, 246–7, 282, 291, 303, 313, 314, 315, 316–9, 324, 330–2, 340, 343, 352

Collins, Benjamin, 87, 115, 178, 182, 363

Colman, George, 11, 18, 20, 126, 127, 128, 129, 137, 157, 223, 224, 225, 229, 231, 234–6, 238–9, 243, 255, 291, 300, 311, 313–21, 322, 329

Connoisseur, The, 127, 129, 137, 139

Contarine, *Revd* Thomas, 49–51, 54, 56, 60–2, 64, 69, 70, 72, 76–81, 85, 86, 110, 267

Cooke, William, 147, 158, 167, 213, 240–1, 276, 279, 311, 324–5, 349, 368

Cornelys, *Mrs* (Therese Imer), 16, 249, 260–3, 270, 316, 328

Cotterell, *Misses*, 23, 188–9

Covent Garden theatre, 10–11, 58, 103, 120, 223, 225, 226–7, 228, 230, 231, 235, 238–40, 298, 305, 312, 317–21

Cox, Joseph, 143–4

Cradock, Joseph, 313, 317, 320, 338, 345, 346, 347, 350

Critical Review, The, 114–5, 118, 119, 121, 130, 157, 183, 223

Cumberland, William Augustus, Duke of, 6, 8

Cumberland, Richard, 318, 319, 320, 349

Daily Advertiser, 332

Dancer, *Mrs*, 11–12, 238

Davies, Thomas, 242, 274, 315, 338, 346, 347–8

Dawson, *Dr* Benjamin, 102

Day, John, 281

Deserted Village, The, 22, 30, 32, 34, 46, 56, 127, 213, 256, 264, 266–75, 280, 290, 292, 306, 325, 329, 335, 347

Dibdin, Charles, 322

Dilly, Charles and Edward, 340–2

Dodd, *Dr* William, 182–3

Dodsley, James, 116, 136, 153, 167, 221

Dodsley, Robert, 104, 116–17, 119–20, 125, 129, 136, 152

Drury Lane theatre, 10–12, 116, 223–4, 225, 226–7, 228, 230, 231, 234, 235, 238, 298, 303, 320, 322, 325, 326

Dyer, Samuel, 189–90, 192, 193, 315, 316–7

East India Company, 106–7

Edgeware, 242

Edinburgh, 70, 71–81, 83

Edwin and Angelina, 221

Ellis, Thomas, 84, 358

Enquiry into the Present State of Polite Learning in Europe, An, 87, 110, 116, 118–20, 124, 137, 149, 224

Evans (publisher of the *London Packet*), 330, 332

Evans, T. fpublisher of Goldsmith's *Poetical and Dramatic Works*, 1780), 359

European Magazine, 147

Eyles, John, 208, 257, 353

Fame Machine, The, 136–7, 335–6

Farr, *Dr* William, 75, 96, 106, 181, 358, 369

Fleming, Miss Elizabeth, 178, 186, 187, 222

Flynn family, 62

Foote, Samuel, 10, 11, 12, 114–5, 117, 224, 252, 320, 325

Fordyce, *Dr* George, 352–4

Forster, John, 105

France, 6, 14, 80, 81, 88–91, 110, 130–1, 138, 159–60, 283–4

Franklin, Benjamin, 215

Garrick, David, 2, 21, 58, 91, 132, 157, 194, 224–31, 234–8, 246, 262, 291, 298, 300, 311–13, 317, 322, 347, 348, 350
  Drury Lane, 10–12
  'the Club', 20, 188, 192, 317, 319, 320, 330–1
  and Goldsmith, 119–20, 149–50, 193, 225, 234, 247, 291–2, 323–7, 348, 349, 350
  The Good-Natured Man, 234–8
  She Stoops to Conquer, 314–5, 317, 319–20, 323–4, 334

Gay, John, 21

Gentleman's Journal, The, 311, 348

Gentleman's Magazine, 22, 106, 212

George II, 3, 162

George III, 3, 5, 6, 7, 8, 114, 160–3, 203, 252, 350, 364

Ginger, John, 353

Ginger, Mary, 353

Glover, *Dr* William Frederick, 19, 86, 88, 90, 276–7, 359

Goldsmith, Anne (mother), 35, 36, 37, 40–1, 49, 50, 54, 64, 67–9, 268–9, 293, 306–8

Goldsmith, Charles (father), 35–7, 39–41, 46, 48, 49–50, 51, 54, 168, 269

Goldsmith, Charles (brother), 40, 68, 110, 269

Goldsmith, Henry (brother), 36, 48, 49, 51, 56, 60, 92, 109, 110, 112–14, 167, 212, 219, 242, 268, 269–70, 325

Goldsmith, John (brother), 40, 68

Goldsmith, Maurice (brother), 40, 68, 269, 280–1, 293–4, 357, 358

Goldsmith, Oliver: Reynolds' portrait of him, 1–2, 19–20, 24, 361; translations of his work, 20, 34; family and background, 21, 35–51, 54, 56, 60, 62–70, 76–7, 79, 92–3, 109, 110, 112–14, 168, 219, 242, 268–70, 280, 293–4, 306–8, 357–8; knowledge of French, 46; fondness for sport, 47; education, 48–51; attendance at Trinity College, Dublin, 52–60, dreams of emigration, 56, 64; weakness for gambling, 57, 69, 84, 346; generosity, 57, 123, 277–82; reluctant to take Orders, 60; becomes a tutor, 62; abortive plan to study law, 69; studies medicine in Edinburgh, 71–9; fondness for music, 75, 85, 87; leaves Edinburgh for Leyden, 80–5; travels in Europe, 85–93; origin of *The Traveller,* 91–2; practices medicine in London, 94–6; teaches in Peckham, 98–9, 110; contributes to the *Monthly Review,* 101–9; plagiarism, 102, 145–7, 300; hopes to visit Palestine, 106; applies for a medical post in India, 106–8, 110, 111–12; translations from French, 109, 112; dispute with Ralph Griffiths, 114–18; contributes to the *Critical Review,* 115, 118, 121, 130; publication of the *Enquiry into the Present State of Polite Learning,* 116–20; offends Garrick, 119–20; moves to Green Arbour Court, 121–3; is arrested for debt, 124; meets the Revd Thomas Percy, 125; his religion, 127, 154, 155, 256, 342; begins to compile *The Bee,* 130; contributes to the *Busy Body,* 130;

invited to write for the *Weekly Magazine*, 130; meets John Newbery, 136; begins the 'Chinese Letters', 138–44; 'dissipation', 144–5; moves to Wine Office Court, 147; meets Garrick, 149; meets Samuel Johnson, 151; *The Rosciad*, 158; memorial to Lord Bute, 161, 174, 175; translates Plutarch, 163, 175; biography of Nash, 175; *History of Miss Stanton*, 164–5; begins *The Vicar of Wakefield* (q.v.), 167; *The Indigent Philosopher*, 172–4; *Survey of Experimental Philosophy*, 175, 187, 221, 346–7; threatened with arrest, 176; moves to Islington, 178, 186; finishes *The Vicar of Wakefield*, 178–82; invited to join the Club, 188; admiration of Johnson, 199–204; publication of *The Traveller*, 209–14; acquaintance with Robert Nugent, 214; interview with Lord Northumberland, 218–20; takes lodgings in the Inner Temple, 221; collection of his essays printed, 222; *The Good-Natured Man*, 232–40; rents a cottage at Edgeware, 242; *History of the Earth and Animated Nature*, 242, 253, 281, 296–8, 315, 337–8, 346, 348, 351, 364; said to have acquired an Oxford degree, 244–6; visits to Vauxhall and Carlisle House, 259–64; *The Deserted Village*, 264–75; visits France with the Hornecks, 282–4; possible attachment to Mary Horneck, 286–8; emotional life, 289–93; visits the West Country, 295; moves to Hyde, 296–8; composition of *She Stoops to Conquer*, 298–308; attack on him by William Kenrick, 308–13; production of *She Stoops to Conquer*, 313–22; friendship with Garrick, 325–7; attack on Evans, 330; coolness between him and Johnson,

332–41; quarrels with Johnson, 342–4; ill health, 345; financial problems, 345–7; *Retaliation*, 350–1; final illness and death, 351–4; Johnson's epitaph, 357;

attitudes to: classicism, 105, 153, 202; his family, 39–41, 56, 67–9, 92, 109, 168, 268–9, 293, 306–8; Johnson, 30, 109, 125, 142, 155, 199, 289–90, 333, 339; luxury, 5, 19, 76, 109, 159, 241, 254–7, 259–60, 270–3, 276; monarchy, 5, 162–3, 180, 203, 364; politics, 83, 150, 159, 162–3, 180, 203, 250, 253–6, 296–7, 341, 364–5; religion, 60, 154, 155, 256, 342; Sterne, 14, 153–4, 202, 335; women, 33, 74, 286–8;

biography by Revd Thomas Percy, 85–6, 90, 94, 181, 220, 232, 246, 331;

memoir by Dr William Frederick Glover, 86, 88, 90.

Good-Natured Man, The, 30, 107–8, 120, 232–41, 290, 316, 317, 325, 329

Grainger, *Dr* James, 102, 125

Grattan, Henry, 281

Gray, Thomas, 104–5, 116, 202, 210, 335

Grecian History, 315

Green Arbour Court, 121–3, 147, 150, 165, 259

Green, Jane, 317, 321

Grenville, George, 6, 7

Griffin, William, 222, 242, 274–5, 311, 315, 356

Griffiths, Ralph, 99–102, 105, 108, 109, 114–19, 137, 167, 187, 278, 310, 328

Grosley, M., 14–15, 259

Grosvenor, *Sir* Richard, 150

Gun, Misses, 287

Hamilton, Duke of, 76, 109

Hamilton, Alexander, 121, 123, 124, 131

Hamilton, William, 294

Hanway, Jonas, 103, 263
Harcourt, 1st Earl, 19, 23, 264–5
Hawes, William, 263, 351–4, 356, 361
Hawkins, *Sir* John, 189, 191, 192, 218–20, 252, 368
Hermti, The, 186
Hickey, Joseph, 283, 349
Hiffernan, Paul, 59, 162, 225, 277–8
History of England, 187, 221, 274, 296, 315, 364
History of Miss Stanton, 164–5, 172, 367
History of the Earth and Animated Nature, 242, 253, 281, 296–8, 315, 337–8, 346, 348, 351, 264
Hodson, Catherine (sister), 36, 37, 38, 47, 48, 49, 54, 56, 60, 74–7, 68, 69, 110, 268, 287, 307, 357
Hodson, Daniel, 49, 54, 62, 63, 64, 69, 71, 93, 110
Hodson, William, 227, 269, 280
Hogarth, William, 3, 7, 10, 123, 150–1, 162, 259, 365
Holberg, Baron, 87
Holland, 80–5, 88
Holland, Charles, 225
Horneck family, 32, 195, 282–8, 313, 318, 328, 330, 346, 356
Horneck, Mary, 195, 283, 286–8, 313, 328, 330
Home, John, 103
Hughes, *Revd* Patrick, 48, 54
Hume, David, 12, 45, 75, 103, 116, 137, 337, 350
Hyde, 297, 351

Idler, The, 129
India, 106–7, 110, 111–12
Indigent Philosopher, 172–3
Infernal Magazine, The, 174
Inner Temple, 221–2, 240–1
Ireland, condition of, 41–6, 104
Islington, 178, 186–8, 222
Italy, 86, 94

Jenner, Charles, 17, 18, 255–6, 336

Johnson, *Dr* Samuel, 2, 13, 22, 23, 24, 32, 52, 75, 77, 102, 105, 106, 114, 116, 126, 128, 129, 132, 137, 142, 144, 151–6, 161, 183, 199–206, 219, 222, 234, 239, 240, 243–7, 250, 254, 257, 258, 264, 277, 289–90, 291, 294, 296, 312, 313, 314, 318, 320, 324, 332–45, 347, 348, 349, 350, 358, 359–60
'the Club', 4, 20, 188–93, 282, 319;
Shakespeare, 13–14, 155, 234, 311;
depression, 14, 29–30, 155–6, 201, 344;
and the poor, 18, 154–5, 254–5;
Dictionary, 23, 116, 155, 219;
and Boswell, 24–7, 158, 199;
and Goldsmith, 26–31, 142, 145–6, 151–6, 181, 193, 195, 200–6, 211, 224, 239, 243–6, 258, 275, 294, 312–3, 318, 325, 332–45, 355–6, 357–8, 360, 361;
The Vicar of Wakefield, 30, 177, 182, 210, 363, 368–9;
Goldsmith's respect for, 30, 109, 125, 142, 155, 199, 289–90, 333, 339;
the *Rambler*, 129, 137, 142, 238, 250;
appearance and mannerisms, 152–3, 193, 196–7;
finishes Goldsmith's poems, 181, 211, 275, 290
Jones, Robert, 106, 107

Kelly (Galway 'squireen'), 59–60
Kelly, Hugh, 162, 173, 222, 235–8, 240, 250, 253, 319, 336, 356
Kennedy, Hugh Alexander, 80
Kenrick, *Dr* William, 108, 137, 213, 231–2, 245, 260, 300, 309–13, 328–30
King's Opera House (Haymarket), 11, 227
Kippis, *Dr* Andrew, 345
Kirkpatrick, *Dr* James, 102
Kirkudbright, *Lord*, 74

Knowles, Admiral, 131

Ladies' Magazine, 149
Langton family, 152, 302–3, 317
Langton, Bennet, 190, 191, 193, 199–
  200, 201, 203, 282, 296, 339, 342
Lawder, James, 50, 77, 78
Lawder, Jane, 50, 77, 78, 110, 111,
  287
LeBlanc, Abbe, 223
Levett, Robert, 94, 199
Lewes, Lee, 317
Leyden, 72, 80–5
Life of Voltaire, 149, 167
Lisburne, Earl of, 274
Lissoy, 37, 38, 46, 49, 54, 62, 68, 69,
  168, 266, 267, 268, 269, 270, 272
Lloyd, Rachel, 326
Lloyd, Robert, 157–9, 225
Lloyd's Evening Post, 132, 163, 172,
  175, 264–5
London, 2–4, 14–19, 121–3, 125–6,
  248–9, 259–62
London Chronicle, The, 211–12, 259
London Packet, The, 328–30
Lucas, Charles, 60
Langton, Bennet, 191, 302
Luttrell, Col. Henry, 251, 262

M'Donnell, M'Veagh, 281–2, 313
Macklin, Charles, 58–9, 228
Maclean, Laughlane, 75, 80
Mallett, Paul Henri, 102
Malone, Edmund, 209
Marivaux, Pierre Carlet de Chamblain
  de, 129, 146–7, 172, 298, 301
Marteilhe, Jean, 109
Martin, Benjamin, 175
Martinelli, Vincenzo, 333, 341
Marylebone Gardens, 4, 260
Mason, William, 300
Maxwell, —, apothecary, 354
Mayo, Dr H., 342
Medicine, 72, 83, 94–5, 175, 351–4,
  356
Memoirs of My Lady B., 109

Middle class, 11, 19, 22, 23, 37, 42, 78,
  99, 105, 122, 126, 128, 150, 226,
  227, 252, 255, 257
Middle Temple, 240–1
Midwife, The, 134
Mills, Edward, 62, 110–1
Milner, Hester, 96–9
Milner, Revd Thomas, 96, 106, 107,
  110, 116
Monarchy, 5, 8, 162–3, 180, 203, 364
Monitor, The, 160
Montesquieu, Charles de Secondat,
  Baron de, 110, 130, 136, 138, 146–7
Monthly Review, The, 101, 102–6, 108,
  110, 114–15, 121, 123, 129, 164,
  183, 212, 310, 322, 332
Moody, —, actor, 228
Moore, Edward, 129
Morning Chronicle, The, 308–9, 312,
  322
Moser, Michael, 339
Munro, Professor Alexander, 72, 76
Murphy, Arthur, 30, 201, 205, 222,
  223–5, 229, 230, 231, 234, 235, 258,
  291, 300, 307, 338, 363
Murray, Miss Nikky, 74
Murray, Richard, 53

Nash, Richard, 163, 175
Newbery, Francis (John Newbery's
  son), 186–7, 356
Newbery, Francis (John Newbery's
  nephew), 182, 316, 322, 347
Newbery, John, 14, 22, 109, 132–6,
  137–8, 145, 147, 152, 163, 164, 167,
  172, 175, 176–9, 181, 182–3, 186–7,
  210, 221, 222, 241, 250, 289, 337,
  346, 347, 363, 364
Newbery, Mrs, 133, 138
Newcastle, 2nd Duke of, 5, 6, 7, 100,
  160
North Briton, The, 6, 162, 179, 248,
  249, 365
Northcote, James, 5, 10, 24, 321, 348,
  360
Northumberland, Hugh Smithson,

1st Earl of, 217–20, 243, 257, 258, 338

Nourse, John, 346

Nugent, *Dr* Christopher, 191, 192

Nugent, *Lieut. Col.* Edmund, *M.P.*, 295

Nugent, Robert, *see* Clare, *Viscount*

Nuneham Courtenay, 19, 264–5

Oglethorpe, *General* James E., 204, 205, 254, 256, 263, 279, 340

Oxford, 243–6, 264

Paine, Tom, 263

Palestine, 106

Pallasmore ('Pallas'), 36, 257, 267

Paoli, *General* Gian Battista, 25, 205, 333, 340

Paris, 80, 81, 88–91

Peckham, 96–9

Percy, *Revd* Thomas (later Bishop of Dromore), 38, 46, 48, 56, 61, 64, 85, 86, 90, 94, 122, 125, 151, 156, 167, 181, 188, 210, 211, 217, 218, 220, 221, 232, 242, 243–6, 264, 265, 267, 282, 295, 307, 331, 334, 349, 351, 354, 357–8, 369

Pilkington, John Carteret, 277–80

Pitt, William, Earl of Chatham, 5, 8–9, 160, 162, 179

Plagiarism, 146–7, 300–1

Plutarch, translation of, 163, 175

Politics, 5–9, 83, 150, 159–63, 180, 203, 243, 248–53, 254, 296–7, 341, 364–5

Pope, Alexander, 21, 116, 215

Pottinger, I., 130, 173

Powell, William, 225–6, 235, 238–9

Prior, *Sir* James, 37, 38, 186, 258, 281, 297

Public Advertiser, The, 16, 95, 354

Public Ledger, The, 4, 19, 20, 83, 132, 137, 147, 149, 153, 164, 167, 361

Purdon, Edward, 130

Quick, —, 317–8, 321

Ralph, James, 102

Rambler, The, 129–32, 137, 142, 238, 250

Ranelagh, 260

Religion, 35, 41, 43, 46, 60, 73, 154, 155, 182, 199, 256, 342

Retaliation, 34, 349–51, 356

Reverie at the Boar's-head-tavern in Eastcheap, 187

Revolution in Low Life, 264–5

Reynolds, Fanny, 23–4, 33, 69, 189, 193, 197, 200, 206, 207, 287, 293, 360

Reynolds, *Sir* Joshua, 1–4, 10, 12, 23–4, 26, 154, 206–10, 241, 243, 247, 257, 260, 277, 282–3, 294, 296, 303, 318, 326, 334–5, 345, 347, 355–6, 357;
portrait of Goldsmith, 1–2, 19–20, 23–4, 361;
house in Leicester Square, 2–4, 16, 297;
'the Club', 4, 20, 188–93, 319;
and Goldsmith, 12, 31–4, 48, 75, 96, 143–4, 193–6, 198, 208–10, 213, 234, 235, 266, 269, 272, 282–5, 286, 290, 293, 294, 298, 313, 345, 350–1, 355, 359;
and Johnson, 23, 188–93, 207, 294

Robertson, *Dr* William, 75, 337

Robin Hood Society, 126–7

Rockingham, Marquis of, 5, 7–8, 243, 249

Roman History, The, 242

Rosciad, The, 157–9, 364

Rose, *Revd Dr* William, 102, 116

Rousseau, Jean Jacques, 12–13, 25, 26, 153, 199, 259, 272

Royal Magazine, The, 149

Rutherford, *Professor* John, 72

St James's *Chronicle, The*, 225, 300, 322

Shakespeare, William, 11, 13, 59, 226, 231, 234, 246, 260, 310

She Stoops to Conquer, 63, 181, 292–3,

298–308, 313–15, 317–24, 329, 353, 357

Sheridan, Thomas, 58–60

Shuter, Ned, 225, 238, 239, 317, 318, 319

Sinclair, *Professor* Andrew, 72

Skelton, *Revd* Philip, 45, 101

Sleigh, Fenn, 75, 80, 95, 99

Smart, Christopher, 134, 136, 137, 187, 311

Smith, 'Gentleman', 225, 317

Smith, Adam, 75, 90, 254

Smollett, Tobias, 89, 91, 94, 115, 121, 123, 125, 131–2, 137, 151, 157, 160, 162, 164, 335, 337

Spectator, The, 22, 129, 299–300

Specimen of a Magazine, 174

Steele, Richard, 12, 22, 129, 226, 299

Steevens, George, 201

Sterne, Laurence, 2, 14, 116, 153–4, 167, 202, 258, 272, 335

Survey of Experimental Philosophy, A, 175, 187, 221, 346–7

Synge, *Bishop*, 61

Temple, Richard, 2nd Earl, 160, 162, 179

Temple, *Sir* William, 263

Theatre, 10–12, 587–60, 103, 119–20, 130, 157–8, 222–40, 298–300, 305–6, 310, 319–20

Thomson, James, 75

Thornton, Bonnell, 127, 129, 255

Thrale, Henry, 30, 224, 257–8, 283, 315, 337, 340, 344

Thrale, *Mrs* Hester (later Piozzi), 23, 26, 30, 31, 151, 154, 156, 181, 193, 197, 198, 203, 206, 224, 230, 233, 243, 252, 257–8, 286, 287, 290, 296, 340, 341, 344, 359, 360, 368–9

Threnodia Augustalis, 316

Tonson, Jacob, 13

Toplady, *Revd* A. M., 343

Townley, *Revd* James, 230, 239

Traveller, The, 20, 28, 30, 56, 81, 91–2, 186, 209–12, 214, 221, 232, 236, 268, 271, 308–9, 329, 335, 347, 356

Trinity College, Dublin, 48–9, 51, 52–62, 73

True Briton, The, 160, 162

Turner, Thomas, 254

Turton, *Dr* J., 353–4

Universal Chronicle, The, 129, 132

Universal Dictionary of the Arts and Sciences, 347–8

Vauxhall, 4, 259–60, 272

Vicar of Wakefield, The, 20, 28, 30, 34, 38, 41, 44, 85, 87, 88–91, 98, 127, 147, 150, 164–72, 174, 177–85, 186–7, 221, 222, 232, 256, 268, 269, 279–80, 290–1, 293, 307, 335, 337, 356;
date, 167, 174, 363–9

Voltaire, Francois Arouet de, 109, 130, 140, 143, 149, 351

Voltaire, Life of, 109, 149, 167

Walpole, Horace, 12, 76, 91, 116, 138, 215, 218, 220, 283, 292, 294, 326, 338, 355, 359, 360

Weekly Magazine, The, 130, 231

Westminster Magazine, 319

Whitefield, George, 256

Whitefoord, Caleb, 349

Wilder, Theaker, 53–5, 56, 72

Wilkes, John, 6–7, 131–2, 151, 160–3, 179–80, 248–53, 322–3, 364–5, 367

Wilkie, J., 130

Wilkinson, Tate, 229

Williams, *Miss*, 27, 197

Wine Office Court, 147–9, 175–7

Woffington, Peg, 227, 228

Woodfall, William, 316, 322, 328

Woodward, Henry, 59, 225, 238, 317, 319

World, The, 116, 129, 137, 139

Young, Edward, 21, 116, 225